A Comparative Syntax of the Dialects of Southern Italy

A Minimalist Approach

D1615136

Publications of the Philological Society, 33

A Comparative Syntax of the Dialects of Southern Italy

A Minimalist Approach

Adam Ledgeway

Publications of the Philological Society, 33

Oxford UK & Boston USA

Copyright © The Philological Society 2000

ISBN 0–631–221–662

First published 2000

Blackwell Publishers
108 Cowley Road, Oxford, OX4 1JF, UK

and
350 Main Street,
Malden, MA 02148, USA.

British Library Cataloguing in Publication Data
A catalogue record for this publication is available from the British Library

Library of Congress Cataloging-in-Publication Data
Applied for

Typeset by Joshua Associates Ltd., Oxford
Printed in Great Britain by
Whitstable Litho Printers Ltd., Whitstable, Kent

Per Alessandra e Luca

CONTENTS

ACKNOWLEDGEMENTS

The preparation of this book, and the original doctoral dissertation (Ledgeway 1996b) out of which many of the ideas for the present research grew, has been made possible thanks to the generous help of many people. I should like to thank Nigel Vincent who first aroused and encouraged my interest in Italian dialectology and theoretical syntax as a graduate student at the University of Manchester. It is thanks to him and Giulio Lepschy, who over recent years has shown particular interest in my work, that this book was written. Expressions of particular gratitude also go to Delia Bentley, Keith Brown, Michela Cennamo, Robert Hastings, Cecilia Goria, Michael Jones, Alessandra Lombardi, Michele Loporcaro, Christopher Lyons, Martin Maiden, Mair Parry, Rosanna Sornicola and Alberto Varvaro for providing invaluable criticisms and comments on parts of this work during the various stages of its preparation. I am also grateful to the members (too many to list) of the audiences of various seminars and conferences at which various parts of the following material were presented. Aspects of chapter 2 were presented at UCL (Ledgeway forthcoming), chapter 3 in Palermo (Ledgeway 1996a), chapter 4 at UCL and Bristol, chapter 5 in Palermo (Ledgeway 1996a, 1998a), chapter 6 in Girona (Ledgeway 1998c), and chapter 7 to audiences in Oxford, Bristol and Padua. Moreover, I would also like to express especial thanks to Keith Brown, Secretary for Publications of the Philological Society, whose generous help proved invaluable in the preparation of the manuscript.

In addition, I owe an enormous debt of gratitude to my informants, who over the past years have shown remarkable kindness and patience in answering my relentless and, at times, annoying inquiries and questions about their dialects. In particular, I should like to thank Delia Bentley, Maria Calzini, Maurizio Carrieri, Francesco Calonico, Anna Maria Cannataro, Eugenio Cannataro, Carmine De Bartolo, Stefania Desideri, Giovanni Esposito, Anna Maria Ferrari, Raffaele Ferrari, Peppino Ferrari, Vienna Gentile, Isa Gimigliano, Stefania Greco, Carlo Iandolo, Antonio Iera, Caterina Laratta, Lorina Lepreti, Marcella Lo Giudice, Alessandra Lombardi, Ciro Manna, Rita Mariani, Stefania Mariani, Salvatore Marra, Gerardo Mazzaferro, Patrizia Orso, Antonio Pacillo, Maria Carla Pagnotta, Irene Pagnotta, Rosa Petramala, Rosetta Rossi, Francesca Spina, Loredana Teresi, Ida Tommasi, Carmela Vitiello and Tersilla Vitiello.

On a personal note, I should like to thank my parents for their continual support and encouragement, and my 'acquired' family in Italy for having provided me with such a welcoming environment in which much of the present work was written. Finally, my deepest gratitude goes to Alessandra for her love and unfailing patience which she heaped on me during the arduous period accompanying the writing of this book. It is to her and our son Luca that this book is dedicated.

LIST OF TABLES

ABBREVIATIONS

a(P)	Light adjective (Phrase)	IMP	Imperative
A(P)	Adjective (Phrase)	INDIC	Indicative
ACC	Accusative case	INF	Infinitive
Agr(P)	Agreement (Phrase)	INFL	Verbal inflection
AgrO(P)	Object agreement (Phrase)	IObj	Indirect object
AgrS(P)	Subject agreement (Phrase)	IP	Inflection Phrase
an.	Animate	IRREG	Irregular
A-P	Articulatory-perceptual	L-A	Latin-American
Appl	Applicative verbal head	LF	Logical Form
arb	with arbitrary reference	LN	Literary Neapolitan
Arg$_{pass}$	Passive morphology argument	M	Mood
		M	Masculine
Asp	Aspect	MLC	Minimal Link Condition
AUX	Auxiliary	N(P)	Noun (Phrase)
C	Complementizer (position)	Neg(P)	Negation (Phrase)
case	Morphological case	NOC	Non-obligatory control
Case	(abstract) Syntactic case	NOM	Nominative case
CFC	Complete Functional Complex	Obj	Object
		OC	Obligatory control
C$_{HL}$	Computational system	PA	Prepositional accusative case
C-I	Conceptional-intentional		
CL	Clitic pronoun	PART	participle
COND	Conditional	pers	Person
CP	Complementizer Phrase	PF	Phonological Form
D(P)	Determiner (Phrase)	PL	Plural
DAT	Dative case	P/N-feature	Person/Number agreement features
DObj	Direct object		
ECM	Exceptional Case Marking	POSS	Possessive
ECP	Empty Category Principle	P(P)	Prepositional (Phrase)
E$_{EV}$	Event time of the embedded verb	PRES	Present tense
		pro	Non-anaphoric null pronominal
E$_{INF}$	Event time of the infinitive		
EPP	Extended Projection Principle	PRO	Anaphoric null pronominal
		reg.	Regional
F(F)	Feature(s)	REG	Regular
F	Feminine	R$_{EV}$	Reference time of the embedded verb
FI	*Faire-Infinitif* (causative construction)		
		R$_{INF}$	Reference time of the infinitive
FP	*Faire-Par* (causative construction)		
		R$_{MV}$	Reference time of the matrix verb
F$_Q$	Question/Interrogative feature		
		Q	Quantifier
GEN	Genitive case	SC	Small clause
GER	Gerund	S.CL	Subject clitic
hum.	Human	SD	Structural dative case

SG	Singular	V(P)	Verb (Phrase)
SIG	Subject In-situ Generalization	X^{max}/XP	Category that does not project any further
SN	Spoken Neapolitan	X^{min}/X^o	Category that does not project at all
Spec	Specifier position		
SR	Subject raising	1	First person
SUBJ	Subjunctive	2	Second person
Subj	Subject	3	Third person
t	Trace (left by moved category)	*	Ungrammatical
T	Tense (features)	?/??	Of marginal/very marginal grammatical status
T-chain	Tense chain	>	Develops into
T(P)	Tense (Phrase)	<	Derives from
UA	Unmarked accusative case	θ	Theta/Thematic
v(P)	Light (performative/causative) verb (Phase)	φ	Nominal/Verbal phi-features
Vb	Verbal complex comprising v and adjoined V(erb)		(variously including person, number and gender)

ABBREVIATIONS OF CITED PROVINCES

AG	Agrigento (Sicily)	LE	Lecce (Apulia)
AQ	L'Aquila (Abruzzo)	LT	Latina (Lazio)
AP	Ascoli Piceno (Marches)	MT	Matera (Basilicata/Lucania)
AV	Avellino (Campania)	NA	Naples (Campania)
BA	Bari (Apulia)	NO	Novara (Piedmont)
BN	Benevento (Campania)	NU	Nuoro (Sardinia)
BR	Brindisi (Apulia)	PA	Palermo (Sicily)
CB	Campobasso (Molise)	PD	Padua (Veneto)
CE	Caserta (Campania)	PZ	Potenza (Basilicata/Lucania)
CH	Chieti (Abruzzo)	RC	Reggio di Calabria (Calabria)
CL	Caltanisetta (Sicily)	RI	Rieti (Lazio)
CS	Cosenza (Calabria)	SA	Salerno (Campania)
CT	Catania (Sicily)	SI	Siena (Tuscany)
CZ	Catanzaro (Calabria)	SR	Siracusa (Sicily)
EN	Enna (Sicily)	TA	Taranto (Apulia)
FG	Foggia (Apulia)	TE	Teramo (Abruzzo)
FR	Frosinone (Lazio)	TO	Turin (Piedmont)
GE	Genoa (Liguria)	TP	Trapani (Sicily)
IS	Isernia (Molise)	VV	Vibo Valentia (Calabria)
KR	Crotone (Calabria)		

1

INTRODUCTION

1.1 AIMS

The present study sets out to investigate from a comparative perspective various aspects of the syntax of the dialects of southern Italy. These dialects, now spoken alongside Italian, a Florentine-based dialect, are the indigenous languages descended from spoken Latin as it evolved naturally and largely unaffected by formal education south of an isogloss running approximately from Rome in the West to Ancona in the East.[1] Though not forming an entirely homogeneous linguistic group, standardly divided into dialects of the Upper South (southern Lazio, Abruzzo, Molise, Campania, Lucania, northern Apulia, northern Calabria) and those of the Extreme South (Salentino peninsula, southern Calabria, Sicily), southern Italian dialects have long been recognized to share a number of common phonetic, morphological and lexical features (see Rohlfs 1972: 9, 27–31). Traditionally, though, considerably less attention has been paid to their syntax which, to the present day, largely remains a poorly understood and unexplored area of Italian dialectology.

The aim of the present book is therefore twofold. On the one hand, the material presented in the following chapters is intended to bring to light, for the first time in many cases, a number of significant and hitherto unexplored syntactic phenomena. In this respect, the results of our investigations offer a valuable insight into the little studied syntax of the dialects of southern Italy, making a significant contribution towards cataloguing the linguistic typology of dialect syntax within the Italian peninsula and, at the same time, bridging the gap between the familiar data of standard Romance and those of lesser known Romance varieties. On the other hand, the southern Italian dialect data present the linguist with a fertile test-bed in which to investigate new ideas about language structure and micro-variation in the syntax of a relatively homogeneous group of dialects. To date, the points of contact between the fields of theoretical syntax and southern Italian dialect data can only be described as, at best, minimal. As a consequence, the potential significance of such dialects for issues in general linguistic theory has been largely overlooked. The results of the following chapters demonstrate, in contrast, that the joint aims of presenting an adequate account of descriptive problems and providing a principled explanation for them can be achieved without compromising either of these two complementary aspects of syntactic research.

The common aim of the following six chapters of this book is then to show how the model of language embodied in Chomsky's (1995) Minimalist Program can be profitably extended to the study of the syntax of southern Italian dialects. Not only will our investigations elucidate significant aspects of the structure of these dialects, they will also have consequences for the general theory, demonstrating how a familiarity with the facts of southern Italian dialect syntax can broaden its empirical domain and shed light on important theoretical issues.

The following provides an overview of the content of this book. Chapter 2 examines the Case-marking of various types of nominal object complement, demonstrating from semantic, morphological and syntactic evidence that it is necessary to distinguish between inherent and structural Case-marked objects. In particular, the analysis will concentrate on the distribution and properties of direct and indirect objects marked by a reflex of Latin AD, investigating a number of phenomena such as the surface neutralization between direct and indirect objects, variation in Case-marking and its semantic correlates, and the behaviour of Case alternations in double-object constructions.

Chapters 3 and 4 explore the syntax of control in finite and (inflected) infinitival complements. These are demonstrated to raise a number of significant issues regarding the distribution of obligatory and non-obligatory control, temporal interpretation, nominative Case-licensing and EPP-checking. In contrast to standard binding- and Case-theoretic accounts in terms of (controlled) PRO, it is argued that obligatory and non-obligatory control structures are best analysed in terms of DP-trace and pro, respectively. The proposed account highlights the central role played by the C position in control, and further accounts for such phenomena as subject-verb agreement and subject clitics in infinitival constructions with overt subjects.

Chapter 5 undertakes an examination of a restricted class of verbal predicates, namely conative verbs and modal-aspectual verbs, whose infinitival complementation structures exhibit a number of special properties alien to main verbs. It is argued that the behaviour of the former, ambivalently incorporating properties of both main verbs and auxiliaries, follows from their status as raising predicates. The behaviour of modal-aspectual verbs, in contrast, is captured by analysing them as the overt realization of temporal, aspectual and modal features merged under T.

Chapter 6 deals with the phenomenon of BE/HAVE auxiliary selection, deriving the distribution of the perfective auxiliaries from an analysis that generalizes the licensing conditions of complement clauses outlined in chapter 3 to that of participial clauses. The proposed analysis will be shown to offer a robust theory of auxiliary selection capable of accounting for the full range of auxiliary alternations common to Romance.

Finally, in chapter 7 the semantico-syntactic properties of want-passives are explored. Questions investigated include the cross-dialectal differences in participial agreement, the availability of dative passivization and the significance of economy conditions on DP-movement.

1.2. The data

The availability of data permitting, the investigations of the following chapters are conducted from a comparative approach, embracing a wide selection of southern Italian dialects. In most cases the analysis starts from a discussion of Neapolitan, widening the field of inquiry to other dialects as the analysis proceeds. The data discussed in the present book are of two principal types: written and live. The former are drawn from a number of different sources, including early and modern dialect texts (prose, plays, poetry, fables, songs, letters, technical manuals), dictionaries, grammars and academic research. As for the live data, these were principally collected *in loco* during numerous fieldwork trips and visits over the past years to southern Italy, in particular Campania, Calabria and Sicily, which figure most in the following chapters. In many cases, the data arose from spontaneous conversations among (often unwitting) native dialect speakers, while in other cases the data were obtained from direct linguistic inquiry by means of specifically designed questionnaires or through discussions with informants resident both in Italy and the UK. Wherever possible, every attempt has been made to consult a broad range of informants in terms of socio-professional status, education, sex and age in order to take account of any significant sociolinguistic factors.

Examples taken from the corpus of live data appear unmarked in the text, whereas those drawn from the corpus of written data appear with their source in parentheses. In addition, the provenance of all examples, where not otherwise specified in the text, is also given in parentheses followed, where relevant, by an abbreviation (see page xvi) indicating the regional province of the locality in question.

Where it proves necessary to illustrate the syntactic structure of the examples, morpheme-by-morpheme glosses have been provided, supplemented, where meaning would otherwise be compromised, with freer English translations. In such cases, glosses generally indicate only information relevant to the points under discussion.

1.3. Theoretical background: the Minimalist Program

In the following section we introduce some of the fundamental concepts of the general theoretic framework within which the present study is couched. The theoretical assumptions adopted throughout are those generally accepted in much recent research carried out within the Minimalist Program (Chomsky 1995).

1.3.1. *The language faculty and the interface levels*

The language faculty is held to consist of two components: the cognitive system and the performance systems. The former stores information which it makes available for interpretation to the articulatory-perceptual (A-P) and conceptual-intentional (C-I) external interfaces of the performance systems. This interaction between the cognitive and performance systems is made possible by two levels of linguistic representation, the level of Phonological Form (PF) at the A-P interface and the level of Logical Form (LF) at the C-I interface. The cognitive system is therefore a mechanism that generates sound-meaning pairs (henceforth derivations), constructed according to a highly restricted set of universal principles and local conditions on economy which at the LF and PF interfaces provide specific instructions for the C-I and A-P systems, respectively.

1.3.2. *The lexicon*

The cognitive system consists of a computational system (C_{HL}) and a lexicon, the latter specifying the lexical items from which the C_{HL} selects to generate linguistic expressions. Within this framework the lexicon is understood to be the 'optimal coding' of lexical idiosyncrasies, providing just sufficient information to construct a phonological and semantic representation at the PF and LF interfaces. The lexicon excludes therefore whatever is predictable by principles of Universal Grammar or language-specific principles of phonology and morphology. In this way, the lexicon is interpreted as the locus of parametric variation, specifying parametric options (see the [±strong] dimension below) and other aspects of language variation not otherwise predictable.

The linguistic items stored in the lexicon are simply collections of three types of features: phonological, semantic and formal (grammatical). In the latter case, we distinguish between intrinsic and optional formal features. The former are those features listed in the lexical entries, such as the categorial features [V], [N], [A] and [P] which are not predictable by universal or language-specific principles. Optional formal features, in contrast, are those which are added arbitrarily in accordance with the particular occurrence of a lexical item. For instance, the Case and φ-features for *book* will have to be specified separately each time the item is drawn from the lexicon to account for its separate occurrences in such sentences as ***books*** *are useful* (NOM.PL) and *I read* ***a book*** (ACC.SG).

A further distinction we draw between formal features is that between those which are semantically interpretable and those which are not. Among the interpretable features are categorial and nominal φ-features. The operations which interpret derivations at the LF interface will need to know, for example, that *read* is a V(erb) and that *book* is a N(oun) with the φ-features [3SG]. In contrast, such operations have no way of interpreting the (abstract) φ-features of *read* or the Case of *book*.[2] Interpretable formal features are thus legitimate objects at LF, whereas uninterpretable features must be eliminated. A derivation is thus said to converge (yield a grammatical derivation) and satisfy the condition of Full Interpretation if its LF representation contains only features interpretable at that particular level. If the LF representation contains uninterpretable features, then Full Interpretation cannot be satisfied and the derivation is said to crash (yield an ungrammatical derivation). In order for the condition of Full Interpretation to be satisfied, uninterpretable features must then be eliminated before they reach the LF interface, a procedure achieved through a checking theory (see section 1.3.4).

1.3.3. *Structure-building operations: Merge and Move*

Lexical items drawn from the lexicon are made available to the C_{HL} by taking them from the numeration (an array of lexical items drawn from the lexicon) and combining them in accordance with the structure-building operations Merge and Move (or, more correctly, Attract).[3] Let us begin by considering Merge, which builds up lexical (for example, V, N, A) and functional (for example, C, T, D) structure in a pair-wise fashion in accordance with the Binarity Condition. This operation selects two syntactic objects {X, Y} from the numeration and replaces them with the new combined category {K, {X, Y}}, where K is a projection of either X or Y. If Y is a complement, then X projects and forms a new category by determining its label. To take a concrete example, imagine we have selected the D(eterminer) *the* and the N *book* from the numeration. We can then combine them to form the new category {the, {the, book}}in (1a):

(1)

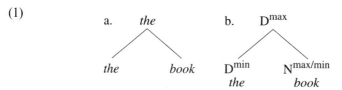

Within Chomsky's (1995: §4.3) bare phrase structure model, maximal and minimal projections are not identified by any specific marking but are interpreted as relational properties of categories determined by the particular structures in which they appear. Retaining the X-bar notation for expository purposes, informally we can distinguish between categories that do not project any further and those that do not project at all. The former we label X^{max} (XP) and the latter X^{min} (X^o), any other intermediate categories (namely X') being invisible to C_{HL} and the LF interface.[4] Under this conception of phrase structure, a category can then be simultaneously X^{min} and X^{max}, as in the case of the noun 'book' in (1b) which does not project any further and which does not project at all.

Remaining with the operation Merge, this can proceed by substitution or adjunction. If Y is a specifier, then X projects (2a). If Y is an adjoined category, then X becomes a two-segment category (2b):

(2)

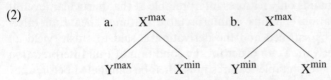

a. X^{max} b. X^{max}

      Y^{max} X^{min} Y^{min} X^{min}

The two cases are exemplified by the indirect interrogative sentences in (3a–b) and their simplified partial representations in (4a–b), respectively:

(3)   a. I wonder [***whether*** *he sees us*]

      b. *I wonder* [***if*** *he sees us*]

(4)

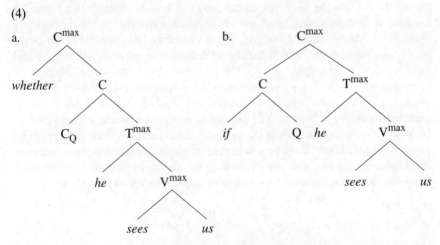

The functional category C(omplementizer) in (4) enters the derivation with an interrogative feature Q(uestion), a variant of a strong [D] or [C] categorial feature, namely D_Q or C_Q, which must be checked by a matching feature within its checking domain. The substitution option is represented by (4a) where the *wh*-phrase *whether* (namely D_Q) substitutes for the empty [Spec, C] position, and the adjunction option by (4b) in which the complementizer *if* (namely C_Q) enters the checking domain of Q by adjoining to the latter.

The second structure-building operation Move, in contrast, is intended to capture the inescapable displacement properties of language. Move targets a merged category and makes it available to the functional structure by raising it within the checking domain of a given functional category. Once again, Move makes use of the substitution and adjunction options, as illustrated by the interrogative structures in (5a–b) and their simplified representations in (6a–b), respectively:

(5) a. *I wonder [**what**$_i$ he can see* t$_i$]^5
    b. ***Can**$_i$ he* t$_i$ *see?*

(6)

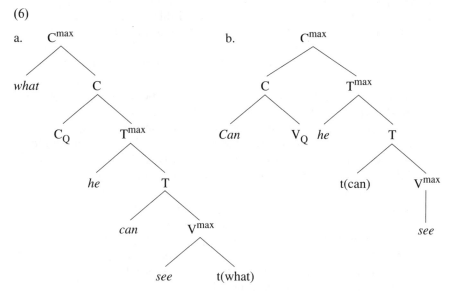

In (6a) the strong D$_Q$ feature on C is checked by raising the *wh*-phrase *what* (namely D$_Q$) from its VP-internal merger position to substitute for the empty [Spec, C] position within the checking domain of C. Alternatively, a category can enter into a checking relation with Q by adjoining to C, as in (6b) where the finite verb *can* (namely V$_Q$) raises to adjoin to V$_Q$ on C.

1.3.4. *Checking theory*

We have seen that formal features may be either interpretable or uninterpretable, the former including categorial features, nominal φ-features, interrogative Q-features and Tense-features, and the latter including verbal, adjectival φ-features and Case features. Among the uninterpretable features, we also recognize the categorial features [V] and [D] of such functional categories as C, T and light *v*, in turn specified as [±strong]. A strong feature is one that a derivation 'cannot tolerate' and which triggers a rule that eliminates it. Thus the [±strong] dimension plays a central role in language variation, determining whether categories raise overtly or covertly into checking configurations. Specifically, the [±strong] dimension is narrowly restricted to categorial features of functional categories, these being the only features that can trigger overt movement. Given that their only function is to trigger movement, [±strong] categorial features cannot be interpreted at LF and must therefore be eliminated.

Above we established that for a derivation to converge, it must satisfy the condition of Full Interpretation which requires that all uninterpretable features be eliminated before they reach LF. This is achieved through a checking theory which places an unchecked feature α (henceforth F[α]) in a checking relation with a matching feature β (F[β]). Checking configurations are established whenever F[β] enters into a Spec-head or Head-head relation (namely the checking domain) with a corresponding F[α]. This is achieved by the operations Merge or Move, by substitution or adjunction. For example, in (4a–b) F[D_Q] and F[C_Q] (namely *whether* and *if*) are merged into the checking domain of C by substitution and adjunction, respectively, whereas in (6a–b) F[D_Q] and F[V_Q] (namely *what* and *can*) are moved into the checking domain of C by substitution and adjunction, respectively. In all four cases, the checking relation results in the elimination of the uninterpretable strong categorial feature on C (namely D, C, V). On the other hand, the interrogative feature Q on C and the corresponding F[Q] on the category inserted into the checking domain of C (namely *whether, if, what, can*) are not eliminated once checked, since they are interpretable and must survive to LF to determine the illocutionary force of the clause.

We see then that while the checking operation eliminates uninterpretable features, it has no effect on interpretable features such as Q, which may enter into multiple checking relations or none at all before they are interpreted at LF. Consider by way of example the following Romanian sentence discussed in Rivero (1989: 290):

(7) *studenţii   trebuiau   să plece*
     students-the$_i$ must.3PL [$_{TP}$ t$_i$ leave.3 [$_{VP}$ t$_i$ . . .]]
     'the students must have left'

The predicate *trebuiau* 'must' subcategorizes for a simple TP complement, a choice which precludes the embedded verb *să plece* 'leave' from checking nominative on its embedded subject *studenţii* 'the students'. Instead, the latter is forced to raise to check nominative on the matrix T, witness the 3PL agreement on *trebuiau*. Yet, notwithstanding the absence of nominative in the embedded clause, the embedded verb continues to display 3rd person agreement with the raised subject. Interpreted in terms of checking theory, these facts find an immediate explanation. The DP *studenţii* in (7) carries interpretable D- and 3PL ϕ-features and an uninterpretable nominative Case feature. Merged with a strong, hence uninterpretable, F[D], the embedded T forces *studenţii* to raise to [Spec, T] within its checking domain, where it can check the strong F[D] on T. The Extended Projection Principle (EPP) of earlier theories, which requires that every sentence have a subject, reduces then to [±strong] D-feature on T. Now, once in a checking configuration with *studenții*, the other uninterpretable features on T, namely 3rd person φ-features, can also be checked 'for free' or as 'free riders'. In contrast, the corresponding categorial and φ-features on *studenții* are not eliminated once checked, since they are interpretable and remain accessible to the C_{HL}.

Subsequently, the strong F[D] on the matrix T must be checked, causing *studenții* to raise to the matrix [Spec, T]. Once inserted within the checking domain of T, *studenții* checks and eliminates the latter's uninterpretable nominative feature (its own uninterpretable nominative feature not having entered into a checking relation with the embedded T). In addition, its categorial and φ-features, which we have established are not eliminated following checking in the embedded clause, can enter into a second checking relation with the matrix T, the latter triggering the 3PL agreement on the matrix verb *trebuiau*. Therefore, raising *studenții* to the embedded and matrix [Spec, T] positions in (7) results in double agreement, double satisfaction of the EPP and a single Case relation with the matrix T.

In addition to overt checking, as in the cases considered above, the checking operation can also apply covertly. Consider the synonymous English and Italian sentences in (8a–b), respectively:

(8) a. [$_{TP}$ *John$_i$* [$_{VP}$ *always* t$_i$ *returns*]]

     b.   *Gianni$_i$*   *torna$_j$*   *sempre*
        [$_{TP}$ Gianni$_i$ returns$_j$ [$_{VP}$ always   t$_i$ t$_j$]]

In both English and Italian the EPP is strong, namely T is drawn from the lexicon with a strong F[D]. Consequently, the subjects *John* and *Gianni* in (8) both raise overtly to [Spec, T] to check this uninterpretable feature, the nominative features on T and *John/Gianni* checked 'for free'. In contrast, the F[V] borne by T is weak in English but strong in Italian. This is revealed by the position of the verb with respect to the VP-adverb *always/sempre* in (8a–b), which follows in English but precedes in Italian. Such linear ordering illustrates that in Italian, but not English, the verb raises overtly out of its merger position within VP. Thus, the strong F[V] on T in the Italian example (8b) forces the verb *torna* to adjoin to T where it can check this feature, as well as its own uninterpretable φ-features 'for free' against those of the subject now raised to [Spec, T]. In the English sentence (8a), on the other hand, F[V] on T is weak, hence verb-movement can and must be delayed until the last minute (see discussion of Procrastinate in section 1.3.6).

At this point in the computation to LF, now that all strong uninterpretable features have been eliminated by checking, an operation called Spell-Out applies to the structures in (8a–b). Spell-Out strips away all those features relevant to the PF representation, leaving the residue which is mapped to LF. The pre-Spell-Out computation we call overt and the subsystem that continues the computation to LF the covert component. It is precisely at this point that any unchecked uninterpretable features must be checked, otherwise the condition of Full Interpretation will not be satisfied causing the derivation to crash at LF. In our Italian example (8b), all uninterpretable features have been checked, such that the derivation can proceed directly to LF where it will converge. In (8a), by contrast, the uninterpretable [-strong] F[V] on T and the uninterpretable φ-features on V (*returns*) have not yet been checked. This is achieved by covert movement which takes the form of pure F(eature)-raising, given that all PF (phonetic) features have been stripped away at Spell-Out. Given that covert movement is always pure F-raising, this will mean that the unchecked features will enter the relevant checking domain by adjunction. Consequently, the unchecked features in (8a) are checked by FF[V] (= *returns*) adjoining to T, yielding the LF representation in (9):

(9)

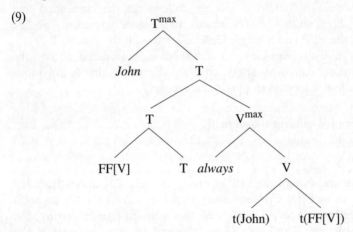

1.3.5. *Functional categories*

Almost all items of the lexicon belong to the substantive (lexical) categories, namely verb, noun, adjective and preposition. Any other items belong to the class of functional categories, a highly (and perhaps universally) restricted class including, at least, C, D, T and (light) *v*. Within the Minimalist Program these assume a central role since they have interpretable features which provide instructions to the PF and LF interfaces. Moreover, they are responsible for feature checking, the procedure which drives Move and, in part, Merge. Consider C. We have seen that this carries information regarding the interpretation of the clause, traditionally termed illocutionary force, determining, for example, whether it is declarative (for example, English *that*) or interrogative (for example, English *if*). In the case of English, we have seen that a strong F[Q] on C requires overt checking by

Merge (4a–b) or Move (6a–b). In addition, C may also encode other interpretable features (see Rizzi 1998: §1), such as reference time, which, if strong, requires overt checking by verb-raising (see section 4.4.2).

Similar considerations apply to D, the functional category which encodes, among other things, interpretable features regarding the definite, referential and animacy properties of its nominal complement. Once again, if D carries a strong F[N], this may trigger overt checking of such a feature. This is the case in the Neapolitan possessive structure (10a) where the kinship term *sora* 'sister' raises overtly to D. In the possessive structure (10b), by contrast, F[N] is weak and N-to-D-raising of *machina* 'car' is delayed until the covert component (see Longobardi 1994):

(10) a.   *sora-ta*
           [$_D$ sister$_i$-your [$_N$ t$_i$]]
           'your sister'

      b.   *'a   machina   toja*
           [$_D$ the [$_{NP}$ car   [$_A$ your]]]
           'your car'

Let us now turn to T. Besides marking interpretable features such as tense, aspect and mood, this functional category also encodes various uninterpretable features such as the (EPP) D-feature, and the nominative and φ-features of the subject, optionally assigned to it as it is drawn from the lexicon for the numeration. Within this system there is then no place for a separate functional category Agr(eement), which assumed a central role in previous theories. Instead, we have an Agr-less model, in many respects similar to that which preceded Pollock's (1989) split-INFL hypothesis.

The final functional category which we shall consider is light *v*, a performative or causative verb which provides the external causative/agentive-role. Consider the English sentences in (11):

(11) a.   [$_{TP}$ *Mary*$_i$ [$_{VP}$ t$_i$ [$_V$ *got a present*]]]

      b.   [$_{TP}$ *John*$_i$ [$_{vP}$ t$_i$ [$_{Vb}$ *got*$_j$-*v*] [$_{VP}$ *Mary* [$_V$ t$_j$ *a present*]]]]

The THEME argument *a present* is merged with the verb *got* to from a V constituent, which is in turn merged with the RECIPIENT argument *Mary* yielding the VP (V^{max}) structure. Subsequently, in (11a) VP is merged with T and the RECIPIENT argument *Mary* is raised to [Spec, T] to check the strong F[D] on T. In (11b), by contrast, the numeration also contains the AGENT argument *John*. This is inserted into the derivation by selecting *v*, a phonetically null verb, from the numeration and merging it with VP. This *v* carries (perhaps universally) a strong F[V] which causes the lexical verb *got* to adjoin to it, forming the verbal complex Vb. Next, *John* is selected from the numeration and merged in [Spec, *v*], where it can be assigned the agentive/causative θ-role by *v* before raising to [Spec, T]. As is evident, it is the presence of *v* in (11b) which provides the external θ-role and the causative reading of *got*, the covert analogue of causative *made* in the equivalent sentence *John made Mary get a present*.

In addition to providing the external (agentive/causative) θ-role, *v* is also responsible for checking the features of the object, in this respect similar to AgrO in the Principles and Parameters model. Consider the sentences in (12) from the Calabrian dialect of Fiumefreddo (CS):

(12) a. *Maria asuliava   a-Cicciu*
       Maria$_i$ listened.PAST.3SG$_j$ [$_{vP}$ ACC-Ciccio$_k$ t$_i$ t$_j$ [$_{VP}$ t$_j$ t$_k$]]
       'Maria was listening to Ciccio'

      b. *Maria asuliava   ru discurzu*
       Maria$_i$ listened.PAST.3SG$_j$ [$_{vP}$ t$_i$ t$_j$ [$_{VP}$ t$_j$ the conversation]]
       'Maria was listening to the conversation'

For reasons which will be explained in chapter 2, the features on the object complement *a Cicciu* 'Ciccio' are checked overtly in (12a), whereas those on *ru discurzu* 'the conversation' in (12b) are checked covertly. We maintain therefore that *v* is drawn from the lexicon with a strong F[D] in (12a) but with a weak F[D] in (12b). Consequently, in the former case the object *a Cicciu* must enter into a checking relation with *v* to eliminate the latter's strong F[D] before Spell-Out. It therefore raises to an outer specifier position of *v* above that of the merger position of the subject, where it enters into a Spec-head relation with *v*, as illustrated by the partial derivation in (13a) where T has not yet been merged:

(13)

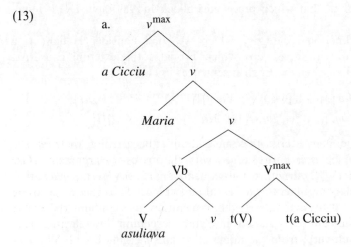

In (12b), by contrast, the weak F[D] and other features (for example, Case) on *v* are checked by covert movement of FF[*ru discruzu*] to *v* (now raised to T) after Spell-Out, as schematized in (13b):

(13) b.

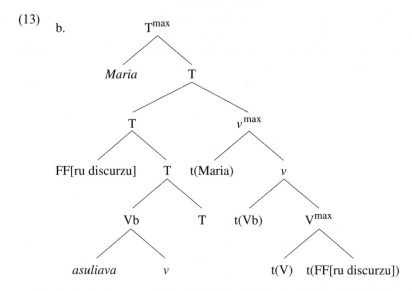

We thus obtain a parallel with EPP checking of the subject: in the same way that the subject raises overtly/covertly to check the strong/weak F[D] on T, objects raise overtly/covertly to check the strong/weak F[D] on v. We can therefore talk about the EPP-checking of T and, by analogy, the EPP-checking of v.

1.3.6. *Economy*

In addition to satisfying conditions on well-formedness such as the condition of Full Interpretation, a derivation must be *optimal*. In other words, it is not sufficient that a derivation converge, it must also satisfy certain natural economy conditions, such as those which impose locality of movement and exclude superfluous steps. The C_{HL} thus chooses among convergent derivations, evaluating their global cost and complexity, ultimately selecting the cheapest derivation. Less economical computations are blocked even if they converge. Naturally, such questions of convergence and economy do not arise for the operation Merge, since insufficient application of Merge would fail to yield an LF representation and no derivation would be generated. The operation Merge is therefore 'costless'. The operation Move, on the other hand, must meet several economy conditions which we take to be part of its definition. One of these is the c-command condition which requires that a category must c-command its trace, thereby excluding 'downwards' and 'sideways' movement.

Another is the Last Resort Condition which requires that movement operations be morphologically driven by feature checking. This has the effect of eliminating superfluous steps in derivations: a step is legitimate only if it is necessary as a 'last resort' for convergence. Had the step not taken place, the derivation would not have been able to converge. This is the case of strong categorial features on functional categories, which if not checked before Spell-Out, cause the derivation to crash.

A related economy principle is Procrastinate which expresses the idea that covert movement is less costly than its overt analogue. This generalization follows from our earlier observation that covert movement is pure F-raising, all PF features having been stripped away following Spell-Out. Overt raising, in contrast, has to carry along whole categories for PF convergence, and not just the relevant unchecked feature, because the PF interface cannot interpret scattered phonological features. Given that shorter derivations blocks longer ones, and assuming that the application of phonological rules counts in evaluating the cost of a derivation, it follows that overt movement which has to pied-pipe along 'excess baggage', is more costly than covert movement. However, a violation of Procrastinate that is required for convergence is not an economy violation. This is the case of strong categorial features on functional categories which, as noted above, cannot be tolerated by the derivation and must be checked before Spell-Out.

The final economy condition on Move is the Minimal Link Condition (MLC) which requires that movement operations proceed by the shortest links permissible. This accounts for the fact that only the closest of two or more potential features can raise to check an unchecked feature.

With these economy conditions in mind, we define the operation Move (Attract) as in (14):

(14)   K *attracts* F if F is the closest feature that can enter into a checking relation with a sublabel of K. (Chomsky 1995: 297)

Suppose β c-commands α and τ is the target of raising, then we define 'close' as in (15):

(15) β is *closer* to K than α unless β is in the same minimal domain as (a) τ or (b) α

To see how these economy conditions work, consider the Neapolitan sentence in (16a) and its partial derivation in (16b):

(16)   a. *Ciro vasaje   a   Cuncetta*
           Ciro kiss.PAST.3SG ACC   Concetta
           'Ciro kissed Concetta'

b.

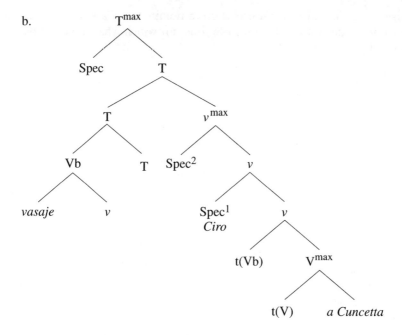

In (16b) all items from the numeration have been selected and merged in the derivation and the verb *vasaje* 'kissed' has raised successively to v and T. Furthermore, both T and v have been drawn from the numeration with a strong F[D] which must be checked before Spell-Out. Let us take first the case of the strong F[D] on v. There are two potential categories in (16b) which could check the strong F[D] on v by raising to [Spec^2, v], namely the object complement *a Cuncetta* and the subject *Ciro* merged in the inner [Spec^1, v]. Initially, it would appear that the subject is the closest category since it c-commands the object. However, the subject and the target of movement [Spec^2, v] are in the same minimal domain, namely they occur within the minimal domain of v. By condition (15a), the subject cannot then be considered closer to [Spec^2, v] than the object. Rather, the target of movement and the subject are said to be *equidistant* from the object. The strong F[D] on v can therefore attract the object, raising it to [Spec^2, v] without violating economy.

Take now the case of the strong F[D] on T. Again both the subject and the object have a categorial F[D] which can potentially check that on T. Although the object, now raised to [Spec^2, v], c-commands the subject merged in [Spec^1, v], it is not closer to the target of movement [Spec, T], since both subject and object are in the same minimal domain and, hence by condition (15b), equidistant from [Spec, T]. Consequently, either object or subject can raise. If the former option is taken, then the derivation will crash since the object cannot check the nominative Case on T.[6] The only convergent derivation is therefore one in which the subject raises to [Spec, T].

2

CASE-MARKING

2.1. INTRODUCTION

In the wake of Chomsky (1995), one of the central topics of much current research has been to determine the role played by functional heads such as C, T and *v* in licensing movement. Within the Minimalist Program, all movement operations are taken to be morphologically driven, a property captured by the Last Resort Condition which requires that 'strong' (uninterpretable) features borne by such functional heads enter into a checking relation with a matching feature prior to LF. The data to be discussed in the present chapter will be shown to bear directly on such a view of movement, inasmuch as we shall derive observed differences in the mechanisms of Case-checking from the properties of such verbal-related functional heads as *v* and Appl(icative). Within such a framework we shall attempt to provide a formal characterization of the various types of object complement found in Neapolitan and a number of other southern Italian dialects, focusing, in particular, on the study of the properties of a specific class of grammatical objects: direct and indirect objects morphologically marked by a reflex of the Latin preposition AD > *a* 'to'. Both from a semantic and syntactic perspective the latter prove particularly interesting in that they exhibit a certain degree of variation in their Case-marking and distribution, correlating with distinct semantic properties. By way of example, consider the contrasts in the Neapolitan sentences (1) and (2):

(1) a. *rispunnetteno a Maria*
       reply.PAST.3PL   to Maria
       'they replied to Maria'

     b. *rispunnetteno â   lettera*
        reply.PAST.3PL   to-the letter
        'they replied to the letter'

(2) a. *nce   l'a   rispunnetteno*
        her.DAT /her.ACC reply.PAST.3PL
        'they replied to her'

     b. *nce   /*'a   rispunetteno*
        it.DAT /it.ACC reply.PAST.3PL
        'they replied to it'

The verb *rispunnere* 'to reply' is traditionally described as a verb which selects for an indirect object marked with dative Case: *a Maria* 'to Maria' in (1a) and *â* (= *a* to' + *'a* 'the') *lettera* 'to the letter' in (1b). However, as witnessed by the parallel pronominal structures in (2), if animate, the indirect object can also surface as a direct object marked by the accusative clitic (2a), an option not available to inanimate indirect objects (2b). A similar example of variation in Case-marking is provided by the sentences in (3):

(3) a. *'a   verette   'a   casa*
       it.ACC see.PAST.1SG the house
       'I saw the house'

   b. *'a   verette   a   Maria*
       her.ACC see.PAST.1SG to Maria
       'I saw Maria'

   c. *appresentaje   (*a) Maria a ll' ate*
       present.PAST.1SG (to) Maria to the others
       'I introduced Maria to the others'

The verb *verette* 'I saw' in (3a–b) is a transitive predicate taking a direct object complement which it marks with accusative, as is confirmed by the doubling accusative clitic *'a* 'it/her'. Nonetheless, it seems legitimate to suppose that the direct objects in (3a–b) are marked with two distinct types of accusative: the inanimate direct object *'a casa* 'the house' in (3a) appears in the unmarked accusative, whereas its animate counterpart *a Maria* 'to Maria' in (3b) is morphologically marked by a reflex of AD. Strangely, though, the latter overt marker disappears in (3c) when the animate direct object co-occurs with an indirect object.

   This kind of behaviour exemplified in (1)–(3) leads us to question the validity in Neapolitan of the traditional Romance classification of direct and indirect objects, standardly interpreted as a DP versus PP distinction, since Neapolitan distinguishes two types of direct object and, in many cases, neutralizes the distinction between direct and indirect objects. In what follows we shall argue, in contrast, that all direct and indirect objects are structural Case-marked DPs and that the observed variation in Case-marking in such examples as (1)–(3) is sensitive to a number of semantic factors determined by the various structural positions that such objects may occupy. Following Chomsky (1995: 352), we suggest that functional heads such as *v* and Appl may host a D-feature on a par with T which, if strong, causes overt raising of the object to an outer specifier position. Concretely, we shall propose that objects associated with such D-related interpretative features as animacy and specificity may under certain circumstances undergo overt object shift to a VP-external specifier position, whereas objects lacking such properties remain within VP,[1] giving rise to a number of Case alternations parallel to the double-object constructions familiar from such languages as English.

An attractive concomitant of this analysis is that it provides a straightforward solution to the Case-marking properties and distribution of Neapolitan objects which can be directly related to the properties of the D-feature on
v and Appl. In this light Romance clitics, often viewed as the spell-out of the
verb's Case feature (see Borer 1984), receive a highly natural interpretation if
they can now be understood as the overt realization of such a D-feature
realized on an independent D-head adjoined to *v* or Appl.[2] Under this
interpretation of Neapolitan clitics, the differing form(s) and distribution of
clitics can be profitably used to establish a number of generalizations about
the functional structure of the clause and the mechanisms of Case-checking
operative in Neapolitan and other southern dialects.

The chapter is organized as the follows. In section 2.2 we review the
behaviour of objects in monotransitive structures, identifying the morphological and syntactic properties that distinguish structural Case-marked
objects from prepositional objects marked with inherent Case. In
section 2.3 we propose a structural interpretation of the distinction between
structural and inherent Case-marked objects in Neapolitan, deriving further
differences in the Case-checking of structural Case-marked objects from the
properties of the functional head *v* and its role in determining overt object
raising. In section 2.4 we turn our attention to ditransitive clauses and the
particular problems they raise for a proper characterization of the distribution of Case-marking, highlighting the range of variations found in the
marking of covert and overt direct and indirect objects, the constraints that
operate on such alternations and the dialectal variation found in this area.
Building on the proposals made for monotransitive clauses, we demonstrate
that the behaviour of objects in ditransitive clauses follows from the
interaction of properties of the functional heads *v* and Appl and the MLC.

2.2. MONOTRANSITIVES: SOME INITIAL OBSERVATIONS

The starting point for our discussion is provided by the Neapolitan sentences
in (4a–e):

(4) a. *veco   'o castiello*
         see.PRES.1SG the castle
         'I can see the castle'

     b. *veco   a   Ciro*
         see.PRES.1SG PA Ciro
         'I can see Ciro'

     c. *telefuno   a   Ciro*
         telephone.PRES.1SG SD Ciro
         'I'll telephone Ciro'

d. *m'   abbetuaje   a Ciro*
   myself accustom.PAST.1SG to Ciro
   'I got used to Ciro'

e. *m'   allicordo   'e Ciro*
   myself remember.PRES.1SG of Ciro
   'I remember Ciro'

We maintain that the verbs in (4a–c) mark their complement with structural Case: (4a) unmarked accusative (henceforth UA), (4b) prepositional accusative (henceforth PA),[3] and (4c) structural dative (henceforth SD),[4] whereas the verbs in (4d–e) mark their complements with an inherent Case realized by the prepositions *a* 'to' (dative) and *'e* 'of' (genitive), respectively. We assume then that verbs traditionally labelled transitive have a single structural accusative Case feature which can license one of two types of accusative object in Neapolitan: UA and PA, the choice between the two being determined essentially by the semantics of the object. Simplifying considerably (though see Ledgeway 1995: S.II.§1.2.2 for a detailed treatment), UA is licensed when the object is inanimate and/or interpreted as non-specific (4a), whereas the PA surfaces whenever the object is animate and specific in reference (4b).[5] Some Neapolitan examples, both from early and modern texts, illustrating the distribution of the PA are given in (5a–h), with additional examples from other southern Italian dialects in (6a–l) highlighting the widespread distribution of the PA throughout southern Italy (see Telmon 1993: 119–20 and references cited there):

(5) a. *li nuostri fereranno [a li Grieci]* (De Blasi 1986: 88, 6)
        'our men will injure [the Greeks]'

     b. *per non offendere [a te]* (Formentin 1987: XXIX)
        'so as not to offend [you]'

     c. *co mmille autre soniette e matricale [a Nnapole] laudanno* (Cortese 1783, in Capozzoli 1889)
        'with thousands of other sonnets and madrigals praising [Naples]'

     d. *ce sta na femmena ca ncanta [all'uommene]* (Vittoria 1990: 35)
        'there is a lady that charms [men]'

     e. *papà pigliaje a schiaffe [a Mastu Nicola]* (Fierro 1989: 199)
        'dad slapped [Mastro Nicola]'

     f. *'o tenite stu barbaro curaggio 'e annummenà [a patemo]?* (Di Giacomo 1991a: 37)
        'you've got the cheek to mention [my father]?'

     g. *acchiappaje [a mammema]* (Bichelli 1974: 290)
        'I grabbed [my mum]'

     h. *nun ringraziate [a Dio]?* (De Filippo 1973: 130)
        'do you not thank [God]?'

(6) a. *cerchieno proprio* [*a tene*] (Rome, Rohlfs 1969: 7)
'they're looking precisely for [you]'

b. *si vvisto* [*a ffràtimo*]? (southern Lazio, ibid.)
'have you seen [my brother]?'

c. *ha lassat'* [*a tté solo*] / *salùtame* [*a ppatrete*] / *vulem'accid'* [*a ffratete*] (Abruzzo, ibid.)
'he left [you alone] / greet me [your father] / we want to kill [your brother]'

d. *sind'* [*a mmé*]! / *vid'* [*a ccustu*]! (Abruzzo, Finamore 1893: 28)
'listen to [me]! / look at [this one]!'

e. ɤward [a nˈnujə]/ˈvekə [a ˈiddə] ka ˈskappa (Calvello (PZ), Gioscio 1985: 63)
'he watches [us/you] / I see [him] run away'

f. sɔ vːɪst/kːjɛt/tʃːɪs [a pːəˈpːɪin] (Altamura (BA), Loporcaro 1986: 269)
'I have seen/found/killed [Peppino]'

g. *facette trasí* [*a Maria*] (Apulia, Rohlfs 1969: 7)
'he had [Maria] shown in'

h. *chiàmame* [*a Nicola*] (Apriligano (CS), Accattattis 1895: §226)
'call [Nicola] for [me]!'

i. *pijja* [*a fràtetta*] (CZ, Scerbo 1886: §236)
'fetch [your brother]!'

j. *jeu aiutài sempri* [*a tia e a tutti i to parenti*] (RC, Meliadò 1994: 129)
'I've always helped [you and all your relatives]'

k. *vitti* [*a to figghia*] (Sicily, Varvaro 1988: 725)
'I saw [your daughter]'

l. *si pigghiarru* [*a na picciridda*] / [*a Paulu*] *u chiamàu Turiddu* (Sicily, Leone 1995: 49)
'they took [the young girl] / Salvatore called [Paolo]'

A potential criticism that might be levelled against our initial classification of the complements in (4a–e) concerns the validity of treating objects in the PA (4b) and SD (4c) as DPs on a par with objects in the UA (4a; see Sornicola 1997b: 66). The *prima facie* evidence would suggest an analysis which treats such objects as PPs marked by some form of inherent dative Case on account of their co-occurrence with *a*, which clearly behaves in many other contexts as a preposition in Romance. In many respects, however, the behaviour of such objects favours analysing them as DPs, a conclusion, moreover, widely proposed for Spanish objects in the PA.[6] In what follows, we shall present extensive morphological and syntactic evidence to substantiate the DP status of objects in the PA and SD, pointing out at the same time how they differ from the prepositional complements in (4d–e) marked with an inherent Case.

2.2.1. *Structural/inherent Case: morphological evidence*

We begin by considering full nominal complements which, as demonstrated by the Neapolitan examples in (7a–b), are morphologically identical, whether they appear in the PA or SD:

(7) a. *vaso   /aspecco   /sento   /chiammo   a   Ciro*
       kiss.PRES.1SG /wait.PRES.1SG /hear.PRES.1SG /call.PRES.1SG PA Ciro
       'I kiss/wait/hear/call Ciro'

   b. *parlo   /rispongo   /dimanno   /riro   a   Ciro*
       speak.PRES.1SG /reply.PRES.1SG /ask.PRES.1SG /laugh-at.PRES.1SG SD Ciro
       'I speak to/reply to/ask/laugh at Ciro'

The identical formal marking of these two types of nominal complement, we suggest, is not arbitrary but reflects a tendency to generalize the Case marker *a* to all structural Case-marked animate objects, irrespective of their accusative or dative status. Indeed, this conclusion is confirmed by a wider examination of the prepositional accusative in Romance, which reveals that it is invariably the dative marker which is pressed into service to mark animate accusative objects.[7]

Furthermore, the observed syncretism between structural accusative and dative evident in examples (7a–b) is not restricted simply to complements which are names, but is also observable in conjunction with DPs headed by a definite article. Since the latter half of the eighteenth century, aphaeresized forms of the definite article *lo > 'o* (M.SG), *la > 'a* (F.SG), *li > 'e* (PL) have been in common use, except before vowels where the velar lateral resurfaces, for example *l'ovo* 'the egg'. Significantly, when the aphaeresized forms of the article co-occur with the PA/SD marker *a*, the latter is absorbed in a process of coalescent assimilation,[8] namely *a + 'o* (M.SG)/*'a* (F.SG)/*'e* (PL) ⇒ *'o/'a/'e*. Consequently, not only is the distinction between DPs in the PA and SD neutralized when headed by the definite article, but DPs in the UA are also formally identical with the latter two. Compare the following examples that adequately illustrate this point:

(8) a. *veco   'o   commune* (UA)
      see.PRES.1SG [DP the town-hall]
      'I can see the town hall'

   b. *veco   'o   scarparo* (PA)
      see.PRES.1SG [DP PA-the cobbler]
      'I can see the cobbler'

   c *parlo   'o   scarparo* (SD)
      speak.PRES.1SG [DP SD-the cobbler]
      'I'll speak to the cobbler'

It follows that structural accusative and dative Case-marking on full DPs, whether animate or otherwise, is in most cases formally identical. Below follow some further examples which amply illustrate the absence of overt marking on DPs in the SD headed by a definite determiner:

(9) a. *io mo nne parlo*   *'o*   *cugnato*
       [_DP_ SD-the brother-in-law]
       'I'm going to speak about it with his brother-in-law' (Di Giacomo 1991a: 98)

    b. *nce ne saglimmo*   *'o*   *Casino*
       [_DP_ SD-the country-house]
       'we are going up to the country house' (De Filippo 1973: 21)

    c. *me fa penzà*   *'o*   *paese nuosto*
       [_DP_ SD-the village our]
       'it makes me think of our village' (ibid., 249)

    d. *Don Pascale dette nu schiaff*   *'a*   *mugliera*
       [_DP_ SD-the wife]
       'Don Pascale gave a slap to his wife' (ibid., 462)

A further consideration which points towards a unified analysis of all objects bearing structural Case, at the same time keeping them distinct from inherent Case-marked complements, concerns the form of their corresponding clitic pronouns:

(10) a. *'o*   *verette*   (*'o castiello*)
         it.ACC see.PAST.ISG (the castle)
         'I saw it (the castle)'

     b. *'o*   *verette*   (*a Ciro*)
         him.ACC see.PAST.ISG (PA Ciro)
         'I saw him (Ciro)'

     c. *(n)ce*   *telefunaje*   (*a Ciro*)
         him.DAT telephone.PAST.ISG (SD Ciro)
         'I telephoned him (Ciro)'

     d. *me*   *(n)ce*   *abbetuaje*   (*a Ciro*)
         myself him.DAT accustom.PAST.ISG (to Ciro)
         'I got used to him (Ciro)'

     e. *me*   *n'*   *allicordo*   (*'e Ciro*)
         myself him.GEN remember.PRES.ISG (of Ciro)
         'I remember him (Ciro)'

From the examples in (10a–e), the following initial generalizations emerge. Firstly, objects marked accusative, whether in the UA or PA, are referenced by the same pronominal form, namely *'o* (10a, b). Similar considerations would appear to apply to objects bearing dative Case, whether structural or inherent, which are uniformly referenced by the pronominal clitic *(n)ce* (10c, d) Finally, verbs which mark their complements with genitive Case reference the latter with the pronoun *n'/ne* (10e). When we consider non-3rd person forms, however, a very different pattern emerges, witness (11a–d):

(11) a. ***te***   *verette*   *(a te)*
      you.ACC see.PAST.1SG (PA you)
      'I saw you'

    b. ***te***   *telefunaje*   *(a te)*
      you.DAT telephone.PAST.1SG (SD you)
      'I telephoned you'

    c. *me* ***(n)ce*** *abbetuaje*   *(a te)*
      myself him.DAT accustom.PAST.1SG (to you)
      'I got used to you'

    d. *me* ***n'***   *allicordo*   *('e te)*
      myself him.DAT remember.PRES.1SG (to you)
      'I remember you'

Now objects in the SD pattern identically to those in the PA, whereas inherent Case clitics remain unchanged. These examples highlight a significant difference between structural and inherent Case in Neapolitan: clitic pronouns referencing structural Case-marked objects encode person and number and, to a lesser extent, also gender (see table 2.1 below), whereas clitics referencing inherent Case-marked objects present an invariable form encoding solely Case.

Following Rizzi (1988: 512–14), we take this difference in the ability of clitics to mark such categories as person, number and gender to underlie a more general difference between nouns and prepositions. In Neapolitan, and Romance more generally, such φ-features are typically marked on nouns but never on prepositions. It follows from this that objects referenced by the structural clitics in table 2.1 are DPs, whereas complements marked by the invariable inherent clitics in table 2.1 are necessarily PPs.

Furthermore, the distribution of the 3rd person structural clitics equally

Table 2.1 Neapolitan clitic proforms

	Structural case		Inherent case	
	accusative	dative	dative	genitive
1SG	*me*	*me*	*(n)ce*	*ne*
2SG	*te*	*te*	*(n)ce*	*ne*
3SG	*lol'o* (M)	*(n)ce*	*(n)ce*	*ne*
	lal'a (F)	*lle* (M/F)		
1PL	*(n)ce*	*(n)ce*	*(n)ce*	*ne*
2PL	*ve*	*ve*	*(n)ce*	*ne*
3PL	*'e* (M/F)	*(n)ce* (M/F)	*(n)ce*	*ne*

provides some strong evidence for the proposed parallel between objects in the
PA and SD on the one hand and the distinction between structural and inherent
dative Case on the other. Though not without important syntactic consequences (see section 2.3.2), a significant and very revealing property of 3rd
person objects common to numerous southern Italian dialects manifests itself
in the optional neutralization of the SD/PA distinction in the 3rd person clitics.[9]
Thus, alongside the unambiguously SD clitic *nce* in (12a), the indirect object
can equally be referenced by the traditional accusative clitic *'o*, as in (12b):

(12) a. *nce   parlo   /rispongo   /dimanno   /riro*
        him.SD_i speak.PRES.1SG /reply.PRES.1SG /ask.PRES.1SG /laugh-at.PRES.1SG
        (*a   Ciro*)
        (SD Ciro_i)

    b. *'o   parlo   /rispongo   /dimanno   /riro*
        him.PA_i SPEAK.PRES.1SG /REPLY.PRES.1SG /ASK.PRES.1SG /LAUGH-AT.PRES.1SG
        (*a   Ciro*)
        (PA Ciro_i)
        'I speak to/reply to/ask/laugh at him (Ciro)'

Below are given some further examples of PA-referencing of indirect objects
in Neapolitan (13a–f) and other Campanian varieties (13g–k).

(13) a. *'a   vanno   appriesso*
        her.ACC go.PRES.3PL after
        'they chase after her' (Di Giacomo 1991a: 56)

    b. *lo   scrivo   sempe*
        him.ACC write.PRES.1SG always
        'I always write to him' (Scarpetta 1992: 387)

    c. *non lo   risponnere*
        not him.ACC reply.INF
        'don't answer him' (Scarpetta 1994: 116)

    d. *vuie 'o   rispunnite   pure?*
        you him.ACC reply.PRES.2PL too
        'will you answer him too?' (De Filippo 1973: 318)

    e. *'o   jett'   incontro*
        him.ACC go.PAST.3SG towards
        'he went up to him' (De Filippo 1975: 177)

    f. o   tələfu'najə
        him.ACC telephone.PAST.1SG
        'I rang him' (Sornicola 1997: 336)

    g. lu   parle'r^aɣɣ^u
        him.ACC speak.FUT.1SG
        'I'll speak to him' (Teggiano (SA), Sornicola 1997: 336)

h. *'o figlio d' 'o Re nun 'o   perdunaie*
the child   of the king not him.ACC forgive.PAST.3SG
'the King's child did not forgive him' (Bacoli (NA), De Simone 1994: 16)

i. *'a   ghjevano   annanze*
her.ACC go.PAST.3PL in-front-of
'they went in front of her' (Castellammare di Stabia (NA), ibid., 340)

j. *'o   curreva   appriesso*
him.ACC run.PAST.3SG after
'he ran after him' (Ferrari (AV), ibid., 356)

k. *'a Rigginella 'o   redeva   'nfaccia*
the princess   him.ACC laugh.PAST.3SG in-face
'the Princess was mocking him' (Ferrari (AV), ibid., 400)

PA-referencing of indirect objects does not, however, operate indiscriminately but proves sensitive to the Case of the object. While the examples in (12)–(13) confirm the acceptability of accusative clitics referencing DPs in the SD, complements marked with inherent dative Case cannot be construed with accusative clitics, witness the sentences in (14) where the complement can only be doubled by the inherent dative clitic *nce*.

(14) a. *me   nce   /*'o   abbetuaje   a Ciro*
myself him.DAT$_i$ /him.ACC$_i$ accustom.PAST.1SG to Ciro$_i$
'I got used to Ciro'

b. *chillo nce   /*'e   teneva   ê   bone manere*
that-one them.DAT$_i$ /them.ACC$_i$ hold.PAST.3SG to-the good manners$_i$
'he insisted on good manners'

c. *nce   /*'o   hadd' âbbadà   ô   cano 'a vicina da casa*
it.DAT$_i$ /it.ACC$_i$ FUT.3SG take-care.INF to-the dog$_i$ the neighbour
'the neighbour will take care of the dog'

d. *nce   /*'a   mpazzesceno pâ   pasta*
it.DAT$_i$ /it.ACC$_i$ go-mad.PRES.3PL for-the pasta$_i$
'they go mad for pasta'

e. *te   nce   /*l'   hêje   stà   accuorto ê   mariuole*
yourself them.DAT$_i$ /them.ACC$_i$ must.PRES.2SG to-be cautious   to-the theives$_i$
'you've got to watch out for thieves'

From the contrasts between (12)–(14) we conclude that an accusative clitic is permitted in conjunction with objects in the SD since, irrespective of the accusative/dative distinction, the clitic always references a structurally Case-marked DP, a requirement which cannot be met in the sentences in (14) where the clitic references a prepositional complement marked with inherent dative Case.

We conclude our discussion with one final observation relating to the difference between objects in the SD and complements marked with inherent dative. Though we have ascertained that the distinction between objects in the PA and SD is neutralized on full DPs marked with the prenominal marker *a*, paralleled by analogous developments in the pronominal paradigm, Neapolitan also presents the option of distinctively marking SD on full DPs by means of the adverbial periphrasis *vicino a*, literally 'close to'.[10] By way of example, consider the following representative sentences:

(15) a. *me vuo' dicere [vicin"e figlie mieie], ca me so' ffiglie?* (De Filippo 1973: 344)
          'do you want to tell [my sons] that they are my children?'

      b. *m'avissev"a fà 'o piacere 'e còsere stu buttone [vicino a sta cammisa]* (ibid., 204)
          'you have to do me a favour and sew this button [onto this shirt]'

      c. *nce 'o piazzammo [vicin"o muro]* (De Filippo 1975: 65)
          'we'll fix it [to the wall]'

      d. *'o sposo ce nfelaje 'a fede [vicino a 'o rito]* (Fierro 1989: 79)
          'the bridegroom placed the ring [on her finger]'

      e. *po' dice [vicino â primma d"e ffiglie]* (Siano (SA), De Simone 1994: 22)
          'then she tells [the first of her daughters]'

      f. *tuzzuliaie [vicin'â porta]* (Castel Morrone (CE), ibid., 38)
          'he knocked [on the door']

Significantly, this adverbial marker is restricted to occurring with objects in the SD, as in (15a–f) above. If used in conjunction with complements marked with inherent dative Case, the sentences invariably prove ungrammatical, witness (16a–b):

(16) a. *m'abbetuo [(*vicin') a sta vita]*
          'I am getting used [(*close) to this life]'

      b. *me stongo attiento [(*vicin') a chillu llà]*
          'I'll watch out [(*close) for him]'

Once again we interpret the contrast between the sentences in (15) and (16) as compelling evidence for distinguishing between two types of dative complement in Neapolitan, one marked with structural Case and the other with inherent Case.

2.2.2. *Structural/inherent Case: syntactic evidence*

We have established that there exists considerable morphological evidence to substantiate our proposed distinction between structural Case-marked DP complements on the one hand and inherent Case-marked PP complements on the other. In what follows we shall turn our attention to various structural differences between these two complement types which lend further support to this distinction.

2.2.2.1. *Co-ordination*

It is standardly assumed that one of the constraints operating on co-ordination is the requirement that both conjuncts be of equal status and, in the case of DP co-ordination, that both DP conjuncts bear the same Case form. On this uncontroversial assumption that only like Cases may be conjoined, we predict that co-ordination proves felicitous whenever the structural Case-marked objects in (4a–c) are conjoined with one another, but that ungrammatical results obtain if we try to co-ordinate one of these structural Case-marked objects with the inherent Case marked objects in (4d–e). The relevant facts are presented below in (17a–d):

(17) a. *avett'â   rummané ê   guagliune e 'e   pazzielle lloro*
       must.PAST.3SG leave.INF [PA-the children] and [UA-the toys   their]
       add' 'a cainata
       at the sister-in-law
       'she had to leave the children and their toys at her sister-in-law's'

      b. *arrivajeno   tutte l' amice nuoste ca avevamo   chiammato*
       arrive.PAST.3PL [all   the friends our]   that have.PAST.1PL call.PART
       e   scritto
       and write.PART
       'all our friends came who we had telephoned and written to'

      c. **cu tuttu ca teneva   e   chiammava a Carmela*
       with all   that hold.PAST.1SG and call.PAST.1SG [to Carmela]
       'although I was fond of and used to call Carmela . . .'

      d. **cu tutto ca teneva   e   scriveva   [a Carmela]*
       with all   that hold.PAST.1SG and write.PAST.1SG [to Carmela]
       'although I was fond of and used to write Carmela . . .'

In (17a) objects in the PA and UA are co-ordinated yielding grammatical results. From this we conclude that both the UA and PA are structural Cases. An analogous conclusion is afforded by (17b) in which the structural Case-marking predicates *chiammà* 'to call' (accusative) and *scrivere* 'to write' (dative) are felicitously co-ordinated. As a consequence, both predicates govern the same object, demonstrating that PA and SD can be formally and structurally conflated. In contrast, a predicate which marks its object PA (17c) or SD (17d) proves incompatible under co-ordination with a predicate like *tené* 'to be fond of' which checks inherent dative. Additional evidence relating to co-ordination comes from sentences (18a–d):

(18) a. *chiammàjeno a Maria e *(a) Teresa*
      call.PAST.3PL   [PA Maria] and [(PA) Teresa]
      'they called Maria and Teresa'

    b. *aggiu   mannato 'a lettera a Maria e   *(a) Teresa*
      have.PAST.1SG send.PART the letter   [SD Maria] and [(SD) Teresa]
      'I've sent the letter to Maria and Teresa'

    c. *m'   abbetuaje   a Maria e (a) Teresa*
      myself   accustom.PAST.1SG to Maria and (to) Teresa
      'I got used to Maria and Teresa'

    d. *v'   allicurdate   'e Maria e ('e) Teresa?*
      yourself remember.PRES.2PL of Maria and (of) Teresa
      'do you remember Maria and Teresa?'

The sentences in (18a–b) demonstrate that in conjunction with verbs that mark their objects with PA and SD, respectively, the second conjunct must be preceded by the structural Case-marker *a* in order for co-ordination to prove felicitous. Given our proposed DP analysis of objects in the PA and SD, the data in (18a–b) follow straightforwardly: we are conjoining two DP complements each of which contains within its internal structural the Case-marker *a*. Consequently, omission of *a* in the second conjunct is to be interpreted as an instance of unbalanced co-ordination in which the second conjunct fails to project to D^{max}. If, in contrast, *a* is not a structural Case marker, but rather a preposition heading a PP taking a DP complement, as indeed we have proposed for the inherent dative Case-marked complement in (18c), as well as the genitive Case-marked complement in (18d), it follows that the presence of the preposition in the second conjunct is optional: either co-ordination occurs at the P^{max} level, in which case the preposition occurs in both conjuncts, or at the intermediate P(-bar) level with one single P realizing Case on each DP.

2.2.2.2. Passivization

In accordance with Burzio's Generalization, it is commonly assumed that a verb's structural Case feature is suppressed under passivization, resulting in the obligatory movement or co-indexation of the verb's complement with the vacant subject position where nominative can be checked. It follows that, if objects in the PA and SD are marked with structural Case, they too should undergo subjectization under passive on a par with objects in UA (19a–b). This prediction is borne out for objects in the PA, as illustrated by the examples (20a–b):

(19) a. *destrujetteno 'a casa*
      destroy.PAST.3PL [the house]
      'they destroyed the house'

b. *'a   casa   fuje   destrutta*
[the house]ᵢ be.PAST.3SG destroy.PART tᵢ
'the house got destroyed'

(20) a *verettemo   a   Ciro*
see.PAST.1PL PA Ciro
'we saw Ciro'

b. *Ciro fuje   visto*
Ciroᵢ be.PAST.3SG see.PART tᵢ
'Ciro was seen'

The facts relevant to objects in the SD prove rather more difficult to interpret, in that passivization does not invariably produce good results, although one cannot exclude here external factors relating to the general avoidance of the canonical BE-passive, especially when the topicalized argument is animate (see Cennamo 1997: 146–53). Nonetheless, in a number of instances SD would appear to be suppressed under passivization, forcing the subjectization of the underlying indirect object (see also Leone 1995: §54 for Sicilian), as confirmed by the active/passive alternations in (21) and (22) and the Calabrian and Sicilian indirect object passives in (23):[11]

(21) a. *'e   /nce   sparavano   a   chille si se ne scappavano*
them.ACC /them.DAT shoot.PAST.3PL PA/SD them . . .
'they would have shot them had they run way'

b. *'a   /nce   telefunaje   a   socrama*
her.ACC /her.DAT telephone.PAST.3SG PA/SD sister-in-law.POSS.1SG
'he telephoned my mother-in-law'

c. *'a   /nce   parlajeno   a   Maria mmiez' â   via*
her.ACC /her.DAT speak.PAST.3PL PA/SD Maria in-middle to-the street
'they spoke to Maria in the middle of the street'

(22) a. *chille erano   sparate   si se ne scappavano*
they   be.PAST.3PL shoot.PART . . .
'they would have been shot had they run away'

b. *socrama   fuje   telefunata*
sister-in-law.POSS.1SG be.PAST.3SG telephone.PART
'my mother-in-law was telephoned'

c. *Maria fuje   parlata   mmiez' â   via*
Maria be.PAST.3SG speak.PART in-middle to-the street
'Maria was spoken to in the middle of the street'

(23) a. *è   stata   parrata   puru mmenz' a ra via*
be.PRES.3SG be.PART speak.PART even in-middle to the street
'she was spoken to even in the middle of the street' (CS)

b. *pe ru sbagliu tua si   statu   ridutu   ntr' a   faccia*
   for the error   your be.PRES.2SG be.PART laugh-at.PART in   the face
   'for your mistake you were laughed at' (CS)

c. *ancora un signu   statu   telefunatu*
   yet   not be.PRES.1SG be.PART telephone.PART
   'I haven't been telephoned yet' (CS)

d. *unni era   statu   nzignatu?*
   where be.PAST.3SG be.PART teach.PART
   'where was he taught/educated?' (Sicily, Leone 1995: 42)

e. *iu ha   statu   parratu*
   I   have.PRES.1SG be.PART speak.PART
   'I was spoken to' (Sicily, ibid., 50)

f. *sono   stato   parlato   da questo Sig. Giudice*
   be.PRES.1SG be.PART speak.PART by this   Mr Judge
   'I was spoken to by this judge' (reg. Italian Sicily, ibid.)

If dative Case were inherent in the examples in (21), an interpretation excluded by the grammaticality of a doubling structural accusative clitic, then the suppression of this Case in the sentences in (22) would remain obscure. Under our structural Case analysis, however, the grammaticality of the passive sentences in (22) and in (23) proves straightforward: marked with a structural Case, the underlying indirect object in (22) and (23) is not subject to the Uniformity Condition and may legitimately receive its Case and θ-role from two distinct heads.

2.2.2.3. *Cliticization*

A further significant and revealing test that we can profitably use to evaluate the status of the complements in (4a–e) concerns their differing behaviour with regard to clitic substitution in conjunction with the quantifier *tutte* 'all'. Consider first the examples in (24):

(24) a. *veretteno   a vuje   tutte* (PA)
        see.PAST.3PL [DP   PA you.PL all]
        'they saw you all'

   b. *parlajeno   a vuje   tutte* (SD)
      speak.PAST3PL [DP   SD you.PL all]
      'they spoke to you all'

   c. *stanno   attiente   a   vuje   tutte* (inherent dative)
      be.PRES.3PL cautious [PP to [DP you.PL all]]
      'they are cautious of you all'

   d. *parlajeno   'e   vuje   tutte* (inherent genitive)
      speak.PAST.3PL [PP of [DP   you.PL all]]
      'they spoke of you all'

In all four sentences in (24) the verb takes a tonic pronominal complement *vuje* 'you', in turn modified by the quantifier *tutte*. Despite their superficial similarity, we have nonetheless argued that the four nominal complements in (24a–d) are structurally very different: the complements in (24a–b) are DPs preceded by the Case-marker *a*, whereas those in (24c–d) are PPs headed by the true prepositions *a* 'to' and *'e* 'of', respectively. The validity of this distinction is all the more evident when we consider what happens to these sentences if the pronominal complement is substituted by a clitic pronoun, as illustrated in (25a–d):

(25) a. *ve   veretteno   a tutte*
          you.ACC see.PAST.3PL [DP PA all]
          'they saw you all'

      b. *ve   parlajeno   a tutte*
          you.DAT speak.PAST.3PL [DP SD all]
          'they spoke to you all'

      c. **nce   stanno   attiente   tutte*
          them.DAT be.PRES.3PL cautious [PP [DP all]]
          'they are cautious of you all'

      d. **ne   parlajeno   tutte*
          it.GEN speak.PAST.3PL [PP [DP all]]
          'they spoke of you all'

In (25a–b) the structural Case clitic *ve* substitutes for the DP *vuje*, stranding the quantifier *tutte*. This proves a licit operation since the clitic substitutes only the DP and not the structural Case marker *a*, its structural Case feature independently marked on the form of the clitic. Consequently, cliticization has no effect on the presence of the Case marker *a* which remains behind to license the matching Case feature of the quantifier *tutte*. In contrast, the inherent Case clitics *nce* and *ne* in (25c–d) are pro-PPs and substitute both the true preposition (*a* 'to' and *'e* 'of') and its DP complement, stranding the quantifier *tutte* illicitly without any Case-marking. Observe furthermore that the grammaticality of (25c–d) does not improve even if the quantifier is preceded by the appropriate inherent Case-marking preposition:

(26) a. **nce   stanno   attiente   a   tutte*
          you.DAT be.PRES.3PL cautious [PP to [DP all]]

      b. **ne   parlajeno   'e   tutte*
          you.GEN speak.PAST.3PL [PP of [DP all]]

Clearly, the ungrammaticality of (26a–b) must be related to the fact that the prepositions preceding the quantifier in such sentences are simply not available, having been substituted by the pro-PP clitics *nce* and *ne*.

2.2.2.4. *Participial agreement*

The distribution of participial agreement in Neapolitan also confirms our proposed distinction between structural and inherent Case-marked complements.[12] Essentially, the overt realization of participial agreement in Neapolitan is rather restricted, given that final unstressed vowels are generally reduced to the central vowel [ə] (see Ledgeway 1995: P.I.§1.1; Loporcaro 1998: 68–70). Nonetheless, in a number of so-called irregular participles a masculine/feminine gender distinction is overtly signalled by the respective presence/absence of metaphony, for example *sciso/scise* [ˈʃisə] (M) versus *scesa/scese* [ˈʃesə] (F) 'descended'. In the light of these observations, consider the following examples:

(27) a. *m'   avite   rotta   (*rutto)   'a machina*
      me.DAT have.PRES.2PL break.PART.F (break.PART.M) the car.F.SG
      'you've have broken my car'

    b. *l'   hê   coperta   (*copierto)   â   nennella?*
      her.ACC have.PRES.2SG cover.PART.F (cover.PART.M) the little-girl.F.SG
      'have you covered the little girl up?'

    c. *a Catia ancora nun l'   aggiu   risposta   (*rispuosto)*
      PA Catia yet   not her.ACC have.PRES.1SG reply.PART.F (reply.PART.M)
      'I still haven't replied to Catia.'

In (27a–c) the absence of metaphony on the participle highlights the agreement relation that holds between the participle and its feminine structural Case-marked object. Similar facts hold of many other southern Italian dialects, witness the analogous behaviour of participial agreement in the Cosentino sentences in (28), where final vowels are clearly articulated:

(28) a. *'i milungiane l'   aju   fritte/*-u*
      the aubergines.F.PL them.ACC have.PRES.1SG fry.PART.F.PL/M.SG
      'as for the aubergines, I've fried them'

    b. *la   baligia   l'   avia   scisa/*-u   patrimma*
      the suitcase.F.SG it.F.SG have.PAST.3SG bring-down.PART.F.SG/M.SG father.POSS.1SG
      'as for the suitcase, my father had brought it down'

    c. *l'   ha   scritti/*-u   a ri   cumpagni?*
      them.ACC have.PRES.2SG write.PART.M.PL./M.SG PA the friends.M.PL
      'have you written to your friends.?'

    d. *Carmela cci   ha   lavuratu/*-a   a ra tesi*
      Carmela it.DAT have.PRES.3SG work.PART.M.SG/F.SG to the thesis.F.SG
      'Carmela has been working on her thesis'

    e. *n'   amu   parratu/*-a   da   guerra*
      it.GEN have.PRES.1PL speak.PART.M.SG/F.SG of-the war.F.SG
      'we spoke of the war'

As with the Neapolitan examples (27a–c), the Cosentino participles in (28a–c) exhibit agreement with a structurally Case-marked object. In contrast, the participles in sentences (28d–e), containing an inherent Case-marked prepositional complement, fail to license any agreement relation with their complement, invariably exhibiting the default M.SG form in -u.

This distribution of participial agreement finds an immediate explanation if we assume that agreement is sensitive to the syntactic nature of the verbal complement: only structural Case-marked complements, namely DPs, license an agreement relation with their associated participle by virtue of occurring in a specific syntactic configuration with their verbal head (see discussion in sections 6.3.2.4 and 7.5). It follows that inherent Case-marked complements, which are clearly PPs, do not enter into such a configuration with the participle and hence do not qualify as legitimate controllers of agreement.

2.2.3. *Summary*

In the preceding sections we have presented extensive morphological and syntactic evidence to support a distinction between nominal complements marked with structural Case and those marked with an inherent Case. The former we have argued are DPs, interpreting the reflex of Latin AD in conjunction with those occurring in the PA and SD as part of the DP structure,[13] and the latter as PPs headed by a true preposition *a* 'to' or *'e* 'of'.

2.3. MECHANISMS OF CASE-CHECKING

In the preceding discussion a number of differences between structural and inherent Case-marked complements were established. In addition, it was ascertained that the marking of structural Case-marked objects is not uniform but, rather, is subject to a certain degree of variation. In what follows, we shall outline a number of proposals to account for the behaviour of objects in monotransitive clauses, demonstrating that the observed variation in this area can be straightforwardly reduced to properties of the functional head *v*. This is a rather pleasing result in that it suggests a natural way of capturing cross-linguistic variation in the Case-marking of objects in terms of the feature composition of *v*, thereby assimilating differences in the syntax of objects to similar observed differences in the syntax of subjects interpreted in relation to the featural content of T.

2.3.1. *Structural accusative Case*

Following Hale and Keyser (1993) and Chomsky (1995), we propose to analyse monotransitive clauses in relation to the clausal structure in (29) below.

(29)

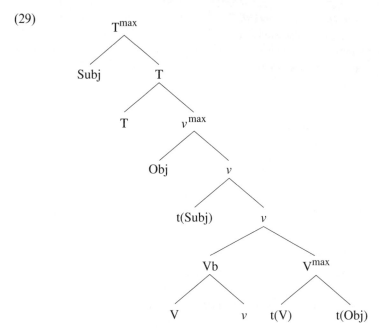

Assuming a 'Larsonian' shell-structure, we take the external argument to be generated not within the VP together with the verb's complement(s), but to be merged in a specifier position of the light verb v (Chomsky 1995: 329ff., 351–2),[14] to which V overtly adjoins forming the complex Vb (= [$_v$ V v]). In addition to assigning the external agentive or causative θ-role to its inner specifier, we further assume that light v, in conjunction with V raised to an adjoined position, is responsible for checking PA, forcing DPs in the PA to raise overtly from within VP to an outer [Spec, v]. We are thus implicitly assuming a structural parallel between the heads T and v, responsible for checking the Case of the subject and object, respectively. In the same way that the EPP may be satisfied by raising of the subject to [Spec, T] to check a strong D-feature on T, simultaneously checking its Case and φ-features 'for free', we propose that a similar EPP feature forces the object to move out of VP to [Spec, v] to check a strong D-feature on v, its PA Case feature and φ-features checked as 'free riders'. This analysis essentially captures the intuition behind Basilico's (1998) VP External Object Hypothesis.

We do not propose however to treat all accusative objects in the same way, observing that objects in the UA present semantico-syntactic properties quite distinct from those in the PA. Instead, we take the accusative Case feature of objects in the UA to be licensed by the verbal complex Vb, to which they adjoin for checking at LF. The observed differences between the UA and PA follow then from their different surface positions within the v-VP complex, as illustrated by the structural representations of (30a–b) in (31a–b), respectively:

(30) a. *isso verette   'o castiello*
        he   see.PAST.3SG the castle
    b. *isso verette   a   Ciro*
        he   see.PAST.3SG PA Ciro

(31) a.

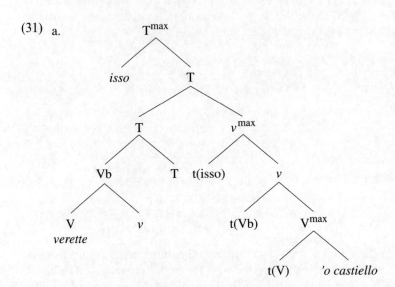

    b.

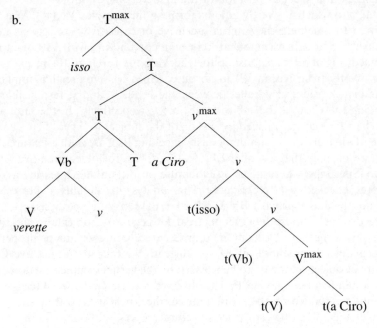

We maintain that overt object shift to [Spec, *v*] in (31b) occurs to satisfy the strong D-feature associated with the head *v*. An attractive and significant consequence of this analysis is that the properties exhibited by objects moved to this position, which are not shared by objects in the UA that remain within the VP, find a natural interpretation in terms of the features of *v* and its associated D-feature. In particular, objects in the PA are associated with the cluster of properties listed in (32):

(32)　i. Clitic doubling
　　　ii. Specificity and definiteness
　　　iii. Animacy

Let us now explore each of these properties in the light of our proposed analysis based on object raising. We begin by noting that a frequently observed characteristic of objects in the PA in Neapolitan, but not those in the UA, is their frequent co-occurrence with a doubling clitic,[15] as is borne out by the representative examples in (33):

(33)　a. *ce　　distruggeno　　a　nnuie?*
　　　　us.ACC$_i$ destroy.PRES.3PL [PA us]$_i$
　　　　'will they destroy us?' (De Filippo 1973: 185)

　　　b. *manna -mi　　-llo　　a　stu nnammurato tuio*
　　　　send.IMP -me.DAT -him.ACC$_i$ [PA this loved-one　　your]$_i$
　　　　'fetch me this fiancé of yours' (ibid., 36)

　　　c. *ll'　　avarisse　　disprezzate all'　ati　duie*
　　　　them.ACC$_i$ have.COND.2SG scorn.PART [PA-the other two]$_i$
　　　　'you would have scorned the other two' (ibid., 346)

　　　d. *v'　　avéssemo　　purtà　ncoppa pure a　vuie?*
　　　　you.ACC$_i$ must.COND.1PL take.INF up　　also [PA you]$_i$
　　　　'do we have to take you up as well?' (Di Giacomo 1991a: 43)

　　　e. *pecchè non lo　　vo　　a　D.Carluccio?*
　　　　why　not him.ACC$_i$ want.PRES.3SG [PA D.Carluccio]$_i$
　　　　'why doesn't he want Don Carluccio?' (ibid., 138)

Indeed, in many southern varieties the use of a doubling clitic has become the norm with the PA (*pace* Telmon 1993: 122).[16] Similar facts have frequently been observed in relation to the Spanish PA (see Jaeggli 1981; Suñer 1988; Demonte 1995, Schmitt 1998; Torrego 1998a) where, subject to dialectal variation, clitic doubling proves considerably more acceptable when the doubled object appears in the PA. Within our present analysis, this fact finds a natural explanation if, along the lines of Borer (1984), we interpret the clitic in examples (33) to be the overt spell-out of the strong D-feature on *v* which has to be checked by raising the DP in the PA to [Spec, *v*].

A further property we pointed out above in relation to objects in the PA concerns their obligatory specific and definite interpretation. Such interpretative notions have recently been the subject of considerable research,[17] which has attempted to capture a correlation between meaning and syntactic configuration by assuming a direct relationship between sentence structure and logical representation (compare Diesing's Mapping Hypothesis). Essentially, the basic insight of this research has been to propose that the specific and definite (or, to borrow Diesing's terminology, *presuppositional*) interpretation of DPs is transparently linked to their syntactic position, typically occurring in a VP-external specifier position (compare Diesing's *restrictive clause*). In light of our proposed analysis of objects in the PA, overt raising to [Spec, *v*] and their concomitant presuppositional reading now follow as a consequence of the strong D-feature on *v*, assuming D to be the locus of such features as specificity and definiteness.

In a similar fashion, the observed animacy restriction on objects in the PA can equally be derived from the properties of *v* and its associated D-feature. Exploiting the parallel suggested above in relation to the heads T and *v*, we assume that *v* variously encodes such features as person and number (see Torrego 1998b), as confirmed by the various forms of the clitics which spell out this D-feature on *v*. Thus, in the same way that in northern Italian dialects T may variously encode person and number features spelt-out in the form of a subject clitic (see Goria in progress), we propose that, in addition to person and number, the D-feature on *v* is also marked for an animacy feature responsible for the observed restriction on objects that overtly raise to [Spec, *v*].

Finally, we note that the properties identified above as characteristic of objects in the PA provide a partial explanation for the fact that tonic pronouns are the most susceptible to occurring in the PA, a fact documented since earliest texts (see Sornicola 1997b: 77–8). Pronominal objects are the most frequently clitic-doubled of all nominal objects and are intrinsically marked for the presuppositional and animate interpretation. Fulfilling all of the typical properties of objects in the PA, it follows that pronominals should prove most felicitous with the PA.

2.3.2. *Structural dative Case*

To conclude our discussion of structural Case, we turn our attention to the SD and the examples in (34a–b):

(34) a. *essa nce   scrivette   (a   Ciro)*
          she   him.DAT   write.PAST.3SG (SD   Ciro)

      b. *essa 'o   scrivette   (a   Ciro)*
          she   him.ACC   write.PAST.3SG (PA   Ciro)
          'she wrote to him (Ciro)'

The verb *scrivere* 'to write' in (34a) marks *Ciro* with SD, whereas in the sentence (34b), to all intents and purposes synonymous with (34a), *Ciro* appears in the PA, witness the change in the co-referential clitic *nce* > *'o*. To account for this difference, we propose that contrary to what happens in (34b), the object in the SD in (34a) fails to undergo object shift but remains in the VP, checking its Case feature at LF against Vb. (34a–b) are assigned the structural representations in (35a–b), respectively (where irrelevant structure above *v*P is omitted for ease of exposition):

(35) a.

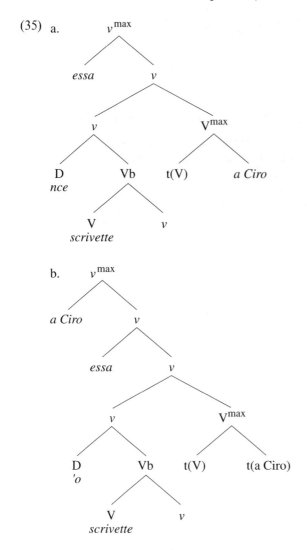

In view of (35a–b), we assume that complements of dative predicates may be marked with SD *in situ* or, alternatively, may appear in the PA if they undergo overt object raising to [Spec, *v*]. In support of this analysis, consider the minimal pairs in (36)–(37):

(36) a. *nce   scrivo   (a Ciro / ô   commune)*
       CL.DAT write.PRES.1SG (SD Ciro / SD-the town-hall)

    b. *'o   scrivo   (a Ciro / *ô   commune)*
       him.ACC write.PRES.1SG (PA Ciro / SD-the town-hall)
       'I'll write to him/to it (to Ciro/the town hall)'

(37) a. *chella nce   pensava   (ê   ffiglie / ê   vacanze)*
       she   them.DAT think.PAST.3SG (SD-the daughters / SD-the holidays)

    b. *chella 'e   pensava   (ê   ffiglie /*ê   vacanze)*
       she   them.ACC think.PAST.3SG (PA-the daughters /SD-the holidays)
       'she always thought about them (her daughters/her holidays)'

The presence of the SD clitic *nce* in the (a) examples does not impose any animacy restrictions on its intended referent, referring freely to both animates (*a Ciro, ê ffiglie*) and inanimates (*ô commune/ê vacanze*) alike. The use of the accusative clitic *'o/'e* in the (b) examples, in contrast, allows only an animate referent. Analogous examples from Altamurano (Loporcaro 1988: 271–2) and Cosentino are given in (38) and (39), and (40) and (41), respectively:

(38) a. la   skrə'vıbː (a sːørm)
       her.ACC write.PAST.1SG (PA sister.POSS.1SG)
       'I wrote to her (my sister)'

    b. ndʒə / ʔla skrə'vibː (a kːɛdːa dıtː)
       it.DAT / it.ACC write.PAST.1SG (SD that   company)
       'I wrote to it (that company)'

(39) a. lʊ   tələfʊ'nɛbː (a 'fːratəmə)
       him.ACC telephone.PAST.1SG (PA brother.POSS.1SG)
       'I telephoned him (my brother)'

    b. ndʒə /ʔlʊ tələfʊ'nɛbː (oː   komːʊu̯n)
       it.DAT /it.ACC telephone.PAST.1SG (SD-the town-hall)
       'I telephoned it (the town hall)'

(40) a. *'a   telefuno   (a Ida)*
       her.ACC telephone.PRES.1SG (PA Ida)
       'I'll telephone her (Ida)'

    b. *cci   / *'a telefuno   (a ra scola)*
       it.DAT / it.ACC telephone.PRES.1SG (SD the school)
       'I'll telephone it (the school)'

(41) a. *l'*   *avianu*   *rispusu*   *(a Cicciu)*
     him.ACC have.PAST.3PL reply.PART (PA Ciccio)
     'they had replied to him (Ciccio)'

    b. *cci*   */ *l'*   *avianu*   *rispusu*   *(a ra littera)*
     it.DAT / it.ACC have.PAST.3PL reply.PART (SD the letter)
     'they had replied to it (the letter)'

Under our analysis, the animacy restrictions observed in such pairs as (38)–
(41) straightforwardly reflect the application or otherwise of object raising in
such structures. In the (b) examples where the clitic indicates that the object
is marked SD, pro remains in VP, while in the (a) examples pro raises to
[Spec, *v*], witness its obligatory animate interpretation and the form of the
clitic. Indeed, the restrictive interpretation of such objects in conjunction
with dative predicates is not limited simply to animacy but reflects the full
array of properties characteristic of objects in the PA reviewed above.

Moreover, the availability of the PA proves sensitive to the thematic
interpretation of the verb. As observed by Torrego (1998a: 27ff.), the PA
in Spanish only yields grammatical results when the subject of the verb
receives an agentive interpretation. Identical considerations hold for the
distribution of the southern Italian PA, witness the Neapolitan, Altamurano
and Trebisaccese sentences in (42):

(42) a. *a Ciro nce*   */ *'o*   *pare*   *ca t'avevano pavato*
     SD Ciro him.DAT / him.ACC seem.PRES.3SG . . .
     'to Ciro, it seems to him that they had paid you' (NA)

    b. *a*   *Maria nce*   */ *'a*   *risurtava*   *nu poco strano*
     SD   Maria her.DAT / her.ACC result.PAST.3SG a   little   strange
     'it struck Maria as a little strange' (NA)

    c. *ndʒə*   */ *u*   *pas'sɔu*   *lu du'laurə də keip*
     him.DAT / him.ACC pass.PAST.3SG the pain   of head
     'his headache went away' (Altamura (BA), Loporcaro 1998: 175)

    d. *nə*   */ *u*   *pa'rɪ*   *b'bɪəllə*
     him.DAT / him.ACC seem.PRES.3SG beautiful
     'it seemed pretty to him' (Trebisacce (CS), ibid.)

    e. *nə*   */ *a*   *su'tʃːɛːdənə*   *'tandə 'kɔːsə*
     her.DAT / her.ACC happen.PRES.3PL so-many things
     'so many things happen to her' (Trebisacce (CS), ibid.)

The athematic raising predicates in (42a, b, d) and the unaccusatives
predicates in (42c, e) mark their indirect complement with SD. Unlike
previous examples of verbs that mark their indirect complement with SD
(38–41), however, these predicates do not present the option of marking
their indirect complement with PA, witness the ill-formedness of the
accusative clitics in (42a–e). If, as we are proposing, checking of PA involves

DP-raising to [Spec, v], then the ungrammaticality of the accusative clitics in these sentences is straightforwardly accounted for since these predicates fail to assign an external θ-role. Following Chomsky (1995: 315), we argued above that the agentive/causative role of the external argument be understood as the interpretation assigned to the v-VP configuration. It follows that in the absence of an external θ-role, v will not be projected in the structure and consequently there will be no [Spec, v] in which to license the PA. Consequently, this correlation between the PA and the verb's agentive interpretation finds an immediate explanation in light of our proposed analysis.

A similar explanation accounts for the semantic differences evidenced by the following Neapolitan and Cosentino sentences (see also Scerbo 1886: 63):

(43) a *nun nce   l'a   parlano*
         not her.DAT / her.ACC speak.PRES.3PL
         'they don't speak to her / give her the time of day' (NA)

      b *cci   l'u   parru*
         him.DAT /him.ACC speak.PRES.1SG
         'I'll speak to him / I'll give him the time of day' (CS, Lombardi 1997: 56)

      c *cci   l'a   ridianu   'nfaccia*
         her.DAT /her.ACC smile.PAST.3PL in-face
         'they were smiling at her / they were mocking her' (CS)

Though the examples in (43) may be synonymous, many speakers note that where the object appears in the PA (compare PA clitics *'a* 'her' and *'u* 'him' above), the verbs *parlà/parrà* 'to speak' and *rida* 'to smile' also permit the idiomatic reading 'to give the time of day, acknowledge' and 'to mock, make fun of', respectively, interpretations absent whenever the object appears in the SD (compare SD clitics *nce/cci* above). We can view this interpretative difference as a direct consequence of the thematic interpretation of the object. When in the SD, the object in (43) is interpreted as the GOAL (of speaking or smiling). On the other hand, when marked by the PA, the object is interpreted as the THEME or PATIENT (of acknowledgement or mockery). The relevant interpretative difference in these examples appears then to be one of affectedness, a reading typical of THEME/PATIENT objects. Building on proposals of Marantz (1993) and Hale and Keyser (1992) which link the licensing of affectedness to the specifier of VP, Torrego (1998a: §2.1.1) argues that affected objects in Spanish must raise out of VP to occupy the outer [Spec, v].[18] Given that we have identified this position with the licensing of PA, the correlation between objects in the PA and their concomitant affected interpretation follows naturally. As expected, when the THEME/PATIENT interpretation obtains in (43), PA-marking of the object is licensed, but not when the object has the GOAL reading.

2.3.3. *Summary*

To summarize our discussion of structural Case, we have argued that the observed differences between the PA and the UA follow from their ability to raise out of the VP before LF. Objects in the PA raise overtly to [Spec, v] to check a strong D-feature on v, a movement operation which explains the frequent appearance of doubling clitics, the specific, animate and affected interpretation of the object and the obligatory presence of an external argument. Objects in the UA, on the other hand, fail to exhibit any of these properties and check their Case feature at LF against Vb. Finally, objects in the SD represent an intermediate case. When they remain within the VP, their Case feature is checked at LF against Vb, but when they move out of the VP to the [Spec, v] before Spell-Out, they check PA against v.[19]

2.3.4. *Prepositional objects: inherent dative and genitive Cases*

Since Chomsky (1981: 170ff.), syntactic theory has distinguished two types of Case: structural and inherent. The former is held to be a purely configurational property that obtains through government at S-structure (typically nominative and accusative), whereas the latter is assigned at D-structure under government and intrinsically associated with θ-marking, for example genitive and oblique. Chomsky (1986a: 194) proposes to account for the more restrictive nature of inherent Case with the Uniformity Condition in (44):

(44) Uniformity Condition on Case Marking
      If α is an inherent Case marker, then α Case marks NP if and only if α theta-marks the chain headed by NP

By way of illustration, consider the Italian passive example in (45):

(45) *Maria viene vista*
      Maria_i comes seen t_i
      'Maria is seen'

Within the Principles and Parameters framework, it was standardly assumed that *Maria* originates at D-structure in the Caseless direct object position where it receives its PATIENT θ-role, but is forced to move at S-structure to the vacant subject position to be Case-marked nominative. Significantly, the argument DP *Maria* receives its Case and θ-role from two distinct heads, namely INFL and V, respectively. Examples such as (45) are therefore taken as providing strong evidence for the independence of θ-marking in structural Case-assignment.

   Now consider the Italian examples in (46):

(46) a. *sono   sicuro di   Maria*
      be.PRES.1SG sure   of [DP Maria]
      'I am sure of Maria'

  b. **sono   sicuro di   Maria   partire*
      be.PRES.1SG sure   of [TP [DP Maria] [T leave.INF]]
      'I am sure of Maria to come'

The adjective *sicuro* in (46a) selects and θ-marks a DP object *Maria* to which it assigns inherent genitive Case, realized at S-structure by the preposition *di* 'of'. However, the same process of Case-assignment cannot apply in (46b) since *Maria* is now subcategorized, and hence θ-marked, by the infinitival verb *partire* 'to leave'. Therefore, (46b) falls foul of the Case Filter, and ultimately the Visibility Condition, since *Maria* cannot be Case-marked.

As it stands, the standard Principles and Parameters account of structural and inherent Cases, which relies on the notion of government, encounters a number of non-trivial problems under minimalist assumptions. From a minimalist perspective, structural Case is now standardly assumed to be licensed by merging or moving D/DP within the checking domain of T or *v*, the Move option applying overtly (pre-Spell-Out) or covertly (at LF). On the other hand, the correct formulation of how the formal licensing of inherent Case is to be interpreted under minimalist assumptions proves more problematic (see Chomsky 1995: 386, n. 55).

One possible line of investigation, which we shall adopt here, is that inherent Case does not have to be checked at all. Indeed, Chomsky (1995: 285) notes that 'an outstanding problem concerning inherent Case . . . [is] how the φ-features of the nominal receiving inherent Case can be checked, in the absence of any plausible functional category; but the question does not arise if they need not be checked.' More specifically, we maintain that inherent Case is assigned and realized by a preposition (at least in the southern Italian cases examined above) within the domain of a θ-marker, thereby capturing the essence of Chomsky's Uniformity Condition (1986b: 192ff.). Unlike structural Case, however, we maintain that inherent Case is not subject to checking, a conclusion derived from several considerations.[20] Firstly, by virtue of being uninterpretable, structural Case is not tied to any particular θ-role and as such must be checked by LF in accordance with the principle of Full Interpretation. Moreover, it is reasonable to suppose that the checking of structural Case-marked DPs equally satisfies the formal licensing condition on their thematic interpretation (the 'Visibility Condition' of Chomsky 1986a). Inherently Case-marked DPs, in contrast, are invariably associated with a particular θ-role, as made explicit in Chomsky's Uniformity Condition which imposes a θ-relation on the inherent Case-assigner. Consequently, we take inherent Case to be an interpretable Case, a sort of 'semantic' case in which syntactic Case and θ-role are rolled into one. It follows that inherent Case-marked DPs are inherently visible and are not subject to checking or any of the overt or covert movement operations outlined above for the licensing of structural Case.

2.4. DITRANSITIVES

The behaviour of Case-marking in ditransitive constructions raises a number of important questions with regard to the mechanisms of multiple Case-checking available to Neapolitan and other southern Italian dialects. The principal reason for this being that, within certain limits which will be defined below, ditransitive verbs permit a considerable degree of variation in the form of Case-marking assumed by their complements, giving rise to a verbal diathesis alternation in many respects similar to the English double-object construction. In what follows, it will be shown that the distribution of Case-marking in ditransitive clauses can be profitably used to throw some light on the finer structure of the clause and the restrictions that operate on DP movement, allowing us to build on our previous analysis of Case-marking in monotransitive structures. To illustrate the difficulties of interpretation posed by ditransitive constructions, we list below in (47)–(49) the typical paradigm of the ditransitive verb *scrivere* 'to write', which appears *prima facie* rather puzzling:

(47) a. *scrivo*   *'a lettera*
write.PRES.1SG the letter
'I'll write the letter'

   b. *'a*   *scrivo*   *'a lettera*
it.ACC write.PRES.1SG the letter
'I write (it) the letter'

(48) a. *scrivo*   *a Ciro*
write.PRES.1SG SD Ciro
'I'll write to Ciro'

   b. *(n)ce scrivo*   *a Ciro*
him.DAT write.PRES.1SG SD Ciro
'I'll write (to him) to Ciro'

   c. *'o*   *scrivo*   *a Ciro*
him.ACC write.PRES.1SG PA Ciro
'I'll write (him) to Ciro'

(49) a. *(n)ce scrivo*   *'a lettera a Ciro*
him.DAT write.PRES.1SG the letter   SD Ciro
'I'll write (to him) the letter to Ciro'

   b. **'o*   *scrivo*   *'a lettera a Ciro*
him.ACC write.PRES.1SG the letter   PA Ciro
'I'll write (him) the letter to Ciro'

   c. *'o   scrivo   'a lettera*
      him.ACC write.PRES.1SG the letter
   'I'll write him the letter'

As indicated by its doubling clitic in (47b), the verb in (47a) marks its inanimate THEME argument with UA. In (48a), on the other hand, the verb selects an animate GOAL argument which it marks with SD or PA, witness the two possible Case forms of its doubling clitic in examples (48b–c), respectively. Finally, the sentences in (49) illustrate what happens when the verb selects both complements. In (49a) the THEME appears in the UA while the dative clitic *nce* on the verb indicates that the GOAL is marked SD. The ungrammatical (49b), on the other hand, would appear to indicate that the GOAL argument cannot appear in the PA if the THEME is also present in the structure. This conclusion, however, is contradicted by the evidence of (49c) in which the use of the accusative clitic demonstrates that, even in the presence of the THEME argument, the GOAL may appear in the PA if covert. In order to make sense of the data in (47)–(49) above, we need to undertake a closer examination of the distribution of the PA and the SD and, in particular, the contexts in which the former can replace the latter in both monotransitive and ditransitive constructions.

2.4.1. *Case alternations*

We begin by examining what others have said about the distribution of the PA and SD in southern dialects. The only grammar of Neapolitan to overtly recognize the use of the PA to mark indirect objects is Bichelli (1974: 128–9), who notes that indirect objects may optionally be marked by the 3rd person accusative clitics *'o* (M.SG), *'a* (F.SG) and *'e* (PL). Bichelli points out that the use of an accusative clitic to reference an indirect object is only possible when the verb does not select in addition a direct object. However, this restriction on the use of the PA is disproven by Bichelli's own example given in (50), in which the accusative clitic *'o* marks the indirect object even in the presence of the direct object *male* 'pain'.

(50) *nun 'o   fà   male*
      not him.ACC do.INF pain
    'don't hurt him'

Moreover, Bichelli's intuition is not supported by the present author's informants who invariably accept sentences such as (49c) above. Some further literary examples are given below (accusative clitic referencing covert indirect object given in bold-type):

(51) a. *nun 'a   facite   mettere appaura!*
        not her.ACC make.INF put.INF fear
      'don't frighten her' (Di Giacomo 1991a: 32)

b. *nun 'o   date   retta*

not him.ACC give.INF heed

'don't take any notice of him' (ibid., 51)

c. *lo   vulevo   mparà la museca*

him.ACC want.PAST.1SG teach.INF the music

'I wanted to teach him music' (Scarpetta 1992: 413)

d. *lo   vuoi   fa'   piglià nu colpo d'aria?*

him.ACC want.PRES.2SG make.INF take.INF a breath of-air

'do want him to take a breath of fresh air?' (De Filippo 1973: 75)

e. *è comme si nunn 'e   facissse   niente*

. . .   not   them.ACC do.PAST.SUBJ nothing

'it's as if it didn't matter to them' (ibid., 83)

f. *'o   dongo   nu piatto nfaccia*

him.ACC give.PRES.1SG a plate in-face

'I'll throw a plate at him' (ibid., 94)

g. *'o   faccio   fa'   marenna*

him.ACC make.PRES.1SG make.INF snack

'I'll give him a horrible surprise' (ibid., 96)

h. *'a   scasso   'a faccia!*

her.ACC break.PRES.1SG the face

'I'll smash her face in!' (ibid., 192)

i. *'e   ddate   a bere   qualche cosa*

them.ACC give.IMP.2PL to drink.INF some thing

'you'll give them something to drink' (ibid. 354)

j. *a chesta nun 'a   dicette   niente*

PA this-one not her.ACC say.PAST.3SG nothing

'to her he didn't say anything' (De Curtis 1989: 22)

k. *nun 'o   deva   mai a mangià*

not him.ACC give.PAST.3SG never to eat.INF

'he never gave him anything to eat' (ibid., 54)

l. *'a   canusce   'a cucina?*

her.ACC know.PRES.2SG the cooking

'do you know her cooking?'

m. *'e   preparaje   na buatta 'e chiochare*

them.ACC prepare.PAST.1SG a jar of peppers

'I prepared for them a jar of peppers in oil'

n. *'o   vulimmo   rialà   nu rilorgio*

him.ACC want.PRES.1PL present.INF a watch

'we want to give him a watch (as a present)'

o. *'o   chiavasse   nu paccaro!*

him.ACC give.COND.1SG a slap

'I would deal him a slap!'

For instance, in sentence (51a) the verb selects both for a direct object (*appaura* 'fright') and a covert indirect object pro, the latter marked with the PA overtly signalled on the verb by the accusative clitic '*o*.

A similar view is echoed by Sornicola (1997a: 335–7) who illustrates with the examples in (52a–g) that indirect objects may be referenced by an accusative clitic in Neapolitan even when the verb selects a direct object complement:

(52) a. o   dumman'najə o   'fattə (*a m'marjə)
    him.ACC ask.PAST.3SG   the fact   (PA Mario)
    'he asked him (Mario) about the matter'

   b. o   pur'tajə   nu 'rjalə (*a m'marjə)
    him.ACC bring.PAST.3SG a   present (PA Mario)
    'he brought him (Mario) a present'

   c. a   ʃkar'fajə   o 'pjattə (*a mma'ria)
    her.ACC heat.PAST.3SG the plate   (PA Maria)
    'he heated her (Maria) the plate up'

   d. a   'rɛttə   na pə'rat (*a mma'ria)
    her.ACC give.PAST.3SG a   kick   (PA Maria)
    'he gave her (Maria) a kick'

   e. o   fa'ʧɛtt   aʃ'ʃi   o s'saŋgə r   o nas (*a Mario)
    him.ACC make.PAST.3SG come-out.INF the blood   from the nose (PA m'marjə)
    'he made the blood come out of his (Mario's) nose'

   f. a   fa'ʧɛttə   las'sa   a ʃkɔl (*a mma'ria)
    her.ACC make.PAST.3.SG leave.INF the school (PA Maria)
    'he made her (Maria) leave school'

   g. o   ʃkas'sajə   nu 'pjattə ŋgap (*a m'marjə)
    him.ACC break.PAST3SG a   plate   in-head (PA Mario)
    'he broke a plate on his (Mario's) head'

Furthermore, Sornicola points out that the PA is only available to mark indirect objects if the latter is covert. If the accusative clitic references an overt indirect object, given in parentheses in (52), the structure proves ill-formed on a par with (49b) above. However, what Sornicola fails to observe is that the sentences in (52a–g) immediately become grammatical if the indirect object is placed before the direct object, witness the examples in (53a–g):[21]

(53) a. o   dumman'najə a m'marjə o   'fattə
    him.ACC ask.PAST.3SG   PA Mario   the fact
    'he asked Mario about the matter'

   b. o   pur'tajə   a m'marjə nu 'rjalə
    him.ACC bring.PAST.3SG PA Mario   a present
    'he brought Mario a present'

c. a   ʃkar'fajə   a mma'ria o   'piattə
  her.ACC heat.PAST.3SG PA Maria   the plate
  'he heated Maria the plate up'

d. a   'rɛttə   a mma'ria na pə'rata
  her.ACC give.PAST.3SG PA Maria   a   kick
  'he gave Maria a kick'

e. o   fa'ʧɛtt   aʃ'ʃi   a m'marjə o s'saŋgə r   o
  him.ACC make.PAST.3SG come-out.INF PA Mario the blood from the
  nasə
  nose
  'he made the blood come out of Mario's nose'

f. a   fa'ʧɛttə   las'sa   a mma'ria a 'ʃkɔlə
  her.ACC make.PAST.3SG leave.INF PA Maria   the school
  'he made Maria leave school'

g. o   ʃkas'sajə   a m'marjə nu 'pjattə ŋgap
  him.ACC break.PAST.3SG PA Mario a   plate in-head
  'he broke a plate on Mario's head'

Far from being exceptional, the system of Case-marking described above for Neapolitan appears to operate in other southern dialects, witness the following examples taken from a selection of other Campanian varieties:

(54) a. *'a Fata a chesta nun 'a   dicette   niente*
  the fairy to this-one not her.ACC say.PAST.3SG nothing
  'the Fairy didn't tell her anything' (Bacoli (NA), De Simone 1994: 21)

 b. *'a   voglio   purta'   nu cumprimento*
  her.ACC want.PRES.1SG bring.INF a   compliment
  'I want to compliment her' (Terzigno (NA), ibid., 88)

 c. *chesta che 'o   pò'   ffa'?*
  this-one what him.ACC be-able.PRES.3SG do.INF
  'what can she do for him?' (Marcianise (CE), ibid., 128)

 d. *p' 'a   fa'   veni'   'o gulio 'e ridere*
  for her.ACC make.INF come.INF the deisre of laugh.INF
  'in order to make her want to laugh' (Ferrari (AV), ibid., 156)

 e. *'a   facette   nu scippo 'nfaccia*
  her.ACC make.PAST.3SG a   scratch in-face
  'she scratched her face' (Castellammare di Stabia (NA), ibid., 238)

 f. *'o   facettero   n' ata paliata*
  him.ACC make.PAST.3PL an other thrashing
  'they gave him another thrashing' (Curti (CE), ibid., 292)

g. *'o   vuleva   fa'   mettere paura*
   him.ACC want.PAST.3SG make.INF put.INF fright
   'he wanted to give him a fright' (Guardia Sanframondi (BN), ibid., 318)

h. *'o   'mparaie   a gghjuca' a ccarte*
   him.ACC teach.PAST.3SG to play.INF to cards
   'he taught him to play cards' (Pietramelara (CE), ibid., 374)

i. *'o Re 'o   dette   la mano*
   the king him.ACC give.PAST.3SG the hand
   'the King shook his hand' (Calitiri (AV), ibid., 618)

Furthermore, Gioscio (1985: §2.34) notes that in the Lucanian dialect of Calvello (PZ), indirect objects can occur in the PA. He provides by way of example the sentences in (55a–b):

(55) a. lu   /la   'rakə   nu ka'vaddə
        him.ACC /her.ACC give.PRES.1SG a   horse
        'I'll give him/her a horse'

     b. lə   d'dakə   nu ka'vaddə
        them.ACC give.PRES.1SG a   horse
        'I'll give them a horse'

As Gioscio's examples demonstrate, the PA-marking of indirect objects appears to be unconstrained by the presence of a direct object in the structure. A similar picture emerges for the Apulian dialect of Mattinata (FG),[22] discussed by Loporcaro (1997b: 346; 1998: 176, n. 199) who provides the following examples of PA-referencing of an indirect object in the presence of a direct object:

(56) a. lu   tur'ʧi   lu 'kuəddə
        him.ACC wring.PAST.3SG the neck
        'he wrung his neck'

     b. la   'dekə   au̯'dɛnʣə
        her.ACC give.PAST.3SG heed
        'he paid heed to her'

One restriction on the PA-referencing of indirect objects which appears to hold of all the above dialects, however, is illustrated by the sentences in (57) and (58) from Neapolitan and Calvello, respectively:

(57) a. nʤ   o   /*o   o   dumman'najə
        him.DAT it.ACC /him.ACC it.ACC ask.PAST.3SG
        'he asked him it'

     b. nʤ   o   /*o   o   pur'tajə
        him.DAT it.ACC /him.ACC it.ACC bring.PAST.3SG
        'he brought him it'

c. ndʒ   o   /*a   o   ʃkar'fajə
her.DAT it.ACC /her.ACC it.ACC heat.PAST.3SG
'he heated her it'

d. ndʒ   a   /*a   a   'rɛttə
her.DAT it.ACC /her.ACC it.ACC give.PAST.3SG
'he gave her it'

e. ndʒ   o   /*o   o   fa'ʧɛtt   aʃ'ʃi   r o   'nasə
him.DAT it.ACC /him.ACC it.ACC make.PAST.3SG come-out.INF of the nose
'he made it come out of his nose'

f. ndʒ   a   /*a   a   fa'ʧɛttə   las'sa
her.DAT it.ACC /her.ACC it.ACC make.PAST.3SG leave.INF
'he made her leave it'

g. ndʒ   o   /*o   o   ʃkas'sajə   ŋgap
him.DAT it.ACC /him.ACC it.ACC break.PAST.3SG in-head
'he broke it on his head'

(58) a. ndʒə   lu   /*lu   lu   'rannə
him.DAT it.ACC /him.ACC it.ACC give.PRES.3PL
'they'll give him it'

b. ndʒə   lu   /*la   lu   'rannə
her.DAT it.ACC /her.ACC it.ACC give.PRES.3PL
'they'll give her it'

c. ndʒə   lu   /*lə   llu   'ranne
them.DAT it.ACC /them.ACC it.ACC give.PRES.3PL
'they'll give them it'

In the ungrammatical versions of (57) and (58), the direct and indirect objects are both referenced by an accusative clitic yielding ungrammatical results. Far from being easy to interpret, the ungrammaticality of these sentences is amenable to at least two possible interpretations. One explanation for the ungrammaticality in (57) and (58) is to assume that the verb's single accusative Case feature is assigned to the direct object, thus precluding the possibility of the indirect object pro raising to [Spec, *v*] to check PA. Initially, this interpretation of the facts would appear confirmed by the grammatical versions of (57) and (58) where the indirect object is marked by the SD clitic *nce* /ndʒə/, which represents the only way of expressing the intended interpretation of these sentences. According to this view, in (57) and (58) the direct object receives the verb's accusative Case feature (compare the accusative clitics *'ollu* (M.SG), *'a* (F.SG)) which forces the indirect object to appear in the only other available Case, namely the SD (*nce* dative).

Though appealing, this explanation of the facts cannot possibly be correct, since it is contradicted by the evidence of sentences such as (49c), (51) and (52), and (54) and (56), the first of these repeated here in (59):

(59) '*o*   *scrivo*   '*a lettera*
     him.ACC write.PRES.1SG the letter
     'I'll write him the letter'

If the THEME argument '*a lettera* receives the verb's sole accusative Case
feature in (59), then the covert GOAL argument, here referenced by the
accusative clitic '*o*, should not be able to occur in the PA, contrary to fact.
We therefore reject this hypothesis. Instead, we interpret the impossibility of
accusative referencing of the GOAL in (57) and (58) as a consequence of the
verb only being able to mark one of its arguments with structural accusative.
Concretely, we argue that in the sentences in (57) and (58) the GOAL
argument checks the verb's sole accusative Case feature, forcing the THEME
argument to be marked with a (default) inherent accusative Case. As a
result, examples such as (57) and (58) do not prove ungrammatical because
the GOAL argument is not able to check PA. On the contrary, we are arguing
that the GOAL argument does check PA and that it is felicitously referenced by
the structural accusative clitic on the verb. Instead, we claim that the
derivation of such sentences crashes simply because a structural accusative
clitic cannot be used to reference the THEME marked with a non-matching
inherent accusative Case. What this amounts to saying is that, like other
southern dialects, Neapolitan does not possess any means of pronominally
marking inherent accusative Case. Consequently, the only way of expressing
the intended pronominal meaning of (57) and (58) is to mark the GOAL with
SD, thus freeing up the verb's structural accusative feature for the THEME
argument. It will be shown below in section 2.4.3 that this particular
interpretation of the facts finds an immediate explanation in terms of our
structural analysis of ditransitive constructions.

We now turn our attention away briefly from Neapolitan and the dialects
of Calvello and Mattinata to examine the different behaviour of Case-
marking in other southern dialects. Although we noted previously that PA
marking of indirect objects is widespread in the dialects of southern Italy, a
number of dialects appear to impose some quite severe restrictions on its
application. By way of example, consider the following sentences from the
Apulian dialect of Altamura (BA) reported by Loporcaro (1988: 270ff.; see
also Loporcaro 1997b: 346; 1998: §11.1.3).

(60) a. jɪ ndʒə   /lʊ   /la   /lɪ   tələfʊ'nɛi̯ʃ
       I CL.DAT.3 /him.ACC /her.ACC /them.ACC telephone.PAST.1SG
       'I telephoned him/her/them'

    b. la mə'gːjerə ndʒə   /lʊ   'kou̯ʃ   /'rii̯t
       'the wife   him.DAT /him.ACC cook.PRES.3SG /smile-at.PRES.3SG
       /'ʃkou̯t   /'spwɛi̯r
       /spit.PRES.3SG /shoot.PRES.3SG
       'his wife cooks for/smiles at/spits at/shoots (at) him'

On the basis of these examples, Loporcaro notes that, in addition to the SD, indirect objects in Altamurano can optionally appear in the PA in unergative clauses. Similar facts also hold of many Calabrian dialects such as Cosentino (61a) and Trebisaccese (CS; 61b), Lucanian varieties (61c), Apulia (61d) and Sicilian (61e and f):[23]

(61) a. *a   Cicciu   cci   l'u   cucinu   lridu*
       to Ciccio him.DAT /him.ACC cook.PRES.1SG /smile.PRES.1SG
       lsparu   ltelefunu   lscrivu
       /shoot.PRES.1SG /telephone.PRES.1SG /write.PRES.1SG
       'as for Ciccio, I'll cook for/smile at/shoot/telephone/write to him'

    b. a mma'rijə rɔːs a   tə'lɛːfənədə
       to Maria   Rosa her.ACC telephone.PRES.3SG
       'as for Maria, Rosa will telephone her' (Loporcaro 1998: 174)

    c. *pensa   i   guai   suoi / lo   sparò   / lo*
       think.PRES.3SG the troubles his   / him.ACC shoot.PAST.3SG / him.ACC
       voglio   bene / non lo   rispondere / non dar   da
       want.PRES.1SG love / not him.ACC reply.INF   / not give.INF to
       mangiare i colombi
       eat.INF   the doves
       'he thinks about his troubles / he shot him / I love him / don't reply to him / don't give food to the doves' (reg. Italian, Anzi (PZ), Ruggieri and Batinti 1992: 87)

    d. *'a   perdunà*
       her.ACC forgive.PAST.3SG
       'he forgave her' (Apulia, Rohlfs 1969: 10)

    e. *a   Cicciu cci   l'u   cucinu   / sparu*
       to Ciccio him.DAT /him.ACC cook.PRES.1SG / shoot.PRES.1SG
       ltelefunu   / vogghiu   beni
       /telephone.PRES.1SG / WANT.PRES.1SG love
       'as for Ciccio, I'll cook for/shoot (at)/telephone/love him'

    f. *lu   'nsignau   a parrari*
       him.ACC teach.PAST.3SG to speak.INF
       'he taught him to speak' (Buccheri (SR), Pitré 1875: II, 122)

Despite the superficial similarity between these dialects and Neapolitan suggested by the examples in (60) and (61), the apparent parallel breaks down when we consider ditransitive clauses. To illustrate this point, consider the examples in (62a–c) from Altamurano, Cosentino and Trebisaccese, respectively.

(62) a. jɪ ndʒə /*lʊ   /*la   'spetːsə   lʊ wʊ'ratːs /'pwɪgːjə
       I CL.DAT /him.ACC /her.ACC break.PRES.1SG the arm   /take.PRES.1SG
       lʊ kwa'pːɪdː /dɪbː   nʊ pʊ'jʊ̯ɲn

        the hat   /give.PAST.3SG a   punch
        'I'll break his/her arm / I'll take his/her hat / I gave him/her a punch'
        (Loporcaro 1988: 272)

  b. *cci / *'u /*'a   cucinu   'a pasta / scrivu   na*
        CL.DAT / him.ACC /her.ACC cook.PRES.1SG the pasta / write.PRES.1SG a
        littera / cuntu   nu fattu / dugnu   'i sordi
        letter   /tell.PRES.1SG a fact / give.PRES.1SG the money
        'I'll cook him/her the pasta / I'll write him/her a letter / I'll tell him/
        her a story / I'll give him/her the money'

  c. nə   /*a   ku'səd   a 'vɛstə
        her.DAT / her.ACC sew.PRES.3SG the dress
        'he sews the dress for her' (Loporcaro 1998: 176)

As all these sentences clearly reveal, as soon as a THEME argument is introduced into the structure, the PA marking of the indirect object proves ungrammatical. Consequently, referencing of the indirect object with an accusative clitic is invariably ruled out. The ill-formedness of such examples suggests therefore that the direct object receives the verb's accusative Case feature, forcing the indirect object to assume SD-marking. What this amounts to saying is that, unlike Neapolitan and the dialects of Cavello and Mattinata, Altamurano, Cosentino, Trebisaccese and Sicilian do not have the option of licensing inherent accusative Case on the direct object. In the absence of inherent accusative Case, the indirect object of a ditransitive clause can consequently only appear in the SD.

Before we offer a structural interpretation of Case-marking in ditransitive clauses, we must finally consider one other restriction on the distribution of the PA in ditransitive clauses which will be demonstrated in section 2.4.3 to have important consequences on our analysis of Case-marking in ditransitive structures. It was ascertained above that in monotransitive clauses southern Italian dialects present the option of marking the indirect object SD or PA. In addition, we noted that some of these dialects, notably Neapolitan, also allow a covert indirect object to appear in the PA in ditransitive clauses. Surprisingly, however, in all dialects, Neapolitan included, the PA is not available to any argument in ditransitive clauses when the direct object is also a potential candidate for the PA, namely specified as animate and specific.[24] By way of illustration, consider the following identical sentences taken from Neapolitan, Altamurano, Cosentino and Sicilian, respectively:[25]

(63) a. *aggiu   appresentato a Maria*
        have.PRES.1SG present.PART   PA Maria

     b. sɔ   p:rəsən'dɛt a m:a'rɪⁱ
        be.PRES.1SG present.PART. PA Maria

     c. *aju   prisintatu a Maria*
        have.PRES.1SG present.PART. PA Maria

d. *prisintai   a   Maria*
present.PAST.ISG PA Maria
'I introduced Maria'

(64) a. *aggiu   appresentato (*a) Maria a chillu guaglione*
have.PRES.ISG present.PART   (PA) Maria SD that   boy

b. *sɔ   pːrəsən'dɛt (*a) mːa'rɪ^i a 'kːʷʊdːʊ wa'ɲːaʊ̯n*
be.PRES.ISG present.PART (PA) Maria   SD that   boy

c. *aju   prisintatu (*a) Maria a   chiru guagliune*
have.PRES.ISG present.PART (PA) Maria SD that   boy

d. *prisintai   (*a) Maria a ddru picciottu*
present.PAST.ISG (PA) Maria SD that boy
'I introduced Maria to that boy'

In the monotransitive sentences in (63), the verb *(ap)presentà(ri)* 'to introduce' selects an animate direct object which, as we should expect, appears in the PA. In the sentences in (64), by contrast, the same verb is used ditransitively and selects in addition to its direct object *Maria* an animate indirect object 'to that boy'. Strangely, however, neither of the objects can appear in the PA. If the direct object *Maria* is preceded by the PA marker *a*, the sentences prove ungrammatical. Equally, the indirect object cannot occur in the PA either in such sentences, as witnessed by its position following the direct object: had the indirect object raised out of the VP to check PA in [Spec, *v*], then it ought to precede the direct object left behind in the VP, contrary to fact. In the examples in (64), the indirect object must therefore be Case-marked SD. We conclude then that the presence of two animate objects in a ditransitive clause, both potential candidates for object raising to [Spec, *v*], precludes the licensing of PA.

2.4.2. *Summary*

We have seen that most southern Italian dialects allow indirect objects to assume the Case-marking of direct objects (namely SD > PA) in monotransitive structures. However, only a smaller number of dialects, including Neapolitan and the dialects of Mattinata (FG) and Calvello (PZ), permit such a phenomenon in ditransitive structures, giving rise to an alternation which parallels in many respects the familiar English dative shift construction. In addition, we observed that such alternations in these dialects are constrained by a number of factors. Firstly, such alternations are always possible when the indirect object is covert and referenced by a clitic pronoun. In these cases, the underlying direct object is marked with a default inherent accusative Case, as witnessed by the ungrammaticality of referencing it with a structural Case clitic. Secondly, the indirect object may be overtly clitic-doubled only if it precedes the direct object. Finally, when the direct object is also a potential candidate for PA-marking (namely, specific, referential and animate), then neither the direct object nor the indirect object can occur in the PA, the former appearing obligatorily in the UA and the latter in the SD. We recapitulate these results by way of table 2.2:

Table 2.2 Case-marking in monotransitive and ditransitive structures

	Direct Object	Indirect Object
Monotransitives	(c)overt UA [−an.] (c)overt PA [+an.]	(c)overt SD (c)overt PA
Ditransitives	overt UA [−an.] overt UA [−an.] overt UA [+an.] covert UA [±an.]	(c)overt SD (c)overt PA (c)overt SD (c)overt SD

2.4.3. *Structural analysis*

In the preceding discussion it was established that in certain contexts ditransitive constructions in Neapolitan and other southern dialects exhibit Case alternations in many ways similar to those found in the English dative shift construction,[26] a diathesis alternation traditionally assumed to be unattested in Romance (*pace* Demonte 1995: 8). Kayne (1984), for instance, attempts to account for the respective presence versus absence of the double-object construction in Germanic and Romance as a consequence of the different Case properties of prepositions in the two language groups: in Romance prepositions assign oblique Case while in Germanic languages like English prepositions assign structural Case. Thus, under Kayne's analysis the existence of the double-object construction in Neapolitan and other southern dialects is entirely expected since, as demonstrated extensively above, AD > *a* variously marks structural (accusative/dative) Case in Neapolitan.[27]

As for the precise structural characterization of Neapolitan ditransitive constructions, there is a long tradition of interpreting the dative alternations as the result of two derivationally related syntactic configurations (though see Oehrle 1976; Kayne 1984; Jackendoff 1990; Pesetsky 1995 for a non-derivational analysis) in accordance with the Uniformity of Theta Assignment Hypothesis (Baker 1988). Following Barss and Lasnik (1986) and Larson (1988; 1990),[28] there are strong reasons to maintain that in the double-object construction the innermost object asymmetrically c-commands the outer object, as is borne out by the pair of English sentences in (65):

(65)   a. *I presented* [*the young girl*]$_i$ [*to her$_i$ new teacher*]
       b. *I presented* [*the new teacher*]$_i$ [*his$_i$ new pupil*]

In Larson's (1988, 1990) seminal analysis of such structures, the asymmetrical c-command relation in (65a) between the direct and indirect object is captured by generating the former in a [Spec, VP] position higher than that of the indirect object which occurs in the complement position of the lower V'. In (65b), on the other hand, Larson proposes a rule of PASSIVE which raises the indirect object to the underlying position of the direct object which, in turn, is demoted to an adjoined V-bar position. The structure that we propose here to account for the Neapolitan data is based on Collins's (1997: 50ff.) analysis of double-object constructions which, though adopting a VP-shell structure, differs in many respects from Larson's analysis. The proposed structure (omitting TP) is given below in (66):

(66)

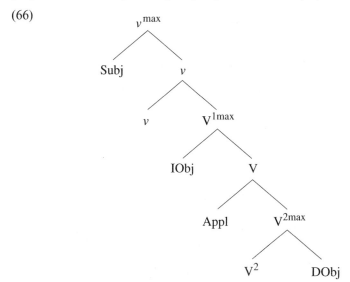

Contrary to Larson's analysis, we follow Collins (1997) in assuming the indirect object to occupy a position higher than that of the direct object: the former merged in the specifier of V^{1max}, whereas the latter is merged in complement position of the lower V^{2max} projection.[29] Based on proposals made in Marantz (1993), Collins suggests that the higher V^{2max} projection is headed by an applicative affix Appl which introduces the indirect object and checks the Case of the direct object, just as *v* introduces the external argument and checks the Case of the indirect object.[30] We thus have two verbal-related functional heads *v* and Appl, responsible for the Case-checking of the indirect and direct objects, respectively. In order to illustrate the adequacy of the structure in (66), consider the derivation of (67a) in (67b):

(67) a. *isso appresentaje nu piatto 'e pasta a Ciro*
      he   present.PAST.3SG a   plate   of pasta SD Ciro
      'he presented Ciro with a plate of pasta'

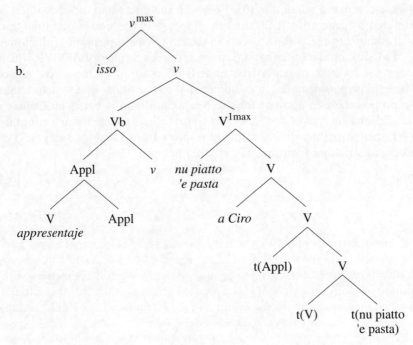

Concretely, the direct object of the verb raises to the outer [Spec, V^{1max}] over the indirect object to check its UA Case feature against Appl, a move independently permitted by the MLC (see section 1.3.6). Observe that we are assuming that objects in the UA raise overtly in ditransitive constructions to check their Case feature, whereas indirect objects check their SD Case feature at LF against v (= Vb), as is confirmed by the superficial linear order DObj + IObj. Let us now turn to consider the sentence in (68a) and its representation in (68b):

(68) a. *isso appresentaje (*a) Ciro a Catia*
      he   present.PAST.3SG (PA) Ciro SD Catia
      'he introduced Ciro to Catia'

b.

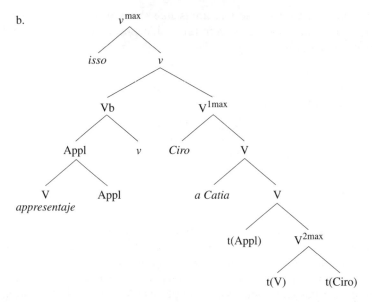

Previously it was noted that sentences such as (68a) highlight an important restriction on the distribution of the PA, insofar as animate and specific direct objects are banned from appearing in the PA when they co-occur with an indirect object. In view of our proposed structure in (68b), this initially puzzling fact regarding the distribution of the PA meets with a highly natural explanation. The only way the direct object *Ciro* can raise to the outer [Spec, *v*] in (68b) to check PA is to move first to the outer [Spec, Appl], since direct raising to [Spec, *v*] over the indirect object *a Catia* is ruled out by the MLC. In particular, *a Catia* in the inner [Spec, Appl] is closer to the outer [Spec, *v*] than *Ciro* merged within V^{2max}. Consequently, *Ciro* in (68b) is forced to move to [Spec, Appl]. From this position *Ciro* could potentially raise further to [Spec, *v*] without violating the MLC, but this possibility is equally ruled out since we have argued that [Spec, Appl] is a Case-checking position. Therefore, once raised to [Spec, Appl], *Ciro* checks the verb's UA Case feature and is 'frozen' in place.

At the same time this analysis precludes raising of the indirect object to [Spec, *v*] to check PA since the verb's accusative feature has already been checked by the direct object in [Spec, Appl], witness the ungrammaticality of (69):

(69) **isso appresentaje a Catia Ciro*
        he   present.PAST.3SG PA Catia   Ciro
        'he presented Catia Ciro'

From the above examples we conclude therefore that the absence of the PA in such structures follows as a direct consequence of the MLC, which conspires to prevent raising of either object to [Spec, *v*].

We now turn to examine structures like those in (70), where the GOAL argument *Ciro* may surface as an indirect object in the SD (70b) or as a direct object in the PA (70c):

(70) a. *isso   mannaje   'a lettera   a   Ciro*
        he   send.PAST.3SG the letter   SD Ciro
        'he sent the letter to Ciro'

    b. *isso nce   mannaje   'a lettera*
        he   him.DAT   send.PAST.3SG the letter
        'he sent the letter to him'

    c. *isso 'o   mannaje   'a lettera*
        he   him.ACC   send.PAST.3SG the letter
        'he sent him the letter'

In (70b) the derivation proceeds much along the lines of (67) above: the direct object *'a lettera* raises to check UA in the outer [Spec, Appl], whereas the covert indirect object (pro) raises to adjoin to *v* at LF to check its SD feature, witness the SD clitic *nce* adjoined to *v*. In (70c), by contrast, we maintain in accordance with our assumptions above that the direct object is marked by V^2 with an inherent accusative Case *in situ*.[31] As a consequence, the verb's structural accusative Case feature can be checked by the indirect object which raises overtly to [Spec, *v*] to be marked PA. We assign to (70c) the structural representation in (71):

(71)

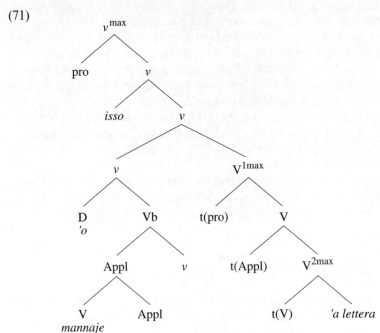

Observe that this analysis only applies to those dialects like Neapolitan examined above in section 2.4.1, and not to dialects such as Altamurano, Cosentino, Trebisaccese and Sicilian which we have seen only allow the indirect object to be marked SD in such examples. To account for these latter dialects, we propose then that V^2 does not license inherent accusative Case. Consequently, in these dialects the direct object in ditransitive sentences must always raise to [Spec, Appl] to check UA, forcing the indirect object to appear in the SD.[32]

Significantly, our proposed analysis also accounts for the behaviour of clitics in ditransitive constructions. Assuming clitics to be a spell-out of the verb's Case feature, we take clitics to signal the presence of a Case-checking verbal head to which D_{CL} is adjoined: accusative clitics referencing UA and PA objects merge with Appl and dative clitics referencing objects in the SD merge with v, as illustrated in (72):

(72)

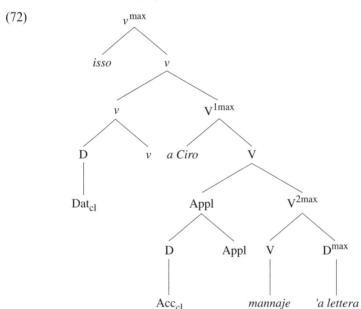

Significantly our interpretation of clitics as merged in an adjoined position to a Case-checking head in (72) has the advantage of capturing the linear ordering of clitics and the co-occurrence restrictions on their distribution. By way of example, consider the sentences in (73), some of which were discussed above in (70):

(73) a. *isso mannaje   'a lettera a Ciro*
       he   send.PAST.3SG the letter SD Ciro
      'he sent the letter to Ciro'

b. *isso   'a   mannaje   a Ciro*
   he   it.ACC send.PAST.3SG SD Ciro
'he sent it to Ciro'

c. *isso   nce   mannaje   'a lettera*
   he   him.DAT send.PAST.3SG the letter
'he sent a letter to him'

d. *isso   nce   'a   mannaje*
   he   him.DAT it.ACC send.PAST.3SG
'he sent it to him'

e. *isso   'o   mannaje   'a lettera*
   he   him.ACC send.PAST.3SG the letter
'he sent him the letter'

f. **isso   'o   'a   mannaje*
   he   him.ACC it.ACC send.PAST.3SG
'he sent him it'

In (73b) the covert direct object (pro) raises to the outer [Spec, Appl] to check its UA feature against the complex verbal head formed by raising V^1 to Appl. This Case feature checked by Appl on the direct object is signalled by the adjoined accusative clitic *'a*. (73c) was discussed above (see 70b), where it was argued that the direct object *'a lettera* raises to [Spec, Appl] to check UA and V^1 undergoes a series of movement operations, adjoining first to Appl (in this instance merged without an accusative clitic) and then to *v*. The SD Case feature borne by the indirect object pro is checked at LF against *v* but is overtly signalled on this head by the adjoined SD clitic *nce*. In light of these facts, the derivation of (73d) in which both objects are cliticized follows straightforwardly: V^1 first left-adjoins to Appl, which has been merged with the UA clitic *'a*, and then raises to left-adjoin to *v*, merged with the dative clitic, correctly yielding the order $+IObj_{CL} > DObj_{CL}$. The derivation of (73d) is given in (74), see below.

Turning now to (73e), we maintained above (see 70c) that the direct object is marked with an inherent accusative Case, freeing up the verb's PA feature which can be checked by the indirect object pro moved to the outer [Spec, *v*]. From this specifier position, the indirect object can enter into a checking relation with the accusative Case feature borne by the head Appl (witness the adjoined accusative clitic *'o*) now adjoined to *v* in the Vb complex. On this view of Case-checking and clitics, the ill-formedness of (73f) is straightforwardly accounted for: the accusative clitic *'a* merged under Appl cannot reference the direct object since the latter does not enter into a Case-checking relation with the head Appl but, rather, is marked with inherent Case by V^2 *in situ*. Instead, we maintain on a par with (73e) that the accusative Case feature borne by Appl is checked when Appl raises to Vb (= [*v* + [Appl +

V]]) against the indirect object pro moved to [Spec, *v*], licensing the PA on the latter.

(74)

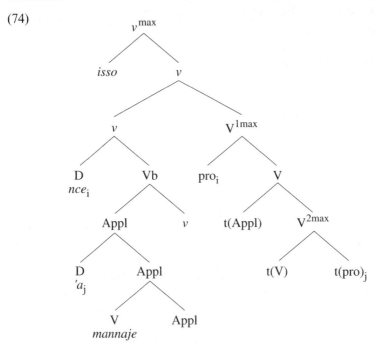

It follows from the present analysis that dative clitics are predicted to precede accusative clitics (see 73d) and that multiple occurrences of identical Case clitics are not permitted (see 73f). In addition, we also have a highly natural account of the distinction between UA and PA. In the core cases, structural accusative is checked by DP raising to [Spec, Appl], where it can check an UA feature against an Appl head. Direct objects in the PA, on the other hand, check their structural Case feature in an outer specifier of *v*, a head which we have argued is canonically responsible for checking SD Case on indirect objects at LF. It follows naturally from this that objects in the PA are simply direct objects in dative clothing, an observation which explains why it is the dative marker which invariably marks such objects. Consequently, the hybrid nature of direct and indirect objects in the PA reflects their exceptional licensing mechanism: full DPs assume dative marking since they occupy the specifier of a dative Case-checking head *v*, but check a structural accusative Case feature since, once raised to [Spec, *v*], they enter into a Case-checking relation with the accusative feature on Appl adjoined to *v* in the Vb complex. Therefore, when referenced by a clitic, such objects are marked by an accusative clitic, and not a SD clitic.

It remains now to consider how we account for sentences such as (75a–d) discussed above in section 2.4.1:

(75) a. *manno*   '*a lettera a   Ciro*
         send.PRES.ISG the letter   SD Ciro
         'I'll send the letter to Ciro'

      b. *'o   manno   'a lettera*
         him.ACC send.PRES.ISG the letter
         'I'll send him the letter'

      c. **'o   manno   'a lettera a   Ciro*
         him.ACC send.PRES.ISG the letter   PA Ciro
         'I'll send (him) the letter to Ciro'

      d. *'o   manno   a   Ciro 'a   lettera*
         him.ACC send.PRES.ISG PA Ciro   the letter
         'I'll send Ciro (him) the letter'

The problem cases are represented by examples (75c–d). As observed by
Sornicola (1997a: 336), although the covert indirect object can be referenced
by a PA clitic in such sentences as (75b), the same clitic is not available to
reference a doubled overt indirect object in sentences like (75c). However, we
noted in section 2.4.1 that (75c) improves if the doubled indirect object
precedes the direct object, as exemplified in (75d). Within our proposed
analysis, these facts are immediately accounted for. As evidenced by the
accusative clitic *'o*, in both (75c–d) the indirect object is marked with PA.
However, only in (75d) is this Case-checked. Recall that previously we
proposed that typical properties of objects in the PA such as animacy and
specificity are related to the properties of a strong D-feature on v, which has
to be checked by overt DP-raising to an outer [Spec, v]. Given the relative
orderings of direct and indirect object in (75c–d), we conclude that only in
(75d) is the strong D-feature on v checked by the raising of the indirect
object to [Spec, v].

2.4.4. *Summary*

Above it was shown that the PA checked by covert and overt indirect objects
in ditransitive structures is made possible by the option of marking the direct
object with inherent accusative Case *in situ*. By virtue of the latter not raising
to check the verb's structural accusative Case in an outer [Spec, Appl],
accusative is freed up and may be checked by the indirect object raising
overtly to the outer [Spec, v], thereby accounting for the linear order IObj +
DObj when the indirect object is overt. Consequently, the direct object
cannot be referenced by a structural accusative clitic merged on Appl, since
it does not enter into a Case-checking configuration with Appl.

Conversely, we have seen that the order DObj + IObj proves ungrammatical if the indirect object occurs in the PA. Clearly, this surface order
indicates that the verb's structural accusative Case is checked by the direct

object raising overtly to the outer [Spec, Appl]. The indirect object is therefore forced to check SD against v at LF.

Finally, the impossibility of PA-marking in ditransitive structures where the direct object is also a candidate for the PA was demonstrated to follow from the MLC. The direct object cannot raise directly to the outer [Spec, v] to be marked PA, since the indirect object in [Spec, Appl] is closer to this position. In order to be equidistant with the indirect object from the outer [Spec, v], the direct object must first raise to the outer [Spec, Appl] within the same minimal domain as the indirect object. However, the outer [Spec, Appl] is the position where the verb's structural accusative (UA) Case is checked. Consequently, once raised to this position, the direct object will check UA and will be 'frozen' in place. By the same token, the indirect object cannot appear in the PA by raising to the outer [Spec, v], since the verb's accusative Case feature has been checked by the direct object in the outer [Spec, Appl].

3

FINITE AND INFINITIVAL COMPLEMENTATION: NULL SUBJECTS AND CONTROL

3.1 INTRODUCTION

In the preminimalist framework the configurational property of government played a central role in the theory of syntax, imposing strict locality conditions on Case-assignment and movement. In the preceding chapter we observed that government no longer has any role to play in the minimalist approach to Case-assignment and movement. Instead, locality conditions are now derived from the definition of minimal domain which restricts Case-checking operations to Spec-head and Head-head configurations and the target of movement to positions reached through minimal links (see the discussion of the MLC in section 1.3.6). By the same token, we must also abandon under minimalist assumptions the notoriously problematic Principles and Parameters account of the distribution of PRO and infinitival complementation embodied in the PRO Theorem,[1] which restricts PRO to ungoverned positions. This state of affairs follows from the contradictory requirements placed on PRO by the binding theory which, as a pronominal anaphor, finds itself subject simultaneously to Principles A and B. However, by virtue of occurring in ungoverned positions, PRO is predicted not to have a governing category and therefore to escape the contradictory requirements of the binding theory.

In response to the problems posed by the PRO Theorem and, in particular, its reliance on government, the minimalist literature has witnessed a number of attempts to capture the distribution of PRO and infinitival complementation which eliminate recourse to government. Arguing from examples like those in (1), Chomsky and Lasnik (1993) observe that PRO behaves like other arguments in moving *to* Case-checking positions (1a) but not *from* positions where Case can be checked (1b):

(1) a. *we never expected* [PRO$_i$ *to be found* t$_i$]

    b. **we never expected* [PRO$_i$ *to seem to* t$_i$ [*that the problems are insoluble*]]

On the basis of such evidence, Chomsky and Lasnik abandon the binding-theoretic account of the distribution of PRO and propose that PRO is Case-marked on a par with other arguments. Specifically, PRO is marked with a null Case, restricted to PRO and checked in a Spec-head configuration with non-finite T. Given these assumptions, both examples in (1) follow from the Last Resort Condition: movement of PRO in (1a) is legitimate since it raises from a Caseless to a null Case position, while (1b) is excluded since PRO originates in a Case position, thereby rendering movement unnecessary.

Even with the elimination of government, this alternative Case-theoretic account fails, as it stands, to predict the distribution of PRO in Neapolitan. In common with a number of related Italian dialects of the Upper South, Neapolitan displays a relatively restricted use of the infinitive in complement clauses.[2] In particular, the problems raised by the distribution of PRO and infinitival complementation centre around the contrast witnessed by the Italian and Neapolitan paradigms in (2)–(3) and (4)–(5), respectively:

(2) a. *Ciro   promette   di   non ubriacarsi*
         Ciro$_i$ promise.PRES.3SG [of PRO$_i$ not get-drunk.INF]
         'Ciro promises not to get drunk'

     b. *Ciro   crede   di   conoscere Mario*
         Ciro$_i$ think.PRES.3SG [of PRO$_i$ know.INF   Mario]
         'Ciro believes that he knows Mario'

(3) a. *Ciro   sta   attento a   non ubriacarsi*
         Ciro$_i$ be.PRES.3SG careful to [PRO$_i$ not get-drunk.INF]
         'Ciro takes care not to get drunk'

     b. *Ciro   è   sicuro di   conoscere Mario*
         Ciro$_i$ be.PRES.3SG sure   of [PRO$_i$ know.INF   Mario]
         'Ciro is sure that he knows Mario'

(4) a. **Ciro prummette   'e   nun se mbriacà*
         Ciro$_i$ promise.PRES.3SG [of PRO$_i$ not get-drunk.INF]

     b. **Ciro   crere   'e   canoscere a Mario*
         Ciro$_i$ think.PRES.3SG [of PRO$_i$ know.INF   PA Mario]

(5) a. *Ciro   sta   attiento a   nun se mbriacà*
         Ciro$_i$ be.PRES.3SG careful to [PRO$_i$ not get-drunk.INF]

     b. **Ciro è   sicuro 'e   canoscere a Mario*
         Ciro$_i$ be.PRES.3SG sure   of [PRO$_i$ know.INF   PA Mario]

When the understood embedded subject, here represented as PRO, is coreferential with that of the matrix clause, the Italian matrix predicates in (2) and (3) subcategorize for an infinitival complement. Yet, when the embedded subject is disjoint in reference from that of the matrix, a finite complement is selected (see 6 and 7) in accordance with the so-called obviation effect:[3]

(6) a. *Ciro   promette   che Gianni non si ubriacherà*
         Ciro   promise.PRES.3SG [that Gianni not get-drunk.FUT.3SG]
         'Ciro promises that Gianni will not get drunk'

b. *Ciro crede   che Gianni conosce   Mario*
   Ciro believe.PRES.3SG [that Gianni   know.PRES.3SG Mario]
   'Ciro believes that Gianni knows Mario'

(7) a. *Ciro sta   attento a che Gianni non si ubriachi*
   Ciro be.PRES.3SG careful   to [that Gianni not get-drunk.PRES.SUBJ.3SG]
   'Ciro makes sure that Gianni doesn't get drunk'

b. *Ciro è   sicuro che Gianni conosce   Mario*
   Ciro be.PRES.3SG sure   [that Gianni know.PRES.3SG Mario]
   'Ciro is sure that Gianni knows Mario'

The grammaticality judgements of the corresponding sentences in (4) and (5), in contrast, demonstrate that quite different principles are at play in determining the distribution of PRO and infinitival complementation in Neapolitan. Apart from the grammatical (5a), the infinitival complements in (4a–b) and (5b) must be substituted by a finite clause introduced by one of the complementizers *ca* or *che*:

(8) a. *Ciro prummette   che nun se mbriaca*
   Ciro promise.PRES.3SG [that not   get-drunk.PRES.3SG]
   'Ciro promises that he'll not get drunk'

b. *Ciro crere   ca canosce   a Mario*
   Ciro believe.PRES.3SG [that know.PRES.3SG PA Mario]
   'Ciro believes that he knows Mario'

c. *Ciro è   sicuro ca canosce   a Mario*
   Ciro be.PRES.3SG sure   [that know.PRES.3SG PA Mario]
   'Ciro is sure that he knows Mario'

Neapolitan complement clauses appear then to escape the obviation effect, insofar as a relation of coreferentiality between matrix and embedded subjects has no effect on the availability of infinitival complementation. Instead, a finite complement is invariably employed in such cases, irrespective of the identity of the embedded subject.

Despite the lack of obviation effects in Neapolitan, it would not, however, be correct to conclude that examples such as (8a–c) do not instantiate a control relation. In this respect, consider the Neapolitan sentences in (9a–b):

(9) a. *Ciro prummette   che Ø Iisso accatta   'e purtualle*
   Ciro$_i$ promise.PRES.3SG [that Ø$_{i/*j}$ /he$_{j/*i}$ buy.PRES.3SG the oranges]
   'Ciro promises that he will buy the oranges'

b. *Ciro se crereva   ca Ø Iisso venceva   'o premio]*
   Ciro$_i$ believe.PAST.3SG [that Ø$_{i/j}$ /he$_{i/j}$ win.PAST.3SG the prize]
   'Ciro believed that he would win the prize'

Verbs like *prummettere* 'to promise' in (9a), which select for the *che* complementizer, impose an obligatory control (OC) relation on the understood subject of their embedded clause (here represented as Ø), such that it can only be interpreted as coreferent with the matrix subject. To be interpreted as disjoint in reference, the embedded subject must be overtly realized (for example, *isso* 'he'). The effects of the presence/absence of OC on the subject of Neapolitan *che*-clauses thus mirrors the behaviour of the Italian infinitival and finite complements in (2)–(3) and (6)–(7): the embedded subject is null when control obtains but overt whenever control is absent.

In contrast, verbs like *crererse* 'to believe' in (9b), which select for the *ca*-complementizer, do not impose such restrictions on the interpretation of the embedded subject. In particular, these verbs yield non-obligatory control (NOC) structures, in which the understood embedded subject may be controlled by an argument of the matrix clause (for example, the matrix subject *Ciro* in (9b)) or receive an independent interpretation. Consequently, if the embedded subject is overtly realized (for example, *isso* 'he'), it too may be freely construed with the matrix subject or not.

Contrary to the predictions of the Case-theoretic approach to PRO, which would lead us to expect the grammaticality of all four sentences in (4) and (5) on a par with their Italian counterparts in (2) and (3), the option of an infinitival complement and hence PRO is only possible in (5a). It emerges therefore that the Neapolitan data pose a number of non-trivial problems for the Case-theoretic approach to PRO. In what follows we shall develop an analysis which derives the distribution of PRO and infinitival/finite complementation in Neapolitan and related southern dialects from the interaction of the Case-checking properties of the matrix predicate and the temporal properties of the embedded verb.

In particular, we shall demonstrate in section 3.2 that the property underlying the contrast between Neapolitan and standard Romance languages, which restricts the use of the infinitive in the former but not the latter, bears in large part on the structural/inherent Case distinction. In Neapolitan and related dialects structural Case-checking predicates fail to license infinitival complementation, thereby ruling out such examples as (4a–b). As for the contrast in infinitival usage displayed by inherent Case-checking predicates (5a–b), we argue in section 3.3 that such facts follow from the role of Tense in the embedded infinitival clause which licenses a null subject, interpreted as DP-trace, in (5a) but not in (5b). The results of this analysis of infinitival complementation, which highlights the importance of Tense in determining the distribution of null subjects, are subsequently shown in section 3.4 to extend straightforwardly to finite clauses. Specifically, we propose that the distribution of null subjects and hence nominative in such examples as (9a–b) falls out as a concomitant of the OC/NOC distinction, wholly independent of the presence of subject-verb agreement. In this respect, the principled distinction between PRO (here interpreted as DP-trace) and pro dissolves, the empty category in subject position now understood as an instantiation of the properties of OC/NOC T. Finally, similar conclusions are drawn in section 3.5 from an examination of the old Neapolitan inflected infinitive, where the repercussions of the OC/NOC distinction on nominative Case-checking are investigated.

3.2. LICENSING OF SENTENTIAL COMPLEMENTS

3.2.1. *Finite complements*

In line with most southern Italian dialects (see Rohlfs 1969: §786; 1972), as well as the Balkan languages (Joseph 1983), Neapolitan boasts two distinct complementizers to introduce finite clauses, namely QU(I)A > ca^4 and QUOD/ QUID > *che*. Broadly speaking (though see section 3.4), *ca* is the complementizer selected by declarative/epistemic predicates that typically s-select for a propositional complement and the indicative. Below follow some examples from the fourteenth century to the present day:

(10) a. *dicevano apertamente* [*cha tutti foro reprisi de grande pazia*] (De Blasi 1986: 176, 28–9)
          'they openly said [that they were all overcome with insanity]'

      b. *considero* [*ca quiste tucte so' miey amice*] (McArthur n.d., 3)
          'I consider [that these are all my friends]'

      c. *nce simme accorgiute* [*ca nce smicciate da no piezzo*] (Cerlone 1825, in Capozzoli 1889: 142)
          'we noticed [that you have been watching us for a while]'

      d. *comprese* [*ca Ciullo era nnammorato*] (Cortese 1783, ibid., 31)
          'he realized [that Ciullo was in love]'

      e. *ce putite giurà* [*ca so' vint'ore*] (Di Giacomo 1991a: 47)
          'you can swear [that it's eight o'clock]'

      f. *che d'è te si scurdata* [*ca facimmo ammore*]? (Scarpetta 1992: 80)
          'why, have you forgotten [that we are courting]?'

   Predicates that typically characterize the state or events of their complements as unrealized at the time of speaking, in contrast, select the *che* complementizer with the verb generally in the subjunctive:

(11) a. *pregaro . . .* [*che devesse concedere questa tregua*] (De Blasi 1986: 180, 22)
          'they asked . . . [that he grant this truce]'

      b. *cossì io te comando da sua parte* [*che tu isse de fore icontinente*] (McArthur n.d., 8)
          'thus I order you on his behalf [that you go out immediately]'

      c. *ordenaje* [*che se desse a li recetante na nforra de cappiello*] (G. Basile 1788, in Capozzoli 1889: 192)
          'he ordered [that the actors' hats be lined]'

   d. *da lo Segnore fuje stabelito* [**che** *non fosse stato co le mmano mmocca*]
      (Rocchi 1783, ibid., 159)
      'it was laid down by the Lord [that he would not stand idle]'

   e. *e quanno vulite* [**che** *vengo?*] (Scarpetta 1992: 196)
      'and when do you want [that I come]?'

   f. *o me prumiette* [**che** *tu te spuse a sorema*] *o si no t'accido* (ibid., 79)
      'either you promise me [that you'll marry my sister] or I'll kill you'

It appears from the data that the core distribution of *ca* and *che* can only be satisfactorily handled if we make reference to the tense of the embedded clause, as demonstrated by Calabrese (1993) for the Salentino congeners of Neapolitan *ca* and *che*. Typically, clauses introduced by *ca* have deictic tense, whereas those introduced by *che* have anaphoric tense. This fact immediately accounts for the distributional properties of the two complementizers with a high degree of accuracy. Predicates that s-select for a propositional complement, and hence *ca*, do not impose any restrictions on the tense specification of their clausal complement. This can be demonstrated by the possibility of embedding a deictic tense such as the preterite under *ca* (12a). On the other hand, predicates that s-select for an irrealis complement, and hence *che*, typically impose severe constraints on the verbal morphology of their embedded complement, since their temporal interpretation is constructed in relation to the temporal specification of the matrix clause. This immediately explains the characteristic use of the subjunctive in such clauses, for the latter typically has anaphoric temporal reference in Romance. A deictic tense such as the preterite therefore proves ill-formed (12b).

(12) a. *saccio/aggiu saputo/sapeva/sapette* [**ca** *ve verette a vuje*]
       'I know/I learnt/I knew/I learnt [that he saw you]'

     b. **voglio/aggiu vuluto/vuleva/vulette* [**che** *ve verette a vuje*]
       'I want/wanted [that he saw you]'

3.2.1.1. *Comparative southern evidence*

Besides Neapolitan, Rohlfs (1969: §786a) reports the distribution of a dual complementizer system (*ca* versus *che/chi*) to be widespread in the dialects of southern Italy, encompassing dialects from Abruzzo as far south as Sicily.[5] However, as Rohlfs' own investigations confirm (see Rohlfs 1972), the fate of such dual complementizer systems in the modern dialects is frequently threatened by a tendency to generalize one of the pair to all contexts.[6] Nonetheless, the examples in (13)–(18) illustrate that there still remain a number of dialects, alongside Neapolitan, which continue to exploit such a distinction in the complementizer system:

Lazio

(13) a. *sənti [ca stevən a ssuná]* (Veroli (FR), Battisti 1921: 74)
      'he heard [that they were playing music]'

   b. *i nnə mmə merdə [chə mmə rechiami fijo tio]* (ibid., 73)
      'I do not deserve [that you call me your son]'

Campania

(14) a. *sə dicə [ca chi nə rrəspetta lu patrə nə rispettə mancu ddivə]*
      (Amaseno (CE), Battisti 1921: 81)
      'they say [that he who doesn't respect his father doesn't respect even
      God]'

   b. *sperə [chə ttu pərdunarai purə mi]* (ibid.)
      'I hope that you will forgive me too'

   c. *vide [ca caca tante belle munete d'oro]* (BN, De Simone 1994: 228)
      'you see [that it produces lots of lovely gold coins]'

   d. *basta [che 'a miette mmiezo â tavula]* (ibid., 228)
      'it suffices [that you put it in the middle of the table]'

   e. *tiene a mmente però, [ca ddoi vote tiene]* (Somma Vesuviana (NA),
      ibid., 1198)
      'bear in mind though [that you have two chances]'

   f. *è meglio [che ghjamo 'a chell'ata parte!]* (ibid.)
      'it is better [that we go to the other place]'

Abruzzo[7]

(15) a. *nə vidə [ca si viecchiə]* (Rohlfs 1972: 153)
      'you cannot see [that you are old]'

   b. *vələtə [kə ccə vajə ji]?* (ibid.)
      'do you want [that I go]?'

   c. *ne' vva penzéte [ca ji' cande pe' vvoje]* (Lanciano (CH), ibid.)
      'don't think [that I'll sing for you]'

   d. *vurreje [che ss'affacciasse la patrone]* (ibid.)
      'I'd like [that the mistress come out]'

   e. *chesta sə nə pənti [ca i era pətutə kellə]* (Arpino (FR), Battisti 1921:
      102)
      'she regretted [that she had asked her for those things]'

   f. *i risse n'auta vota [che se fussə rəcurdata ca n'i aveva ra pəti nientə*
      (ibid.)
      'she told her [that she was not to ask her for anything]'

   g. ts a'krɑde [ka lɪ sa] (Tollo (CH))[8]
      'he thinks [that he knows it]'

h. nnɪ v'vujjə [**kɪ** vve a p'pidə] (ibid.)
'I don't want [that he come on foot]'

Lucania
(16) a. *crèdisi* [*ca lu truvamu*]? (Maratea (PZ), Rohlfs 1972: 153)
'do you think [that we shall find him]?'

b. *vogliu* [*chi scúmbisi*] (ibid.)
'I want [that you finish]'

Calabria
17 a. *t'accurgi* [*ca durante l'anni ha fattu tante fissarie*] (Mendicino (CS), Barca 1996: 11)
'you realize [that over the years he has got up to so many stupid things]'

b. *ti prumintu* [*chi juri ara tombiceddu tua un ti fazzu mancare*] (ibid., 110)
'I promise you [that I won't fail to place flowers on your grave]'

c. *s'ha fattu 'u cuntu* [*ca putie restari*] (Amantea (CS), Launi 1980: 12)
'he worked out [that you could stay]'

d. *lu prieju de li figli e d'a mugliera* [*chi la stanchizza me fanu scordare*] (ibid., 17)
'I ask of my children and wife [that they make me forget my tiredness]'

Sicily[9]
(18) a. *ti dicu* [*ca è accussì*] (Varvaro 1988: 725)
'I tell you [that is like that]'

b. *vogghiu* [*chi l'accattanu*] (ibid.)
'I want [that they buy it]'

c. *finciti* [*ca muriu*] (Borgetto (PA), Pitré 1875: I, 64)
'pretend [that he has died]'

d. *dati ordini* [*chi tutti li fimmini di la citati vinissiru a chianciri*] (ibid.)
'order [that all the women of the city come and cry]'

e. *cci dissi* [*ca si vulia maritari*] (Acireale (CT), ibid., 348)
'he told him [that he wanted to marry]'

f. *cci dissi idda a lu 'Mperaturi* [*chi si ni jèvanu tutti li cirusichi*] (ibid., 347)
'she told the Emperor [that all the surgeons should leave]'

In the Laziale, Campanian and Abruzzese examples in (13)–(15), predicates which s-select for a propositional complement introduce the latter with the *ca* complementizer, whereas irrealis complements are headed by the *che* complementizer. Similar contrasts in the distribution of *calchi* are observable in the Lucanian, Calabrian and Sicilian examples in (16)–(18). It would appear then that the distinct type of finite complementation outlined above for Neapolitan also characterizes the dialects of southern Italy more generally.

3.2.1.2. *Licensing*

Following in essence Stowell (1981), we assume that, by virtue of their [+finite] specification, tensed clausal complements, whether introduced by *ca* or *che*, are headed by an intrinsic structural Case feature, which places them outside of the Case Filter.[10] Consider the examples in (19):

(19) a. *eo doveto*   *(*de) che fuorze per la   ventura voy non*
      I   doubt.PRES.1SG (of) [that perhaps for the chance   you not
      sapite   tutto lo convenente]
      know.PRES.2PL all   the facts]
      'I suspect that perhaps, by chance, you don't know all the facts' (De Blasi 1986: 59, 17–18)

   b. *non potite   stare secure(*de) ca   non me tenarrate*
      not be-able.PRES.2PL be.INF sure   (of) [that not me keep.FUT.2PL
      maje p' amico
      ever for friend]
      'you cannot be sure that you will never have me as your friend' (Spassatiempo 1875, in Capozzoli 1889: 98)

   c. *isso è   cuntento (*e) ca   esce   d' 'o*
      he   be.PRES.3SG happy   (of) [that come-out.PRES.3SG of the
      manicomio?
      mental-asylum]
      'is he happy that he is coming out of the mental asylum?' (De Filippo 1973: 11)

The matrix predicates in (19) are inherent Case-checkers. Yet, when they subcategorize for a finite complement, the latter fails to be Case-marked, witness the impossibility of the bracketed prepositions in (19). For instance, although the predicate *dubbetà* 'to doubt' marks its nominal and infinitival complements in (20a–b) with inherent genitive Case, witness the preposition *'e* 'of', the same preposition fails to surface before the finite CP complement in (19a).

(20) a. *dubbetaje   d'   'a parola soja*
      doubt.PAST.1SG of [DP the word   his]
      'I doubted his word'

   b. *dubbeteaje 'e   puté   venì   ê   seje*
      doubt.PAST.1SG of [CP be-able.INF come.INF at-the six]
      'I doubted that I could come at six o'clock'

These facts confirm our proposal that finite CP complements are inherently visible, marked with an intrinsic structural Case feature licensed by their finite specification.

3.2.2. *Infinitival complements*

An unmistakable feature of Neapolitan, in contrast to most standard Romance varieties, manifests itself in the restricted distribution of the infinitive. The problem of pinpointing its precise distribution in complement clauses finds however a partial explanation in terms of Case-checking. On a par with DPs, it has been proposed (Raposo 1987, Acquaviva 1989) that Romance infinitival CPs require abstract Case, occurring solely as arguments to the Case-checking heads T (21a), V (21b) and P (21c).

(21) a. *bere   troppo   alcool è   pericoloso* (nominative)
         [CP drink.INF too-much alcohol] be.PRES.3SG dangerous
         'to drink too much alcohol is dangerous'

   b. *decisero   di incontrarsi* (accusative)
      decide.PAST.3PL [CP of meet.INF]
      'they decided to meet up'

   c. *aspirò   a.   diventare ricca* (inherent dative)
      aspire.PAST.3SG to [CP become.INF rich]
      'she aspired to become rich'

In contrast to the Italian examples in (21), the Case-licensing requirement on infinitival CPs is only partially confirmed by Neapolitan:

(22) a. *guardandose **de**   non bevere   acqua fredde*
        refrain.GER   from [CP not drink.INF water cold]
        'refraining from drinking cold water' (Percopo 1887: I, 8–10)

   b. *nce resistero   **a**   nno lo fare   recoperare*
      it resist.PAST.3PL to [CP not it have.INF recover.INF]
      'they fought against letting it be recaptured' (De Blasi 1986: 102, 39)

   c. *io so'   atto **a**   servire*
      I be.PRES.1SG fit   to [CP serve.INF]
      'I am fit to serve' (McArthur n.d., 22)

   d. *la speranza **de**   trovare confuorto l'ha movuto*
      the hope   of [CP find.INF comfort]   . . .
      'the hope of finding comfort moved him' (Oliva, in Capozzoli 1889: 141)

   e. *vuie site   pronta **a**   ripetere in tribunale chello che avite
      ditto?*
      you be.PRES.2PL ready   to [CP repeat.INF . . .]
      'are you willing to repeat in court what you've just said?' (De Filippo 1973: 148)

> f. *nun te   miette   scuorno 'e   me venì   a. dicere pure chello*
>   not you put.PRES.2SG shame   of [CP me come.INF to say.INF . . .]
>   *ch'e' fatto?*
>   'aren't you ashamed to come and tell me what you did as well?' (Di
>   Giacomo 1991a:161)

The infinitival complements in (22) occur as the complement of an inherent
Case-checking predicate, introduced by the preposition that co-occurs with a
nominal complement. For instance, in (22b) and (22f) the predicates *resistere*
'to resist' and *metterse scuorno* 'to be ashamed' mark their respective
infinitival complements with the prepositions *a* 'to' and *'e* 'of', the same
prepositions which surface in conjunction with a nominal complement in
(23a–b):

> (23) a. *Maria nun ha   pututo   resistere a   'e moine 'e Ciro*
>   Maria not have.PRES.3SG be-able.PART resist.INF to [DP the caresses of Ciro]
>   'Maria couldn't resist Ciro's caresses'
>
>   b. *'a mamma 'e Maria se mette scuorno d'   'a figlia*
>   the mum   of Maria be-ashamed.PRES.3SG of [DP the daughter]
>   'Maria's mother is ashamed of her daughter'

Prepositions with predicates like those in (23) were interpreted in chapter 2
as the overt realization of inherent Case on the DP complement. It follows
from this that the infinitivals in (22) are indeed Case-marked by their
subcategorizing predicates, otherwise the presence of the preposition
would remain unexplained.

On the other hand, infinitivals as complements to structural Case-checkers
prove systematically ungrammatical (24a–b).[11] In order to rescue such
structures, the infinitival complement must be substituted by a finite
complement (25a–b):

> (24) a. **rico   /respongo   /crero   nun canoscere*
>   say.PRES.1SG /reply.PRES.1SG /believe.PRES.1SG [not know.INF
>   *a sorata*
>   PA SISTER.POSS.2SG]
>   'I say/reply/believe that I do not know your sister'
>
>   b. **deciretteno /prummettetteno /speravano lle   spiecà*
>   decide.PAST.3PL /promise.PAST.3PL /hope.PAST.3PL [him.DAT explain.INF
>   *tutta cosa*
>   all   thing]
>   'they decided/promised/hoped to explain everything to him'
>
> (25) a. *rico   /respongo   /crero   ca nun canosco*
>   say.PRES.1SG /reply.PRES.1SG /believe.PRES.1SG [that not know.PRES.1SG
>   *a sorata*
>   PA SISTER.POSS.2SG]

b. *deciretteno   /prummettetteno /speravano   che lle*
decide.PAST.3PL /promise.PAST.3PL   /hope.PAST.3PL [that him.DAT
spiecavano   tutta cosa
explain.PAST.3PL all   thing]

If Neapolitan infinitivals are subject to Case-checking, as would appear confirmed by examples (22), their incompatibility with structural Case-checkers in (24) suggests *a priori* that it is structural Case checked by the infinitival complement that causes such structures to crash. We can directly test this claim by considering the behaviour of subject infinitivals, the other context in which structural Case is checked:

(26) a. *sufficiente fosse   **ad** potérescence   lavare   tucte*
sufficient   be.PAST.SUBJ.3SG to [be-able.INF-oneself-there wash.INF all
l'   autre   menbra]
the other   limbs]
'to be able to wash all one's other limbs in it was sufficient' (Percopo 1887: III, 8–9)

b. *forria   lo plu securo **de** ne   astinere   da   questa*
be.COND.3SG the more safe   of [ouselves abstain.INF from this
impresa
undertaking]
'to abstain from this undertaking would be safest' (De Blasi 1886: 82, 16)

c. *multo   le   piaccea   **a** vedere Costancio*
much   him.DAT please.PAST.3SG to [see.INF Constantius]
'it pleased him much to see Constantius' (McArthur n.d., 42)

d. *comm' è   bello **a** fumà   dopo mangiato*
how   be.PRES.3SG nice   to [smoke.INF after   eat.PART]
'how nice it is to smoke after eating' (Di Giacomo 1991b: 32)

e. *ma è   difficile **a** truvà   sta medicina?*
but be.PRES.3SG difficult to [find.INF this medicine]
'is it difficult to find this medicine?' (De Filippo 1973: 238)

The subject infinitivals in (26) fail to check nominative and are marked instead with inherent Case realized by a dummy preposition, generally *a(d)* 'to'. This suggests that the nominative feature of T in examples (26) is checked, not by the infinitival, but by an expletive pro merged in subject position. This conclusion is substantiated by the fact that in such structures Neapolitan, like many other southern dialects,[12] also allows an overt expletive in the form of the masculine singular demonstrative *chillo* or, more commonly, the so-called neuter demonstrative *chello*:

(27) a. ***chillo* è**   meglio /è   cchiù facele /cummene
      that   be.PRES.3SG better   /be.PRES.3SG more easy /be-wise.PRES.3SG
      a   se nne ji
      to [leave.INF]
      'it is better/is easier/is wiser to leave'

   b. **'kell-** ab'bast-   a ka'noʃʃər- a 'strata
      that-   suffice.PRES.3SG- to [know.INF-   the road]
      'it is enough just to know the way' (Sornicola 1996: 332)

   c. **'kell-** ɛ   f'fatʃil- a ppar'la
      that- be.PRES.3SG easy-   to [speak.INF]
      'it is easy to speak' (ibid.)

It is not therefore structural Case which is incompatible with the subject infinitivals in the Neapolitan examples (26) and (27): nominative is checked by a covert/overt expletive and hence not available to the infinitival.[13] By the same line of reasoning, it cannot be structural Case which is incompatible with the infinitival complements in (24). Rather, their ungrammaticality is due to the fact that structural accusative/dative is simply not available, an idea we shall justify further in section 3.2.2.2

3.2.2.1. *Comparative southern evidence*

The sensitivity of the Neapolitan infinitive to the structural/inherent Case distinction is not unique among southern Italian dialects. For instance, Trumper and Rizzi's (1985) investigation of complementation in Calabrian dialects points to a number of dialects exhibiting the same properties as Neapolitan (see also Trumper 1996: 352). Specifically, they observe that dialects north of the Nicastro-Catanzaro-Crotone line, the present-day dialect of Crotone included, exhibit a restricted use of the construction verb + infinitive. Instead, such dialects make greater use of finite complements. Similarly, Trumper (1997: 363) observes that in dialects of northern Calabria 'infinitives are not used in subordinate clauses whose subject is coreferential with that of the main clause: ['sattʃu k 'aju 'dittu u 'vɛru] = 'I know that I'm telling the truth'. In this regard consider the following Calabrian examples from Trumper and Rizzi (1985) and Trumper (1996: 352):

(28) a. *sacciə [ca dichə u verə]* (Lausberg area, northern Calabria)
      'I know [that I am telling the truth]'

   b. *creghə [ca canoschə a cquillə]* (Lausberg area)
      'I believe [that I know him]'

   c. *aggə decisə [ca parchə crajə]* (Lausberg area)
      'I have decided [that I am leaving tomorrow]'

   d. *e' decidutu [ca partu dumane]* (CS)
      'I decided [that I will leave tomorrow]'

   e. *sacciu* [*ca dicu u veru*] (CS)
     'I know [that I am telling the truth]'

   f. *criju* [*ca canusciu a chiddu*] (CS)
     'I believe [that I know him]'

   g. *e' dittu* [*ca e' partutu*] (KR)
     'I said [that I left]'

   h. *criju* [*ca pozzu veniri*] (KR)
     'I believe [that I can come]'

   i. *speru* [*ca ti truovu bbonu*] (KR)
     'I hope [that I'll find you well]'

In all the above examples, an infinitival complement would prove ungrammatical. A similar situation is reported for Abruzzese dialects by Finamore (1893: 25), who observes that the Italian infinitive corresponds to a finite clause in examples like (29a). Furthermore, Robert Hastings (personal communication) observes that, though the dependent infinitive does occur in the Abruzzese dialect of Tollo (CH),[14] it is less common than the use of a finite clause (see 29b–e). Analogously, De Vicentis (1872: 18) reports that in the dialect of Taranto Italian infinitival clauses are rendered with an indicative finite clause (29f–g):

(29) a. *nne' je putive dice'* [*ch'avéss' aspettate?*]
      'couldn't you have told him [that he wait?]'

    b. 'diʧə   [dɪ vu'larlə] / [ka lɪ vɔ]
       say.PRES.3SG [of want.INF-it] / [that it want.PRES.3SG]
      'he says that he wants it'

    c. 'pɛnʣə   [dɪ tɪ'narlə] / [ka lɪ te]
       think.PRES.3SG [of have.INF-it] / [that it have.PRES.3SG]
      'he thinks he's got it'

    d. a   'dittə [kɪ lɪ vɔ   fa]
       have.PRES.3SG say.PART [that it want.PRES.3SG do.INF]
      'he said that he wants to do it'

    e. mɪ   mbaʊ'riʃʃə [kɪ p'pɛrdə   'tuttə 'kosə]
       myself frighten.PRES.1SG [that lose.PRES.1SG all   thing]
      'I'm frightened of losing everthing'

    f. *creggio* [*ca l'agghio visto*]
      'I believe [that I have seen him]'

    g. *penso* [*cu voco*]
      'I think [that I shall go]'

Significantly, all verbs in (28) and (29) which do not admit an infinitival complement check structural Case, an observation which suggests that infinitival complementation in these dialects is also sensitive to the structural/inherent Case distinction. This is further supported by the fact that infinitival complements in southern dialects are restricted to inherent Case-checking positions (Case preposition given in bold-type):

(30) a. *la   ntenzione mea era   **dde** aé   una fija   l' anno*
         the intention   my be.PAST.3SG of [have.INF one daughter the year]
         'my intention was to have one daughter a year' (RI, Battisti 1921: 62)

      b. *quannə fu   pə la via, i   vennə   nə ulíə   r*
         when be.PAST.3SG for the way her.DAT come.PAST.3SG a   desire of
         arapr'   chella scatəla
         [open.INF that   box]
         'on her way, she was taken by a desire to open that box' (Arpino (FR), ibid., 103)

      c. *n'   n   é   ddégne **de** l' avé*
         not of-it   be.PRES.3SG worthy of [it have.INF]
         'he is not worthy of having it' (Abruzzo, Finamore 1893: 22)

      d. *ha   mutive **de** le   mmaledì*
         have.PRES.3SG reason of [them criticize.INF]
         'he has reason to criticize them' (ibid.)

      e. *pənzó   di seji   **a** rrkorrə   a u re*
         think.PAST.3SG of herself to [have-recourse.INF to the king]
         'she thought to herself to try with the king' (Ferrandina (MT), Battisti 1921: 164)

      f. *u   latr næn z'   a   vvrgignei **a** ssroi   a ttutt ch'*
         the thief not himself have.PRES.3SG shame.PART to [shout.INF to all   that . . .
         avai accattot a ændre
         'the thief was not ashamed to shout to all that he had bought the horse' (Bisceglie (BA), Battisti 1921: 149)

      g. *aiutu   a Cicciu **a** purtà   'u paccu*
         help.PRES.1SG PA Ciccio to [carry.INF the package]
         'I'll help Ciccio to carry the package' (CS)

      h. *'un tena   u curaggiu 'i m' 'u dicia*
         not have.PRES.3SG the courage   of [me it say.INF]
         'he hasn't the courage to tell me' (CS)

From this, admittedly summary, examination of complementation in some related southern dialects, we conclude that such dialects pattern with Neapolitan inasmuch as infinitival clauses only occur in inherent Case-checking positions.

3.2.2.2. Licensing

Above we observed how, as non-finite arguments, infinitival CPs do not bear an intrinsic structural Case feature and must therefore be Case-marked like

DPs. However, unlike DPs, Neapolitan infinitival CPs can only be licensed by inherent (31a) and not structural (31b) Case. Consequently, infinitivals in structural Case-checking positions must be replaced by a finite CP (31c):

(31) a. *se metteva appaura 'e* [CP *caré*]
'he was frightened [CP to fall over]'

  b. **deciretteno* [CP *lle spiecà tutta cosa*]
'they decided [CP to explain everything to him]'

  c. *deciretteno* [CP *che lle spiecavano tutta cosa*]
'they decided [CP that they would explain everything to him]'

How then do we account for the contrast in acceptability illustrated by the infinitival complements in (31a–b)? Our proposed explanation capitalizes on the fact that Neapolitan and similar dialects make extensive use of finite clauses, as highlighted by their dependence on a dual complementizer system. Consequently, in the core cases a predicate does not check Case on its subcategorized sentential complement, since finite complements do not require Case-marking. We propose then that, when subcategorizing for a sentential complement, structural Case-checking predicates enter the derivation without an objective Case feature by default; this represents the unmarked option in accordance with the predominant use of finite complements. It follows from this that structural Case-checking predicates like *decirere* 'to decide' are restricted to selecting finite CPs (31c) which do not require Case-checking. We thus identify in Neapolitan and related dialects a distinct class of 'unaccusative' verbs which, though discharging an external θ-role, fail to mark their sentential complement with structural Case.[15]

It remains then to explain how inherent Case-checking predicates like *mettere appaura* 'to be frightened' in (31a) can Case-mark a subcategorized infinitival complement. This contrast between structural and inherent Case-checkers follows from the different nature of structural and inherent Case identified in chapter 2. Unlike inherent Case, structural Case is divorced from subcategorization in that the availability of a structural Case-checking feature does not imply a thematic relation between Case-checker and argument, as evidenced by raising and ECM structures. By the same token, the ability of a predicate to subcategorize for an argument does not necessarily presuppose the concomitant availability of an appropriate structural Case feature, witness canonical unaccusative structures. Inherent Case, on the other hand, is narrowly tied to subcategorization, as made explicit in Chomsky's (1986b: 194) *Uniformity Condition* which interprets inherent Case-checking as parasitic on θ-marking: a predicate checks inherent Case only if it discharges a θ-role to its complement. If an inherent Case-checking predicate subcategorizes then for a complement, be it nominal or sentential, this presupposes the concomitant availability of an inherent Case feature. On this view, the grammaticality of the infinitival complement in (31a) finds an immediate explanation since the predicate which θ-marks it also has, by implication, an inherent Case feature.

The present analysis predicts that the restricted distribution of the infinitive in Neapolitan and related dialects, in contrast to its wider distribution in standard Romance, follows from the different behaviour of Case-checking in relation to sentential complements in these two language groups. This prediction is borne out by the contrast exhibited by the French and Italian examples in (32) and their Neapolitan and Cosentino equivalents in (33):

(32) a. *fais*   *attention*   *(à)* *ce que* *les étudiants* *soient*
          fa   *attenzione* *(a)* *che*   *gli studenti*   *siano*
          pay.IMP.2SG attention   (to)   [that   the students   be.PRES.SUBJ.3PL
          préparés (French)
          preparati (Italian)
          prepared]
          'make sure that the students are well prepared'

      b. *je tiens*   *(à ce)* *qu'elle* *soit* *avertie* (French)
          tengo   *(a)*   *che*   *sia*   *avvertita* (Italian)
          be-anxious.PRES.1SG (to) [that be.PRES.SUBJ.3SG informed]
          'I am anxious that she be informed'

(33) a. *statte* *attiento* *(*a)* *che* *'e sturiente fosseno* *appriperate* (NA)
          statti *attientu* *(*a)* *ca* *'i studenti fussaru*   *priperati* (CS)
          be.IMP.2SG careful   (to)   [that the students be.SUBJ.3PL prepared]

      b. *tengo*   *(*a)* *che fosse* *avvertita* (NA)
          tiegnu *(*a)* *ca fussa*   *avvertita* (CS)
          be-anxious.PRES.1SG (to) [that be.SUBJ.3SG informed]

Notwithstanding the finite specification of the complement clause, in the French and Italian examples in (32) the matrix predicate checks inherent Case on its complement, spelt-out in the preposition *à/a* 'to'. Such examples demonstrate that the subcategorization of a sentential complement, whether finite or otherwise, does not entail the absence of the matrix predicate's Case-checking feature in French and Italian. The impossibility of the same preposition in the corresponding Neapolitan and Cosentino examples in (33), in contrast, highlights the inability of the matrix predicate to Case-mark a finite complement. The evidence of such examples lends further support to our claim that in Neapolitan and related dialects a matrix predicate's Case-checking feature is suppressed whenever it subcategorizes for a sentential complement.

3.2.2.3. *Restructuring*

Neapolitan boasts a number of structural Case-checking predicates, so-called restructuring verbs, that apparently contradict our conclusion restricting infinitival complements to inherent Case-checking positions.

Restructuring, a term originally introduced by Rizzi (1982) for Italian, refers to the increased dependency and integration induced by a process of clause combining that produces an extreme case of interlacing (see Lehmann 1988) between matrix and dependent infinitival clauses. The effects of such interlacing in the restructuring process are manifested in the obscuring of surface clausal boundaries, such that clitic pronouns of the infinitival complement surface adjacent to the matrix predicate, a process termed clitic climbing:[16]

(34) *vulimmo   'o   vedé*   ⇒   *'o   vulimmo   vedé*
      want.PRES.1PL [him see.INF]] ⇒ [him want.PRES.1PL see.INF]
      'we want to see him'

Verbs that permit restructuring are listed below:[17]

(35) a. *vulé(re)* 'to want', *preferí(re)* 'to prefer', *desiderà(re)* 'to desire';
      b. *gire>jì(re)* 'to go', *venì(re)* 'to come', *mannà(re)* 'to send', *riuscì(re)* 'to manage';

The verbs listed in (35a) check structural accusative, whereas those in (35b) mark their complement with SD, as witnessed by the distinctive SD clitics they license in examples (36):[18]

(36) a. *nun te   va   propeto*
          not you.DAT go.PRES.3SG right
          'you don't fancy it at all'

      b. *mo'lle   vene   a mente*
          now him.DAT come.PRES.3SG to mind
          'now it comes to his mind'

      c. *me   riesce   difficele*
          me.DAT turn-out.PRES.3SG difficult
          'I find it difficult'

      d. *chillo   ve   mannaje   na lettera*
          that-one you.DAT send.PAST.3SG a   letter
          'he sent you a letter'

    Despite the accusative/dative distinction exhibited by the predicates in (35a–b), Neapolitan restructuring verbs form a homogeneous class, all licensing structural Case and OC structures. Yet, contrary to many Romance varieties where restructuring proves optional, in Neapolitan restructuring is always obligatory. Thus, (37a) is a well-formed structure but (37b), in which restructuring fails to obtain, witness the failure of the clitic *lo* 'him' to climb to the matrix verb, is excluded:

(37) a. *'o   jamm'   a chiammà*
          [him go.PRES.1PL to call.INF]

b. *jamm'   a   lo   chiammà
[go.PRES.1PL to [him call.INF]]
'we are going to call him'

Below follow a selection of examples which reinforce this point (clitic pronouns given in bold type):

(38) a. se **ncze** vole   intrare in quisto bangno
if there want.PRES.3SG enter.INF in this   bath
'if one wants to enter into this bath' (Percopo 1887: XXIX, 11–12)

b **lo** andao   a vedere
him go.PAST.3SG to see.INF
'she went to see him' (De Blasi 1986: 67, 5)

c. io **ve** voria   incarecare
I   you like.COND.1SG involve.INF
'I would like to involve you' (Parenti 1978: 203)

d. che aspiette, che **te** vengano   a ccacare nzi lloco mmocca?
. . .   you come.PRES.SUBJ.3PL to shit.INF
'what are you waiting for, for them to come and shit in your
mouth?' (Lombardi 1783, in Capozzoli 1889: 221)

e. iàte**la**   a cunzula
go.IMP.2PL-her to console.INF
'go and console her' (Di Giacomo 1991a: 38)

Not coincidentally, other southern Italian dialects are widely reported to behave analogously to Neapolitan,[19] insofar as restructuring is equally obligatory and restricted to structural Case-checking predicates. Below follow some examples from a variety of dialects:

Lazio
(39) a. **lu** mannó   a cchiamà
him send.PAST.3SG to call.INF
'he sent for him to be called' (RI, Battisti 1921: 61)

b. cco questo **te** olevi   avvelenà?
with this   you want.PAST.2SG poison.INF
'with this you wanted to poison yourself?' (Rome, ibid., 65)

c. jate**ci**   a ttolla   la vesta ppiu bbella
go.IMP.2PL-him to fetch.INF-it the suit   more fine
'go and fetch him the finest suit' (Ceccano (FR), ibid., 79)

Campania
(40) a. nun **ce** **'o** riuscimmo   a spartere
not ourselves it manage.PRES.1PL to divide.INF
'we can't manage to divide it up among ourselves' (Bacoli (NA), De
Simone 1994, 138)

b. *craie*   ***m' 'e***   *vvaco*   *a*   *ppiglià*
tomorrow   me them   go.PRES.1SG   to   take.INF
'tomorrow I'll go and fetch them' (Ferrari (AV), ibid., 474)

c. *tuttiquanti* ***ve*** *vèneno*   *a*   *trová*
everyone   you come.PRES.3PL   to   find.INF
'everyone comes to see you' (Pomigliano d'Arco (NA), ibid., 554)

d. *io* ***ve*** *vulesse*   *aiutà*
I   you   like.COND.1SG   help.INF
'I'd like to help you' (Palma Campania (NA), ibid., 622)

e. *io* ***m' 'o*** *voglio*   *accattà*
I   me it   want.PRES.1SG   buy.INF
'I want to buy it' (AV, ibid., 1156)

Abruzzo/Molise

(41) a *ze*   ***ne***   *vuló*   *ji*
himself   from-there   want.PAST.3SG   go.INF
'he wanted to leave' (TE, Savini 1881: 99)

b. *nə tə woja*   *səntí*   *chiù*
not you want.PRES.1SG   hear.INF anymore
'I don't want to listen to you any more' (Arpino (FR), Battisti 1921: 104)

c. *ni juorn cə enn'*   *un a ffa*   *la*   *domanda də*
one day   her come.PAST.3SG one to do.INF the   proposal   of
matrəmoniə
marriage
'one day somebody came to make her a proposal of marriage' (Pescoscolido (FR), ibid., 107)

d. ***se*** *sarrá*   *jita*   *a*   *ccummunicá*
herself   be.FUT.3SG   go.PART   to   confess.INF
'she's probably gone to confession' (AQ, ibid., 118)

e. *l' ajjə*   *jut*   *a*   *chiamà je*
him have.PRES.1SG   go.PART   to   call.INF   I
'I went to call him' (Vasto (CH), ibid., 137)

f. *s'*   *avriaja*   *wuliut*   *abbutteà*
himself   have.COND.3SG   want.PART   stuff.INF
'he would have wanted to stuff himself' (Agnone (IS), ibid., 139)

g. *zi Valter se*   ***la*** *mnett*   *a piglià*
uncle Valter himself   it   come.PAST.3SG   to take.INF
'uncle Valter came to fetch it' (IS, Bagaglia 1997)

Calabria

(42) a. *l' hanno   mannata a pigliare ncarozza?*
      him have.PRES.3PL send.PART to take.INF in-carriage
      'have they sent for her to be fetched in a carriage?' (CS, De Marco
      1986b: 139

   b. *neputimma   ca **me**   venuto   a pigliare*
      nephew.POSS.1SG who me-be.PRES.2SG come.PART to take.INF
      'my nephew who came to fetch me' (Mendicino (CS), Barca 1996:
      11)

   c. *forse **tu** riesciu   a dire*
      perhaps you-it succeed.PRES.1SG to say.INF
      'perhaps I'll manage to explain it you' (Belmonte (CS), Vespucci
      1994: 89)

   d. ***nci lu** mandaru   a diri   a la rigina*
      her it send.PAST.3PL to say.INF to the queen
      'they had word sent to the queen' (RC, Falcone 1979: 28)

   e. ***a** vogghiu   vinciri sta partita*
      it want.PRES.1SG win.INF this game
      'I want to win this game' (RC, Meliadò 1994: 95)

Apulia

(43) a. ***nne** və lojə   addəmanné a ccrestə*
      some want.PAST.3SG ask.INF   to Christ
      'he wanted to ask Christ for some' (Andria (BA), Battisti 1921: 146)

   b. *mo s'   **u** vəleivə   mancé*
      now himself it want.PAST.3SG eat.INF
      'now he wanted to eat it' (ibid.)

   c. *t' aɣɣ   vleut   mett' a la prouv*
      you have.PRES.1SG want.PART put.INF to the test
      'I wanted to put you to the test' (Bisceglie (BA), ibid., 150)

Sicily

(44) a. ***a** vuogghiu   vìriri*
      her want.PRES.1SG see.INF
      'I want to see her' (Leone 1995: §66)

   b. ***u** spieru   i' truvari*
      him hope.PRES.1SG of find.INF
      'I hope to find him' (ibid.)

   c. *lu nicu   nun **lu** vulievanu   fari   vèniri*
      the small-one not him want.PAST.3PL make.INF come.INF
      'as for the the smallest one, they didn't want to have him come
      along' (Vallelunga Pratameno (CL), Pitré 1875: II, 196)

d. *si   jeru   a pigghiari la manta*
themselves go.PAST.3PL to take.INF   the blanket
'they went to fetch the blanket' (Erice (TP), ibid., 376)

e. *mi vogghiu   mettiri 'a giacca*
me want.PRES.1SG put.INF   the jacket
'I want to put on the jacket' (Belpasso (CT), Martoglio 1978b)

Restructuring predicates appear then to represent a major exception to our previous conclusion restricting infinitivals to inherent Case-checking positions. Above we noted that such predicates canonically check structural Case, which leads us to expect that restructuring predicates, on a par with verbs like *decirere* 'to decide' (compare 31b), fail to license an infinitival complement. By way of illustration, consider the example in (45a):

(45) a. *m' 'o   voglio   leggere*
me it   want.PRES.1SG [$_{CP}$ read.INF]

b.   *m' 'o voglio   leggere*
[$_T$ me it   want.PRES.1SG$_j$ [$_{v\text{-}VP}$ t$_j$ read.INF$_i$ [$_{CP}$ t$_i$]]]
'I want to read it'

As it stands, the structure in (45a) is ill-formed in that the matrix verb *voglio* 'I want' lacks accusative Case to license its infinitival CP complement. Given the obligatory climbing of clitics (namely *m''o* 'me it') with these verbs, we interpret restructuring as underlying an incorporation structure. Concretely, we propose that as a last resort operation in order to rescue the structure, a restructuring process takes place whereby the infinitive raises out of the embedded CP to incorporate by adjunction into the matrix predicate. In turn, the latter excorporates to raise to adjoin to the matrix T, as illustrated in (45b). We maintain that it is precisely restructuring by means of the incorporation process which licenses the infinitive in (45b), an idea originally proposed by Baker (1988: 108ff.) who treats incorporation as an alternative to Case-marking (in his terms 'Case-indexing'). Following incorporation into the matrix verb, the infinitive in (45b) is then licensed and the potential Case Filter violation is avoided. It follows that all clitics in such constructions will appear on the matrix verb, for they raise to the matrix clause together with their associated infinitive.

Consequently, we abandon arbitrary restructuring rules such as that proposed by Rizzi (1982) for Italian, deriving Neapolitan restructuring from independently motivated principles on argument licensing. Similarly, Roberts (1994) and Moore (1994) adopt the position that Romance restructuring verbs form an arbitrary class of verbs with *special* properties, which they fail to derive from other properties of the grammar. Under our analysis, by contrast, restructuring falls out as a concomitant of the independently motivated Case-licensing condition on infinitival complements. It thus follows in a principled manner that the class of restructuring verbs is exclusively made up of structural Case-checkers, without there being any need to attribute *special* properties to such verbs.[20]

3.2.3. *Summary*

Significant generalizations regarding the distribution of finite and infinitival complements in Neapolitan and related dialects have been demonstrated to follow as a direct consequence of Case Theory. In particular, sentential complements are licensed by one of the three mechanisms in (46):

(46) a. Intrinsic structural Case: finite CPs
      b. Incorporation: restructured infinitival CPs
      c. Inherent Case: infinitival CPs

Finite CPs are inherently visible, bearing an intrinsic structural Case feature licensed by their [+finite] specification which allows them, unlike infinitival complements, to freely occur in Caseless positions. Infinitival complements to structural Case-checkers prove ill-formed since the latter lack an appropriate licensing Case feature whenever they subcategorize for a sentential complement. This explains, in addition, why only these predicates give rise to restructuring-incorporation, a marked last resort option which provides infinitival complements with an alternative licensing mechanism. Inherent Case-checking predicates, by contrast, variously license an infinitival complement since the availability of their Case feature is inextricably tied to θ-marking. Subcategorization of an infinitival complement necessarily presupposes therefore the availability of inherent Case.

Despite the merits of our proposed Case-theoretic account, it fails to provide an entirely comprehensive account of infinitival distribution in Neapolitan. In particular, examples such as (5b), repeated below, prove recalcitrant to the Case-theoretic account:

(5) b. *Ciro è   sicuro 'e   canoscere a Mario*
        Ciro$_i$ be.PRES.3SG sure of [PRO$_i$ know.INF PA Mario]
        'Ciro is sure that he knows Mario'

Though the matrix predicate marks its infinitival complement with inherent genitive Case (witness the preposition *'e* 'of'), the sentence still proves ungrammatical. We cannot therefore appeal to the absence of Case to exclude (5b). Rather, there must be another reason which causes such structures to crash. Below we shall argue that their ungrammaticality is related to the licensing conditions operative on the understood subject of the infinitival clause. In what follows, we shall therefore investigate null infinitival subjects.

3.3. INFINITIVAL SUBJECTS

3.3.1. *Case-theoretic accounts*

3.3.1.1. *Watanabe (1996)*

Watanabe (1996) proposes a number of modifications to the minimalist mechanisms of Case-checking with the elaboration of a theory of Layered Case Checking. According to his proposal, Case-checking instantiates an asymmetrical checking process. For instance, in (47a) the nominative feature borne by *he* is eliminated from the derivation once it raises to the embedded subject position, where it enters into a checking relation with the nominative feature on T.

(47) a. *Mary believes* [$_{CP}$ *that* [$_{TP}$ *he$_i$* T [$_{v\text{-}VP}$ t$_i$ *ate an apple*]]]

  b. *Mary believes* [$_{CP}$ T$_j$-*that* [$_{TP}$ *he$_i$* t$_j$ [$_{v\text{-}VP}$ t$_i$ *ate an apple*]]]

On the other hand, Watanabe argues that the nominative Case feature on T is not eliminated in this checking configuration. Rather, it has to undergo subsequent checking with a higher functional head in order to be eliminated. Essentially, this amounts to saying that there must be a follow-up process to Case-checking in (47a), interpreted by Watanabe as adjunction of T to C (see 47b), a checking configuration in which C can eliminate the nominative feature borne by T.

On the assumption that licensing of null Case involves an analogous follow-up process of Case-checking of T adjoined to C, Watanabe successfully derives the distribution of PRO in examples (48) from c-selection:

(48) a. *John tried* [$_{CP}$ PRO *to understand the lesson*]

  b. **John believed* [$_{TP}$ PRO *to know the truth*]

  c. *John believed* [$_{TP}$ *Mary to know the truth*]

  d. **John seemed* [$_{TP}$ PRO *to know the truth*]

  e. *John$_i$ seemed* [$_{TP}$ t$_i$ *to know the truth*]

In the control sentence (48a), the null Case on PRO is checked against T which, in turn, raises to adjoin to C where its own null Case feature can be checked. In the ungrammatical ECM and raising structures in (48b, d), in contrast, the null Case on PRO can be checked against the embedded T but the null Case feature on T itself cannot be eliminated by a follow-up Case-checking process, since the infinitival only projects to TP. Consequently, a DP merged in this position can only be legitimately Case-marked if subsequently raised (at LF/pre-Spell-Out) to the matrix clause where accusative (48c) or nominative (48e) can be checked.

Further support for this analysis comes from well-known differences between control and raising in the Romance languages:

(49) a. *Jean   décide   l'essaye   de   revenir* (French)

b. *Gianni decide   /tenta   di   tornare* (Italian)

John   decide.PRES.3SG /try.PRES.3SG [CP of PRO return.INF]

'John decides/tries to come back'

(50) a. *Jean   semblait   (*de)   comprendre* (French)

b. *Gianni sembrava   (*di)   capire* (Italian)

John$_i$ seem.PAST.3SG (of)   [TP t$_i$ understand.INF]

'John seemed to understand'

The appearance of an overt infinitival complementizer *de/di* 'of' in the French and Italian control structures in (49) signals the CP status of the infinitival complement and the availability of C to undertake the follow-up checking of the null Case feature on T. In the corresponding raising structures in (50), by contrast, the non-finite complementizer is excluded, highlighting the TP status of the embedded infinitival and the impossibility of PRO.

According to Watanabe's analysis, the distribution of PRO reduces essentially to c-selection, along similar lines to the binding-theoretic approach: PRO is predicted to occur in non-finite CPs but not in non-finite TPs. Under these assumptions, we should expect PRO to be invariably licensed in the Neapolitan infinitivals in (4) and (5), contrary to fact. On Watanabe's analysis, the ungrammaticality of (4a–b) and (5b) must be attributed to c-selection and the failure of such complements to project to CP. However, the evidence of the corresponding grammatical sentences (see 8a–c), in which the same predicates c-select for a finite CP speak against such an analysis. Furthermore, if such predicates did c-select for TP, we should expect them to license an ECM infinitival on a par with (48c), an expectation not borne out. We conclude therefore that Watanabe's Layered Case Checking account of the distribution of PRO fails to predict the distribution of PRO in Neapolitan on several counts.

3.3.1.2. *Martin (1992)*[21] *and Bošković (1997)*

Building on Chomsky and Lasnik's (1993) Case-theoretic account of PRO, Martin (1992) proposes to derive the distribution of PRO from significant interpretative properties of control infinitivals first noted by Stowell (1982). Arguing from English, Stowell maintains that finite and control infinitival CPs have an internally determined Tense, the former specified as [±Past] and the latter, lacking the morphological feature [±Past], receiving an 'unrealized future' interpretation with respect to the time frame of the matrix verb. ECM and raising infinitivals, in contrast, lack an internally determined Tense insofar as their temporal interpretation can only be externally fixed by the Tense of the matrix verb. These facts are exemplified by the sentences in (51):

(51) a. *John tries* [$_{CP}$ PRO *to bring the wine*] (control)

   b. *John considers* [$_{TP}$ *himself to be the smartest*] (ECM)

   c. *John$_i$ appears* [$_{TP}$ t$_i$ *to like poker*] (raising)

Stowell convincingly accounts for these interpretative facts by arguing that control infinitivals contain a temporal operator at the head of CP, which provides the infinitival with an internally organized 'unrealized future' Tense. On the standard assumption that ECM and raising infinitivals only project to TP, they lack the necessary CP structure to host a temporal operator and can only be evaluated by default in relation to the matrix Tense.

In a principled fashion, Martin (1992) relates the differences in the temporal interpretation of control versus ECM/raising infinitivals to the ability of non-finite T to check null Case. Accordingly, he draws a distinction between [+tense] and [-tense] non-finite T, where [+tense] is to be interpreted as denoting an unrealized future. The former is associated with control infinitivals checking null Case on PRO, whereas the latter characterizes ECM and raising infinitivals lacking all Case-checking properties whatsoever. On this view the presence/absence of PRO in the French and Italian control and raising structures in (49) and (50) is a direct consequence of the temporal interpretation of the infinitival clauses.

Martin's Case-theoretic account is further developed by Bošković (1997), who maintains that such an approach makes it possible to dispense with the stipulative c-selection analysis associated with the binding-theoretic account of PRO. Specifically, Bošković demonstrates that the control predicate *try* in (52a–b) can take either a TP or CP complement, the possibility of PRO and the impossibility of DP-trace in such sentences falling out as a consequence of the Case-checking properties of the embedded infinitive. Irrespective of whether the infinitival complement is a TP or CP, its [+tense] specification enables it to check null Case on PRO in (52a). On the other hand, DP-trace in the embedded [Spec, T] is excluded in (52b), since raising of *John* would involve movement from one Case-checking position to another in violation of the Last Resort Condition on movement.

(52) a. *John tried* [$_{CP/TP}$ PRO *to lock the door*]

   b. **John$_i$ is tried* [$_{CP/TP}$ t$_i$ *to lock the door*]

Potentially problematic for the Case-theoretic approach proposed by Martin (1992) and Bošković (1997) is the distribution of PRO in the Neapolitan infinitival clauses in (4) and (5). As with Watanabe's account, the ungrammaticality of (4a–b) and (5b) is unexpected. In particular, the impossibility/possibility of PRO in (4a) versus (5a) meets with a serious problem. As predicates which s-select for a non-propositional complement, in Bošković's terms an 'irrealis' complement, both *prummettere* 'to promise' and *stà attiento* 'to take care', should subcategorize for a [+tense] infinitival T capable of checking null Case on PRO. In light of the grammaticality of (5a), the ungrammaticality of (4a) remains therefore unexplained.

3.3.1.3. *Summary*

Despite the superficial differences observed above with regard to the various Case-theoretic accounts of PRO proposed by Watanabe (1996) on the one hand and Martin (1992) and Bošković (1997) on the other, the results of both approaches are not irreconcilable. Watanabe's Layered Case Checking account reduces essentially to c-selection, restricting the distribution of PRO to non-finite CPs and DP-trace in ECM/raising structures to non-finite TPs. On the other hand, Martin and Bošković identify the temporal properties of infinitivals as the sole discriminant in accounting for the distribution of PRO: [+tense] T checks null Case (namely control), while [-tense] T is inert for Case (namely ECM/raising). As these authors explicitly note, this observation regarding the temporal properties of infinitivals is based on Stowell (1982), who relates such interpretative differences to the availability of C in the infinitival clause: control infinitivals project to CP whose head hosts a temporal operator which fixes the understood temporal frame of the infinitive as 'unrealized' with respect to the matrix Tense, while ECM/raising infinitivals only project to TP and therefore lack a temporal operator. Consequently, the understood Tense of ECM/raising infinitivals is determined externally by the semantics of the matrix verb.

Notwithstanding the importance attributed to c-selection under Stowell's account, Martin fails to make reference to the relevance of the TP/CP distinction (see Watanabe 1996: 34–5), even though under his account the availability of null Case is derived from the semantic content of non-finite T. Similarly, Bošković dismisses the significance of the CP/TP distinction on the availability of null Case, arguing instead that control infinitivals may project to either TP or CP. To remain consistent with Stowell's account of infinitival Tense, on which both Martin's and Bošković's Case-theoretic accounts rest, we propose to restrict the [-tense] and [+tense] specifications of non-finite T to TP and CP, respectively, a possibility neither excluded nor incompatible with these authors' analyses. Moreover, such a move provides a natural way of subsuming the results of Watanabe's analysis, restricting DP-trace and PRO to non-finite TPs and CPs, respectively.

Despite the problems raised by the Case-theoretic accounts of the distribution of PRO in Neapolitan, there emerges an inescapable correlation between the different temporal properties exhibited by control versus ECM/raising infinitivals, in turn inextricably related to the TP/CP distinction and the availability of DP-trace and OC PRO. In short, we too shall exploit such temporal distinctions in our movement-based account of the distribution of OC PRO below. However, in contrast to the Case-theoretic account, we do not take [Spec, T] in control infinitivals to be a Case-checking position.[22]

3.3.2. *Movement accounts*

3.3.2.1. *Hornstein (1999)*

An alternative to the Case-theoretic approach to PRO is advocated by Hornstein who, drawing on the similarities between OC PRO and locally bound anaphors, analyses the former as the residue of A-movement displaying all the characteristics of DP-trace. In particular, Hornstein follows Williams (1980) in distinguishing between OC and NOC PRO, a distinction substantiated by the contrasts witnessed in (53) and (54):

(53) a. **it was expected* PRO *to shave himself*

  b. **John thinks that it was expected* PRO *to shave himself*

  c. **John's campaign expects* PRO *to shave himself*

  d. *John expects* PRO *to win and Bill does too* (= Bill will win)

  e. **John$_i$ told Mary$_j$* PRO$_{i+j}$ *to wash themselves/each other*

  f. **the unfortunate expects* PRO *to get a medal*

(54) a. *it was believed that* PRO *shaving himself was important*

  b. *John$_i$ thinks that it was believed that* PRO$_i$ *shaving himself is important*

  c. *Clinton's$_i$ campaign believes that* PRO$_i$ *keeping his sex life under control is necessary for electoral success*

  d. *John thinks that* PRO *getting his resume in order is crucial and Bill does too* (= John gets his resume in order)

  e. *John$_i$ told Mary$_j$ that* PRO$_{i+j}$ *washing themselves/each other would be fun*

  f. *the unfortunate believes that* PRO *getting a medal would be boring*

The ungrammaticality of the OC structures in (53) and the grammaticality of the corresponding NOC structures in (54) illustrate the differing behaviour of PRO in these two very distinct contexts. Specifically, OC PRO, but not NOC PRO, must have an antecedent (see (a) examples) which is local (see (b) examples) and c-commands it (see (c) examples). In addition, contrary to NOC PRO, OC PRO only allows the sloppy reading under VP ellipsis (see (d) examples), does not permit split antecedence (see (e) examples) and has an obligatory *de se* interpretation (see (f) examples). In view of such contrasts and the fact that OC PRO in (53) and NOC PRO in (54) can be replaced by the anaphor *himself* and pronoun *his*, respectively, Hornstein argues that the differences between OC and NOC PRO reduce to the differences between locally bound anaphors and pronouns, respectively. This observation thus speaks against the binding-theoretic account which interprets PRO simultaneously as an anaphor and a pronoun but, rather, makes it possible to treat PRO as an anaphor in OC structures and a pronoun (namely pro) in NOC structures.

Interpreting PRO in terms of a movement analysis, OC structures are now viewed as a subtype of raising structure, only differing from canonical raising structures in that A-movement targets a θ-position. Crucially, Hornstein's analysis of OC PRO as the residue of A-movement rests on treating θ-roles as morphological features on predicates which, in line with standard minimalist assumptions, are checked off by a DP under Merge. Given this interpretation of θ-assignment, DP movement to a θ-position is now allowed in accordance with the last resort nature of movement. Furthermore, it is predicted that chains may bear more than one θ-role in cases of OC PRO, since OC establishes a relation between at least two θ-positions.

Given this package of assumptions, analysing OC PRO in terms of movement yields a considerable simplification of the grammar of control. By way of example, consider the control and raising structures in (55a–b), respectively:

(55)   a. [$_{TP}$ John$_i$ [$_{v-VP}$ t$_i$ decides [$_{TP}$ t$_i$ to [$_{v-VP}$ t$_i$ ring Mary]]]]

      b. [$_{TP}$ John$_i$ [$_{v-VP}$ seemed [$_{TP}$ t$_i$ to [$_{v-VP}$ t$_i$ ring Mary]]]]

In (55a) John is merged with win in [Spec, v] where it checks its external θ-role before raising to the embedded [Spec, T] to satisfy the embedded EPP. From this position, John raises to the matrix [Spec, v] to check the external θ-role on decides and then to the matrix [Spec, T] where it checks its categorial and nominative features against T. Significantly, John enters only into one Case-checking relation in (55a) since, unlike the Case-theoretic accounts, the embedded [Spec, T] is not a Case-checking position. Equally, under the present analysis the typical properties of OC PRO reviewed above (see 53), imposing, for example, a local, c-commanding antecedent on OC PRO, follow straightforwardly from interpreting PRO as an intermediate (minimal) link in an A-chain. As for the corresponding raising structure in (55b), within the present approach it only differs minimally from the OC structure in (55a) in that John targets an athematic position.[23]

3.3.2.2. A-movement and T-chains

3.3.2.2.1. English and standard Romance

While Hornstein's account of OC PRO accounts well for English, it is not immediately obvious how the same analysis can be extended to Romance OC structures. For instance, consider the simplified representations of the French and Italian equivalents of (55a) given in (56a–b):

(56)   a. Jean   décide   de   téléphoner à Marie (French)

      b. Gianni decide   di   telefonare a Maria (Italian)

         John$_i$ decide.PRES.3SG [$_{CP}$ of t$_i$ telephone.INF to Mary]

In contrast to English *decide*, French and Italian *décider/decidere* select for a CP infinitival, as witnessed by the presence of the infinitival complementizers *de/di* (scc Vincent 1997a: 171–2; Rizzi 1998: 119–20). The empty category in the embedded [Spec, T] in (56a–b) cannot therefore be analysed as DP-trace on a par with (55a), since movement of *Jean/Gianni* to the matrix through the embedded [Spec, T] would cross a CP boundary, thereby violating locality conditions on anaphors (see Watanabe 1996: 35ff.; Bošković 1997: 180, n. 13). Indeed, under Hornstein's account one would be forced to analyse the Romance sentences in (56a–b) as instances of NOC structures, the empty category in the embedded [Spec, T] filled by pro, 'a formative used as a last option to save an otherwise doomed derivation . . . licensed *at a cost* in [Spec, IP] of nonfinite CP complements' (Hornstein 1999: 93). Clearly, this would be an undesirable result since the empty category in the embedded [Spec, T] in (56a–b) fails to display any of the interpretative characteristics of NOC PRO examined above (see 54).

The main problem for the movement analysis of OC PRO in Romance is then how to account for the apparent non-local nature of A-movement out of a control infinitival across CP. This also proves a problem for English control infinitivals on our assumption that [+tense] non-finite T invariably implies a CP structure (see section 3.3.1.3). To illustrate the problem, consider the English and Italian OC structures in (57), where we omit irrelevant details of DP-movement through the embedded and matrix *v*-VP:

(57) a. *John*$_i$ *tries* [$_{CP}$ t$_i$ *to get up*]

  b. *Gianni*$_i$ *cerca* [$_{CP}$ *di* t$_i$ *alzarsi*]

As it stands, the grammaticality of (57a–b) is unexpected, since both sentences contain an offending DP-trace in the embedded subject position. In the system of Chomsky (1986b), the offending DP-trace is ruled out because movement crosses a CP barrier, causing an ECP violation on the assumption that C does not qualify as a proper governor. From a minimalist perspective, the same conclusion can be derived from economy conditions on movement if, following Manzini (1994), movement must proceed through the domain of each head. Under such an approach, DP-movement from the embedded to the matrix subject positions in (57) requires *John/Gianni* to pass through the embedded [Spec, CP], thereby giving rising to a case of improper movement (see Bošković 1997: 180, n. 13; Collins 1997: 111–14).

Informally then, the problem raised by the DP-trace ensuing from the movement of *John/Gianni* in (57) reduces to a case of long-distance binding: as an anaphor, DP-trace (namely OC PRO) in [Spec, T] must in accordance with Principle A be locally bound by its antecedent *John/Gianni* situated in the matrix clause. Within the literature a number of cases of long-distance binding have been noted, leading to a variety of theoretical interpretations of such phenomena (for an overview, see Harbert 1995: 193ff.). For instance, the same problem is addressed by Manzini (1983) who treats OC PRO as a pure anaphor but which, by virtue of occurring in ungoverned positions, lacks a governing category.[24] In order for OC PRO to be bound by its antecedent in the matrix clause, Manzini proposes an extended Principle A which allows PRO to be bound within the governing category of the CP containing it.

Under minimalist assumptions we cannot appeal to Manzini's analysis which crucially relies on government to account for the distribution of PRO/DP-trace. Instead, within a restrictive theory of locality we propose to derive this apparent phenomenon of long-distance A-movement out of control CP infinitivals as a consequence of the latter's temporal properties. The idea that Tense plays a role in the characterization of binding domains has been highlighted by a large body of research,[25] which has identified the effects of the different Tense features of indicative and subjunctive clauses on long-distance binding.[26] Consider the Icelandic and Italian examples in (58) and (59), taken from Thráinsson (1990) and Giorgi (1983–4), respectively:

(58) a. *Jón   upplýsti   hver hefði   barið sig*
          John$_i$ reveal.PAST.3SG [who have.PAST.SUBJ.3SG hit.PART self$_i$]

      b. **Jón$_i$ upplýsti   hver hafði   barið sig*
          John$_i$ reveal.PAST.3SG [who have.PAST.INDIC.3SG hit.PART self$_i$]
          'John revealed who had hit him'

(59) a. *Gianni suppone   che tu sia   innamorato della*
          Gianni$_i$ suppose.PRES.3SG [that you be.PRES.SUBJ.2SG in-love   of-the
          propria moglie
          self$_i$ wife]

      b. **Gianni suppone   che tu sei   innamorato della*
          Gianni$_i$ suppose.PRES.3SG [that you be.PRES.INDIC.2SG in-love   of-the
          propria moglie
          self$_i$ wife]
          'Gianni supposes that you are in love with his wife'

The grammaticality of the (a) examples demonstrates that the reflexive *sig/propria* 'self' can be bound by the matrix subject across the finite subjunctive clause, in apparent violation of Principle A. On the other hand, in the (b) examples long-distance binding is excluded when the embedded verb appears in the indicative. Such facts lead Anderson (1982) and Manzini and Wexler (1987) to conclude that the definition of governing category may make reference to Tense. Specifically, Anderson proposes a rule of Tense agreement which has the effect of extending the governing category of the anaphor to include the matrix clause. Capitalizing on the fact that subjunctive complements (in Icelandic), but not necessarily indicative complements, usually have the same tense as their matrix clause, Anderson successfully derives the fact that long-distance binding is only possible when there is Tense agreement between matrix and embedded clauses.

In a similar vein, Manzini and Wexler (1987) propose that the definition of governing category be understood to include a local domain containing a referential Tense. It follows that subjunctive, unlike indicative, complements do not qualify as a governing category for an anaphor since they have anaphoric Tense. Moreover, Giorgi (1983–4: 335–41) makes similar claims with her treatment of the indicative and subjunctive as independent and dependent moods marked by a [-dep] INFL and [+dep] INFL, respectively. Being dependent on the matrix clause, the governing category of subjunctive complements is therefore understood to include the matrix clause, thereby accounting for the grammaticality of (59a).

Significantly, these proposals regarding the temporal properties of the embedded complement come very close to our conclusions about the role of infinitival Tense. Above we established that infinitivals do not encode absolute tense, their temporal evaluation being invariably determined in relation to the matrix Tense. Since den Besten (1983) and Stowell (1981; 1982), it has been standardly assumed that the C position hosts Tense features (see also Enç 1987). Adopting a Reichenbachian theory of tense, we propose that the embedded C position hosts features encoding the reference time of the infinitive (R_{INF}), which serve to mediate a T(ense)-chain between the reference time of the matrix verb (R_{MV}) and the event time of the infinitive (E_{INF}).[27] In the case of control infinitivals, R_{INF} coincides with E_{INF} ($R_{INF} = E_{INF}$) and locates the reference time of the infinitive after that of the matrix verb ($R_{MV} \rightarrow R_{INF}$), thereby fixing the understood temporal frame of the infinitive as unrealized with respect to the matrix Tense.

Such an analysis captures the anaphoric temporal interpretation of control infinitivals whose Tense, like that of subjunctive clauses, is anchored to the matrix T, rather than to the moment of speech. Significantly, the construction of such a T-chain between the matrix and embedded Tenses has the effect of extending the binding domain of the embedded clause to include that of the matrix. It follows from this that A-movement out of the embedded control infinitival in (58a–b) is a licit operation, since the trace left in the embedded [Spec, T] is licensed by the extended locality conditions arising from the construction of a T-chain between the matrix and embedded Tenses.[28,29]

ECM and raising infinitivals, on the other hand, lack the irrealis interpretation associated with control infinitivals and, as we have seen, do not project the higher CP functional layer. Consequently, ECM and raising infinitivals lack an independent R_{INF}. Instead, the temporal location of E_{INF} is constrained by default by the R_{MV} with which it coincides ($R_{MV} = E_{INF}$). Therefore, ECM and raising infinitivals pose no problems for locality conditions on A-movement to an external Case-checking position since they project only to TP.

3.3.2.2.2. Southern Italian dialects

Adapting Hornstein's (1999) proposals, we have outlined a movement-based theory of OC PRO which successfully accounts for the distribution of PRO and infinitival complementation in both English and standard Romance languages. At this point, let us take a closer look at how the southern Italian dialect data square with our proposed analysis. We repeat the Neapolitan paradigm in (4) and (5):

(4) a. *Ciro prummette   'e   nun se mbriacà
         Ciro$_i$ promise.PRES.3SG [of PRO$_i$ not   get-drunk.INF]
         'Ciro promises not to get drunk'

     b. *Ciro crere   'e PRO canoscere a Mario
         Ciro$_i$ think.PRES.3SG [of PRO$_i$ know.INF   PA Mario]
         'Ciro believes that he knows Mario'

(5) a. Ciro sta   attiento a   nun se mbriacà
         Ciro$_i$ be.PRES.3SG careful   to [PRO$_i$ not get-drunk.INF]
         'Ciro is careful not to get drunk'

     b. *Ciro è   sicuro 'e   canoscere a. Mario
         Ciro$_i$ be.PRES.3SG sure   of [PRO$_i$ know.INF   PA Mario]
         'Ciro is sure that he knows Mario'

Examples (4a–b) have already been excluded on Case-theoretic grounds. However, the same reasoning would incorrectly lead us to expect the grammaticality of (5b) on a par with (5a). The contrast between examples like (5a) and (5b) must therefore underlie a significant difference between such structures, which we propose to interpret as s-selection. In particular, the matrix predicate in (5a) s-selects for an irrealis sentential complement, whereas in (5b) the matrix predicate s-selects for a propositional complement (see further Bošković 1997: 13). This distinction between irrealis and propositional infinitivals has important consequences on the temporal properties of the embedded Tense. In this respect, consider the differences illustrated in (60) between standard Romance and English propositional infinitivals:

(60) a. Jean$_i$ croit   [t$_i$ gagner   le   prix]   (French)
      b. Gianni$_i$ crede   [di t$_i$ vincere   il   premio] (Italian)
      c. o João$_i$ acredita [t$_i$ conseguir o   prêmio] (Portuguese)
      d. Juan$_i$ cree   [t$_i$ conseguir el   premio] (Spanish)
      e. *John$_i$ believes [t$_i$ to win   the prize]

Unlike their English counterparts, Bošković (1997: 63ff., 196, n. 20, 21) observes that Romance propositional infinitivals to believe-class verbs allow a non-habitual interpretation. Even in the absence of an auxiliary or an adverb of quantification (see 60a–d), such infinitivals denote a possible future event specified as unrealized with respect to the matrix Tense. Assuming with Enç (1991b) that eventive predicates contain a temporal argument which must be bound, the Romance propositional infinitivals in (60a–d) must have an internally organized Tense, otherwise the temporal argument would remain illicitly unbound. We interpret this internally organized Tense as R_{INF} in C, anchoring a T-chain between the matrix and embedded Tenses. As a concomitant of this T-chain, the binding domain of the embedded clause is extended to include that of the matrix and thereby license long-distance A-movement. In this respect, propositional infinitivals in the standard Romance languages pattern with control infinitivals, both projecting to CP and hence hosting an internally organized Tense (R_{INF}) in C.

In the English sentence in (60e), by contrast, the temporal reference of the propositional infinitival is directly determined by the time frame of the matrix clause. Lacking the unrealized interpretation and hence C and R_{INF}, English propositional infinitivals are in the relevant sense Tenseless. Consequently, the use of an eventive predicate in (60e) proves ill-formed since the temporal argument borne by the latter cannot be bound. From these observations, we conclude that the possibility of subject control, and hence long-distance A-movement sanctioned by a T-chain, is fully predicted in standard Romance propositional infinitivals but not in their English counterparts, which lack an internally organized Tense.

Bošković (1997: 178–9, n. 9) suggests that such differences in the temporal properties of English and standard Romance propositional infinitivals are related to further differences in the temporal interpretation of present tense in the two language groups. Following Enç (1991), he notes that English has no 'present tense'.[30] For example, in (61a) the simple present tense verb form *dances* does not allow the continuous imperfective interpretation. Instead, it forces the habitual reading, the temporal argument of *dances* being bound by an implicit habitual/generic adverb of quantification. In order to obtain the non-habitual reading, an explicit *be* + gerund continuous periphrasis must be employed, as in (61b):

(61) a. *John dances*

   b. *John is dancing*

Italian and other standard Romance varieties, on the other hand, do have 'present tense'.[31] For instance, the Italian simple present *balla* in (62) allows either the habitual or continuous interpretation:

(62) *Gianni balla*
    'John dances/is dancing'

In a principled fashion, Bošković relates these differences in the interpretation of the English/Romance 'present tense' to analogous temporal differences displayed by propositional infinitivals: English propositional infinitivals only allow the habitual interpretation (60e), whereas their standard Romance counterparts allow both the habitual and non-habitual readings (60a–d).

Significantly, Neapolitan and related southern dialects appear to pattern with English, rather than standard Romance, in the relevant respects (see Posner 1999: 133). Consequently, the Neapolitan simple present *abballa* in (63a) favours the habitual interpretation, the non-habitual reading being more readily expressed by the *stà* 'be' + gerund periphrasis in (63b):

(63) a. *Giuanne abballa*
     'Gianni dances'

   b. *Giuanne sta abballanno*
     'Gianni is dancing'

Contrary to the Italian *stare* + gerund periphrasis, which stresses imperfectivity and durativity (see Maiden 1995: 156–7), the Neapolitan periphrasis has to a large extent lost its strictly durative value, tending to oust the simple present as the unmarked means of expressing on-going activity simultaneous with the moment of speech (see Ledgeway 1995: S.III.§1–1.2.1).[32] This development may be further linked to the frequent use of the simple present as a marker of future time, leading to its specialization 'as a "performative", representing especially habitual and future situations.' (Posner 1999: 134–5). Consequently, the periphrasis proves equally compatible with stative predicates, yielding structures whose Italian equivalents would be judged ungrammatical (see Bertinetto 1991: 132ff.):

(64) a. *tu he 'a vedé 'a pacienza che sto tenenno io* (De Filippo 1973: 51)
     'you ought to see the patience that I've got (literally 'am having')'

   b. *addò steva abbetanno la reggina* (Bertoni 1916: §119)
     'where the queen was living'

   c. *se sta addunanno ca è tardo assaie*
     'she realizes (literally 'is realizing') that it's very late'

   d. *stanno capenno tutta cosa*
     'they understand (literally 'are understanding') everything'

   e. *sta materia nun me sta piacenno pe niente*
     'I don't like (literally 'am not liking') this subject at all'

   f. *no, nuje stammo stanno ccà 'ngopp'â spiaggia*
     'no, we are staying here on the beach'

Similarly, the periphrasis is used to refer to present time which extends beyond the immediate moment, again a function expressed by the simple present in Italian:

(65) a. *è no mese che me sta cuffianno, che me sta portanno ncarrozza!*
          (Scarpetta, 1992: 499)
          'he's been mocking and cheating me for a month!

      b. *'a quanno ha avuto chillu posto, sta viaggianno nu sacco*
          'since he got that job, he's been travelling a lot'

      c. *Ciro sta sturianno scienze politiche all'università*
          'Ciro studies (literally 'is studying') political sciences at university'

      d. *chê belle ghjurnate 'e chistu periodo stamme jennu sempe ô mare*
          'with the fine weather during this period, we're always going to the
          seaside'

A preference for the continuous periphrasis over the simple present is
widely reported to hold of all southern Italian dialects,[33] due allowance
being made for variation in choice of auxiliary/prefix (for an overview, see
Rohlfs 1969: 133). Indeed, Rohlfs (1969: §720) describes the use of *stare* +
gerund as 'usatissima' ('very frequent') in the South.[34] Piecing these facts
together, we observe that Neapolitan and related dialects lack 'present tense'
in the relevant sense. Correlatively, propositional infinitivals in these dialects
are predicted to lack an internally organized Tense, namely R_{INF} in C,
behaving in this respect like English propositional infinitivals. The failure of
DP-trace in examples like (5b) is then fully expected since, in the absence of
R_{INF} in C, a T-chain between the matrix and embedded clauses cannot be
constructed. As a consequence, long-distance A-movement from the
embedded subject position will be excluded by local economy conditions
on movement.

3.4. NULL SUBJECTS IN FINITE CLAUSES

In addition to Case-theoretic considerations, the distribution of OC PRO/
DP-trace and control infinitivals has been demonstrated to derive in large
part from the temporal properties of the embedded clause. Formally this was
captured by attributing Tense features (R_{INF}) to the embedded C position,
responsible for fixing the understood temporal frame of the infinitive (E_{INF})
as unrealized with respect to the reference time of the matrix verb (R_{MV}) by
means of a T-chain, namely $R_{MV} \rightarrow R_{INF}$, $R_{INF} = E_{INF}$. ECM and raising
infinitivals, on the other hand, lack the CP functional layer and hence an
internally organized Tense, their reference being determined externally by
R_{MV}. In line with a long tradition (see Stowell 1981, 1982; den Besten 1983;
Safir 1985; Enç 1987; Rizzi 1998), we are therefore assuming a relationship
between C and T. For instance, since den Besten (1983) the dependency
between C and T has been widely recognized in a number of Germanic
varieties, where Tense features in C are interpreted as the locus of

nominative Case and responsible for overt V-to-T-to-C movement in main clauses.[35] Such evidence leads to the view that inflectional categories of the verbal system may, in accordance with parametric variation, be encoded in the C-system (see Rizzi 1998: §1), spelling out such categories as tense/ finiteness (English *that* + tensed clause, *for* + infinitival clause), subject agreement (in Germanic; see Zwart 1997: 136ff.), mood (in Balkan languages) and negation (in Latin and Celtic).

Though lacking the full distribution of infinitival clauses, Neapolitan and related southern dialects display in finite clauses a dependency between C and T analogous in many respects to that found in conjunction with propositional and irrealis infinitivals. Concretely, the distribution of *ca* versus *che/chi* in dialects of the Upper South correlates with the temporal interpretation of the embedded clause, the former typically heading propositional complements and the latter irrealis complements. We therefore interpret the shape of the complementizer in finite clauses as the reflex of an agreement rule between C and T, spelling out the reference time of the embedded verb (R_{EV}).

Under this view, we take the *ca* complementizer to mark a neutral or unconstrained relation between the reference time (R_{EV}) and the event time (E_{EV}) of the embedded verb, allowing the former to precede ($R_{EV} \rightarrow E_{EV}$), coincide with ($R_{EV} = E_{EV}$) or follow ($E_{EV} \rightarrow R_{EV}$) the latter. On the other hand, the *che/chi* complementizer equates the reference time of the embedded verb with that of the event time ($R_{EV} = E_{EV}$), locating the reference time of the embedded verb after that of the matrix verb ($R_{MV} \rightarrow R_{EV}$).

These facts account for our earlier observation (see section 3.2.1) regarding the differences in the range of tense forms displayed by verbs embedded under *ca* and *che/chi*. In the former case, the embedded verb is capable of marking the full range of temporal distinctions, since the embedded T is unconstrained by the reference time marked in C. As for clauses headed by *che/chi*, the embedded verb is restricted to marking aspectual distinctions (presence/absence of aspectual auxiliary) since its time frame its tied to the reference time encoded in C, itself located after that of the matrix clause. The traditional use of the subjunctive in such clauses therefore falls out naturally, for the subjunctive typically has anaphoric temporal reference in Romance.

Following the widespread loss of the present subjunctive in the modern dialects (see Rohlfs 1968: §559; 1969: §681), the morphological restrictions placed on verb forms embedded under *che/chi* are even more severe. Though this is not the place to enter into a discussion of subjunctive usage in southern Italy, an area in urgent need of investigation, a cursory examination of the available evidence demonstrates the wide-spread use of a temporally unmarked verb form in *che/chi*-clauses.[36] Essentially, there are two cases to be noted. In the first, the expected subjunctive paradigms, including the imperfect subjunctive, are replaced by the present/imperfect indicative (see Rohlfs 1969: §681), a tendency particularly frequent in conjunction with volitional predicates,[37] witness (66a–k):

(66) a. *voglio*   /*vulevo*   *che tu me sinte*   /*senteva*

want.PRES.ISG /want.PAST.ISG that you me hear.PRES.INDIC /hear.PAST.INDIC.2SG

'I want/wanted you to listen to me' (Celano (AQ), Villa 1992: 97–98)

      b. *è*   /*era*   *necessario che tu remane*   /*remaneva*

be.PRES.3SG /be.PAST.3SG necessary   that you stay.PRES.INDIC /stay.PAST.INDIC.2SG

'it is/was necessary for you to stay' (ibid.)

      c. *voglio*   /*vuleva*   *che tu viene*   /*venive*

want.PRES.ISG /want.PAST.ISG that you come.PRES.INDIC /come.PAST.INDIC.2SG

'I want/wanted you to come' (NA, Iandolo 1994: 272)

      d. *'vɔʎʎə*   *ka 'vɛnənə*

want.PRES.ISG that come.PRES.INDIC.3PL

'I want them to come' (Calvello (PZ), Gioscio 1985: 77)

      e. *tʃə sfur'tunə ka nun dzo*   *bbə'nutə*

what misfortune that not be.PRES.INDIC.3PL come.PART

'what a shame that they have not come' (ibid.)

      f. *ve*   *spagnati   ca sientu?*

yourselves fear.PRES.2PL that hear.PRES.INDIC.ISG

'are you afraid that I will hear?' (CS, De Marco 1986a: 95)

      g. *ha*   *sempre speratu ca ti ricuglìe*

have.PRES.3SG always   hope.PART that return.PRES.INDIC.2SG

'he has always hoped that you would come home' (Mendicino (CS), Barca 1996: 11)

      h. *spero*   *che se ne va*   *presto*

hope.PRES.ISG that go.PRES.INDIC.3SG soon

'I hope that he leaves soon' (reg. Italian, Apulia, Stehl 1988: 7)

      i. *speravo*   *che ci venivi*   *a trovare*

hope.PAST.ISG that us come.PAST.INDIC.2SG to find.INF

'I hoped that you would come to see us' (ibid.)

      j. *vuliti*   *ca si pigghianu?*

want.PRES.2PL that self- take.PRES.INDIC.3PL

'do you want them to be fetched?' (Sicily, Varvaro 1988: §8.6)

      k. *vogghiu*   *c' u fannu*

want.PRES.ISG that it do.PRES.INDIC.3PL

'I want them to do it' (ibid.)

In such cases, the distribution of the present versus imperfect indicative in the embedded *che/chi*-clause cannot be said to mark temporal distinctions. Rather, their distribution is simply determined by the temporal specification of the matrix verb, instantiating the so-called sequence of tense rule, as with the subjunctive in standard Romance.

The other case, particularly common in optative, directive, dubitative and concessive clauses, consists in the generalized use of the imperfect subjunctive paradigm (67) or, less commonly, the pluperfect subjunctive paradigm (68). In such cases the verb is once again unmarked for tense and presents the further peculiarity of exhibiting the same verb form irrespective of the temporal specification of the matrix verb.[38]

(67) a. *dijje   che cce jésse*
      tell.IMP.2SG-him that there go.PAST.SUBJ.3SG
      'tell him to go there' (Abruzzo, Finamore 1893: 25)

   b. *mamme ne' vvó   che cce jésse   sóle*
      mum   not want.PRES.3SG that there go.PAST.SUBJ.3SG alone
      'mum doesn't want that I go alone' (ibid.)

   c. *so   minut'   a prigarti   che m' insignissi*
      be.PRES.1SG come.PART to pray.INF-you that me teach.PAST.SUBJ.2SG
      'I've come to ask that you teach me' (Abruzzo, Rohlfs 1969: §682)

   d. *ularría   ca ussería me nzegnasse*
      want.COND.1SG that you   me teach.PAST.SUBJ.2SG
      'I'd like that you teach me' (CB, Battisti 1921: 142)

   e. *permettete che dicessi   due parole*
      allow.IMP.2PL that say.PAST.SUBJ.1SG two words
      'allow me to say my piece' (NA, Scarpetta 1992: 72)

   f. *raccomannatele   che non facesseno   chiasso*
      remind.IMP.2PL-them that not do.PAST.SUBJ.3PL noise
      'impress upon them that they are not to make any noise' (NA, Scarpetta 1994: 82)

   g. *um pò   èssi ca ji l' avissi   dittu*
      not can.PRES.3SG be.INF that I it have.PAST.SUBJ.1SG say.PART
      'it can't be that I have said it' (Maratea (PZ), Rohlfs 1969: §682)

   h. *dubito   pur' ca veníss'   pàtrit'*
      doubt.PRES.1SG even that come.PAST.SUBJ.3SG father.POSS.2SG
      'I doubt that you father will come' (Muro Lucano (PZ), Mennonna 1977: 123)

   i. *digli   che venissero   /entrassero*
      tell.IMP.2SG-them that come.PAST.SUBJ.3PL /enter.PAST.SUBJ.3PL
      'tell them to come/enter' (reg. Italian, Anzi (PZ), Ruggieri and Batinti 1992: 85)

   j. *illu vo   chi jissi   all' America*
      he want.PRES.3SG that go.PAST.SUBJ.1SG to-the America
      'he wants me to go to America' (Aprigliano (CS), Accattatis 1895: §209)

k. *si pretienni   ca   illu te scrivissi   supra a   carta*
if   claim.PRES.2SG that he   you write.PAST.SUBJ.3SG on   the paper
bullata
stamped
'if you insist that he write to you on official note paper' (CS, De
Marco 1986a: 28)

l. *mi   scantava   ca   trasissi*
myself fear.PAST.1SG that enter.PAST.SUBJ.3SG
'I was afraid that he would come in' (Sicily, Leone 1995: §40)

m. *spieru   ca   vinissi*
hope.PRES.1SG that come.PAST.SUBJ.3SG
'I hope that he will come' (ibid.)

(68) a. *mamme ne' vvó   che cc-i avésse   jite   sóle*
mum   not want.PRES.3SG that there have.PAST.SUBJ.1SG go.PART alone
'mum doesn't want that I go alone' (Abruzzo, Finamore 1893: 25)

b. *m' à   ⁓   ditte   c' avisse   menute subbete*
me have.PRES.3SG say.PART that have.PAST.SUBJ.2SG come.PART at-once
'he told me that you should come at once' (ibid.)

c. *nne' je putive   dice' ch' avéss'   aspettate?*
not him be-able.PAST.2SG say.INF that have.PAST.SUBJ.3SG wait.PART
'couldn't you order that he wait?' (ibid.)

d. *dəciavə   la mamm' a lu fijj' ô cchə s'avessə   'mbaratə*
say.PAST.3SG the mother to the son that   have.PAST.SUBJ.3SG learn.PART
qualchə artə
some   trade
'the mother told her son that he learn a trade' (Abruzzo, Rohlfs
1969: §683)

e. *disse   che lo fosse   juto a   vennere*
say.PAST.3SG that it be.PAST.SUBJ.3SG go.PART to sell.INF
'he ordered that he go and sell it' (NA, Rohlfs 1969: §683)

f. *facivə   nnu tələgrammə a Pəppinə chə fussə*
do.PAST.1SG a   telegram   to Peppino that be.PAST.SUBJ.3SG
turnatə subbətə
return.PART at-once
'I sent Peppino a telegram informing him that he come back at
once' (Lucania, Rohlfs 1969: §683)

g. *n' autra cartelluzza scrissi   a Ntuoni, chi m' avissi*
an other note   write.PAST.1SG to Antonio that me have.PAST.SUBJ.3SG
mannatu u panaru
send.PART the basket

'I wrote Antonio another note telling him that he send me down the basket' (Calabria, ibid.)

It emerges that the temporal frame of verbs embedded under *che/chi*, whether indicative (66) or subjunctive (67) and (68), is marked exclusively by the choice of complementizer, the embedded verb itself encoding solely agreement and aspectual features.[39] In a parallel fashion to control infinitivals, we conclude then that verbs introduced by the complementizer *che/chi* are not morphologically marked for Tense, their temporal interpretation in both cases being determined by properties of the C position. In examples (66)–(68) we therefore assume, on a par with control infinitivals, the construction of a T-chain between the matrix and embedded Tenses mediated by the referential temporal features hosted by C (see Giorgi 1983–4: 339, and note 28 below).

In the light of these similarities between control infinitivals and *che/chi*-clauses, we might expect to find further affinities between both types of clause. Indeed, the construction of a T-chain in control infinitivals was demonstrated above to license the presence of DP-trace in the embedded subject position. In this respect we considered in section 3.1 Neapolitan examples such as those in (69), where an OC relation between the embedded subject and an argument of the matrix was demonstrated to preclude the possibility of an overt subject in the embedded clause:

(69) a. *Ciro prummette   che Ø   /isso accatta   'e purtualle*
         Ciro$_i$ promise.PRES.3SG [that Ø$_{i/*j}$ /he$_{j/*i}$ buy.PRES.3SG the oranges]
         'Ciro promises that he will buy the oranges'

      b. *Ciro ha   deciruto   che Ø   /isso fatica   ogge*
         Ciro$_i$ have.PRES.3SG decide.PART [that Ø$_{i/*j}$ /he$_{j/*i}$ work.PRES.3SG today]
         'Ciro decided that he will work today'

      c. *Stefania ordenaje   a   Ciro che Ø   /isso venesse*
         Stefania   order.PAST.3SG PA Ciro$_i$ [that Ø$_{i/*j}$ /he$_{j/*i}$ come.PAST.SUBJ.3SG]
         'Stefania ordered Ciro to come'

A rather natural assumption would be to interpret the empty category (namely Ø) in the embedded subject position in (69) as pro, its content readily recovered, and hence licensed, by the agreement features of the embedded verb. Under current assumptions (Rizzi 1986) which identify a Case requirement on pro, the embedded [Spec, T] must then be a position in which nominative is licensed. However, there is reason to believe that in OC structures the embedded [Spec, T] is not a Case-checking position. Consider the behaviour of the *ca*-clauses in (70):

(70) a. *Ciro se crereva   ca Ø   /isso venceva   'o premio]*
         Ciro$_i$ believe.PAST.3SG [that Ø$_{i/j}$ /he$_{i/j}$ win.PAST.3SG the prize]
         'Ciro believed that he would win the prize'

b. *Ciro è   sicuro ca Ø lisso s'   ha   perz'*
Ciro$_i$ be.PRES.3SG sure [that Ø$_{i/j}$ /he$_{i/j}$ himself have.PRES.3SG lose.PART
'a chiave
the key]
'Ciro is sure that he has lost the key'

c. *Ciro ricette   ca Ø lisso veneva   cchiù doppo*
Ciro$_i$ say.PAST.3SG [that Ø$_{i/j}$ /he$_{i/j}$ come.PAST.3SG more   after]
'Ciro said that he would come later'

Despite a possible control relation with an argument of the matrix predicate, the embedded subject of the *ca*-clauses in (70) may surface as a null (presumably pro) or overt (*isso* 'he') pronoun. Given the non-complementary distribution of pro and *isso* in examples (70), we conclude that nominative can be checked in the embedded subject position of *ca*-clauses. In contrast, the complementary distribution of covert and overt DPs in the *che/chi*-clauses in (69) under their control reading suggests that nominative cannot be checked in the embedded subject position, thereby precluding the presence of pro. Rather, as a Caseless position, the embedded [Spec, T] in (69) must therefore host DP-trace (namely OC PRO). Indeed, the distribution of PRO/DP-trace versus pro in terms of the OC/NOC distinction is further supported by the contrasts evidenced in (71) and (72), which we observed in section 3.3.2.1 distinguish between structures containing pro and those containing PRO/DP-trace:

(71) a. **Ciro$_i$ prummette [che* PRO$_j$ *se sose priesto]* (obligatory antecedent)
'Ciro$_i$ promises [that PRO$_j$ gets up soon]'

b. **'a sora$_j$ 'e Ciro$_i$ prummette [che* PRO$_i$ *se sose priesto]* (c-commanding antecedent)
'Ciro$_i$'s sister$_j$ promises [that PRO$_i$ gets up soon]'

c. *Ciro$_i$ prummette [che* PRO$_i$ *se sose priesto e Giuanne pure]* (TP-ellipsis)
'Ciro$_i$ promises [that PRO$_i$ gets up soon and Gianni does too]' (= Gianni gets up)

d. *Giuanne$_j$ prummette a Ciro$_i$ [che* PRO$_{k/*j+i}$ *nce jevano cchiù doppo]* (split-antecedence)
'Gianni$_j$ promises Ciro$_i$ [that PRO$_{k/*j+i}$ would go later]'

(72) a. *Ciro$_i$ crere [ca* pro$_{i/j}$ *se sose priesto]* (optional antecedent)
'Ciro$_i$ believes [that pro$_{i/j}$ gets up soon]'

b. *'a sora$_j$ 'e Ciro$_i$ se crere [ca* pro$_i$ *se sose priesto]* (non-c-commanding antecedence)
'Ciro$_i$'s sister$_j$ believes [that pro$_i$ gets up soon]'

c. *Ciro$_i$ crere [ca* pro$_i$ *se sose priesto e Giuanne pure]* (TP-ellipsis)
'Ciro$_i$ believes [that pro$_i$ gets up soon and Gianni does too]' (= Ciro or Gianni gets up)

    d. *Giuanne$_j$ ricette a Ciro$_i$ [ca pro$_{k/j+i}$ nun avevan'a pavà subbeto]* (split-
      antecedence)
      'Gianni$_j$ told Ciro$_i$ [that pro$_{k/j+i}$ didn't have to pay at once]'

Given our observations regarding the temporal properties of verbs embedded under *chelchi*, which pattern in all relevant respects with control infinitivals, we suggest that OC structures like (69a) have the simplified structure in (73):

(73)   *Ciro prummette*   *che*   *accatta*   *'e purtualle*
      Ciro$_i$ promise.PRES.3SG [that t$_i$ buy.PRES.3SG$_j$ [*v*-VP t$_i$ t$_j$ the oranges]]
      'Ciro promises that he will buy the oranges'

After checking its external θ-role against *accatta* 'buys' within the embedded *v*-VP, *Ciro* moves to the embedded [Spec, T] to check its D-feature on T, its 3SG φ-features checked as 'free riders' against *accatta* now raised to T. The nominative Case feature borne by *Ciro* is not checked at this point, since the embedded [Spec, T] is not a Case-checking position. Subsequently, *Ciro* raises to the matrix clause to check the external θ-role of *prummette* 'promises' and its D-feature, nominative and φ-features in [Spec, T]. As with control infinitivals, raising of *Ciro* to the matrix subject position is a legitimate step sanctioned by the construction of a T-chain extending the binding domain of the embedded clause to include the matrix clause.

    In spite of its rich array of φ-features, the embedded verb *accatta* does not check nominative in conjunction with the embedded T. We maintain that there is no strict correlation between the availability of nominative Case and the presence of subject-verb agreement. This point is persuasively argued by Vincent (1998) in his comparison of the early Tuscan gerund and the old Neapolitan inflected gerund. He observes that the former frequently licenses a nominative subject just like the old Neapolitan inflected gerund, though lacking the overt subject agreement of the latter. On the strength of such evidence, Vincent (1998: 146) concludes that 'it is the subject which licenses the inflection rather than vice versa.' (see further the discussion of the inflected infinitive in section 3.5).

    By the same token, we have seen that the presence of subject-verb agreement in *chelchi*-clauses does not presuppose the availability of nominative Case. Rather, it is the establishment of a checking relation between the embedded T and the subject raised to [Spec, T] which licenses such agreement. Indeed, similar cases have recently been discussed in the literature in relation to a number of languages, in particular Greek and Romanian (see discussion of example (7) in section 1.3.4 and Chomsky 1995: 285).[40] Within the minimalist framework, structures like (73) find an immediate explanation. The D- and φ-features of *Ciro* in (73) are interpretable. Consequently, once checked against the embedded T, they are still accessible to the C_{HL} and hence free to enter into subsequent checking relations. On the other hand, the nominative feature borne by *Ciro* is unintepretable but cannot be checked in the embedded clause. Therefore, raising of *Ciro* to the matrix subject position follows in accordance with the last resort nature of movement, resulting in double agreement, double satisfaction of the EPP and a single Case relation in conjunction with the matrix T.[41]

3.4.1. *Summary*

In light of the above discussion, the traditional distinction between pro and PRO/DP-trace in terms of finite versus non-finite T cannot be upheld. Instead, the distribution of the two empty categories falls out as a consequence of the OC/NOC distinction (see Hornstein 1999): verbs like *crerere* 'to think' license NOC structures and hence pro, whereas verbs like *prummettere* 'to promise' license OC structures and hence PRO/DP-trace. In turn, we have established that these control properties are related to further differences in the temporal properties of the embedded T, the head responsible for nominative.[42]

3.5. OLD NEAPOLITAN INFLECTED INFINITIVE

In addition to the canonical infinitive, old Neapolitan texts as late as the seventeenth century document the existence of an infinitive inflected for person and number agreement, although the singular persons bear no overt marking (see table 3.1).[43]

Table 3.1 Old Neapolitan inflected infinitive

1SG	*cantare*	I-to-sing
2SG	*cantare*	you-to-sing
3SG	*cantare*	s/he-to-sing
1PL	*cantar(e)mo*	we-to-sing
2PL	*cantar(e)vo*	you-to-sing
3PL	*cantar(e)no*	they-to-sing

The inflected infinitive presents then somewhat of a problem for the traditional binary classification in terms of finite and non-finite verb forms, falling somewhere between the two, if we take subject agreement to be an indicator of relative finiteness (Koptjevskaja-Tamm 1993: 256). Indeed, in contrast to the canonical infinitive (see though chapter 4), the inflected infinitive may co-occur with an explicit subject, which may either precede or follow the infinitive:

(74) a. *per tanto pizola accaysune, quale fo   chesta de esserenno*
          for so   small   reason   which be.PAST.3SG this   of [be.INF.3PL
          *licenciati **li Greci** (De Blasi 1986: 53, 14–15)*
          free.PART   the Greeks]

      b. *per tanto pizola accaysune quanto fo   quella de **li   Grieci***
          for so   small   reason   which be.PAST.3SG that   of [the Greeks
          essereno licenciate (ibid., 75, 10–11)
          be.INF.3PL free.PART]
          'for such a minor reason, as was that of the Greeks being freed'

However, it is not true that the inflected infinitive can in all instances co-occur with an explicit subject. Rather, the latter possibility hinges on the control properties of the subcategorizing predicate (see also Vincent 1996: 396). Concretely, in OC structures the embedded subject is invariably null, witness the examples in (75):

(75) a. *determenaro   ancora in concordia de se repartireno in tutto da*
          determine.PAST.3PL again   in agreement of [re-leave.INF.3PL in all   from
          Troya
          Troy]
          'they decided again in agreement to all leave Troy once more' (De Blasi 1986: 259, 18)

      b. *ll' altri se apprestaro tutti de combattere co   li   Grieci per*
          the others prepare.PAST.3PL all   of fight.INF   with the Greeks for
          volereno   defendere la   lloro libertate
          [want.INF.3PL defend.INF the their freedom]
          'the others all prepared to fight with the Greeks to defend their freedom' (ibid., 123, 9–10)

      c. *scelcero   plu toste de volereno   morire cavallarusamente in*
          choose.PAST.3PL rather   of [want.INF.3PL die.INF honourably   in
          terra che de annegareno in mare nén de volereno   fugire
          land   than of drown.INF.3PL in sea   nor of want.INF.3PL flee.INF]
          'they decided to die honourably on land rather than to drown at sea or to flee' (ibid., 142, 37–9)

      d. *non refinerranno de ve assaltare e   de ve dareno   tempesta*
          not finish.FUT.3PL of [you attack.INF and of you give.INF.3PL turmoil
          e   briga
          and strife]
          'they will not cease to attack you and to cause you turmoil and strife' (ibid., 264, 35–6)

e. *allora li Grieci se   incorayaro   follescamente de*
   then   the Greeks themselves encourage.PAST.3PL madly   of
   se partirenno colle   nave lloro da   Troya
   [leave.INF.3PL   with-the ships their from Troy]
   'then the Greeks were wildly encouraged to leave Troy in their
   ships' (ibid., 267, 10–11)

f. *quilli prisuni, li   quali tu   commanderray de liberarenosse*
   those   prisoners the which you command.FUT.2SG of [free.INF.3PL-themselves]
   'those prisoners, whom you will order to free themselves' (ibid., 104,
   20–1)

In (75a–e) the understood null subject of the inflected infinitival clause can
only be construed with that of the matrix, giving rise to a subject-control
structure. Similarly, in (75f) the understood subject of the inflected infinitive
is necessarily coreferent with the matrix object *li quali* 'whom', *commandare*
'to command' being an object-control verb.

Where an inflected infinitive does co-occur with an explicit subject, in
contrast, the matrix predicate does not impose an OC relation on its
embedded subject. Rather, explicit subjects only occur in NOC structures:

(76) a. *ave   plazuto   ai   nuostri Diey de **nuy** esseremo in*
        have.PRES.3SG please.PART to-the the our   Gods of [we be.INF.1PL in
        questa parte
        this   part]
        'it has pleased out Gods for us to be in these parts' (De Blasi 1986:
        69, 35)

   b. *non possendo la toa   dimanda dolcissima adimpire per esserno*
      not be-able.GER the your request   most-sweet fulfil.INF for [be.INF.3PL
      ***li mei pensieri** con li   affannati mei spiriti in cotal modo*
      the my thoughts with the   worried my spirits in such   way
      contristati et oppressi
      saddened   and burdened
      'not being able to fulfil your most kind request because my thoughts
      together with my worried spirits are so saddened and burdened'
      (Formentin 1987: XLIII)

   c. *me   maravellava   multo forte de **quisto cavalire** avire*
      myself surprise.PAST.3SG very   strong of [this   knight   have.INF.SG
      tacto   potere
      so-much power]
      'I was extremely surprised at this knight's having so much power'
      (McArthur n.d., 46)

For example, in (76a) the understood reference of the embedded subject is
not constrained by the semantics of the matrix predicate *ave plazuto* 'it has

pleased' but, rather, is free to refer to any set of individuals, in this instance the speaker King Peleus and his soldiers.

In most instances, however, the subject position in such NOC structures is null, the overt person and number agreement on the infinitive proving sufficient to reference the identity of the understood subject:

(77) a. *da poy che ave*   *plazuto*   *a la contraria*   *nostra fortuna*
from then that have.PRES.3SG please.PART to the unfavourable our   fortune
de esseremmo reducti a cquisto presente stato
of [be.INF.1PL reduced to this   present   state]
'since it has pleased our unfavourable fortune for us to be reduced to this present state' (De Blasi 1986: 264, 29–30)

    b. *non credevano*   *de may lo*   *vedereno plu*
not believe.PAST.1PL of [never him see.INF.3PL anymore]
'they did not believe they would ever see him again' (ibid., 66, 33)

    c. *se nde tornaro . . . per se reposareno*
return.PAST.3PL   for [rest.INF.3PL]
'they returned . . . in order to rest' (ibid., 171, 24–5)

    d. *che era*   *meglyo a sseglyre oy de se partireno dall'*   *assieyo*
that be.PAST.3SG better   to ascend.INF or of [leave.INF.3PL from-the siege
e no plu vattaglyare, oy de puro durareno a la vattaglya
and no more battle.INF   or of even last.INF.3PL to the battle]
'whether it was better to join or to abandon the siege and to battle no more, or to continue the battle' (ibid., 230, 21–2)

    e. *serrà*   *leya cosa ad averemonde*   *grande avantayo*
be.FUT.3SG light thing to [have.INF.1PL-of-it great   advantage]
'it will be easy for us to have the advantage over them' (ibid., 88, 5–6)

    f. *non se*   *voleano*   *ponere a periculo de gerino*   *spierti*
not themselves want.PAST.3PL put.INF to danger of [go.INF.3PL lose.PART]
'they did not want to put themselves in danger of going astray' (ibid., 183, 32)

    g. *ormay èy*   *hora de nne*   *levaremo da lo liecto*
now   be.PRES.3SG hour of [ourselves raise.INF.1PL from the bed]
'now it is time for us to get up' (ibid., 63, 2–3)

    h. *quisti danno*   *sta provenda per potereno*   *cavalcare*
these give.PRES.3PL this fodder   for [be-able.INF.3PL ride.INF]
'these men give (the horses) this fodder in order for them to be able to ride' (De Jennaro, cited in Rohlfs 1969: 92)

Particularly revealing in this respect is the contrast illustrated by the near minimal pair (76a) and (77a), in which the infinitival subject is overt in the former but covert in the latter, despite both infinitival clauses being embedded under the same matrix predicate. Such pairs highlight then the availability of nominative Case in NOC inflected infinitival complements like (77), even though the subject is not overtly realized.

In light of these facts, we are forced to recognize once again that there is no one-to-one relationship between the presence of person/number marking and the presence of nominative Case. Rather, the ability of an inflected verb form, in both infinitival and *chelchi*-clauses, to check nominative is related to the OC/NOC distinction. In OC structures like that in (78a), the inflected infinitive fails to Case-mark its subject *le nave* 'the ships' nominative. Raising of the latter to the embedded subject position results solely in the checking of the D- and ϕ-features borne by the embedded T, nominative being exclusively checked in conjunction with the matrix T. In the NOC inflected infinitival example in (78b), in contrast, nominative is indeed checked in the embedded subject position, variously licensing *nuy* or pro and excluding subsequent raising to the matrix clause:

(78) a. *le nave   siano   preste a   moverenose de   lo   puorto*
          the ships$_i$ be.PRES.SUBJ.3PL swift   to [$_{TP}$ t$_i$ leave.INF.3PL from the port]
          'the ships are quick to leave the port' (De Blasi 1986: 120, 34)

      b. *ave   plazuto   a li   nuostri Diey /a la contraria   nostra*
          have.PRES.3SG please.PART to the our   Gods /to the unfavourable our
          *fortuna de nuy /*pro *esserem(m)o . . .*
          fortune of [we /pro be.INF.1PL   ...]
          'it has pleased our Gods/our unfavourable fortune for us to be . . .'
          (ibid., 69, 35; ibid., 264, 29–30)

The presence of pro, rather than DP-trace (namely PRO), in NOC structures like (77) and (78b) is further confirmed by examples (79), where only a partial relation of identity obtains between matrix and embedded subjects:

(79) a. *io v' aio   qua fate   congriare per nuy averemo*
          I$_i$ you$_j$ have.PRES.1SG here make.PART gather.INF for [we$_{i+j}$ have.INF.1PL
          ordene
          orders]
          'I have assembled you here for us to receive orders' (McArthur n.d., 24)

      b. *meglyo credo   che fosse   stato pre tene e   pre*
          better believe.PRES.1SG that be.COND.3SG be.PART for you$_i$ and for
          mene de   averemo   facta   la vita nostra in uno luoco
          me$_j$ of [pro$_{i+j}$ have.INF.1PL do.PART the life our   in a   place
          solitario
          solitary]
          'I believe that it would have been better for you and myself to have led our lives in a solitary place' (De Blasi 1986: 186, 33–187, 1)

c. *ayo*   *ià*   *certa speranza de*   *lo*   *poteremo*
have.PRES.1SG$_i$ already certain hope   of [pro$_{i+j}$ him be-able.INF.1PL

avere   *alle*   *mano nostre*
have.INF to-the hands our]

'I have hopes for us to be able to capture him' (ibid., 250, 24)

Clearly, these examples highlight the possibility of split antecedence for the null subject in such NOC structures, an option which we observed above is not compatible with PRO/DP-trace.

3.5.1. *Summary*

The results of our discussion of the old Neapolitan inflected infinitive lend further support to our analysis of nominative Case-checking in *che/chi*-clauses. In both instances, it has been established that control relations play a central role in licensing nominative. The latter can be checked in NOC but not OC structures, where subject-raising to the matrix obtains, yielding double agreement, double satisfaction of the EPP and a single Case relation. The presence of subject-verb agreement, on the other hand, has been demonstrated to be independent of nominative Case-checking, a conclusion that we shall subsequently reinforce with our discussion of the personal infinitive in chapter 4.

4

THE PERSONAL INFINITIVE

4.1. INTRODUCTION

Within the traditional approach to finiteness (see Koptjevskaja-Tamm 1993: 256; Vincent 1998: §3),[1] Romance infinitives are treated as non-finite verb forms, marked by the absence of tense and agreement inflections which typically characterize finite verb forms. We thus find contrasts like those in (1a–b) from Neapolitan:

(1) a. *lloro teneno   gulìo 'e   cantà*
       they$_i$ have.PRES.3PL desire of [t$_i$ sing.INF]
       'they feel like singing'

    b. *lloro cantaieno*
       they sing.PAST.3PL
       'they sang'

In (1a) the infinitive *cantà* 'to sing' fails to inflect for the categories of person/number and tense. Infinitives are then in the relevant sense inflectionally impoverished, inasmuch as the interpretation of their understood subject (namely 3PL) and time reference (future relative to the speech moment) are referenced implicitly by the matrix verb. In view of their reduced semantic autonomy, infinitives are typically resticted to occurring as embedded verb forms. In contrast, the finite verb form *cantaieno* 'they sang' in (1b) inflects for person/number (*-no* 3PL) and tense (*-aie-* PAST), inflections which license a full lexical subject *lloro* 'they' and afford it greater semantic autonomy, as witnessed by its ability to occur as a matrix predicate.

Within the generative tradition these differences are commonly held to follow from properties of the functional heads T and Agr, in turn correlatively responsible for the availability of nominative Case-checking (see Ledgeway 1998b). In particular, infinitives are marked [-T, -Agr], an impoverished INFL specification which underlies the impossibility of nominative Case-assignment to the subject position and, at the same time, correctly predicts that a null anaphoric pronominal subject (PRO) is licensed. Finite verb forms, in contrast, exhibit both tense and person/number marking, hence specified as [+T, +Agr]. Consequently, either T (Chomsky 1980: 250) or Agr (Chomsky 1981: §4.3) may be taken as responsible for the assignment of nominative to the subject position (see Koopman and Sportiche 1991).

However, the evidence of the personal infinitive, a species of infinitive which will form the focus of our attention in the present chapter, raises some fundamental questions about the proper characterization of finiteness in relation to the infinitive and, in particular, the licensing of nominative Case and the role of control and subject-verb agreement in such processes. Consider the following examples of the personal infinitive from a number of southern Italian varieties:

(2) a. *primme de succedere* **chesto**, *ha*   *ditto*   *che*   *fa cose de*
      [before   of   happen.INF   this]   have.PRES.3SG   say.PART   that   ...
      pazze!
      'before that happens, he said that he'll get up to wild things' (NA, Scarpetta 1992: 49)

    b. *ne*   *jemmo*   *prima de farse*   **notte**
      ourselves   go.PRES.1PL   [before   of   fall.INF   night]
      'we left before nightfall' (Celano (AQ), Villa 1992: 86)

    c. *chi si alzava*   *alle tre per trovarsi*   *al*   *posto di*
      who self- get-up.PAST.3SG at-the three for find.INF-oneself at-the place of
      lavoro   *prima*   *di uscire*   **il sole**
      work   [before   of come-out.INF the sun]
      'those who got up at three to get to work before sunrise' (reg. Italian, Cerignola (FG), Rinaldi and Sobrero 1974: 94)

    d. *pi mangià* **Massimiliano** *'a carne, hadd'*   *essa propiu*
      [for eat.INF   Massimiliano   the meat]   must.PRES.3SG be.INF really
      bona
      good
      'for Massimiliano to eat the meat, it must be really good' (CS)

    e. *si nni iju dintra a curcari*   *senza sèntilu*   **sò mugghieri**
      go.PAST.3SG inside   to lie-down.INF [without hear.INF-him his wife]
      'he went inside to go to bed without his wife hearing him' (Salaparuta (TP), Pitré 1875: I, 246)

Though morphologically identical to the canonical Romance infinitive in (1a), failing to inflect for any of the so-called finite categories, the personal infinitive licenses a subject (given in bold type) with independent reference that is not controlled by an argument of the matrix predicate. Such infinitival forms therefore differ from OC (canonical) infinitivals like (1a) where the absence of nominative Case forces raising of the infinitival subject to the matrix clause. Such differences would appear to bear directly on the OC/NOC distinction, inasmuch as nominative-licensing is restricted to NOC (personal) infinitivals like (2). The existence of the personal infinitive construction therefore challenges the traditional dichotomy between finite and non-finite verb forms and, in particular, the presumed correlation between nominative Case-checking and the presence of person/number marking (see also Vincent 1998).

In what follows we shall provide a formal characterization of the syntax of the personal infinitive, investigating subject positions, nominative Case-licensing and the effects of verb raising in constraining the possible checking configurations for the EPP. Though our investigation will concentrate predominantly on the dialects of southern Italy, our analysis will also integrate comparative data from a number of other Romance varieties.

The chapter is organized as follows. In sections 4.2 to 4.5 we explore the fundamental properties of the personal infinitive construction, investigating its distribution and the characteristics of the infinitival verb and its subject. This is followed in section 4.6 by an examination of the restrictions operative on the various positions occupied by overt and covert infinitival subjects. In section 4.7 we propose an account of such restrictions in terms of EPP-checking configurations and the derived position of the infinitive.

4.2. DISTRIBUTION

The distribution of the personal infinitive, unlike like that of the canonical and inflected infinitive, appears to be restricted to non-subcategorized positions in southern Italian dialects, namely subject (3) and adverbial (4) clauses:

(3) a. *cummene   a ce   ne   parlà   tu*
        be-better.PRES.3SG to [him.DAT of-it speak.INF you]
        'it is better for you to speak about it with him' (NA)

     b. je   d:ə'f:ɪtʃəl ad a'k:jal:ə **pə'p:ɪnə**
        be.PRES.3SG difficult   to [find.INF-it Peppino]
        'it'll be difficult for Peppino to find it' (Altamura (BA), Loporcaro 1988: 261)

     c. *cummena   a num benire   **tu**
        be-better.PRES.3SG to [not come.INF you]
        'it is better for you not to come' (CS)

     d. *ora pari   chi fussi   di giustu di jirivinni*
        now seem.PRES.3SG that be.SUBJ.3SG of just   of [leave.INF-yourself₁ pro₁]
        'now it seems that it is time for you to leave' (Polizzi-Generosa (PA), Pitré 1875: III, 7)

(4) a. *primma 'e venì   tu   'o dottore proprio chesto m' ha*
        [before of come.INF you] the doctor   precisely this   me have.PRES.3SG
        ditto
        tell.PART
        'before you came, the doctor told me precisely that' (NA, De Filippo 1973: 15)

b. *'u   purcile avia   ri scifi   vasci pi ci   mangià i **gallini***
the   pigsty   have.PAST.3SG the troughs low   [for there eat.INF   the hens
   e   ri puorci
   and the pigs]
   'the troughs in the pigsty were low enough for the hens and the pigs
   to eat from them' (San Fili (CS))

c. *stɛm   a pːrəpaˈrɛ pə mːanˈʤɛ pur **aˈtːandə** kə nːu^u*
   be.PRES.1PL to prepare.INF [for eat.INF   also dad   with us]
   'we are preparing for your dad to eat with us' (Altamura (BA),
   Loporcaro 1988: 261)

d. *stu magasenu avia   la porta cu   lu pirtusu tunnu tunnu*
   this warehouse have.PAST.3SG the door with the hole   round round
   *pi tràsiri e   nesciri **li gatti***
   [for enter.INF and go-out.INF the cats]
   'this warehouse had a door with a perfectly round hole for the cats to
   go in and out of' (Ficarazzi (PA), Pitré 1875: IV, 162)

Though semantically the subject of the matrix predicate, the personal
infinitive in (3) does not occur in subject position but appears in an
adjunct position to the right of the matrix verb,[2] a conclusion substantiated by evidence from Case-marking: as discussed in section 3.2.2, the
infinitive in subject clauses in southern dialects is invariably preceded by a
prepositional inherent Case-marker, typically *a* 'to'. Such facts demonstrate that the nominative Case feature, as well as the EPP D-feature, of
the matrix T are not checked by the infinitive but by an expletive (albeit
overt in some dialects) merged in [Spec, T]. It follows from this that
subject infinitivals occur in adjunct positions where they are Case-marked
by a preposition.

   Turning now to the examples in (4), here the personal infinitive is not
selected by the verb but appears in an adverbial clause. Its adverbial status is
confirmed by its ability to occur in a variety of positions with respect to the
matrix verb and any verbal complements, as illustrated in the Cosentino
sentences in (5):

(5) a. *prima 'i si fà **notte**, Stefania vulissa   ca si ricuglissaru*
      [before of fall.INF night] Stefania like.COND.3SG that come-home.SUBJ.3PL
      'before night falls, Stefania would like them to come home'

   b. *Stefania vulissa,   prima 'i si fà **notte**, ca si ricuglissaru*
      Stefania like.COND.3SG [before of fall.INF night] that come-home.SUBJ.3PL
      'Stefania would like, before night falls, for them to come home'

   c. *Stefania vulissa   ca si ricuglissaru   prima 'i si fà **notte***
      Stefania like.COND.3SG that come-home.SUBJ.3PL [before of fall.INF night]
      'Stefania would like them to come home before night falls'

On the uncontroversial assumption that adverbial clauses are not arguments, it follows that the personal infinitive is restricted to non-subcategorized positions, a conclusion further substantiated by the ill-formedness of the structures in (6), where the personal infinitive illicitly occurs in complement position:

(6) a. *dubitammo 'e telefunà **Maria**
   doubt.PRES.1PL of [telephone.INF Maria]
   'we doubt that Maria will telephone' (NA)

   b. *nannuzza fora   cuntenta 'i jucà   **Luca**
   granny   be.COND.3SG happy   of [play.INF Luca]
   'granny would be happy for Luca to play' (CS)

Analogous considerations hold for the distribution of the personal infinitive in other Italo-Romance varieties.[3] For instance, in the Tuscan variety of San Gimignano (SI; Cresti 1994: 39–40) and the Ligurian dialect of Cicagna (GE; Cuneo 1997: §3.1, 3.2), the distribution of the personal infinitive is reported to be limited to non-argument positions, namely subject (7a–c) and adverbial (7d–g) clauses, never occurring in complement position (7h) (see Cuneo 1997: §4).

(7) a. li   garbava   più esse **la donna civile** pe tenè   bottega
   him.DAT please.PAST.3SG more [be.INF the lady   civilian for run.INF shop]
   'he preferred a city woman to run the shop' (Cresti 1994: 38)

   b. l'   üsu   l'è   d' acatâ tütu u **padrùn**
   the custom be.PRES.3SG of [buy.INF all the boss]
   'it is customary for the boss to buy everything' (Cuneo 1997: 107)

   c. nu sèrve   egnî   **u vìgile!**
   not serve.PRES.3SG [come.INF the traffic-warden]
   'it's not necessary for the traffic warden to come' (ibid.)

   d. pe   un marcì **i' grano**, si pigliava   un copertone
   [for not rot.INF the wheat] one take.PAST.3SG a   large-blanket
   'so that the wheat would not rot, we would take a large blanket'
   (Cresti 1994: 36)

   e. ci   guardavano da fidanzati a un rimanè incinta **la ragazza**
   themselves watch.PAST.3PL as fiancés   [to not remain   pregnant the girl]
   'when they were courting, they would simply look at one another so that the girl wouldn't get pregnant' (ibid., 37)

   f. l'à   fatu   tütu sènsa saîlu   e **sō'gènte**
   have.PRES.3SG do.PART all [without know.INF-it the his parents]
   'he did everything without his parents knowing' (Cuneo 1997: 106)

   g. invece de vengî   **a stâ**,   végne   de l' ægua
   [instead of come.INF the summer] come.PRES.3SG of the water
   'instead of summer coming, it's raining' (ibid., 107)

h. *l'è   stô   atèntu a nu case e sêsce
be.PRES.3SG be.PART careful to [not fall.INF the cherries]
'he was careful that the cherries did not fall' (ibid., 111)

Though subject to considerable regional and individual variation (see Bertuccelli Papi 1991: 824–5; Manzini 1991: 496–7; Cuneo 1997: §2.9), the distribution of the personal infinitive in colloquial Italian obeys identical restrictions, occurring solely in subject (8a–b) and adverbial (8c–e) clauses:

(8) a. *non sarà   facile, diventare direttore **Roberto***
    not be.FUT.3SG easy [become.INF manager Roberto]
    'it won't be easy for Roberto to become manager' (Cuneo 1997: 104)

   b. *è   una cosa strana, essere in chiesa **Giovanni***
    be.PRES.3SG a thing strange [be.INF in church Giovanni]
    'it's strange for Giovanni to be in church' (ibid.)

   c. *a furia di andarci   sempre **lui**, gli altri nemmeno si*
    [by dint of go.INF-there always he] the others not-even   themselves
    muovono
    move.PRES.3PL
    'because he always goes, the others don't even bother' (ibid.)

   d. ?*Gianni è   partito   prima di poterlo   salutare*
    Gianni_i be.PRES.3SG leave.PART [before of be-able.INF-him_i pro_j greet.INF]
    'Gianni left before I/you/(s)he/we/they could say good-bye to him'
    (Manzini 1991: 496)

   e. ?*a Gianni è   passato di mente dopo averlo*
    to Gianni_i be.PRES.3SG pass.PART of mind [after have.INF-him_i pro_j
    salutato
    greet.PART]
    'it slipped Gianni's mind after I/you/(s)he/we/they had greeted him'
    (ibid.)

Besides Italo-Romance, the personal infinitive is similarly attested in a number of other Romance varieties.[4] Of these the Spanish personal infinitive has undoubtedly attracted the greatest attention.[5] In line with the dialects of southern Italy, the Spanish personal infinitive is restricted to non-subcategorized positions,[6] occuring in subject (9a–b) and adverbial (9c–d) clauses, but never in complement position (9e):

(9) a. *ir   **yo** a la facultad mañana va   a ser   imposible*
    [go.INF I to the faculty tomorrow [go.PRES.3SG to be.INF impossible]
    'for me to go to to university tomorrow will be impossible'
    (Fernández-Lagunilla 1987: 125)

   b. *telefonear **tú** primero sería   un error*
    [telephone.INF you first] be.COND.3SG an error
    'for you to telephone first would be a mistake' (Piera 1987: 153)

c. *después de actuar* **Caballé**, *cantó* *Carreras*
[after of perform.INF Caballé] sing.PAST.3SG Carreras
'after Caballé performed, Carreras sang' (Rigau 1995: 280)

d. *para celebrar* **Rita** *su cumpleaños, se fue de viaje al*
[for celebrate.INF Rita her birthday] go.PAST.3SG of trip to-the
Caribe
Caribbean
'to celebrate her birthday, Rita went on a trip to the Caribbean'
(Torrego 1998b: 209)

e. **Marta está contenta de venir* **tú**
Marta be.PRES.3SG happy of [come.INF you]
'Marta is happy for you to come' (Pérez-Vázquez 1997: 135)

Identical facts hold for Catalan, witness the following subject (10a–b) and
adverbial (10c–d) clauses:[7]

(10) a. *cantare* **nosaltres** *ara no seria mala idea*
[sing.INF we now] not be.COND.3SG bad idea
'for us to sing now wouldn't be a bad idea' (Hualde 1992: 28)

b. *rentar-se* **ell** *la roba era l' únic que podia*
[wash.INF-self he the clothes] be.PAST.3SG the only that be-able.PAST.3SG
fer
DO.INF
'doing the washing himself was the only option' (Wheeler, Yates
and Dols 1999: 399)

c. *després d' actuar* **la Caballé**, *va cantar en Carreras*
[after of perform.INF the Caballé] go.PRES.3SG sing.INF the Carreras
'after Caballé performed, Carreras sang' (Rigau 1995: 280)

d. *es van casar just en acabar* **la guerra**
themselves go.PRES.3PL marry.INF [just in finish.INF the war]
'they got married just when the war ended' (ibid., 282)

The available evidence for Occitan (11a–b) and Romanian (11c–f)
suggests a parallel distribution of the personal infinitive in these varieties:[8]

(11) a. *sense l' avé* **digùn** *bist*
[without him have.INF anyone see.PART]
'without anyone having seen him' (Ronjat 1937: 595)

b. *se plorava dempuei tres jorns sens* **degun** *lo poder*
himself cry.PAST.3SG since three days [without anyone him be-able.INF
consolar
console.INF]
'he wept for three days without anyone being able to console him'
(Wheeler 1988: 270)

c. *este   de trebuinţă a   intra   si **Roşiorii-de-Vede** în lanţul*
be.PRES.3SG of necessity [to enter.INF also Rosiorii-de-Vede   in chain-the
căilor ferate
rail-way]
'it's necessary for Rosiorii-de-Vede to also enter into the rail network' (Sandfield and Olsen 1936: 270)

d. *pentru a curge **apa**,   apasaţi pe pedală*
[for   to run.INF water-the] press.IMP on pedal
'in order for the water to run, push down on the pedal' (Körner 1983: 81)

e. *fără   veni   **Radu** nu putem   face   nimic*
[without come.INF Radu] not be-able.PRES.1PL do.INF nothing
'unless Radu comes, we cannot do anything' (Lombard 1974: 294)

f. *Ion a   mîncat înainte de a pleca   **mama***
Ion have.PRES.3SG eat.PART [before of to leave.INF mother-the]
'John ate before his mother left' (Dobrovie-Sorin 1993: 115)

4.2.1. Control

As appears clear from our examination of the above examples, the relation of control plays a significant role in determining the distribution of the personal infinitive *vis-à-vis* the canonical infinitive. Considering the Romance languages as a whole, when left unexpressed, the subject of an infinitival clause is generally obligatorily construed as coreferent with an argument of the matrix clause, typically the subject (12a–b) or, less frequently, the direct (13a) or indirect (13b) object, as evidenced by the following Italian examples:

(12) a. *il   criminale convinse   la polizia di   essere innocente*
the criminal$_i$ covince.PAST.3SG the police$_j$ [of Ø$_i$ be.INF innocent]
'the criminal convinced the police that he was innocent'

b. *il   criminale disse   alla polizia di   essere innocente*
the criminal$_i$ tell.PAST.3SG to-the police$_j$ [of Ø$_i$ be.INF innocent]
'the criminal told the police that he was innocent'

(13) a. *il   criminale convinse   la polizia a   lasciarlo   andare*
the criminal$_i$ covince.PAST.3SG the police$_j$ to [Ø$_j$ let.INF-him$_i$ go.INF]
'the criminal convinced the police to let him go'

b. *il   criminale disse   alla polizia di   lasciarlo   andare*
the criminal$_i$ tell.PAST.3SG to-the police$_j$ [of Ø$_j$ let.INF-him$_i$ go.INF]
'the criminal told the police to let him go'

In both (12) and (13) the matrix verb imposes an OC relation on the subject of its embedded clause, such that the reference of the latter is immediately retrievable from the semantics of the matrix verb. In short, the OC relation is a property of the matrix verb's subcategorization frame, inasmuch as the subcategorization of an infinitival complement triggers an obligatory relation of identity between the embedded subject and an argument of the matrix. It follows from this that OC characterizes complement clauses, namely argument positions, since these are s-selected by the matrix verb.

In contrast, personal infinitives are used when the reference of the infinitival subject is not predetermined by properties of the matrix verb (see Pountain 1995: §2). In other words, the personal infinitive occurs in NOC contexts (see also Cuneo 1997: 111–17), restricted to marking non-coreferentiality (14) and never surfacing in contexts of coreferentiality (15), where subject reference is already independently recoverable (Fernández-Lagunilla 1987: 134–5; Piera 1987: 160):

(14) a. *Maria appicciaje 'a luce pe ce veré meglio **Giuanne***
         Maria   light.PAST.3SG the light [for see.INF better   Gianni]
         'Maria turned on the light for Gianni to see better' (NA)

      b. *María se descalzó   al   llegar   **Juan** a casa*
         Maria   remove-shoes.PAST.3SG [to-the arrive.INF Juan at home]
         'María took her shoes off when Juan arrived home' (Spanish, Fernández-Lagunilla 1987: 135)

(15) a. *Maria appicciaje 'a luce pe ce veré meglio (*****Maria*****)* (NA)
         Maria   light.PAST.3SG the light [for see.INF better   (Maria)]
         'Maria turned on the light to see better'

      b. *María se descalzó   al   llegar   (*****Maria*****) a casa* (Spanish)
         Maria   remove-shoes.PAST.3SG [to-the arrive.INF (Maria)   at home]
         'María took her shoes off when she arrived home'

The familiar tests (see section 3.3.2.1) that distinguish pro from PRO (= DP-trace) in NOC and OC structures, respectively, also substantiate the NOC character of the personal infinitive.

(16) a. *chesta è   stata   na bella   combinazione pe ve*
         this   be.PRES.3SG be.PART a beautiful coincidence [for yourself$_i$
         spusà   proprio a Luigi Belfiore
         marry.INF pro$_i$ precisely PA Luigi Belfiore]
         'that was lucky for you to marry Luigi Belfiore of all people' (NA, Scarpetta 1992: 31)

      b. *nce   simme   nfucate   talmente che è   impossibile e*
         ourselves$_i$ be.PRES.1PL$_i$ heat.PART so-much   that be.PRES.3SG impossible of
         ce   lassà
         [ourselves leave.INF pro$_i$]
         'we got so heated up that it was impossible for us to leave one another' (ibid., 78)

    c. *comme, io me   l'   aggia   spusà e chella me tratta*
        what   I myself her$_i$ must.PRES.1SG marry and she$_i$ me treat.PRES.3SG
        de chesta manera. Na serata sana senza guardarme   manco
        of this   manner an evening whole [without look-at.INF-me pro$_i$ even
        nu poco
        a bit]
        'what, I'm to marry her and she treats me like this. A whole evening
        without her looking at me even for a second' (ibid., 82)

    d. *aviamu   cunzatu   'a stanza 'i Cicciu pi si   ripusà*
        have.PAST.1PL prepare.PART the room of Ciccio$_i$ [for himself rest.INF pro$_i$]
        'we had prepared Ciccio's room for him to rest in' (CS)

    e. *iju   a cunfiriri cu sò maritu pri cumminari   lu*
        go.PAST.3SG$_i$ to confer.INF with her husband$_j$ [for plot.INF   pro$_{i+j}$ the
        comu ci l' avissiru   a pigghiari, dda pupidda
        how her it must.COND.3PL to take.INF   that child]
        'she went to speak with her husband in order to plot how they
        should take that child from her' (Borgetto (PA), Pitré 1875: IV,
        245)

These examples demonstrate that the infinitival subject does not require an antecedent (16a), or if present, it need not be local (16b) or occur within the same sentence (16c), or even c-command the infinitival subject (16d). In addition, (16e) indicates that the infinitival subject can have split antecedents. Such facts are clearly only compatible with a NOC structure.

    Moreover, we have seen that personal infinitives are restricted to non-subcategorized positions, in particular adverbial and subject clauses. As adjuncts, such clauses are not selected by the matrix verb but, rather, function as optional modifiers of the sentence which do not enter into a direct selectional relation with the matrix verb.[9] Consequently, the reference of the subject in the personal infinitive is not inherently determined by properties of the matrix verb but, rather, is referentially free. From this follows the generalization that NOC (personal) infinitives predominantly occur in non-subcategorized positions, while OC (canonical) infinitives occur only in subcategorized positions.[10] We conclude therefore that the presence of a subject with independent reference in the personal infinitive can be straightforwardly derived from the latter's restriction to NOC environments.

    However, there are some apparent counterexamples of personal infinitives in subcategorized positions. For instance, following Loporcaro (1988: 261), Cuneo (1997: §2.2) claims that the Sicilian personal infinitive may also occur in subcategorized positions, a claim corroborated by Delia Bentley (personal communication; see also Bentley 1997: 229, n. 42). The relevant examples are given below:

(17) a. *si dícinu   di **tu** mangiarmi, mi mangi*
         if say.PRES.3PL [of you eat.INF-me]   me eat.PRES.2SG
         'if they order that you eat me, you will eat me' (Etna (EN), Pitré
         1875: IV, 165)

      b. *Maria cunsigghiau di véniri   **Giuvanni***
         Maria   advise.PAST.3SG [of come.INF Giovanni]
         'Maria advised that Giovanni come' (Loporcaro 1988: 261)

Observe firstly that the significance of these sentences should not be
overstated, for they represent only two examples out of a total corpus of
171 examples of Sicilian infinitival clauses with non-controlled subjects.
Moreover, we have established that the correct generalization regarding the
distribution of the personal infinitive is not that it occurs only in non-
subcategorized positions but, rather, that it occurs only in NOC
contexts.[11,12] The frequent distribution of the personal infinitive in non-
subcategorized positions is thus simply a concomitant of the fact that NOC
infinitivals predominantly occur in such positions. Indeed, the sentences in
(17a–b) confirm this interpretation of the facts. In particular, the predicates
diri 'to tell' and *cunsigghiari* 'to advise' canonically license OC infinitival
structures whose understood subject is interpreted as coreferent with the
GOAL argument of the matrix verb, witness (18a–b):

(18) a. *quannu mè patri ti   dici   di   fari   chissu*
         when   my father you₍ᵢ₎ tell.PRES.3SG [of Ø₍ᵢ₎ do.INF this]
         'when my father tells you to do this' (Vallelunga Pratameno (CL),
         Pitré 1875: I, 135)

      b. *figghiu, vi cunsigghiu di   iirivinni*
         son   you₍ᵢ₎ advise.PRES.1SG [of Ø₍ᵢ₎ leave]
         'son, I advise you to leave' (Acireale (CT), ibid., II, 288)

In (17a–b), in contrast, these same verbs fail to subcategorize for a GOAL
argument. Consequently, the content of the infinitival subject cannot be
controlled, and hence recovered, by an argument of the matrix clause, for it
is not provided in the verbs' subcategorization frame. Consequently, a NOC
structure obtains and the infinitival subject has to be overtly realized. The
NOC status of the structures in (17a–b) is further substantiated by the
interpretative differences between (17a–b) and (18a–b). Whereas the understood infinitival subject in the latter is understood as directly involved in the
verbal activity, namely the RECIPIENT of the 'order' (18a) or 'advice (18b), the
explicit infinitival subject in (17a–b) can only be construed as indirectly
involved in the ordering/advising. Hence, (17a–b) are only compatible with
the translations given above, and not with the respective OC translations 'if
they order you to eat me' and 'Maria advised Giovanni to come'.

4.3. Properties of the subject

4.3.1. *Position*

As is borne out by the preceding examples, one of the most salient features of the personal infinitive is the obligatory postverbal position of the infinitival subject. Any attempt to place the subject in preverbal position invariably results in ungrammaticality,[13] as illustrated by the following Campanian example:

(19) *me faceva   muri'. . . invece 'e (*essa) muri' essa!*
me make.PAST.3SG die   instead of (her)   die.INF her
'I almost died . . . instead of her dying' (Montesano Scalo (SA), De Simone 1994: 636)

In this respect, however, Sicilian diverges somewhat from other southern Italian dialects (see La Fauci 1984: 122; Varvaro 1988: 725; Leone 1995: §67; Bentley 1997: 216, 229, n. 42), exhibiting both postverbal (20) and preverbal (21) subjects:

(20) a. *prima d' arrispigghiarisi l' acidduzzi, era   a lu scogghiu*
[before of wake.INF   the birds] be.PAST.3SG at the rock
'before the birds would wake, he would be at the rock' (Borgetto (PA), Pitré 1875: II, 355)

   b. *me patri morsi   prima di arrivari la figghia*
my father die.PAST.3SG [before of arrive.INF the daughter]
'my father died before his daughter arrived' (Varvaro 1988: 725)

   c. *pi jirisinni li fati, com' haju   a fari?*
[for go.INF the fairies] how have.PRES.1SG to do.INF
'in order for the fairies to go away, what do I have to do?' (PA, Pitré 1875: I, 155)

   d. *mè patri pi nasciri io fici   un vutu di sett' anni di cuccagna*
my father [for be-born.INF I] make.PAST.3SG a vow of seven years of
plenty
'my father, so that I would be born into the world, vowed not to enjoy himself for seven years' (PA, ibid., I, 130)

   e. *non ci nn' ha   a èssiri caccia 'nt' 'e ressi ppi non nn' ammazzari tu*
not there any have.PRES.3SG to be.INF game in the area [for not
any kill.INF you]
'for you not to kill anything must mean that there is no game in these parts' (Belpasso (CT), Martoglio 1978b)

(21) a. *arrivau   prima di **tu** aviri   nisciutu*
      arrive.PAST.3SG [before of you have.INF go-out.PART]
      'he arrived before you went out' (La Fauci 1984: 122)

   b. *si nni iu   senza **tu** avirici   parratu?*
      leave.PAST.3SG [without you have.INF-him.DAT talk.PART]
      'did he leave without you having talked to him?' (ibid.)

   c. *hai   nigatu   li toi parenti pir **ipsi** essiri poviri?*
      have.PRES.2SG deny.PART the your family   [for they be.INF poor]
      'did you disown your family because they are poor?' (ibid.)

   d. *per **lui** andare nel   dottore, vuol   dire   che sta*
      [for he go.INF   in-the doctor]   want.PRES.3SG say.INF that be.PRES.3SG
      vero male
      real ill
      'for him to go to the doctor's must mean he is really sick' (reg.
      Sicilian Italian, Bentley 1997: 216)

   e. *mé patri morsi   prima   di **vui** veniri*
      my father die.PAST.3SG [before of you come.INF]
      'my father died before you came' (Cerda (PA), Pitré 1875: IV, 26)

   f. *senza **io** essiri oblicato*
      [without I be.INF obliged]
      'without my having to' (Mòcciaro 1991, cited in Leone 1995: 59)

Nonetheless, the preverbal position is not freely available, being restricted
to pronominal subjects (21), though these may equally occur in postverbal
position (20d–e) without any apparent difference in interpretation.[14,15]
Consequently, nominal subjects always occur postverbally and never
preverbally:

(22) *prima d' (***lu Suli**) affacciari **lu Suli** affaccia   un sirpenti*
      [before of (the sun) appear.INF the sun] appear.PRES.3SG a snake
      'before the Sun comes out, there appears a snake' (Salaparuta (TP),
      Pitré 1875: I, 249)

Though most studies highlight the obligatory postverbal position of the
subject, examples of preverbal subjects in peninsular Spanish are found in
sentences like (23):[16]

(23) a. *lo hizo   sin   **yo** saberlo*
      it do.PAST.3SG [without I know.INF-it]
      'he did it without my knowing' (Fernández-Lagunilla 1987: 127,
      footnote 3)

   b. *María salió   de la sala sin   **yo** verla*
      María go-out.PAST.3SG of the room [without I see.INF-her]
      'María went out of the room without my seeing her' (Yoon and
      Bonet-Farran 1991: 355)

Contrary to appearances, however, the preverbal position in peninsular Spanish proves highly restricted. According to the *Grámatica de la Real Academia de la lengua* (1973: 486), it is very infrequent, although not totally excluded in the colloquial example (23a), which occurs alongside of *sin saberlo yo* with a postverbal subject. This view is echoed in Gili y Gaia (1955: 169), who considers examples such as (23a) 'poco frecuente' ('infrequent') and less usual than those with a postverbal subject. Similarly, Fernández-Lagunilla (1987: 127, n. 3) observes that the availability of the preverbal position is contingent on several factors: (i) that the personal infinitive be introduced by the preposition *sin* 'without' (less frequently *con* 'with'); (ii) that the subject be pronominal (see also Keniston 1937b: 234, 237–8); and (iii) that the infinitival verb be of a restricted class, typically *saber* 'to know'. On the basis of such evidence, she concludes that examples like (23) are felt by most speakers to be lexicalized. Moroever, both Fernández-Lagunilla (1987) and Torrego (1998b: 207, n. 3) note that when a nominal subject does appear before the infinitive (24a), it carries narrow focus, unlike a postverbal subject (24b):[17]

(24) a. *al*   **EL JUEZ** *leer*   *el verdicto, todo el mundo se levantó*
[to-the the judge   read.INF the verdict]   all   the world   get-up.PAST.3SG
'when THE JUDGE read out the verdict, everyone stood up'
(Torrego 1998b: 207)

b. *todo el mundo se levantó*   *al*   *leer*   *el juez el veredicto*
all   the world   get.up.PAST.3SG [to-the read.INF the judge the verdict]
'everyone stood up when the judge read out the verdict' (ibid.)

Such facts lead Fernández-Lagunilla to propose that the subject in preverbal position in peninsular Spanish examples like (24a) occupies a Focus position (in her terms a 'Topic' position).

In contrast, Latin American Spanish and, in particular Caribbean varieties,[18] appear to favour the preverbal position,[19] a phenomenon which in Caribbean varieties, according to Suñer (1986: 191), 'is widespread in all socioeconomic levels' and which 'does not spearate classes or levels, nor does it stigmatize the user.'[20] Below follow some examples:

(25) a. *como . . . se me puede*   *morir Luisa en las manos, sin*   **yo**
as   if me can.PRES.3SG die.INF Luisa in the hands [without I
verlo, sin   **yo** *sentirlo!*
see.INF-it without I   feel.INF-it]
'as if Luisa can die in my arms, without my realizing it, without my sensing it' (Argentinia, Kany 1951: 126)

b. *me daba*   *la oportunidad de yo comunicarme en mi idioma*
me give.PAST.3SG the chance   of [I communicate.INF in my language]
'it gave me the chance to communicate in my own language'
(Ovalle, Chile, Lipski 1991: 203)

c. *¿qué tú   me recomiendas para **yo** entender   la   lingüística?*
   what you me recommend   [for   I   understand.INF the   linguistics]
   'what do you recommend for me to understand linguistics?' (Cuba,
   Lipski 1994: 233)

d. *deme   para **yo** criarle*
   give.IMP.2SG-me [for   I   raise.INF-him]
   'give me him so that I can bring him up' (Ecuador, Mateus 1953: 268)

e. *cuando me empezaron   a dar   trabajo para **yo** hacer   maquinilla*
   when   me begin.PAST.3PL to give.INF work   [for   I   make.INF shaver]
   'when they began to give me work, with me making shavers'
   (Puertorico, Morales 1988: 93)

With the exception of a few apparent counterexamples to be discussed below
in section 4.7.1, the examples in (25) illustrate that, on a par with Sicilian,
only pronominal subjects may occur preverbally in Latin-American varieties. However, even pronominal subjects can occur in postverbal position
(26a–b), the only position available to nominal subjects (26c–e):[21]

(26) a. *semejante expresión no hubiera   salido   de mis labios*
         similar   expression not have.COND.3SG come-out.PART of my   lips
         *al   no saber   **yo** que mi cuenta estaba   cancelada*
         [to-the not know.INF I   that my   account be.PAST.3SG cancelled]
         'such an expression would have never left my lips if I had known
         that my account was closed' (Colombia, Kany 1951: 27)

      b. *no me hubiese   afeitado hasta el domingo de no haberme*
         not me have.COND.ISG shave.PART until the sunday   [of not have.INF-me
         *convidado **ustedes***
         invite.PART you]
         'I wouldn't have shaved until Sunday if you had not invited me'
         (Chile, ibid., 361)

      c. *al   no tenerlo **la biblioteca**, podría   comprarlo aquí*
         [to-the not have.INF-it the library]   be-able.COND.ISG buy.INF-it   here
         'if the library doesn't have it, I could buy it here' (Chile, ibid., 26)

      d. *al   ser **pulmonía** no hubiera   durado tres días*
         [to-the be.INF pneumonia] not have.COND.3SG last.PART three days
         'if it had been pneumonia, it wouldn't have lasted three days'
         (Ecuador, ibid., 27)

      f. *al   no querer **nadie** hablarnos, tampoco teníamos   nada*
         [to-the not want.INF nobody speak.INF-us] neither   have.PAST.IPL nothing
         que decirnos entre nosotros
         that say.INF-us among ourselves
         'if nobody wanted to speak to us, we neither had anything to say to
         one another' (Cuba, ibid., 1951: 28)

We therefore conclude that the unmarked position of subjects in conjunction with the personal infinitive is generally postverbal, the preverbal position found in Sicilian and Latin-American Spanish being restricted to pronominal subjects.

4.3.2. Case

Turning, to the Case of the infinitival subject, all varieties present a consistent behaviour in this regard. When a pronoun, the subject invariably occurs in the nominative,[22] as evidenced by the following representative examples:

(27) a. *si   è   accorto   che nel   letto invece 'e ce   sta'   io,*
himself be.PRES.3SG realize.PART that in-the bed   [instead of there be.INF I]
ce   steva   Mario Bertolini
there be.PAST.3SG Mario Bertolini
'he realized that instead of me being there in the bed, there was Mario Bertolini' (NA, De Filippo 1973: 144)

b. *je   'mːegːj a 'pːerdə tu   e 'nːaunə jɪ*ⁱ
be.PRES.3SG better   to [lose.INF you.NOM and not   I]
'it is better for you to lose and not I' (Altamura (BA), Loporcaro 1988: 261)

c. *pi essa tu   cuntientu, basta   ca ti dugnu   nu*
[for be.INF you.NOM happy]   suffice.PRES.3SG that you give.PRES.1SG a
piattu 'i pasta
plate of pasta
'for you to be happy, I just have to give you a bowl of pasta' (CS)

d. *a locu d' arrispunniri tu,   m' arrispunni la sèggia*
[to place of reply.INF   you.NOM] me reply.PRES.3SG the chair
'instead of you answering me, I'm answered by the chair' (PA, Pitré 1875: I, 111)

e. *per dirlo   io, deve   essere così*
[for say.INF-it I] must.PRES.3SG be.INF thus
'for me to say it, it must be true' (colloquial Italian, Cresti 1994: 41)

f. *en entrar jo, tots es   van   aixecar*
[in enter.INF I] all   themselves go.PRES.3PL get-up.INF
'when I entered, everyone got up' (Catalan, Hualde 1992: 251)

g. *am   plecat înainte de a ajunge ea*
have.PRES.1SG leave.PART [before of to arrive.INF she.NOM]
'I left before she arrived' (Romanian, Dobrovie-Sorin 1993: 89)

The obligatory nominative Case form assumed by such infinitival subjects demonstrates that the subject is Case-licensed by the infinitive. If the Case of the subject were licensed by the preposition which introduces the infinitival, then the pronominal subject would be marked oblique, contrary to fact. Moreover, as we shall see in sections 4.4.2 and 4.4.3, the mechanism for licensing nominative in such structures is related to verb-raising (see also De Miguel 1996: 45–6, n. 17).

4.3.3. *Lexical versus null*

In the examples in (16) above, we noted that the personal infinitive licenses a null pro subject. Such parallelism with finite verb forms is to be expected, since all languages which exhibit the personal infinitive are also pro-drop. In contrast to finite verbs, however, the occurrence of a null subject in conjunction with the personal infinitive is frequently driven by pragmatic considerations. Specifically, the presence of a pro subject is only possible if the pragmatic conditions are such that the content of the infinitival subject is salient elsewhere in the discourse and can be appropriately recovered (Pountain 1995: 20).

For example, in the Cosentino example in (28a) the prominence of the subject in the preceding question is such that the 3SG reference of the infinitival subject is immediately deducible, albeit with some degree of ambiguity. In the Sicilian examples in (28b–c), in contrast, the identification of the infinitival subject is pragmatically retrievable from the presence of a coreferential adjunct in the matrix clause, namely *cu iddu* 'to him' and *cci* 'for him'. A similar case is presented by the Italian example in (28d), where the 1PL reference of the infinitival subject is constructed in relation to the 1SG object clitic *mi* 'to me' in conjunction with the null 3SG matrix subject. Finally, in the Catalan and Occitan sentences in (28e–f) the identification of the 1SG pro subject is not overtly signalled anywhere in the sentence. Instead, its reference is pragmatically picked up by the discourse prominence associated with the speaker.

(28) a. *illu parte   lu prufessure? Lu vuogliu   vidire primu de*
        it leave.PRES.3SG the teacher_i   him_i want.PRES.1SG see.INF [before of
        partire
        leave.INF pro_i]
        'is the teacher leaving? I want to see him before he leaves'
        (Aprigliano (CS), Accattatis, 1895: §221)

   b. *si   vota   cu iddu p' aiutallu*
      himself_i turn.PRES.3SG with him_j [for help.INF-him_i pro_j]
      'he turns to him so that he will help him' (Sicily, Leone 1995: §85)

   c. *cci   ddumàiu   u luci ppi nun sèntiri   friddu*
      him.DAT_i light.PAST.1SG the light [for not feel.INF pro_i cold]
      'I lit him the fire so that he would not feel cold' (ibid.)

d. *mi ha   telefonato   per andare   al   mare*
me$_i$ have.PRES.3SG$_j$ telephone.PART [for go.INF pro$_{i+j}$ to-the sea
domenica prossima
sunday   next]
'he rang me for us to go to the seaside next Sunday' (colloquial Italian, Bertuccelli Papi 1991: 825)

e. *en /al   mirar-te,   vas   envermellir*
[in /to-the watch.INF-you$_i$ pro$_j$] go.PRES.2SG$_i$ blush.INF
'when I looked at you, you turned red' (Catalan, Rigau 1995: 284)

f. *on   as   tu demorat despuei non t'   aver   vist?*
where have.PRES.2SG you$_i$ stay.PART [since not you$_i$ have.INF see.PART pro$_j$]
'where have you been since I last saw you?' (Occitan, Wheeler1988: 270)

Alternatively, the reference of the infinitival subject may be overtly marked within the infinitival clause by morphosyntactic means. Such a case arises in the following examples, where the content of pro is identified by the overt agreement borne by a coreferent clitic anaphor:

(29) a. *vih,   che c'   è   vuluto   pe me   ricordà   stu*
see.IMP that it.DAT be.PRES.3SG want.PART [for myself$_i$ remember pro$_i$ this
nomme
name]
'you see what it took for me to remember this name' (NA, Scarpetta 1992: 270)

b. *ma nun è   decente, de t'   apprufittà   de na*
but not be.PRES.3SG decent of [yourself$_i$ take-advantage.INF pro$_i$ of a
furastera
foreigner]
'but is is not honest for you to take advantage of a foreign girl' (CS, Ziccarelli 1988: 61)

c. *t'   u ricu   p' un t'   u scurdari*
you it say.PRES.1SG [for not yourself$_i$ it forget.INF PRO$_i$]
'I'll tell you it so that you won't forget it' (Sicily, Leone 1995: §85)

d. *al   desmayarte,   empezaron a chillar*
[to-the faint.INF-yourself$_i$ pro$_i$] begin.PAST.3PL to shout.INF
'when you fainted, they began to shout' (Spanish, Rigau 1995: 286)

e. *en agenollar-me,   es sentí   una música celestial*
[in kneel.INF-myself$_i$ pro$_i$] itself hear.PAST.3SG a music celestial
'when I knelt down, celestial music was heard' (Catalan, Rigau 1995: 286)

4.4. PROPERTIES OF THE INFINITIVAL VERB

4.4.1. *Class*

As with finite adjunct clauses, there are no restrictions on the class of verb which can occur in personal infinitival clauses (Pérez-Vázquez 1997: §2), which may be copular (30a), auxiliary (30b), modal (30c), impersonal (30d), monotransitive (30e), ditransitive (30f), unergative (30g), unaccusative (30h), reflexive (30i), or impersonal passive (30j):

(30) a. *sa'   chi cci   vurrissi   pi **tu** essiri vera filici?*
       know.PRES.2SG what it.DAT want.COND.3SG [for you be.INF real   happy]
       'do you know what it would take for you to be really happy?' (PA, Pitré 1875: I, 320)

   b. *de haberlo   corregido   yo, . . .*
      [of have.INF-it correct.PART I]
      'if I had corrected it, . . .' (Spanish, Rigau 1995: 300)

   c. *p'   'a pute'   piglia', ve   dongo   io stu spicchietiello*
      [for proᵢ her be-able.INF take.INF] youᵢ give.PRES.1SG I this little-mirror
      'in order for you to catch her, I'll give you this little mirror' (Pomigliano d'Arco (NA), De Simone 1994: 452)

   d. *pi chiova   mo' cu stu cavudu, ci   vulerra   nu mirculu*
      [for rain.INF pro now with this heat] it.DAT want.COND.3SG a   miracle
      'for it to rain now would take a miracle' (CS)

   e. *stɔk   a fːɛ   lɪ rəkːjə'tedːə pə pːurtarə'tɪlːə **tu** a 'rːɔum*
      be.PRES.1SG to do.INF the orecchiette   [for take.INF-you-them you to Rome]
      'I am making orecchiette (pasta) for you to take them to Rome' (Altamura (BA), Loporcaro 1988: 261)

   f. *nun sgarrava   mai l' uri soi, senza dàricci corda **nuddu***
      not err.PAST.3SG never the hour its [without give.INF-it wind nobody]
      'it always kept time without ever having to be wound up' (Borgetto (PA), Pitré 1875: I, 406)

   g. *si unn' u   mancu canuscite   è   'nutile a chiangia **vua***
      if not him even know.PRES.2PL be.PRES.3SG useless to [cry.INF you]
      'if you don't even know him it's ridiculous for you to cry' (CS)

   h. *ce   vonno   10 minute pe partì **lo treno***
      it.DAT want.PRES.3PL 10 minutes [for leave.INF the train]
      'it'll take 10 minutes for the train to leave' (NA, Scarpetta 1992: 161)

   i. *l' unico mezzo pe' se   salvà **lloro** avit'   'a murì vuie*
      the only means [for themselves save.INF they] have.PRES.2PL by die.INF you
      'the only way for them to save themselves is for you to die' (NA, De Filippo 1973: 403)

j. *cci stava   sempri chiantata la furca, senza livarisi*
there be.PAST.3SG always planted   the gallows [without remove.INF-itself
mai
never]
'the gallows always stood erected without ever being removed'
(Ficarazzi (PA), Pitré 1875: IV, 109)

4.4.2. *Temporal properties*

Following proposals originating in Stowell (1982), we established in chapter
3 that OC infinitivals are characteristically marked by an obligatory
unrealized future reading (31a). Formally, we captured this generalization
by proposing that infinitival C hosts temporal features marking the reference
time (R_{INF}). Via a T-chain with the matrix Tense, the latter fixes the temporal
frame of the infinitive (E_{INF}) posterior to the matrix reference time (R_{MV}). The
presence of these temporal features in C was demonstrated to be overtly
marked by the choice of complementizer (namely *che/chi*) in dialects of the
Upper South, which predominantly use so-called finite clauses in OC
structures (31b). In NOC structures, by contrast, the tense of the embedded
verb does not carry the obligatory irrealis interpretation. Once again, in
dialects of the Upper South this difference in temporal interpretation is
replicated in the morphology of the complementizer, namely *ca*. Unlike *che*,
the reference time (R_{EV}) encoded by *ca* may locate the temporal frame of the
embedded verb (E_{EV}) as simultaneous (31c), anterior (31d) or posterior (31e)
to the matrix reference time (R_{MV}).

(31) a. *Gianni decide   di tornare*
Gianni$_i$ decide.PRES.3SG [$_{CP}$ t$_i$ of return.INF]
'Gianni decides to return' (Italian)

b. *Giuanne decire   che   torna*
Gianni$_i$ decide.PRES.3SG [$_{CP}$ that t$_i$ return.PRES.3SG]
'Gianni decides that he will return' (NA)

c. *Giuanne rice   ca sta   turnanno*
Gianni say.PRES.3SG [$_{CP}$ that be.PRES.3SG return.GER]
'Gianni says that he is returning' (NA)

d. *Giuanne rice   ca steva   turnanno*
Gianni say.PRES.3SG [$_{CP}$ that be.PAST.3SG return.GER]
'Gianni says that he was returning' (NA)

e. *Giuanne rice   ca torna*
Gianni say.PRES.3SG [$_{CP}$ that return.PRES.3SG]
'Gianni says that he will return' (NA)

In a similar fashion the tense of the personal infinitive, which we have demonstrated to be an NOC structure, displays identical referential freedom. Consider the following Cosentino examples:

(32) a. *pi sagliere Cicciu fin' a ccà c' è bulut' 'a man'*
   [for ascend.INF Ciccio up to here] it.DAT be.PRES.3SG want.PART the hand
   'i Dio
   of God

   b. **pi ra sagliuta 'i Cicciu fin' a ccà c' è bulut'*
   [for the ascension of Ciccio up to here] it.DAT be.PRES.3SG want.PART
   'a man' 'i Dio
   the hand of God
   'for Ciccio to come up all this way required divine intervention'

In (32a) the infinitive *sagliere* 'to come up' refers to a specific event as having occurred. In contrast, the event nominal *'a sagliuta* 'the coming up' in (32b) proves incompatible with the meaning of a specific event. This contrast can be straightforwardly accounted for if we assume that the personal infinitive, but not the event nominal, expresses tense (see Elordieta 1993; De Miguel 1996: 32–3). More specficially, we take the personal infinitive to express a non-specific tense, relative to the matrix predicate, unlike OC structures which carry an obligatory irrealis interpretation. This captures the fact that the tense of the personal infinitive is always interpretatively bound by that of the matrix. For instance, in (33) the temporal frame of the infinitive may be interpreted as past, present or future in accordance with the temporal specification of the matrix verb:

(33) *ascette /esce /hadd' âscì senza 'e*
   go-out.PAST.3SG /go-out.PRES.3SG /must.PRES.3SG go-out.INF [without of
   se n'addunà 'a mamma
   realize.INF the mother]
   'she went out/goes out/will go out without her mother realizing' (NA)

Lacking the overt inflections of *ca*-clauses, we maintain then that the personal infinitive has a 'weak' Tense, the content of which has to be specified. Rigau (1995: 287, 289) argues along similar lines for Spanish and Catalan, maintaining that the 'weak' Tense of the personal infinitival 'is the minimal expression of tense, a tense to be determined by an operator' (p. 287). Once related to such an operator, she argues that the latter can give content to this 'weak' Tense which then, in conjunction with (abstract) Agr, can license the infinitival subject's nominative Case (see also Pérez-Vázquez 1997: 137). In a similar vein, we suggest that, by virtue of being 'weak', Tense in the personal infinitive clause must raise overtly to C from where it can enter into a T-chain with the matrix Tense.[23] By raising to C, the content of the 'weak' infinitival Tense can then be determined by the matrix verb, an operation which endows the infinitival Tense with the necessary features to Case-mark its subject.

Nominative Case-licensing within the personal infinitive then falls out as a property of the C-T complex, perhaps related to the residual Verb-Second phenomena of Romance (Rizzi 1990a, b). On this view, we equate a 'weak' infinitival Tense with a strong V-feature on C which forces overt T-to-C raising to check this uninterpretable feature. By virtue of entering into this checking configuration with C, the 'weak' infinitival Tense can then be bound by the referential temporal features borne by C and license a well-formed T-chain.

4.4.3. Position

Finally, let us briefly review some evidence to illustrate that the infinitive raises overtly to C. Above we established that the personal infinitive is restricted to NOC environments, therefore typically occurring in non-subcategorized positions. If the personal infinitive raises to C, then this will also exclude it from appearing in complement position, since in many of the Romance languages (though not Spanish and Portuguese) infinitival complements are introduced by prepositional complementizers descended from AD and DE (Vincent 1988: 67–9). Therefore, a raised personal infinitive would be competing for the same position as that of the prepositional complementizer.[24,25] A parallel argument accounts for the incompatibility of the personal infinitive with the indirect interrogative complementizer se/si 'if':

(34) a. *'Ntoniu un sa   se   accettà o no*
         Antonio not know.PRES.3SG [CP if [TP accept.INF or not]]
         'Antonio doesn't know whether to accept or not' (CS)

      b. **Ntoniu un sa   se accettà   l'   atri   o no*
         Antonio not know.PRES.3SG [CP if accept.INF_i [TP t_i the others or not]]
         'Antonio doesn't know whether the others will accept or not' (CS)

The behaviour of wh-operators also supports the raising analysis of the infinitive. In Chomsky and Lasnik (1977) a structural condition known as the Doubly-Filled COMP Filter was proposed to exclude structures in which the C position is filled and [Spec, C] simultaneously hosts a wh-operator. Putting aside the question of how the Filter should be integrated within minimalist assumptions, we simply note that the generalization it expresses holds for the dialects of southern Italy, witness the Neapolitan example in (35a). The personal infinitive should therefore prove incompatible with wh-operators, since raising of the infinitive to C will give rise to a violation of the Doubly-Filled COMP Filter. This prediction is borne out by the ungrammaticality of (35b).

(35) a. *un saccio   comme (*che) Maria l'*
    not know.PRES.1SG [$_{SpecC}$ how [$_C$ (that) [$_{TP}$ Maria him
    acchiappaie
    seize.PAST.3SG]]]
    'I don't know how (*that) Maria seized him'

    b. **un saccio   comme l'   acchiappà   Maria*
    not know.PRES.1SG [$_{SpecC}$ how [$_C$ him seize.INF$_i$ [$_{TP}$ t$_i$ Maria]]]
    'I don't know how Maria seized him'

4.5. SUMMARY

Below we summarize the results of the preceding discussion.

- The personal infinitive is restricted to NOC environments, a fact which accounts for its general restriction to non-subcategorized positions;
- The infinitival subject may be null (pro) or lexical, is invariably Case-marked nominative and always occupies the postverbal position, except in Sicilian and Latin-American Spanish varieties where pronominal subjects may optionally occur in preverbal position;
- The infinitival verb may be of any semantico-syntactic class;
- The Tense of the infinitive is underspecified and must be interpreted by raising to C, where its temporal reference can be determined by the matrix verb via a T-chain;
- As a consequence of the latter operation, nominative Case can be licensed by the infinitival T now raised to C.

4.6. SUBJECT POSITIONS

4.6.1. *Preverbal pronominal subjects*

Having established that Sicilian and a number of Latin-American varieties optionally allow preverbal pronominal subjects, we now turn to examine what structural position they occupy. One possible analysis would be to treat such pronominals as topicalized or focused subjects. Typically, topicalized elements express old information salient in the previous discourse. While this is generally true of preverbal pronominal subjects, topichood is also a common property of all preverbal subjects, thereby rendering this test inconclusive. In addition, topicalized constituents are generally separated from the rest of the sentence by a comma-type intonation, which is lacking in conjunction with preverbal pronominal subjects. On the other hand, focused elements carry new information bearing a focal (typically contrastive) stress, an interpretation which does not hold of preverbal pronominal subjects, as highlighted by Suñer (1986: 193) who argues that it would be incorrect 'to suggest that these pronouns are emphatic/focused in any way'. Moreover, Morales (1988: 95, n. 6) argues that preverbal pronominal subjects in Puerto Rican Spanish 'se "cliticalizan" al infinitivo y forman con él una especie de unidad léxica' ('cliticize to the infinitive with which they form a type of lexical unit'). If this is so, then such pronominal subjects prove incompatible with a topicalized or focused reading.[26]

The topicalized or focused intepretation of the preverbal pronominal subject is not substantiated by syntactic evidence either. For instance, it is well known that quantifiers cannot be topicalized (Benincà 1988: §2.1.1.3; Rizzi 1998: 122). Yet, as the Sicilian (36a–b) and Latin-American (36c–d) examples below demonstrate,[27] bare quantifiers can occupy the preverbal position:

(36) a. *arristassuvi   patruni di tuttu 'u miu, senza **nuddu** sapillu!*
       remain.COND.2PL master of all   the mine [without nobody know.INF-it]
       'you would have all that is mine, without anybody knowing!'

    b. *chiudìu   'a porta pi **nuddu** nésciri*
       close.PAST.3SG the door [for nobody go-out.INF]
       'he closed the door so that nobody could go out'

    c. *una alma es   algo   demasiado delicado demasiado frágil,*
       a   soul be.PRES.3SG something too   delicate   too   fragile
       *para **uno** comprometerse   a mantenerla limpia de esta fangal*
       [for anyone compromise.INF-oneself to maintain.INF-itclean of this mud
       de la vida
       of the life]
       'a soul is something too delicate, too fragile, for anyone to commit oneself to keeping it clean of the mire of life' (Colombia (Antiquia), Kany 1951: 26)

    d. *lo hizo   sin   **nadie**   mandárselo*
       it do.PAST.3SG [without nobody order.INF-him-it]
       'he did it without anybody ordering him to' (ibid.)

Rizzi (1998) argues for an articulated structure of the CP-domain, in which focused and topicalized elements are held to respectively occupy a [Spec, Foc] and [Spec, Top] position, sandwiched between ForceP and FinP, as illustrated in (37):

(37)

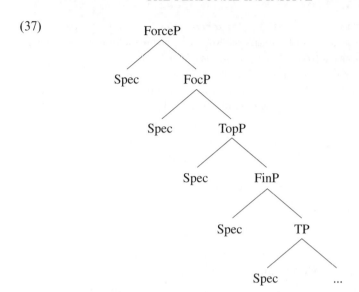

Given this structure, he argues that prepositional complementizers like *di/de* 'of' and *a* 'to' introducing infinitival clauses occupy the head of FinP. Therefore topicalized (henceforth underlined) and focused (henceforth capitalized) elements precede complementizers. This can be seen in the Italian example (38a), where the topic *il tuo libro* 'your book' precedes the complementizer *di* 'of'. By the same token, if preverbal pronominal subjects were topicalized or focused, then they too should precede so-called prepositional complementizers, contrary to fact (see 38b–c):

(38) a. *credo,*   *il   tuo   libro,*   *di apprezzarlo   molto*
         believe.PRES.1SG [SpecTop the your book [Fin of appreciate.INF-it much]]
         'as for your book, I believe that I appreciate it a lot' (Rizzi 1998: 120)

      b. *ni nni iemmu   pi ttu ristari sulu*
         leave.PAST.1PL [Fin for you stay.INF alone]
         'we left so that you could remain alone' (Sicily, La Fauci 1984: 122)

      c. *se fué   antes   de yo llegar*
         leave.PAST.3SG [before [Fin of I   arrive.INF]
         'he left before I arrived' (Colombia (Antiquia), Kany 1951: 126)

Instead, when an element is topicalized or focused, subject or otherwise, it precedes the prepositional introducer in all varieties, witness the following examples:

(39) a. *io capisco*   *so'*   *femmene, e*   *li*   *femmene pe fà*
     I   understand.PRES.1SG be.PRES.3PL women   and the women   [for do.INF
     toletta, nce   *vò*   *la mano de lo Cielo*
     wash]   it.DAT want.PRES.3SG the hand   of the heavens
     'I understand they are women, and for women to get ready requires
     divine intervention' (Scarpetta 1992: 213)

     b. *lu*   *figghiu pi livarisillu*   *di*   *supra cci dissi*   *'na vota . . .*
     the son   [for remove.INF-him from above] him tell.PAST.3SG one time
     'his son, to get rid of him, he told him one day. . .' (PA, Pitré 1875:
     II, 153)

     c. *per cierto mello ey*   *QUESTA BATALLA a spinire* **lui** **e**
     for certain better be.PRES.3SG this   battle   to [finish.INF he and
     io
     I]
     'certainly it is better for he and me to finish THIS BATTLE' (Old
     Neapolitan, McArthur n.d., 26)

     d. *e*   **TU** *pe t'*   *ascì*   *na parola da*   *la vocca nce*
     and you [for you come-out.INF a   word   from the mouth] it.DAT
     vonno   *de spuntunate*[28]
     want.PRES.3PL of urging
     'and YOU, to get a word out of your mouth takes some encour-
     agement' (Scarpetta 1992: 411)

It follows from this that preverbal pronominal subjects cannot be interpreted as topicalized or focused, since they should occur to the left of the
prepositional introducer, contrary to fact.

Finally, if preverbal subjects are indeed topicalized or focused in Sicilian
and Latin-American Spanish, this fails to explain why they have to be
pronominal. While topics do typically tend to be definite (Croft 1990: 161;
Lyons 1999: §6.1.2), this would still leave us without an account of why
definite nominals cannot be preverbal.

We conclude then that neither the semantic nor the syntactic properties of
preverbal pronominal subjects in Sicilian and Latin-American Spanish
supports treating them as topicalized or focused. Instead, we have seen
that such subjects are in semantic terms canonical subjects which form a
tight nexus with the infinitival verb (see Morales 1988: 95, n. 6). Below in
section 4.7.1 we shall provide a straightforward explanation for the restriction of the preverbal position to pronominal subjects in terms of the position
they occupy within the clause.

4.6.2. *Lexical and null subjects*

In section 4.4.3 we presented evidence to demonstrate that the infinitive
under T moves to C, from where it can enter into a T-chain and license

nominative Case. Consequently, the surface linear order infinitive + subject proves ambiguous, in that the subject could be in its merger position [Spec, *v*], or could have raised to [Spec, T].[29] In what follows, we shall present conclusive evidence to demonstrate that lexical subjects occupy the former position, whereas null subjects (namely pro) raise out of *v*-VP, though not to [Spec, T].[30]

We begin by considering negation. Adopting standard assumptions about the functional structure of the clause, we take the functional projection NegP to be sandwiched between TP and *v*-VP. On this view negative polarity elements like southern Italian *cchiù* 'no more' and *mai(e)* 'never', occupying the specifier position of NegP (Belletti 1994: §1; Rowlett 1998: ch. 3),[31] are predicted to precede the infinitival subject if the latter fails to raise to [Spec, T], as is borne out by the following examples:

(40) a. *pe nu fummà (*Giuanne) cchiù Giuanne, nce vô*
     [for not smoke.INF (Gianni) anymore Gianni] it.DAT want.PRES.3SG
     'a fine do monno
     the end of-the world
     'for Gianni not to smoke any more, you'll have a long wait' (NA)

   b. *mi ni fricava dua senza 'e mi vida (*nonnu) mai*
     mysyself some steal.PAST.1SG two [without of me see.INF (grandad) never
     nonnu
     grandad]
     'I would take a few without grandad ever seeing me' (CS)

Identical results obtain in relation to adverb position. As argued in Alexiadou (1997: §5.2), Laenzlinger (1998: 101–2) and Cinque (1999: §4.2.4), manner adverbs like southern Italian *buono/-u* 'well' are taken to mark the left-periphery of the *v*-VP configuration, occurring in a position higher than that of the merged subject and shifted PA-objects in an outer [Spec, *v*] (see section 7.5.2.1). We should then expect such adverbs to precede the infinitival subject in [Spec, *v*], as confirmed by (41a–b).[32]

(41) a. *pe se cocere (*'a torta) bona 'a torta, l' hêja fà*
     [for self- cook.INF (the cake) well the cake] it must.PRES.2SG make.INF
     stà rint' ô fuorno
     stand in the oven
     'for the cake to cook well, you must let it stand in the oven'
     (Boscotrecase (NA))

   b. *l' avia a tena pi ra manu prima 'e sapé camminà*
     him have.PAST.1SG to hold.INF by the hand [before of know.INF walk.INF
     *(*iddru) buonu iddru*
     (he) well he]
     'I had to hold him by the hand before he knew how to walk well'
     (San Biase (CS))

Burzio (1986: 129ff.) argues that existential constructions only license postverbal subjects. Under present assumptions this means that existential subjects must be in [Spec, *v*]. Consequently, pro, which must always raise out of [Spec, *v*] (see Cardinaletti 1997), proves ungrammatical. This is shown by the Italian example in (42):

(42) *(*io / *pro)* ci   sono   **io** alla festa
    (I   /pro)   there be.PRES.1SG I   at-the party
    'I am at the party'

Lexical infinitival subjects should then prove grammatical in existential constructions, for they remain *in situ*, whereas pro, which we claim moves out of *v*P, should be ungrammatical. The contrast in examples (43a–b) versus (43c) confirm this prediction:

(43) a. *si   è   accorto   che nel letto invece 'e ce   sta' **io**,*
       himself be.PRES.3SG realize.PART that in-the bed [instead of there be.INF I]
       ce   steva   Mario
       there be.PAST.3SG Mario
       'he realized that instead of me being in the bed, there was Mario'
       (NA, De Filippo 1973: 144)

    b. *si 'nveci di essirci **iu**, cca, c' era   suo fratello, o so'*
       if [instead of be.INF-there I   here] there be.PAST.3SG his brother or his
       patri
       father
       'if instead of me being here, there were his brother or father'
       (Belpasso (CT), Martoglio 1979)

    c. **pe   ce stà ncopp' ô   commune hadda   esse na*
       [for pro there be.INF up   at-the town-hall] must.PRES.3SG be.INF a
       questione mpurtante
       question important
       'for me/you/him/her/us/them to be at the town hall, it must be something important' (NA)

Similar contrasts arise in conjunction with copular sentences. Following Moro (1993), we take copular sentences to consist of a copula + small clause (SC), as in (44a). In the canonical case, the copular subject position is filled by the small clause subject (44b), whereas in inverse copular sentences it is the predicative nominal which raises (44c). Significantly, in the former case, but not the latter, the small clause subject may be pro:

(44) a. *è   Marco /pro 'o prufessore* (NA)
       be.PRES.3SG [SC Marco /pro the teacher]

    b. *Marco / pro è   'o prufessore* (canonical copula)
       Marco$_i$ / pro$_i$ be.PRES.3SG [SC t$_i$ the teacher]
       'Marco / pro is the teacher'

c. *'o   prufessore è*   *Marco* / *pro   (inverse copula)
the teacher$_i$ be.PRES.3SG [$_{SC}$ Marco / pro t$_i$]
'the teacher is Marco/pro'

Now consider the following Neapolitan copular sentences embedded within
a personal infinitival clause:

(45) a. *pe essere   Marco prufessore ce   vulesse   nu miraculo*
[for be.INF [$_{SC}$ Marco   teacher]]   it.DAT want.COND.3SG a   miracle
'for Marco to be a teacher would require a miracle'

b. **pe essere prufessore Marco   . . .*
[for be.INF teacher$_i$ [$_{SC}$ Marco t$_i$ . . .]]
'for Marco to be a teacher. . .'

c. *pe essere   prufessore . . .*
[for pro$_i$ be.INF [$_{SC}$ t$_i$ teacher   . . .]]
'for pro to be a teacher. . .'

As it stands, (45a) is ambiguous in that it is impossible to tell whether *Marco*
remains within the small clause, as indicated in (43a), or whether it has raised
to [Spec, T]. However, the ungrammaticality of (45b), where the order
prufessore + Marco demonstrates that the predicative nominal has raised
to [Spec, T], proves that neither argument can raise out of the small clause.[33]
Consequently, *Marco* in (45a) must be *in situ*. In contrast, the grammaticality
of pro in (45c) indicates once again that it must have raised out of [Spec, *v*].

Another sure indicator of the *v*P-internal position of lexical subjects is
provided by their position with respect to various object complements. In
chapter 2 we established that objects in the PA move overtly to an outer
[Spec, *v*] above that occupied by the merged subject, whereas objects in the
UA or SD remain within VP. Now consider the Cosentino sentences in (46)
and (47):

(46) a. *pi si spusà a Lisandra **Cicciu**, ci   vo   ra fine du*
[for marry.INF PA Lisandra Ciccio]   it.DAT want.PRES.3SG the end of-the
munnu
world
'for Ciccio to marry Lisandra, you'll have a long wait'

b. *pi si spusà **Cicciu** A LISANDRA, ci   vo   ra fine du*
[for marry.INF Ciccio PA Lisandra]   it.DAT want.PRES.3SG the end of-the
munnu
world
'for Ciccio to marry LISANDRA, you'll have a long wait'

(47) a. *?m'   era   azatu   prima 'i sparà **mamma** 'a tavula*
myself be.PAST.1SG get-up.PART [before of clear.INF mum   the table]
'I got up before mum cleared the table'

b. *m'   era   azatu   prima 'i sparà   'a tavula* **MAMMA**
  myself be.PAST.ISG get-up.PART [before of clear.INF the table   mum
'I went out before MUM cleared the table'

(46a) demonstrates the unmarked word order for objects in the PA which raise to the outer [Spec, *v*], where they precede the *v*P-internal subject. The reverse word order evidenced in (46b) only proves grammatical with a right-focus interpretation of the object in the PA. Though proving somewhat marginal, the order subject + object in (47a) presents the unmarked position of objects in the UA, an order consistent with the *v*P-internal analysis of the infinitival subject. Once again, the reverse order (47b) is only possible if the infinitival subject carries narrow focus.

Let us now turn to the less than perfect status of (47a) in which the object in the UA follows the infinitival subject. Why should it be that objects in the PA (see 46a) yield perfectly acceptable structures, whereas those in the UA produce, at best, marginal results? The answer, we suggest, lies in some form of a transitivity restriction, as proposed by Alexiadou and Anagnostopoulou (1998a, b, c) to account for the fact, as observed in a wide range of languages, that subject and object cannot both remain *in situ*. Consider by way of example the following English expletive sentences taken from Alexiadou and Anagnostopoulou (1998c: 3):

(48) a. *there arrived* [$_{VP}$ *a man*]

   b. **there finished* [$_{VP}$ *somebody the assignment*]

In (48a) the logical subject *a man* remains VP-internal and the D-feature on T is checked by merging the expletive *there* in [Spec, T]. An identical derivation obtains in the ungrammatical (48b), with the exception that VP also contains an object complement *the assignment*. To account for these and similar data, Alexiadou and Anagnostopoulou propose the Subject In-situ Generalization (SIG), which amounts to saying that at least the subject or object must vacate the *v*-VP complex before Spell-Out. Essentially, the SIG is derived from Case-theoretic considerations which prevent T (+Vb) from being able to check two Case features (that of the subject and of the object) at LF. It follows from this that either the subject or object, if not both, must raise overtly to check its Case features.[34]

Returning to the contrast in grammaticality judgements evidenced by such pairs as (46a) and (47a), these can now be interpreted in terms of the SIG. In the former, the accusative Case feature on the object in the PA is checked overtly in the outer [Spec, *v*], allowing the subject to check its nominative feature at LF. In (47a), by contrast, neither the Case feature of the subject nor that of the object is checked before Spell-Out. Consequently, neither argument can check its Case feature at LF, resulting in the marginal status of this example. Clearly, such facts only find an explanation if the lexical infinitival subject remains in [Spec, *v*].

Note, on the other hand, that if pro in the personal infinitive raises out of *v*-VP before Spell-Out, as we are claiming, then objects in the UA should prove entirely grammatical in these contexts. This prediction is borne out, as the following examples demonstrate:

(49) a. *ma che volete,   è   stato il desiderio di   me*
but what want.PRES.2PL be.PRES.3SG be.PART the desire   of [pro$_i$ myself$_i$

   fà   na bella fumata!
do.INF a lovely smoke]
'but what do you expect, I just felt like having a nice smoke!' (NA, Scarpetta 1992: 132)

b. *unn' è   statu pussibile a   ni   vida   'u filmi*
not be.PRES.3SG be.PART possible to [pro$_i$ ourselves$_i$ see.INF the film]
'it wasn't possible for us to watch the film' (CS)

c. *ddà Gesù Cristu cci   fabbricau 'na Chiesa pi   fari*
there Jesus Christ him.DAT$_i$ build.PAST.3SG a church [for pro$_i$ make.INF

   orazioni a sò piaciri
speeches to his pleasure]
'there Jesus Christ built him a church so that he could preach to his heart's content' (Resuttano (CL), Pitré 1875: III, 39)

d. *al   tocar   la pòrta, lo gos se botèt   a jaupar*
[at-the pro$_{arb}$ knock.INF the door] the dog begin.PAST.3SG to bark.INF
'when there was a knock at the door, the dog began to bark' (Occitan, Wheeler 1988: 270)

By the same token, we predict that objects in the UA should prove grammatical in Sicilian whenever a pronominal subject appears preverbally in a *v*P-external position, as confirmed by (50a). Naturally, objects in the PA also prove grammatical in such contexts (50b):

(50) a. *pi iu fari   tantu   beni a lu Cummentu ci   haju*
[for I do.INF so-much good to the covent]   it.DAT have.PRES.1SG

   appizzatu la saluti[35]
attach.PART the health
'because of my doing so much good for the Convent, I have neglected my health' (Polizzi-Generosa (PA), Pitré 1875: III, 233)

b. *comu mai è   possibili, voscenza pigghiari a mè figghia,*
how ever be.PRES.3SG possible [you take.INF PA my daughter]

   menticchi jeu nun haju   nè tegnu?
while   I   not receive.PRES.1SG nor have.PRES.1SG
'how is it possible for you to take my daughter while I am left with nothing?' (Marsala (TP), Pitré 1875: IV,230)

Significantly, Cresti (1994: 40–1) notes in her analysis of the personal infinitive in the Tuscan variety of San Gimignano (SI) that the infinitive is predominantly of the unaccusative class. In a similar fashion, Cuneo (1997: 109) maintains that in the dialect of Cicagna (GE) transitive infinitives with full lexical objects prove ungrammatical (see 51a–b):

(51) a. *prüma de purtâ   i   franchi u Giôśe   /u Giôśe   i   franchî],
        [before of bring.INF the money the Giuseppe /the Giuseppe the money]
        pasià   dū   tènpu
        pass.FUT.3SG some time
        'before Giuseppe brings the money, some time will pass'

     b. *nu l' è   guâi fàsile, aî   u s-ciöpu in prâe /in
        not s.CL be.PRES.3SG not easy [have.INF the rifle   a priest /a
        prâe u s-ciöpu
        priest the rifle]
        'it is not very likely for a priest to have a rifle'

On our assumption that the subject is νP-internal, the ungrammaticality of (51a–b) ensues from the SIG: at LF neither the Case of the subject nor of the object can be checked. In contrast, Cuneo observes that transitive infinitives with clitic objects prove grammatical, as is also true of the other varieties under consideration:[36]

(52) a. me   piglio   'o giurnale primma 'e s'   'o leggere
        myself take.PRES.1SG the paper [before of himself it read.INF
        fratema
        brother.POSS.1SG]
        'I'll take the paper before my brother reads it' (NA)

     b. avia   cacciatu   'a corchia pi s'   'a mangià 'u cane
        have.PAST.1SG remove.PART the skin [for itself it eat.INF the dog]
        'I had removed the skin so that the dog could eat it' (CS)

     c. 'nta stu modu s'aliticavanu senza purtariccilla   nuddu
        in this way argue.PAST.3PL [without take.INF-her.DAT-it nobody]
        'in this way they continued to argue among themselves without anybody taking it to her' (Polizzi-Generosa (PA), Pitré 1875: III, 318)

     d. l' è   ina côsa fàsile da capîla   i   fènti]
        s.CL be.PRES.3SG a thing easy of [understand.INF-it the kids]
        'it is easy for the kids to understand it' (Cicagna (GE), Cueno 1997: 106)

     e. per avertelo   detto Luigi, devono   saperlo   proprio
        [for have.INF-you-it say.PART Luigi must.PRES.3PL know.INF-it precisely
        tutti
        everyone
        'for Luigi to have told you, absolutely everybody must know' (colloquial Italian, ibid., 104)

f. *on   as   tu demorat despuei   non t' aver   vist?*
where have.PRES.2SG you be.PART [since   pro not you have.INF see.PART]
'where have you been since I last saw you?' (Occitan, Wheeler 1988: 270)

g. *en /al   mirar-te,   vas   envermellir*
[in /to-the pro look-at.INF-you] go.PRES.2SG blush.INF
'when I looked at you, you turned red' (Catalan, Rigau 1995: 284)

These facts follow from our arguments in section 2.3 that clitics represent the overt spell-out of the verb's D-feature and other related features such as Case. On this view, examples like those in (52) prove grammatical because the Case of the object is checked before Spell-Out on the clitic. Hence, the nominative Case feature of the infinitival subject in [Spec, *v*] can be legitimately checked at LF.[37]

To sum up, the evidence reviewed above is entirely consistent with the proposed *v*P-internal analysis of lexical infinitival subjects and the *v*P-external analysis of pro subjects. Note that in the latter case, raising of pro out of *v*P falls out in accordance with the 'general cross-linguistic fact that pronouns tend to move overtly' (Collins 1997: 34). Indeed, Cardinaletti and Starke (1994) and Cardinaletti (1997: 35) suggest that pro is a 'deficient' (namely clitic-like) pronoun which must move to a Case-checking position before Spell-Out.

4.7. EPP: MERGE/MOVE D^{max}/D^{min}

So far we have established that in the personal infinitive construction the infinitive moves to C and that lexical nominal subjects always remain *in situ* within *v*P. Pronominal subjects, on the other hand, behave differently. In Sicilian and Latin-American varieties overt pronominal subjects may remain in [Spec, *v*] or move to a position preceding the infinitive raised to C. In contrast, null pronominals, namely pro, always move out of [Spec, *v*] in all varieties. These facts are summarized in Table 4.1:

Table 4.1 Infinitival subject positions

	Preverbal	Postverbal
Lexical nominal subjects	none	all varieties
Overt pronominal subjects	Sicilian, L-A Spanish	all varieties
Null pronominal subjects	all varieties	none

There arise then two questions: To what position do overt (Sicilian, Latin-American Spanish) and null preverbal pronominals raise? And, why is this preverbal position restricted to pronominals? The answers to both of these questions, we suggest, lie in the various ways that the EPP (namely the D-feature on infinitival T) may be checked.

4.7.1. *Lexical preverbal pronominal subjects*

According to general minimalist principles (see section 1.3.4 and Chomsky 1995: §4.3), checking configurations are established by one of the two operations Merge and Move, which introduce a feature into the checking domain of a given head by substitution (X^{max}) or adjunction (X^{min}). Beginning with Merge, this operation can only obtain when the EPP checker is an expletive element, since θ-related categories are merged within the *v*-VP configuration (Chomsky 1995: 313). Consider the substitution option, as exemplified in (53a). The thematic subject *a letter* remains within *v*-VP and the strong D-feature on T is checked by merging the expletive DP *there* in [Spec, T]. The adjunction option is exemplified by expletive subject clitics in northern Italian dialects. For example, in the Turinese example (53b), the EPP is checked by merging an expletive clitic *a* [a] (< ILLAM) on T within the latter's checking domain. The Move operation, in contrast, obtains when the EPP feature on T is checked by a thematic element raised from its merger position within the *v*-VP configuration into the checking domain of T. The substitution case is exemplified by (53c), where the subject *a letter* raises to [Spec, T].

(53) a. [$_{\text{SpecT}}$ ***there*** T [$_{v\text{-VP}}$ *arrived a letter*]

   b.   **a** 'vɛŋa   ka'tɛjɛ

      [$_\text{T}$ it be-necessary.PRES.3SG$_i$ [$_{v\text{-VP}}$ t$_i$] buy.INF-them

      'it is necessary to buy them' (TO, Parry 1997: 243)

   c. [$_{\text{SpecT}}$ ***a letter***$_i$ T [$_{v\text{-VP}}$ *arrived* t$_i$]

What then of the corrresponding case of Move by adjunction, namely raising of a D to adjoin to T? We suggest that this case is instantiated by the examples of preverbal pronominals in the Sicilian and Latin-American Spanish personal infinitive, as exemplified by the derivation of the Sicilian example in (54a):

(54) a. *chi cci   voli   pi   **tu** libbiràriti?*

      what it.DAT want.PRES.3SG for [$_\text{CP}$ you$_i$ free.INF-yourself$_j$ [$_\text{TP}$ t$_j$ [$_{v\text{-VP}}$ t$_i$ t$_j$]]]

      'what will it take for you to free yourself?' (PA, Pitré 1875: II, 240)

   b. *lu patri ci   avia   fattu   fari un puzzu pi (*l'*

      the father them.DAT have.PAST.3SG make.PART make a well   [for (the

      acqua) *'un cci   ammancari l' acqua*

      water) not them.DAT be-lacking.INF the water]

      'the father had had built a well for them so that they would have water' (PA, ibid., 370)

In (54a) The infinitive raises out of v-VP through T and up to C. In order to check the strong D-feature on T, the pronominal *tu* 'you' raises from [Spec, v] to adjoin to T now in C. Recall that within the bare phrase structure approach (see section 1.3.3; Chomsky 1995: §4.3), we distinguish between categories that do not project any further (X^{max}) and those that do not project at all (X^{min}). Within this conception of phrase structure, a category can then be simultaneously classed as X^{min} (head) and X^{max} (phrasal). This is the case of pronominals like Sicilian *tu*, which do not project any further and which do not project at all, as schematized in (55a):[38]

(55)

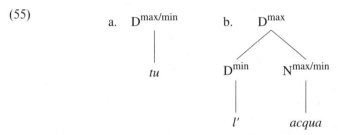

It follows from this that only pronominals in Sicilian and Latin-American Spanish structures like that in (54a) can raise overtly to adjoin to T, since these are heads (that do not project any further).[39] In contrast, nominal subjects like *l'acqua* 'the water' in (54b) are D^{max} categories (see 55b) and cannot therefore adjoin to the X^{min} category T, as formalized in Chomsky's (1995: 253) Chain Uniformity Condition in (56):

(56) A chain is uniform with regard to phrase structure status

Observe that if we were to maintain that preverbal pronominals in these varieties moved to [Spec, C], a move in any case independently ruled out by the Doubly-Filled COMP Filter, then this would fail to explain why nominal subjects cannot occur preverbally. Essentially, therefore, raising of the infinitival verb to C has the effect of constraining the type of subject (namely D^{min}) that can overtly raise to check the strong D-feature on T.[40] The present analysis also provides us with a principled account of the ungrammaticality of preverbal subjects in sentences like (57):

(57) *chistu t'   havi   a   sèrviri   pri (*tu sulu e   li   toi)*
      this   you have.PRES.3SG to serve.INF [for (you only and the yours)
      mangiare tu sulu e   li   toi
      eat.INF   you only and the yours]
      'this will have to do for your parents and you alone to eat' (Polizzi-Generosa (PA, Pitré 1875: 273)

If EPP-checking involves head-adjunction to T, it is clear that subjects like *tu sulu e li toi* 'you alone and your parents' cannot raise overtly, even if they contain a pronominal, since they are phrasal categories and not heads.

However, the Sicilian and Latin-American corpora present a number of apparent exceptions to this claim. Consider first the Latin-American examples in (58):

(58) a. *no encuentro razón para **a** **gente** murmurar*
       not find.PRES.1SG reason [for   the people gossip.INF]
       'I see no reason for anybody to gossip' (Panama, Kany 1951: 126)

   b. *este salón es   para **la gente** bailar*
      this room be.PRES.3SG [for   the people dance.INF]
      'this room is for dancing' (ibid.)

In (58) the preverbal infinitival subject is the quantifier *(l)a gente* 'one, people, everybody'. Its literal meaning, however, is 'the people', consisting of the definite article *(l)a* 'the' + noun *gente* 'people', apparently then an X^{max} category (DP) and hence unable to head-adjoin to T under C. It is reasonable to assume, though, that in this usage *l(a) gente* is a fossilized expression, more felicitously analysed, synchronically at least, as a bare $Q^{max/min}$.

Now consider the following Sicilian and Latin-American examples:

(59) a. *partì   senza (so pa') virillu   **so pa'***
       leave.PAST.3SG [without (his father) see.INF-him his father]
       'he left without his father seeing him' (Sicily, Leone 1995: §85)

   b. *Maistà, pi (so' figghia) stari bona so' figghia cci*
      Majesty [for (your daughter) be.INF well your daughter] it.DAT
      voli   ca sparassinu   li so' fraati
      WANT.PRES.3SG that shoot.SUBJ.3PL the her brothers
      'Majesty, for your daughter to get well, you have to have her brothers shot' (PA, Pitré 1875: II, 21)

   c. *a los tres meses de **mamá** morir*
      at the three months [of mum   die.INF]
      'three months after mum died' (Santo Domingo, Kany 1951: 126)

The Sicilian examples in (59a–b) appear in their source texts with a postverbal subject. However, as pointed out by Delia Bentley (personal communication), the preverbal position given in parentheses is also an option for these subjects. The problem presented by the examples in (59) is then how a phrasal category (DP) can adjoin to a head category T, in apparent violation of the Uniformity Condition. Significantly, the infinitival subject in all three examples in (59) is a kinship term. It is well known that kinship terms display a strong cross-linguistic tendency to undergo overt N-to-D raising, presumably as a consequence of their intrinsic referential value (see Longobardi 1994). A similar tendency is observable in many of the Romance languages. By way of example, consider the following Sicilian possessive structures:

(60) a.   *('u)   mè   libbru
            [D (the) [NP [A my] book]]
            'my book'

      b.   (*'u) mè   patri
            [D (the)   my [N father]i [NP ti]]
            'my father'

      c. *   mè   beddu patri
            [D my [NP lovely   father]i [NP ti]]
            'my lovely father'

In the possessive structure (60a), the D position is filled by the definite
article 'u, which takes a nominal complement mè libbru 'my book'. Non-
kinship terms like libbru do not then raise overtly to D, since this position is
always obligatorily filled by the article. In (60b), on the other hand, the
definite article proves ungrammatical, a behaviour peculiar to kinship
possessive structures. The complementary distribution of the definite article
and kinship terms suggests that in (60b) the D position is filled by the
proclitic possessive mè 'my', to which the kinship term patri 'father' adjoins
in the syntax.[41] Overt N-to-D raising in (60b) is further confirmed by the
impossibility of inserting a prenominal adjective like beddu 'lovely' between
possessive and kinship term in (60c). Such structures are excluded by the
Chain Uniformity Condition, which precludes raising of a phrasal category
(NP) to a head (D). If the kinship term in (60b) did not raise to D, then the
ungrammaticality of (60c) would remain obscure.

Returning to our examples in (59a–c), we now have a principled account
of the availability of the preverbal position with kinship (possessive) phrases,
since these raise overtly to D. Adjoined to D^{min}, the kinship term therefores
qualifies as a legimite candidate for head-adjunction to T under C.

Analysing preverbal pronominal subjects as adjoined to the infinitival
verb under C also explains why they must follow prepositional inherent Case
markers (for example, reflexes of AD, DE) and (prepositional) adverbs (for
example, equivalents of 'without') which introduce the personal infinitive, as
well as focused and topicalized elements. Moreover, the proposed analysis
captures the fact that only negation can separate the adjoined pronoun from
the infinitive.

Finally, we also have a straightforward account for Morales' (1988: 95,
n. 6) observation that in Puerto Rican Spanish preverbal pronominal
subjects 'cliticize to the infinitive with which they form a type of lexical
unit.' Like clitics, which are also simultaneously $D^{max/min}$, preverbal
pronominal subjects adjoin to a verbal head, namely T, before Spell-Out.
We are thus led to the controversial conclusion that preverbal pronominals
in the Sicilian and Latin-American Spanish personal infinitive are in fact
subject clitics.[42] In light of their clitic status, an even stronger conclusion,
that appears justified, would be to treat such infinitival forms with preverbal

pronominal subjects in Sicilian and Latin-American Spanish not as personal infinitives at all but, rather, as inflected infinitives.

4.7.2. Null subjects: referential and expletive pro

In the previous section we saw how the EPP can be checked by Merge or Move, by substitution or adjunction. The various cases are presented in table 4.2:

Table 4.2 Overt EPP-checkers

	Substitution	*Adjunction*
Merge	***there** arrived a letter*	a_{clitic} 'veŋta
Move	***a letter** arrived*	tu_{clitic} *libbiràriti*

The examples in table 4.2, however, all involve instances of phonetically overt categories which check the D-feature on T. Nonetheless, the operations Merge and Move are neutral to the overt/covert distinction. We should therefore also expect examples of covert categories in these same cases, as exemplified in table 4.3:

Table 4.3 Covert EPP-checkers

	Substitution	Adjunction
Merge	***pro** vengono tante donne*	pro_{clitic} *escere u maritu*
Move	***pro** vengono*	pro_{clitic} *me puté sanà*

Beginning with the Merge operation, the substitution and adjunction cases are given in (61a–b), rspectively:

(61) a. *vengono   tante   donne*
      [$_{SpecT}$ **pro** come.PRES.3PL$_i$ [$_{v\text{-}VP}$ t$_i$ so-many women]]
      'lots of women are coming' (Italian)

   b. *ppe   escere   u   maritu   cce   vuonnu*
      for [$_{CP}$ pro$_{clitic}$ go-out.INF$_i$ [$_{TP}$ t$_i$ [$_{v\text{-}VP}$ t$_i$ the husband]]] it.DAT want.PRES.3PL
      n'atri   vint'   anni
      another twenty years
      'you'll have to wait another twenty years before my husbands comes out' (CS, De Marco 1991: 28)

In the Italian example (61a), the logical subject *tante donne* 'lots of ladies' remains *in situ* within *v*-VP. The EPP feature on T is therefore checked by a null expletive pro merged in [Spec, T]. Similarly, in the Cosentino personal infinitival clause in (61b), the logical subject *'u maritu* 'my husband' is *v*P-internal and the infinitive raised to C has an unchecked D-feature. As we have seen, the nominal subject cannot raise to [Spec, T], since this position is not projected in personal infinitives (see n. 40). Neither can the nominal subject raise to adjoin to T under C because it is a D^{max} category. Once again, raising of the infinitive to C restricts the type of category which can check the D-feature on T. The only way the derivation can converge is if an expletive pro is merged to an adjoined position on T. As in the Sicilian and Latin-American Spanish examples of preverbal pronominal subjects, this expletive pro is a clitic since it is a $D^{max/min}$ category adjoined to a verbal head.[43]

Let us, finally, consider the Move operation. The substitution and adjunction options are illustrated in (62a–b), respectively:

(62) a.   *vengono*

        [$_{SpecT}$ pro$_i$ come.PRES.3PL$_j$ [$_{v\text{-}VP}$ t$_i$ t$_j$]]

        'they come' (Italian)

   b. *a me nisciuno dà*   *la vera medicina pe*   *me*

     to me nobody   give.PRES.3SG the real   medicine   for [$_{CP}$ pro$_{clitic_i}$ myself

     puté   *sanà*

     be-able.INF   cure.INF$_j$ [$_{TP}$ t$_j$ [$_{v\text{-}VP}$ t$_i$ t$_j$]]]

     'nobody will give me the real medicine for me to be able to cure myself' (NA, Scarpetta 1992: 368)

As argued above, the particular properties and licensing conditions of referential pro are such that it must always raise overtly out of [Spec, *v*] to check its Case and D-features on T before Spell-Out (Cardinaletti and Starke 1994; Cardinaletti 1997). This is the case in both (62a) and (62b). In the former, pro raises to [Spec, T], whereas in the latter it adjoins to T under C, a possibility sanctioned by its ambivalent $D^{max/min}$ categorial status. In other words, referential pro in (62b) is a covert subject clitic, the raising of which is analoguous to that of overt pronominal clitics in Sicilian and Latin-American Spanish. We thus have a case of an inflected infinitive with abstract agreement, the latter taking the form of a preverbal pro cliticized to the infinitive.

Observe that the option of merging an expletive clitic pro under T in (62b), as in examples like (61b), forcing referential pro to remain *v*P-internal, is excluded since referential pro would not be licensed, causing the derivation to crash. Therefore, in cases like (62b) considerations of economy which otherwise favour the less costly option of merging an expletive clitic pro are overriden by the particular licensing conditions of referential pro.[44]

4.7.3. *Summary*

We have established that overt raising of the infinitive (in T) to C in the personal infinitive construction restricts EPP-checking to the Head-head configuration. This explains why only D^{min} categories (namely overt/covert pronouns, bare quantifiers and kinship terms) can occur in the preverbal position and why D^{max} categories must remain v-VP-internal. Furthermore, the option of raising overt categories (pronominals, bare quantifiers and kinships terms) in Sicilian and Latin-American Spanish, but not in other Romance varieties, follows from the optional versus obligatory selection of an expletive pro, respectively. In the latter an expletive pro is always drawn from the lexicon in forming the numeration, but only optionally so in the former.

5

AUXILIARY INFINITIVAL CONSTRUCTIONS

5.1. INTRODUCTION

In the present chapter we shall investigate the syntax of infinitival complements of a closed class of verbal predicates which, broadly speaking, are distinguished by their reduced semantico-syntactic autonomy and, hence, potential candidates for auxiliary status. Such verbs can be further divided into two classes: (i) modal-aspectual verbs, and (ii) conative verbs. We shall approach the question of the syntax of such verbs from two distinct angles. In the first part of the chapter, we shall establish a number of criteria to distinguish modal-aspectuals from conative verbs, and to distinguish both of these, in turn, from main verbs which also take an infinitival complement. In the final part of the chapter, we shall investigate the appropriate structural representations to be attributed to infinitival complements to such verbs.

5.2. AUXILIARY VERB STATUS

As a preliminary working hypothesis, we shall invoke the following two properties to individuate auxiliaries. Firstly, auxiliary + dependent infinitive constructions invariably instance a monoclausal structure, contrary to the OC verbs examined in chapter 3 which, when combined with an infinitival CP, yield a biclausal structure. Secondly, we assume that the auxiliary does not alter the argument frame of the infinitival verb (see Ramat 1987: 16; and The Heir-Apparent Principle of Harris and Campbell 1995: 193), in that the auxiliary inherits and governs the syntax of the infinitival complement. Based on these two properties, we can determine *a priori* whether a given verb is an auxiliary or not by considering a range of local phenomena, namely whether such auxiliary constructions can license certain operations which are assumed to hold exclusively of simplex clauses. The verbs that we initially propose for auxiliary status in Neapolitan are given below:

    (i) a. **Modals**: *puté(re)* 'can, may' (epistemic/deontic), *dovere* (obsolete)/ *avé(re d)'a* 'must (epistemic/deontic); future marker', *sapé(re) (a)* 'can, know how', *vulé(re)* 'future marker';

b. **Aspectuals**: *stà(re) pe'* 'to be about to', *stà(re) a* 'to be X-ing', *cessà(re) de* (obsolete)/*terminà(re) de* (obsolete)/*fernì(re) 'e* 'to finish', *(i)ncommenzare/accummencià a* 'to begin', *cuntinuà(re) a* 'to continue', *turnà(re) a* 'to keep on X-ing, do again';

(ii) **Conatives**: *pru(v)à(re) a/vedé(re) 'e/truvà(re) 'e/cercà(re) 'e* 'to try to';

In order to create a controlled experimental environment and highlight the particular syntactic behaviour of the potential auxiliaries above, in the following discussion we shall compare the behaviour of the auxiliaries with that of main verbs that take OC infinitival CPs.

5.2.1. *Cliticization*

As in all Romance varieties, Neapolitan clitic pronouns must cliticize to the verb of their clause, as in (1):

(1) *liggette   'o libbro* ⇒ *'o liggette*
    read.PAST.1SG the book   it$_i$ read.PAST.1SG pro$_i$
    'I read the book' ⇒ 'I read it'

However, as the example in (2a) indicates, cliticization is a local operation in that the clitic *'o* 'it' is blocked from climbing to the matrix OC verb *se fida* 'feels like'. Instead, the clitic must cliticize to its associated verb in the embedded CP (2b):

(2) a. **nun s'   'o fida   'e   leggere*
      not   himself it$_i$ feel-like.PRES.3SG of [$_{CP}$ t$_i$ read.INF pro$_i$]

   b. *nun se   fida   'e   'o leggere*
      not himself feel-like.PRES.3SG of [$_{CP}$ it$_i$ read.INF pro$_i$]
      'he doesn't feel like reading it'

Now, in conjunction with modals (3a–b) and aspectuals (4a–b), clitics must invariably climb to the modal-aspectival verb (see Sornicola 1997a: 337):

(3) a. *nce   pô   /hadda   /sà   /vô*
    them.DAT$_i$ be-able.PRES.3SG /must.PRES.3SG /know.PRES.3SG /want.PRES.3SG
    parlà
    [speak.INF pro$_i$]

   b. **pô   /hadda   /sà   /vô   nce*
    be-able.PRES.3SG /must.PRES.3SG /know.PRES.3SG /want.PRES.3SG them.DAT$_i$
    parlà
    [speak.INF pro$_i$]
    'he can/must (will)/knows how to/will speak to them'

(4) a. *nce   accummenci' a /cuntinu'   a /fernesce   'e*
        them.DAT$_i$ begin.PRES.3SG to /continue.PRES.3SG to /finish.PRES.3SG of
        /stà   pe' /stà   a parlà
        /be.PRES.3SG for /be.PRES.3SG to [speak.INF pro$_i$]

    b. **accummenci' a /cuntinu'   a /fernese   'e /stà   pe'*
        begin.PRES.3SG to /continue.PRES.3SG to /finish.PRES.3SG of /be.PRES.3SG for
        /stà   a nce   parlà
        /be.PRES.3SG to [them$_i$ speak.INF pro$_i$]
        'he begins to/continues to/finishes/is about to/is speak(ing) to them'

These data imply that such verbs yield a monoclausal structure. However, the aspectual *turnà a* allows both the clitic to climb (5a) and to remain *in situ* (5b) proclitic to its associated infinitive:

(5) a. *nce   torna   a parlà*
        them.DAT$_i$ return.PRES.3SG to [speak.INF pro$_i$]
        'he keeps on speaking to them'

    b. *torna   a nce   parlà*
        return.PRES.3SG to [them.DAT$_i$ speak.INF pro$_i$]
        'he is going back to speak to them'

As the glosses demonstrate, the examples with *turnà* in (5a–b) are not synonymous. As a lexical main verb of motion meaning 'to return' (5b), the clitic must surface with its associated infinitive on a par with (2b). By contrast, the clitic must climb when *turnà* is an exponent of iterative aspect (5a). We conclude therefore that *qua* aspectual predicate *turnà* patterns identically to the other aspectual verbs in (4).

   Let us finally examine conative verbs:

(6) a. *nce   prov'   a /vede   'e /cerca   'e parlà*
        them.DAT$_i$ try.PRES.3SG to /see.PRES.3SG of /search.PRES.3SG of [speak.INF pro$_i$]

    b. *prov'   a /vede   'e /cerca   'e nce   parlà*
        try.PRES.3SG to /see.PRES.3SG of /search.PRES.3SG of [them.DAT speak.INF pro$_i$]
        'he tries to speak to them'

These verbs apparently exhibit an ambivalent status between main verbs and auxiliaries in that clitic climbing is entirely optional.

5.2.2. Binding

Another local process that we can employ as a diagnostic is the binding of anaphors. According to Principle A of the Binding Theory (see Chomsky 1981 and subsequent work), an anaphor must be bound within its *complete functional complex* (CFC). For our present purposes, we can interpret the

CFC to simply mean the clause within which the anaphor itself occurs. Consider first the example in (7):

(7)　　*lavo　　　　a me stesso　/*a isso stesso　/*a lloro stesse*
　　　pro$_i$ wash.PRES.1SG PA me self$_i$　/PA him self$_j$　/PA them selves$_k$
　　　'I wash myself/*himself/*themselves'

Only the 1SG anaphor *a me stesso* 'myself' gives grammatical results in (7), since it finds an appropriate agreeing binder within its clause, namely the pro subject co-indexed with *lavo*, equally endowed with 1SG ϕ-features. Perhaps surprisingly, a sentence such as (7) embedded under a main verb like *fidarse* 'to feel like' is also well-formed:

(8)　　*nu mme fido　　　　'e　　　lavà　　a me stesso*
　　　pro$_i$ not myself feel-like.PRES.1SG of [$_{CP}$ t$_i$ wash.INF PA me self$_i$]
　　　'I don't feel like washing myself'

However, the subject position of the dependent infinitival clause contains DP-trace, co-indexed with the matrix subject, which can bind the anaphor within its clause. If we embed (7) under an object control verb such as *avvisà* 'to warn, inform', by contrast, the anaphor cannot be licensed since its only potential binder is in the matrix clause:

(9)　*　*avviso　　a Giuanne 'e　　lavà　　a me stesso*
　　　pro$_i$ warn.PRES.1SG PA Gianni$_j$　of [$_{CP}$ t$_j$ wash.INF PA me self$_i$]
　　　'I warn Giuanne to wash myself'

　　Example (9) therefore provides incontrovertible proof that the binding of anaphors is subject to strict locality conditions. Consequently, we can profitably exploit this aspect of binding as a diagnostic for identifying monoclausal structures. As can be seen, if (7) is embedded under a modal (10a) or aspectual (10b) verb, the same anaphor proves grammatical:

(10)　a.　*pozzo　　　/aggia　　　/saccio　　　/voglio*
　　　　　pro$_i$ be-able.PRES.1SG /must.PRES.1SG /know.PRES.1SG /want.PRES.1SG
　　　　　lavà　　a me stesso
　　　　　[wash.INF PA me self$_i$]
　　　　　'I can/must/know how to/will wash myself'

　　　b.　*accummenci' a　/cuntinuo　　　a /fernesco　　'e /sto*
　　　　　pro$_i$ begin.PRES.1SG to /continue.PRES.1SG to /finish.PRES.1SG of /be.PRES.1SG
　　　　　pe' /sto'　　a /torno　　a lavà　　a me stesso
　　　　　for /be.PRES.1SG to /return.PRES to [wash.INF PA me self$_i$]
　　　　　'I begin to/continue to/finish/I am about to/I am/I carry on wash(ing) myself'

Therefore, in order for the anaphor *a me stesso* to be bound in the examples in (10), the auxiliary + dependent infinitive must instance a monoclausal structure. Analogously, grammaticality obtains in conjunction with conative predicates:

(11)   *provo   a /cerco   'e /vedo   'e lavà   a me stesso*
         pro$_i$ try.PRES.1SG to /search.PRES.1SG of /see.PRES.1SG of [wash.INF PA me   self$_i$]
         'I'll try to wash myself'

5.2.3. *Middle-passivizer se*

Unlike the related Italian *si* construction, Neapolitan middle SE > *se* is a passivizer morpheme and as such is exclusively used in conjunction with transitives,[1] invariably triggering verb agreement with the underlying object which surfaces as subject in either [V, DP] (12a) or [Spec, T] (12b):

(12) a.   *se portano   /*se porta   tanta   cate*
             [pro$_i$] se carry.PRES.3PL /se   carry.PRES.3SG [so-many buckets]$_i$

      b. *tanta   cate   se portano   /*se porta*
             [so-many buckets]$_i$ se carry.PRES.3PL /se   carry.PRES.3SG [t$_i$]
             'so many buckets are carried'

Yet, in conjunction with main verbs that take an infinitival complement, a complement of the latter retains its object status, failing to trigger agreement with the matrix verb, and *se* acquires an indefinite [+generic] interpretation:[2]

(13) *se ajuta   /*se ajutano   a   purtà   'e cate*
       se help.PRES.3SG /se   help.PRES.3PL to [$_{CP}$ carry.INF the buckets]
       'one helps to carry the buckets'

Therefore, the domain of application of passivizer *se* is unmistakably local like the canonical passive, restricted to promoting its clausal object. It follows that if modal-aspectuals and conative verbs do yield monoclausal structures, they ought to license passivizer *se*. Indeed, this prediction is borne out by the following examples:

(14) a. *'e cate   se ponno   /s' hanna   /se vonno   purtà*
          the buckets se be-able.PRES.3PL /se   must.PRES.3PL /se   want.PRES.3PL carry.INF
          'the buckets can be/must be/will be carried'

      b. *'e cate   s' accummencian' a /se cuntinuan'   a /se fernesceno*
          the buckets se begin.PRES.3PL   to /se continue.PRES.3PL to /se finish.PRES.3PL
          'e /se tornan'   a /se stanno   pe' purtà
          of /se return.PRES.3PL to /se be.PRES.3PL for carry.INF
          'the buckets begin/continue/finish/keep on/are about (to) be(ing) carried'

      c. *'e cate   se provan'   a /se cercano   'e /se veden'   'e*
          the buckets se try.PRES.3PL to /se search.PRES.3PL of /se see.PRES.3PL of
          purtà
          carry.INF
          'one tries to carry the buckets'

5.2.4. *Focalization*

In Neapolitan, arguments (DPs, CPs) of main verbs may be moved into clause initial position to occupy a focus position, where they receive a contrastive reading:

(15) a. *'O FRANGESE me   mparo,   nun l' ingrese*
     the French$_i$ myself teach.PRES.1SG t$_i$ not the English
     '(it's) FRENCH I'll learn, not English'

   b. *A NUTÀ me   mparo,   unn' âbballà*
      to swim.INF$_i$ myself teach.PRES.1SG t$_i$ not to-dance.INF
      'TO SWIM I'll learn, not to dance'

However, such a device is not available in conjunction with modals and aspectuals:

(16) a. **NUTÀ pozzo   /aggia   /saccio   /voglio,*
      swim.INF$_i$ be-able.PRES.1SG /must.PRES.1SG /know.PRES.1SG /want.PRES.1SG t$_i$
      unn' abballà
      not   dance.INF
      'TO-SWIM I can/must/know how to/will, not dance'

   b. **A /E' /PE' NUTÀ accummencio /cuntinuo   /fernesco*
      to /of /for swim.INF$_i$ begin.PRES.1SG /continue.PRES.1SG /finish.PRES.1SG
      /sto'   /torno   unn' a /'e /pe abballà
      /be.PRES.1SG /return.PRES.1SG t$_i$ not to /of /for dance.INF
      '(TO) SWIM(MING) I begin/continue/finish/am (about to)/keep on, not dance(ing)'

It would appear that the examples in (16) prove ungrammatical on account of a general morphological constraint (see below) that requires the modal-aspectual verb to invariably occur contiguous to a dependent infinitive. Given our assumption that such verbs are auxiliaries in a monoclausal structure with their following infinitive, the ungrammaticality of (16a–b) follows.

As for conative verbs, they give rise to an ambivalent structure, neither wholly ill-formed nor well-formed:

(17) *?A /'E NUTÀ provo   /cerco   /vedo,   unn' a /'e*
     to /of swim.INF$_i$ try.PRES.1SG /search.PRES.1SG /see.PRES.1SG t$_i$ not to /of
     abballà
     dance.INF
     'TO SWIM I'll try, not dance'

As for the clitic climbing test, it would appear again that the conative verbs share both properties of auxiliaries and main verbs.

5.2.5. *Summary*

The results of the four preliminary tests that we have proposed to identify auxiliary status in Neapolitan are summarized in table 5.1:

Table 5.1 Tests for monoclausality

Test	Modal/Aspectual	Conative	Main verb
Clitic climbing	+	±	−
Anaphor binding	+	+	−
Middle-Passivizer *se*	+	+	−
Focalization	−	±	+

The tests constructed to individuate a monoclausal structure, and hence auxiliary verb status, substantiate that the modal-aspectuals have auxiliary status. In contrast, conative verbs produce ambivalent results, exhibiting auxiliary properties with respect to binding and middle-passivizer *se*, and main verb properties with respect to clitic climbing and focalization. However, even in the latter two tests, auxiliary behaviour is not entirely excluded insofar as clitic climbing appears to be optional and focalization of the infinitival complement proves marginal. Clearly, the intermediate position between auxiliary and main verb status displayed by conative verbs should equally be captured in structural terms, in such a way that the properties of infinitives to conative verbs can be derived straightforwardly. It is to this question that we now turn.

5.3. REDUCED INFINITIVAL CLAUSES

The point of departure and conclusion of the proposed analysis is based on the assumption that modal-aspectuals select for a *v*P infinitival complement, a non-argument, whereas conative verbs select for a TP infinitival complement, equally a non-argument. In this respect, both classes of verb differ from the OC infinitival clauses of chapter 3 which invariably project to CP and have argument status, in that they exhibit a reduced clausal structure. In order to highlight this difference, we shall once again compare the behaviour of modal-aspectuals and conatives with that of main verbs that take an infinitival CP. We begin then by presenting various pieces of evidence in support of the claim that the infinitival complements to modal-aspectual and conative verbs are reduced clauses, namely they do not project to CP.

5.3.1. *Infinitival wh-extraction*

Main verbs take an argument infinitival clause, namely a CP, which, as expected, can be extracted by the pro-argument *wh*-phrase *che* 'what':

(18) a. *Giuanne se mette scuorno 'e   dicere bucìe*
   Gianni   be-ashamed.PRES.3SG of [CP tell.INF lies]
   'Gianni is ashamed of telling lies'

   b. *'e che se mette scuorno Giuanne?*
   of what$_i$ be-ashamed.PRES.3SG Gianni   [CP t$_i$]
   'of what is Gianni ashamed?'

However, modal-aspectuals (19) and conative verbs (20) pattern differently with respect to the possibility of allowing *wh*-extraction of the infinitive:

(19) a. *Giuanne pô   /hadda   /sà   /vô*
   Gianni   be-able.PRES.3SG/must.PRES.3SG /know.PRES.3SG /want.PRES.3SG
   dicere bucìe
   [vP tell.INF   lies]
   'Gianni may/must/knows how to/will tell lies'

   b. **che   pô   /hadda   /sà   /bô*
   what$_i$ be-able.PRES.3SG /must.PRES.3SG /know.PRES.3SG /want.PRES.3SG
   Giuanne?
   [vP t$_i$] Gianni
   'what can/must/knows/will Gianni?'

(20) a. *Giuanne accummenci' a /cuntinu'   a /fernesce   'e*
   Gianni   begin.PRES.3SG to /continue.PRES.3SG to /finish.PRES.3SG of/
   /turn'   a /stà   pe' /stà   a   dicere bucìe
   /return.PRES.3SG to /be.PRES.3SG for /be.PRES.3SG to [vP tell.INF lies]
   'Gianni begins/continues/finishes/keeps on/is about to/is (to) tell(ing) lies'

   b. **a /'e /pe' che   accummencia /cuntinua   /fernesce*
   to /of /for what$_i$ begin.PRES.3SG /continue.PRES.3SG /finish.PRES.3SG
   /turna   /stà   Giuanne?
   /return.PRES.3SG /be.PRES.3SG [vP t$_i$] Gianni
   'what does Gianni begin/continue/finish/keep on/is about to?'

Infinitival extraction is only possible with main verbs as in (18) because their infinitival complements are arguments, namely CPs. Consequently, extraction is ruled out in (19b) and (20b) since we are arguing that these infinitival complements are not arguments, namely *v*Ps. Moreover, it is a known fact of Romance that *v*P extraction is an illicit operation (see Zagona 1988).

A parallel behaviour obtains when the infinitival complement to a conative is *wh*-extracted, since these are TPs:

(21) a. *Giuanne prov'*   *a*   */cerca*   *'e*   */trova*   *'e*
   Gianni   try.PRES.3SG to /search.PRES.3SG of /find.PRES.3SG of
   /vede   *'e*   *dicere bucìe*
   /see.PRES.3SG of [TP say.INF lies]
   'Gianni tries to tell lies'

   b. **a /'e che prova   /cerca   /trova   /vede*
   to /of what$_i$ try.PRES.3SG /search.PRES.3SG /find.PRES.3SG /see.PRES.3SG
       Giuanne?
   [TP t$_i$] Gianni
   'what does Gianni try?'

5.3.2. *Clitic referencing*

This is similar to *wh*-extraction, only the infinitival complements of main verbs can be substituted and referenced by a clitic pronoun since these have argument (CP) status:

(22) a. *Giuanne se   mette   scuorno 'e   dicere bucìe*
   Gianni   himself put.PRES.3SG shame   of [CP tell.INF lies]
   'Gianni is ashamed of telling lies'

   b. *Giuanne se   ne   mette   scuorno*
   Gianni   himself of-it$_i$ put.PRES.3SG shame [CP t$_i$]
   'Gianni is ashamed of it'

If we are correct in maintaining that infinitival complements to modal (23) and aspectual (24) verbs are *v*Ps, they ought not allow clitic substitution, as is indeed borne out:

(23) a. *Giuanne pô   /hadda   /sà   /vô*
   Gianni   be-able.PRES.3SG /must.PRES.3SG /know.PRES.3SG /want.PRES.3SG
       dicere bucìe
   [vP tell.INF lies]
   'Gianni may/must/can/will tell lies'

   b. **Giuanne 'o pô   /hadda   /sà   /bô*
   Gianni   it$_i$ be-able.PRES.3SG /must.PRES.3SG /know.PRES.3SG /want.PRES.3SG
   [vP t$_i$]
   'Gianni may/must/can/will it'

(24) a. *Giuanne accummenci' a /cuntinu'   a /fernesce   'e*
   Gianni   begin.PRES.3SG to /continue.PRES.3SG to /finish.PRES.3SG of
   /turn'   a /stà   pe' /stà   a   dicere bucìe
   /return.PRES.3SG to /be.PRES.3SG for /be.PRES.3SG to [vP tell.INF lies]
   'Gianni begins/continues/finishes/keeps on/is about to/is (to) tell(ing) lies'

    b. *Giuanne ce accummencia /ce cuntinua   /ne fernesce
       Gianni   it$_i$ begin.PRES.3SG /it$_i$ continue.PRES.3SG /it$_i$ finish.PRES.3SG
       /ce turna   /ce stà
       /it$_i$ return.PRES.3SG /it$_i$ be.PRES.3SG [$_{vP}$ t$_i$]
       'Gianni begins/continues/finishes/keeps on/is about it'

As for conative verbs, these yield ambivalent results in that cliticization of the infinitival complement ranges from marginal to downright ungrammatical:

(25) a. Giuanne prov'   a /cerca   'e /trova   'e
       Gianni   try.PRES.3SG to /search.PRES.3SG of /find.PRES.3SG of
       /vede   'e   dicere bucìe
       /see.PRES.3SG of [$_{TP}$ tell.INF lies]
       'Gianni tries to tell lies'

      b. Giuanne ?ce prova   /*ne cerca   /*ne trova   /*ne
       Gianni   it$_i$ try.PRES.3SG /it$_i$ search.PRES.3SG /it$_i$ find.PRES.3SG /it$_i$
       vede
       see.PRES.3SG [$_{TP}$ t$_i$]
       'Gianni tries it'

      c. Giuanne prova/*cerca/*trova/*vede
       'Gianni tries to'

However, a perfectly acceptable way to achieve the same results, at least with pruvà, is to simply delete the infinitival constituent, as illustrated in (25c). On the assumption that infinitival complements to conatives are TPs, the infelicitous use of a clitic in (25b) follows straightforwardly since such clitics only reference arguments.

5.3.3. Impersonal passivization

As a relation-changing operation, passivization promotes the underlying object complement to subject status. Clearly, we may use impersonal passivization as a diagnostic to test for argumenthood of the infinitival complements to modal-aspectual and conative verbs:

(26) a. *è   stato pututo   /avut''a /saputo /vuluto magnà
       be.PRES.3SG be.PART be-able.PART /must.PART /know.PART /want.PART   eat.INF
       'it was able to/had to/known to/wanted to eat'

      b. *è   stato fernuto 'e /cuntinuat' a /accummenciat' a
       be.PRES.3SG be.PART finish.PART of /continue.PART to /begin.PART   to
       /turnat' a magnà
       /return.PART to eat.INF
       'it was finished/continued/begun/kept on (to) eat(ing)'

c. *è   stato   pruvat' a /truvat'   'e /cercat'   'e /vedut'   'e
be.PRES.3SG be.PART try.PART to /find.PART of /search.PART of /see.PART of
magnà
eat.INF
'it was tried to eat'

The fact that impersonal passivization yields ill-formed results across the board provides incontrovertible proof that modal-aspectuals and conatives do not subcategorize for an infinitival CP argument.

5.3.4. *Tensed complements*

The possibility of selecting a tensed CP complement is available to main verbs since they invariably subcategorize for a CP complement, be it tensed or infinitival:

(27) a. *me mecco scuorno 'e /voglio   fà   l' ammore cu*
be-ashamed.PRES.1SG of /want.PRES.1SG [CP make.INF the love   with
chella   llà
that-one there]
'I am ashamed of/I want to court(ing) her'

b. *me mecco scuorno /voglio   che Giuanne fà   l'*
be-ashamed.PRES.1SG /want.PRES.1SG [CP that Gianni   make.PRES.3SG the
ammore cu   chella   llà
love   with that-one there]
'I am ashamed/want that Gianni courts her'

Modal-aspectuals and conatives, by contrast, never allow a tensed CP complement since they only subcategorize for a constituent smaller than CP:

(28) a. **pô   /hadda   /sa   /vô   che*
be-able.PRES.3SG /must.PRES.3SG /know.PRES.3SG /want.PRES.3SG that
parte
leave.PRES.3SG
'he can/must/knows how (= can)/will that he leave'

b. **accummencia /cuntinua   /fernesce   /torna   (a l'e)*
begin.PRES.3SG /continue.PRES.3SG /finish.PRES.3SG /return.PRES.3SG (to /of)
che parte
that leave.PRES.3SG
'he begins/continues/finishes/keeps on that he leaves'

c. **prova   /vede   /trova   /cerca   (a l'e) che*
try.PRES.3SG /see.PRES.3SG /find.PRES.3SG /search.PRES.3SG (to /of) that
parte
leave.PRES.3SG
'he tries that he leaves'

5.3.5. *Functional structure*

The discussion in sections 5.3.1 to 5.3.4 has been principally concerned with demonstrating that main verbs subcategorize for a CP complement, whereas modal-aspectuals and conatives subcategorize for a constituent smaller than CP. So far we have taken this constituent to be *v*P and TP, respectively. In what follows, we shall provide some evidence for this view. The most natural way to test this claim and to differentiate between a *v*P and a TP constituent is to adduce evidence for the presence or absence of an inflectional projection, namely T, in the infinitival complements in question from visible surface phenomena. For example, if such infinitival complements can be shown to overtly manifest functional categories associated with verbal inflection, then we can conclude that they must contain a T node in order to host such categories.

We begin therefore by considering whether infinitival complements to the verbs in question can exhibit temporal or aspectual distinctions. If so, this will indicate that the infinitival constituent projects to at least TP. Consider first the modal-aspectuals in (29)-(32):

(29) a. *ha'   vut''a   piglià 'e sorde*
     have.PRES.3SG must.PART take.INF the money

   b. **hadda ' vé   pigliato 'e sorde*
     must.PRES.3SG have.INF take.PART the money
     'he must have taken the money' (epistemic)
     'he had to take the money' (deontic)

(30) a. *nn' ha   pututo   astipà tanta sorde*
     not have.PRES.3SG be-able.PART keep.INF so-much money

   b. **num pô   avé   astipato tanta sorde*
     not be-able.PRES.3SG have.INF keep.PART so-much money
     'he couldn't have put by much money' (epistemic)
     'he was not able to put by much money' (deontic)

(31) a. *l' hâ   'ccummenciat' a capì*
     it have.PRES.3SG begin.PART   to understand.INF

   b. **l' accummencia âvé   capito*
     it begin.PRES.3SG to-have.INF understand.INF
     'he has begun to understand it'
     'he begins to have understood it'

(32) a. *ha   cuntinuat'   a sgarrà*
     have.PRES.3SG continue.PART to err.INF

   b. **cuntinua   âvé   sgarrato*
     continue.PRES.3SG to-have.INF err.PART
     'he has continued to be mistaken'
     'he continues to have been mistaken'

The evidence of examples (29)-(32) indicates that all temporal and aspectual distinctions must appear on the modal-aspectual and never on the infinitive.[3] This pattern is immediately accounted for under the proposed *v*P analysis of such infinitival constituents, since there is no inflectional node to host such temporal/aspectual distinctions. Consequently, all temporal/ aspectual distinctions necessarily appear on the modal-aspectual. Observe furthermore that the epistemic/deontic uses of *avé(re d)'a* 'must' and *puté(re)* 'can' are not formally distinguished as they are, say, in the corresponding Italian examples in (33) and (34):[4]

(33) a. *deve   avere   preso   i   soldi*   (epistemic)
          must.PRES.3SG have.INF take.PART the money

      b. *ha   dovuto   prendere i   soldi*   (deontic)
          have.PRES.3SG   must.PART take.INF   the money

(34) a. *può   avere   messo   da parte tanti   soldi* (epistemic)
          be-able.PRES.3SG have.INF put.PART by side   so-much money

      b. *ha   potuto   mettere da parte tanti   soldi* (deontic)
          have.PRES.3SG   be-able.PART put.INF by side   so-much money

Rather, the epistemic/deontic distinction found with such verbs, which in Italian corresponds to a discrete structural distinction in terms of raising versus control predicates,[5] respectively, finds no structural correlate in Neapolitan (compare also French *il a dû prendre l'argent* 'he must have taken/he had to take the money'). This does not hold, however, of infinitives to main verbs which can host temporal/aspectual oppositions:

(35) a. *comme si dubbetammo 'e l'   avé   visto   cu ll' uocchie*
          as   if doubt.PRES.1PL of [him have.INF see.PART with the eyes
          nuoste
          our]
          'as if we doubt having seen him with our own eyes'

      b. *comme si ammo   dubbetato 'e 'o   vedé cu ll' uocchie*
          as   if have.PRES.1PL doubt.PART of [him see.INF with the eyes
          nuoste
          our]
          'as if we have doubted seeing him with our own eyes'

Examples (35a–b) are not synonymous. If the aspectual auxiliary is realized on the control verb (35b), then the temporal/aspectual specifications of the latter are directly affected by a concomitant past time reading of the following infinitive. In (35a), in contrast, the auxiliary has temporal/ aspectual scope only over its embedded clause and not over the matrix clause predicate. This follows as an immediate consequence of our proposal that infinitives to main verbs are CP complements, which therefore contain a

T projection within which such temporal/aspectual oppositions are generated.

Finally, let us look at the behaviour of conatives in conjunction with such temporal/aspectual distinctions:

(36) a. *pruvamm' âvé   aggiustat' 'a seggia primma che se ne turna*
    try.PRES.1PL [to-have.INF repair.PART the chair   before   that return.PRES.3SG
    'a   'o   spitale
    from the   hospital]
    'we'll try and have repaired the chair before he comes out of hospital'

   b. *ammo   pruvat' âggiust'   â seggia primma che se ne turna*
    have.PRES.1PL try.PART [to-repair.INF the chair   before   that return.PRES.3SG
    'a   'o   spitale
    from the   hospital]
    'we've tried to repair the chair before he comes out of hospital'

Given our preliminary assumptions regarding conative verbs, the results of (36) are fully expected. They behave like main verbs in that they too contain a T projection capable of generating such temporal/aspectual distinctions. On the basis of this first test, we tentatively conclude that the infinitival constituents to modal-aspectuals are indeed *v*Ps, whereas those to the conative verbs are TPs.

The final test that we shall adopt concerns negation. It is standardly assumed that negation is represented by a functional head Neg generated between TP and VP (Belletti 1990; 1994). It stands to reason, therefore, that if such infinitival constituents are able to host a Neg head, namely *nun* (or one of its various allomorphs), we shall have another piece of evidence for the presence of a T node. The correctness of this approach is confirmed by (37):

(37) *dubbeto   'e   num puté   venì*
    doubt.PRES.1SG of [CP [TP not   be-able.INF come.INF]]
    'I doubt that I won't be able to come'

The main verb *dubbetà* 'to doubt' selects for a CP complement. Consequently, the embedded infinitive may be independently negated since it contains a position for the Neg head *num* within its functional structure. Similarly, conative verbs equally allow their infinitival complement to be independently negated, as expected given their proposed TP status:

(38) a. *cerca   'e   nun te fa'   abberé quanno nce*
    search.IMP.2SG of [TP not you make.INF see.INF when   there
    trase!
    enter.PRES.2SG]
    'try not to get yourself seen when you enter in there'

b. *heja   pruvà a   nun spennere tutti chilli sorde*
must.PRES.3SG try.INF to [TP not   spend.INF all   that   money]
'you must try not to spend all that money'

On the other hand, modal-aspectuals do not permit independent negation of their infinitival complement in line with their proposed *v*P status:

(39) a. **putimmo   /amma   /sapimmo   /vulimmo   num*
be-able.PRES.1PL /must.PRES.1PL /know.PRES.1PL /want.PRES.1PL [vP not
fa'   tropp'   ammuina
make.INF too-much noise]
'we may/must/know how to/will not make too much noise'

b. **accummenciamm' a /cuntinuamm' a /fernimmo   'e*
begin.PRES.1PL   to /continue.PRES.1PL to /finish.PRES.1PL of
/turnamm'   a   num fa'   tropp' ammuina
/return.PRES.1PL to [vP not   make.INF too-much noise]
'we begin/continue/finish/keep on not (to) make(ing) too much noise'

To conclude, on the basis of a series of tests, we have established that the infinitival complements of modal-aspectuals and conatives do not exhibit any of the properties of argumenthood. As a consequence, we have shown that the infinitival complements of such verbs exhibit a reduced clause structure. Specifically, infinitival complements to modal-aspectuals lack any functional structure, as confirmed by the ungrammaticality of infinitival temporal/aspectual distinctions and independent negation of the infinitive. On the other hand, infinitival complements to conative verbs do license such inflectionally-related categories and are therefore more appropriately analysed as TP constituents.

5.4. COMPARATIVE SOUTHERN EVIDENCE

So far our discussion has been restricted to Neapolitan, highlighting a number of differences displayed by infinitival complements to modal-aspectual and conative verbs *vis-à-vis* infinitival complements to main verbs. Although this area of southern Italian infinitival complementation still remains largely unexplored, the available, albeit scanty, evidence of related southern dialects also points to a similar tripartite distinction between infinitival complements to modal-auxiliaries, conatives and main verbs. In what follows, we shall therefore bring together some evidence from the behaviour of infinitival complementation in conjunction with modal-aspectual and conative verbs in such dialects, suggesting that our conclusions regarding Neapolitan hold more generally of southern dialects.

We begin our discussion with an examination of the syntax of modal-aspectual predicates. Like their Neapolitan counterparts, such predicates license a number of strictly local phenomena, which can be understood as a consequence of their taking a *v*P infinitival complement in a monoclausal structure. For instance, discussing clitic climbing in conjunction with these verbs, Rohlfs (1968: 173) observes that in literary registers of Italian clitic climbing does not generally obtain, a tendency which he also ascribes to northern Italian dialects. In contrast, he describes clitic climbing as the norm in southern dialects, citing by way of example the sentences in (40) (clitics given in bold type):

(40) a. *se   potaría   levá*
          himself be-able.COND.3SG get-up.INF
          'he could get up' (Campania)

    b. ***lu** pozzu   dimenticare*
          it be.able.PRES.1SG forget.INF
          'I may forget it' (Calabria)

    c. ***se**   vaci   a piazzà*
          himself go.PRES.3SG to place.INF
          'he goes to sit down' (Apulia)

    d. ***ce**   vuleme   arrubbà lu porche?*
          him.DAT want.PRES.1PL steal.INF the pig
          'do we want to steal his pig?' (Abruzzo)

    e. ***jə   lə** vujjə   mannà*
          him.DAT it want.PRES.1SG send.INF
          'I want to send it to him' (Abruzzo)

Analogous conclusions are reported for the Abruzzese dialect of Teramo by Savini (1881: 101–2) who notes that in conjunction with *puté* 'can' the clitic 'si prefigge sempre al verbo che regge l'infinito, e non si suffigge mai all'infinito' ('is always prefixed to the matrix verb, never attaching to the infinitive'). Thus, irrespective of the presence/absence of the negator *n'* 'not' in (41), which determines proclisis (41a–b) versus enclisis (41c–d), respectively, the clitics *ze/se* 'one' and *(l)u* 'it' invariably attach to *puté* 'can':

(41) a. *n' **ze** pó   fá*
          not one be-able.PRES.3SG do.INF
          'it cannot be done'

    b. ***nu** pó   fá*
          not-it be-able.PRES.3SG do.INF
          'he cannot do it'

    c. *po**se**   fá*
          be-able.PRES.3SG-one do.INF
          'it can be done'

d. *polu*   *fa*
   be-able.PRES.3SG-it   do.INF
   'he can do it'

Similarly, Meliadò (1994: 95) observes that in the dialect of Reggio Calabria '[n]elle espressioni in cui l'azione di un verbo è completata da un verbo servile, nel nostro dialetto il pronome oggettivo precede sempre il verbo servile: Es. *u pozzu rrivari*' ('in expressions in which the action of a verb is supplemented by an auxiliary verb, in our dialect the object pronoun always precedes the auxiliary: e.g. *u pozzu rrivari* "I can reach him" (literally "I him can reach")'). This view is echoed by Leone (1995: §66) for Sicilian, who notes 'una certa tendenza a trasferire a sinistra il pronome o altra particella atona in casi come . . . *cci potti iri* ("ci son potuto andare")' ('a definite tendency to transfer pronouns or other clitic particles to the left in cases like . . . *ci potti iri* "I could go there" (literally "I there could go")').

By far the most comprehensive study of infinitival complementation in conjunction with aspectual-modal verbs is provided by Lombardi's (1997: ch. 2, 3; 1998a) investigations of such structures in Calabrian dialects. She argues that in Calabrian dialects, including those southern dialects which also present the option of a MODO-clause alongside a traditional infinitival clause, infinitival complements display a high degree of grammatical integration in conjunction with such auxiliaries. In particular, Lombardi demonstrates on the basis of a number of locally constrained phenomena like those examined above for Neapolitan that aspectual-modal predicates subcategorize for a VP infinitival complement, giving rise to a monoclausal structure.[6] It follows from this that clitic climbing from the infinitive to the aspectual-modal predicate proves obligatory, witness the northern and southern Calabrian examples in (42) and (43), respectively:

(42) a. *e*   *poterano*   *mbentare megliu*
     them be-able.COND.3PL invent.INF   better
     'they could invent them better' (Lombardi 1997: 146)

   b. *t'*   *e*   *trovari prontu a cci jettari 'nu bicchieri 'e*
      yourself must.PRES.2SG find.INF ready   to on-it throw   a   glass   of
      acqua
      water
      'you must be ready to throw a glass of water on it' (ibid.)

   c. *'u 'ncignava*   *a ffravicare nu cummentu*
      it begin.PAST.3SG to build.INF   a   convent
      'he began to build (it) a convent' (ibid., 149)

   d. *Maruzzu s'*   *a finiscia*   *'i mangià*   *prim' 'i nescere*
      Maruzzu himself it finish.PRES.3SG of eat.INF   before of go-out.INF
      'Maruzzu will finish eating before going out' (ibid.)

e. *si ancora **mi** cuntinua   a fa   mal' a   capu, aju*
if still   me continue.PRES.3SG to make.INF pain the head   have.PRES.1SG
'i jì   addr' 'u   miedicu
of go.INF to   the doctor
'if my head continues to hurt, I'll have to go to the doctor's' (ibid.)

(43) a. *'on t' 'u pozzu   dira*
not you it be-able.PRES.1SG tell.INF
'I cannot tell you' (CZ, Lombardi 1997: 207)

b. *non **'a** seppa   fara   mancu iddhu*
not it know.PAST.3SG do.INF not-even he
'even he couldn't do it' (CZ, Colacino 1994: 55)

c. *v' a pozzu   fari   'na domanda?*
you it be-able.PRES.1SG do.INF a   question
'can I ask you a question?' (Nicotera (CZ), Caré 1982)

d. *nun **nd'** haju de   rendere cuntu a nessunu*
not of-it must.PRES.1SG give.INF account to nobody
'I don't have to explain it to anybody' (Soveria Mannelli (CZ),
Pascuzzi 1982: 22)

e. ***si***   *tornau   a lavari   la facci*
himself return.PAST.3SG to wash.INF the face
'he washed his face again' (RC, Falcone 1979: 81)

f. ***si***   *cominciau   ad armari*
himself begin.PAST.3SG to arm.INF
'he began to arm himself' (ibid., 67)

Analogous results confirming the monoclausal status of such constructions emerge from the behaviour of anaphor binding (44), middle-passivizer
si (45) and focalization (46) (following examples from dialect of Cosenza):

(44) a.   *po   /haddi   lavà   a iddu stessu*
pro$_i$ be-able.PRES.1SG /must.PRES.3SG [wash.INF PA him self$_i$]
'he can/must wash myself'

b.   *ncigna   a /finiscia   'i lavà   a iddu stessu*
pro$_i$ begin.PRES.3SG to /finish.PRES.3SG of [wash.INF PA him   self$_i$]
'he begins to/finishes wash(ing) myself'

(45) a. *'i cati   si puonnu   /s' hanna   purtà*
the buckets si be-able.PRES.3PL /si must.PRES.3PL carry
'the buckets can be/must be carried'

b. *'i cati   si ncignanu   a /si finisciunu   'i purtà*
the buckets si begin.PRES.3PL to /si finish.PRES.3PL of carry.INF
'the buckets begin/finish (to) be(ing) carried'

(46) a. *_NATÀ puozzu_   _/aja,_   _unn' âbballà_
          swim.INF_i be-able.PRES.1SG /must.PRES.1SG t_i not   to-dance.INF
          'SWIM I can/must, not dance'

      b. *_A /'I NATÀ ncignu_   _/finisciu,_   _unn' a /'i abballà_
          to /of swim.INF_i begin.PRES.1SG /finish.PRES.1SG t_i not   to /of dance.INF
          '(TO)SWIM(MING) I begin/finish, not dance(ing)'

In addition, the non-argumental status of such infinitival complements (see Lombardi 1997: 160–1) is highlighted by the impossibility of _wh_-extraction (see (b) examples), clitic referencing of the infinitival complement (see (c) examples), impersonal passivization (see (d) examples) and a tensed complement (see (e) examples) in the Cosentino sentences (47) and (48):

(47) a. _Giuvanni po_   _/hadda_   _dicere bugìe_
          Giuvanni   be-able.PRES.3SG /must.PRES.3SG [_vP_ tell.INF lies]
          'Giovanni may/must tell lies'

      b. *_cchi po_   _/hadda_   _Giuvanni?_
          what_i be-able.PRES.3SG /must.PRES.3SG [_vP_ t_i] Giovanni
          'what can/must Giovanni?'

      c. *_Giuvanni u po_   _/hadda_
          Giovanni   it_i be-able.PRES.3SG /must.PRES.3SG [_vP_ t_i]
          'Giovanni it may/must'

      d. *_è_   _statu   pututu_   _/avut'a_   _dicere bugìe_
          be.PRES.3SG be.PART be-able.PART /must.PART [_vP_ tell.INF lies]
          'it was able to/had to tell lies'

      e. *_Giuvanni po_   _/hadda_   _ca   parta_
          Giovanni   be-able.PRES.3SG /must.PRES.3SG that leave.PRES.3SG
          'Giovanni can/must that he leave'

(48) a. _Giuvanni ncigna_   _a /finiscia_   _'i_   _dicere bugìe_
          Giovanni   begin.PRES.3SG to /finish.PRES.3SG of [_vP_ tell.INF lies]
          'Giovanni begins/finishes (to) tell(ing) lies'

      b. *_a /'i cchi ncigna_   _/finiscia_   _Giuvanni?_
          to /of what_i begin.PRES.3SG /finish.PRES.3SG [_vP_ t_i] Giovanni
          'what does Gianni begin/finish?'

      c. *_Giuvanni cci ncigna_   _/ni finiscia_
          Giovanni   it_i begin.PRES.3SG /it_i finish.PRES.3SG [_vP_ t_i]
          'Giovanni begins/finishes it'

      d. *_è_   _statu   ncignatu a /finisciutu 'i_   _dicere bugìe_
          be.PRES.3SG be.PART begin.PART to /finish.PART of [_vP_ tell.INF lies]
          'it was begun to/finished (to) tell(ing) lies'

    e. *Giuvanni ncigna   a /finiscia   'i ca parta
       Giovanni   begin.PRES.3SG to /finish.PRES.3SG of that leave.PRES.3SG
       'Giovanni begins/finishes that he leaves'

Furthermore, the VP status of the infinitival complement is confirmed by the impossibility of independently negating the latter, witness the following Cosentino examples (see Lombardi 1997: 152–3):

(49) a. *putimu   /amu 'e   um fa'   troppu casinu
         be-able.PRES.1PL /must.PRES.1PL [$_{vP}$ not make.INF too-much noise]
         'we may/must not make too much noise'

      b. *ncignamu a /finiscimu   'i   um fa'   troppu casinu
         begin.PRES.1PL to /finish.PRES.1PL of [$_{TP}$ not make.INF too-much noise]
         'we begin/finish not (to) make(ing) too much noise'

As for the inability of the infinitival complement to host an aspectual auxiliary, thereby neutralizing the deontic/epistemic distinction, Rohlfs reports (1969: §702, n. 4; see also n. 3 below) such behaviour to be widespread throughout the South, witness his Abruzzese examples in (50):[7]

(50) a. essə l' a   'vut   accidə
         she him have.PRES.3SG must.PART kill.INF
         'she must have killed him'

      b. mə l' a   vut'a   tòjjə lu tavernə
         me it have.PRES.3SG must.PART take.INF the innkeeper
         'the innkeeper must have taken it from me'

Stehl (1988: §5.3.2) also reports that:

c'è da segnalare una particolarità per i nessi dei verbi servili *dovere* e *potere* con un infinito che l'area pugliese e salentina condivide con altre regioni meridionali. Quando l'azione si riferisce a un passato compiuto, la solita costruzione del tipo *deve aver osservato* può essere invertita, per la stretta connessione sintattica, nel tipo *ha dovuto osservare*. Quest'ultima costruzione si trova anche nei nostri dialetti che esprimono il concetto di *dovere* tramite *avere a* + infinito.

(the auxiliary verbs *dovere* 'must' and *potere* 'can' + infinitive present a feature which Apulian and Salentino dialects share with those of other southern regions. When the action refers to a completed past action, the usual construction *deve aver osservato* 'he must have observed' can be inverted, on account of the tight syntactic cohesion (between auxiliary and infinitive), to yield *ha dovuto osservare* 'he has had to observe'. This latter construction is also found in dialects which express the concept of *dovere* 'must' with *avere a* 'have to' + infinitive.)

Interestingly, Lombardi (1997: 155–8; 1998a: 620–1) also argues that the VP status of such infinitivals in Cosentino precludes the presence of an aspectual auxiliary in the infinitival complement (see also Trumper and Rizzi 1985). Instead, the auxiliary is hosted by the modal-aspectual verb. Significantly, however, the deontic/epistemic distinction, at least with *putí* 'can' + unaccusative infinitive, is not obscured but, rather, is signalled by the choice of perfective auxiliary. Use of the *avire* 'have' auxiliary gives rise to the deontic value (51a), whereas selection of the *essare* 'be' auxiliary forces the epistemic reading (52a–b):

(51) a. *avia   persu   i   chiavi e   nun **ha**   **pututu***
       have.PAST.3SG lose.PART the keys   and not have.PRES.3SG be-able.PART
       escia   d'   a   casa
       go-out.INF from the house
       'he had lost his keys and wasn't able to leave the house' (Lombardi 1998a: 620)

    b. *ccu stu strusciu nunn' **aju**   **pututu**   **dorma** mancu nu*
       with this racket   not   have.PRES.1SG be-able.PART sleep.INF not-even a
       pocu
       little
       'with all this racket, I haven't been able to sleep a wink' (ibid.)

    c. *ara bon' ura **aju**   **pututu**   pulizzà*
       to-the good hour have.PRES.1SG be-able.PART clean.INF
       'finally I've been able to do some cleaning' (ibid.)

(52) a. *nun c'   è   **pututu**   escia   iddru?*
       not there be.PRES.3SG be-able.PART go-out.INF he
       'couldn't he have gone out?' (Lombardi 1998a: 620)

    b. *è   **pututa**   escia   ch' è   na minz' ura*
       be.PRES.3SG be-able.PART go-out.INF that be.PRES.3SG a half   hour
       'she could have been gone (out) for half an hour' (ibid., 621)

    c. *l' **a**   **pututa**   chiamà Giuvanni e nua 'un c'*
       her have.PRES.3SG be-able.PART call.INF Giovanni and we not there
       eramu
       be.PAST.1PL
       'Giovanni could have called her and we wouldn't have been there' (ibid., 620)

Turning, finally, to infinitival complements to conative verbs, the paucity of available evidence prevents us from drawing any firm conclusions. However, there are some clues. Leone (1995: §66) reports that in Sicilian clitic climbing is optional in conjunction with *circà 'e* 'to try to', behaving on a par with Neapolitan in this respect:

(53) a. *i   ciercu   'i cummìnciri*
       them$_i$ try.PRES.1SG of [convince.INF t$_i$]

b. *ciercu* '*i cummincilli*
try.PRES.ISG of [convince.INF-them]
'I'll try to convince them' (Leone 1995: §66)

Equally, Alessandra Lombardi (personal communication) reports clitic climbing to be optional in conjunction with conatives in dialects of northern Calabria:[8]

(54) a. *l' amu   pruvatu a   leja*
it$_i$ have.PRES.IPL try.PART to [t$_i$ read.INF]

b. *amu   pruvatu a   ru leja*
have.PRES.IPL try.PART to [it read.INF]
'we tried to read it'

In addition, she reports that infinitival clauses to this class of verbs may also host aspectual auxiliaries (55a) and negation (55b):

(55) a. *provanu   ad avire   cunzat'   a   machina prima 'i vena   tu*
try.PRES.3PL to [have.INF repair.PART the car   before of come.INF you]
'they'll try to have repaired the car before you arrive'

b. *aju   pruvatu a num mbacchià 'a machina ma m'*
have.PRES.ISG try.PART to [not crash.INF   the car   but me
è   fujut'   'a frizione
be.PRES.3SG slip.PART the clutch]
'I tried not to crash the car but the clutch slipped'

Failing further and more detailed investigations, the preceding discussion has succeeded, despite its admittedly limited range, in identifying a number of differences between infinitival complements to modal-aspectual and conative verbs which broadly appear to mirror those examined above in relation to Neapolitan. In particular, we conclude that both types of infinitival complement are non-arguments, characterized by a reduced clausal structure smaller than CP. Based on their respective ability to occur with inflectionally-related elements such as perfective auxiliaries and negation, we have further identified infinitival complements to modal-aspectual predicates as bare *v*P complements and those to conative predicates as TP constituents.

5.5. STRUCTURE OF MODAL-ASPECTUAL AND CONATIVE CONSTRUCTIONS

5.5.1. *Modal-aspectuals*

On the basis of the preceding discussion and the evidence of a range of strictly local phenomena, we have established that the combination of a modal-aspectual verb and its dependent infinitive yields a monoclausal structure. In addition, it was demonstrated that the dependent infinitive exhibits a reduced clausal structure, incapable of hosting any of the categories associated with functional structure. Accordingly, we are led to the undeniable conclusion that infinitival complements to modal-aspectuals are vP constituents. The analysis that we propose therefore is that, while in morphophonological terms modal-aspectual verbs are clearly discrete independent words with full inflectional paradigms, they behave morphosyntactically as bound-affixes in conjunction with the lexical main verbs with which they occur (see Zubizarreta 1985). Specifically, modal-aspectuals originate in periphrastic constructions in conjunction with a following infinitive which, following independently motivated syntactic operations, result in what morphologically appears to be a single unitary complex (see Heine 1993: §1.5). That is to say, superficially modal-aspectuals enter with a linearly adjacent infinitive into a type of relation characteristic of morphological inflection, spelling out categories such as tense, mood and aspect. Such an account, therefore, allows us to capture the desired idea that such auxiliaries are in fact of a syntactic nature, although, at the same time, they typically contrast with morphological elements such as inflectional formatives of tense, modality and aspect (Ledgeway 1996a).[9]

Now, although there exists no explicit and consistent definition of what is meant by auxiliary in universal terms (Heine 1993: §1.2.4), there is some general agreement as to what the archetypal characteristics of auxiliaries should be (see Ramat 1987, Hopper and Traugott 1993: §5.3.2; Harris and Campbell 1995: §7.4). It is generally held that auxiliaries exhibit a specialized syntactic behaviour and tend to carry markers of tense, mood and aspect (Steele 1978: 13; Heine 1993: §1.3). What this means for our present purposes is that the category AUX, considered to be a category dominating tense, mood and aspect, should be equated with T, namely C → DP T (= AUX) VP. Thus, whereas AUX may not be a universal category, T is indeed argued to be universal, such that the category of AUX is simply reduced to a particular case of T. This does not mean, however, that AUX is necessarily the only marker of tense, mood or aspect in a clause, as witnessed by a number of languages (for example, Warlpiri) where such markers may be represented discontinuously within the clause (Heine 1993: 25, 43, 121). Similarly, although these Neapolitan modal and aspectual verbs may mark modality and aspect, respectively, tense at least continues to be marked by inflections on the modalizer-aspectualizer. Thus, we propose that at some point in the derivation, a sentence like (56a), will have the structure in (56b):

(56) a. *Ciro pô   scrivere a   Maria*
     Ciro be-able.PRES.3SG write.INF SD Maria
     'Ciro can write to Maria'

b.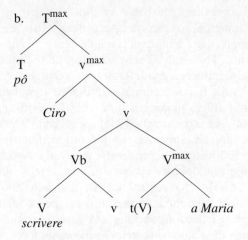

We maintain that *pô* 'he-can', as is true of all modal and aspectual verbs, is essentially a bundle or amalgam of functional features, namely Agr, T, M, Asp, in that it is merged under T and not under VP like lexical main verbs. As such, *pô* is rather like an affix with a morphological subcategorization frame [__+V], spelt-out as a strong V-feature that causes the embedded lexical verb *scrivere* 'to write' to selectionally incorporate into the structural slot created for it under T. By raising to T, the lexical infinitive satisfies the morphological properties of the incorporation host checking the strong V-feature on T and picks up its various agreement, tense, mood and aspect markings (Roberts 1991: 213). This rule of morphological incorporation gives the superficial impression that a verb embedded under *pô* restructures with the latter, whereas at bottom it is a straightforward case of V-raising to T. Consequently, at Spell-out (56b) will have the representation in (57):

(57)

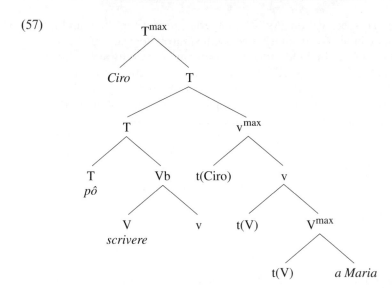

The derivation in (57) is therefore parallel to that of a canonical inflected verb form such as '*vene*' come.PRES.3SG, which following merger in the embedded *v*-VP raises overtly to check the V-feature on T. This explains the surface morphosyntactic properties of such auxiliary constructions. The modal-aspectual verb and its following infinitive are correctly predicted to form a single complex verbal predicate, namely [$_T$ *pô* + *scrivere*]. The fact that inflectional categories end up on the leftmost side of the complex verbal predicate, as opposed to the canonical right-side position, namely [[*pô*] *scrivere*] versus [*ven*[-*e*]], is indicative of the general analytic tendencies of Neapolitan as a VO language.

Typically, incorporation by selected substitution results in a visible amalgam of two underlying heads, as in (57) where Vb has raised to incorporate into T to unite with its tense, modal and Agr features. Essentially, we assume that, by virtue of its morphological properties, the incorporation host (T) morphologically subcategorizes for the incorporee Vb, creating a structural slot for the latter into which the incorporee must move. Following Roberts (1991) and Guasti (1993), in such cases both the incorporation host and incorporee are bound heads, namely of the category X^{-1}, and not free heads (X°).

Not only does this conclusion seem to be intuitively correct, but it is also supported by morphological facts: X^{-1}s are not well-formed words, typically non-autonomous categories which do not have independent word status. This appears to be true of many modal-aspectual predicates which cannot occur in isolation (at least in their grammatical functions), for example, **pozzo* 'I can', **aggia* 'I must'. Equally, we are maintaining that the infinitival main verb is deficient in that it is a verbal root, lacking any type

of inflectional specification. As X^{-1} categories, modal-aspectual and infinitive cannot be individually interpreted by the morphological component (PF)
and must therefore combine with one another in order to form a well-formed
word, namely $X^{-1} + X^{-1} \rightarrow X^{min}$ (*pô* + *scrivere*), the latter with independent
word status.[10] The resultant complex head formed by substitution incorporation is then characterized by a high degree of morphological fusion
between the underlying X^{-1}s, as witnessed by the following examples:

(58) a. *pô*   *scrivere   Ciro   a   Maria?*
    [be-able.PRES.3SG write to.INF]ᵢ Ciro   tᵢ   PA   Maria

   b. **pô*   *Ciro   scrivere   /*scrivere   Ciro   pô*   *a*
    [be-able.PRES.3SG]ᵢ Ciro   tᵢ write to.INF / [invite.INF]ᵢ Ciro be-able.PRES.3SG tᵢ SD
    Maria?
    Maria
    'can Ciro invite Maria?'

In (58a) the complex finite verb form [*pô scrivere*], formed via selectional
incorporation, has raised from within TP to the vacant C position to form the
question 'can Ciro invite Maria?' The ungrammaticality of (58b), where only
the modal or infinitive raises to C, illustrates that the incorporation host and
incorporee are firmly fused, inseparable, and must therefore invariably move
together. Consequently, the analysis outlined above enables us to retain the
conclusion that modal-aspectual constructions sit astride of the morphology/
syntax distinction. On the one hand, such constructions appear to be
morphological insofar as the verbal complex formed by incorporation is
morphologically analogous to a simple autonomous verb form. On the other,
such constructions appear syntactic in that the verbal complex is formed in the
syntactic component by head-movement of one distinct head into another.

Presumably, the emergence of a series of modal-aspectual auxiliaries in
Neapolitan must be seen within the context of more general tendencies at
force within the dialect. Specifically, the correlation between the loss and
decline of inflectionally expressed modal[11] and aspectual oppositions and the
emergence of a series of discrete modal-aspectual auxiliaries is undeniable.[12]
Moreover, the morphophonological behaviour of such verbs generally
confirms their auxiliary status, in that when these verbs are reduced to
tense, mood or aspect markers, they frequently present extremely reduced
phonetic forms, exhibiting various degrees of attrition and clitichood, for
example, 3SG *ha(dda)* (clitic, AUX) 'must, will' versus *ave* (tonic, lexical)
'receives', both from HABET, and similarly for *sà* (clitic, AUX) 's/he can' versus
sape (tonic, lexical) 's/he knows', *pote* (tonic) > *pô* (clitic) 's/he can, may', *sto'*
(clitic, progressive AUX) 'I am' versus *stongo* (tonic, lexical) 'I am'. In fact,
the property of clitichood is generally held (Bybee and Dahl 1989, Heine
1993: §3.3; Hopper and Traugott 1993: §5.3.2) to represent one of the
conclusive stages on the main verb $\rightarrow$ affix cline, whereby original main

verbs are progressively desemanticized in an on-going process of gramma-ticalization, ultimately reduced to synthetic agglutinative formatives.

Now the so-called obligatory phenomenon of clitic climbing is accounted for in a principled manner. There is in fact no clitic climbing as such since clitic pronouns are restricted to attaching to verbal hosts, of which there is only one in the clause, namely the complex verbal predicate (for example, $[_T$ *pô scrivere*$]$).

5.5.2. *Conative verbs*

Previously we established that, while exhibiting a number of strictly local phenomena in common with modal-aspectual auxiliaries, conative verbs also share similarities with main verbs. Furthermore, it was demonstrated that the infinitival complements to such verbs exhibit a reduced clausal structure in that they lack argument status, but yet retain the possibility of hosting T-related categories. Quite neatly, we are led to conclude that conatives select for a TP infinitival complement, a constituent structurally intermediate between the *v*P infinitivals of modal-aspectuals and the CP infinitivals of main verbs.[13]

The analysis that we propose is that, contrary to the auxiliaries, conative verbs enter into a more transparent and looser relationship with their infinitival complement, a fact congruent with their more lexical nature. When such verbs give rise to interlacing with a following infinitive, this is not motivated by inflectional features as with modal-aspectuals but, rather, is motivated by Case Theory. Just like the OC CP infinitival complements examined in chapter 3, the T of infinitives embedded under conative verbs is incapable of licensing nominative, thus forcing the embedded subject to raise to the matrix [Spec, T] where it can check nominative Case.[14]

This raising analysis allows us to capture all the relevant properties of such verbs. Firstly, the observed interlacing between the matrix and dependent clauses in terms of locally constrained phenomena follows a consequence of subject raising. For example, it was previously demonstrated that in accord-ance with Principle A of the Binding Theory, an anaphor of the dependent infinitive can be locally bound by an argument of the matrix clause, as in (59):

(59) *'o ninno prova   a   lavà   a isso stesso*
      the child$_i$ try.PRES.3SG to $[_{TP}$ t$_i$ wash.INF PA him self$_i$]
      'the child tries to wash itself'

Despite locality conditions on binding, the anaphor *a isso stesso* 'himself' can still be bound in (59) by an appropriate local binder, namely *'o ninno*, although the latter is in the matrix clause by Spell-out. Crucially, the binding domain of the anaphor is extended to include the matrix clause following movement of *'o ninno*, since the latter leaves a co-indexed trace in its base position in the embedded clause. Consequently, the anaphor can connect with the surface matrix clause subject via the local intermediate trace in the embedded [Spec, T].

As for the obligatory verb agreement displayed by conatives in conjunction with passivizer *se*, this requires no further explanation, since the
underlying object raised to the embedded Caseless [Spec, T] will have to
move to the matrix subject position to be Case-marked, a position which will
naturally trigger agreement with the matrix conative verb (60a):

(60) a. *'e cate   se provan'   a   purtà*
     the buckets$_i$ se try.PRES.3PL to [$_{TP}$ t$_i$ carry.INFt$_i$]
     'one tries to carry the buckets'

    b. *se ajuta   a   purtà   'e cate*
     se$_i$ help.PRES.3SG to [$_{CP}$ t$_i$ carry.INF the buckets]
     'one helps to carry the buckets'

Observe that in conjunction with main verbs like *ajutà* 'to help' in (60b),
the matrix verb does not license verbal agreement with the THEME argument
of the infinitive. This is a rather surprising result given our previous analysis
in chapter 3 of OC structures as a subtype of raising structure. However,
previously we noted that main verbs like *ajutà* 'to help' fail to license the
middle-passivizer *se*, the *se* morpheme in examples like (60b) only allowing
an indefinite arbitrary reading 'one'. It follows that in such examples, we
have two distinct instances of *se* which, along the lines of Cinque (1988), can
be identified as [-arg] middle-passivizer *se* and [+arg] indefinite *se* (see also
Dobrovie-Sorin 1998). In the former case, as in example (60a), *se* is a
passivizing formant which has the effect of suppressing the infinitival's
external θ-role and its accusative Case feature. As a consequence, the
THEME argument *'e cate* 'the buckets' is forced to raise to the matrix subject
position, passing *en route* via the embedded [Spec, T], where it can check
nominative. In (60b), by contrast, *se* is [+arg] and as such has no effect on
the infinitival's Case and thematic properties, leaving the THEME argument *in
situ* marked accusative. As an argument, however, indefinite [+arg] *se*$_{arb}$
must raise to the matrix subject position where it can check nominative, a
position in which it licenses default 3SG agreement.

Finally, we return to clitic climbing which we previously noted proves
entirely optional:

(61) a.   *pruvasseve a   'o scarfà   'o lietto?*
     pro$_i$ try.COND.2PL to [$_{TP}$ t$_i$ it$_j$ warm.INF the bed$_j$]

    b.   *'o pruvasseve a   scarfà   'o lietto?*
     pro$_i$ it$_j$ try.COND.2PL to [$_{TP}$ t$_i$ t$_j$ warm.INF the bed$_j$]
     'would you warm (it) the bed?'

In light of our analysis, there is no reason why clitic climbing should not be
available in such structures, since head-movement of the clitic to the matrix in
(61b) follows in accordance with the MLC. At the same time, there is no
reason why it should be necessary (see 61a), as was the case with restructuring

verbs or the modal-aspectual auxiliaries. It is thus predicted that clitic climbing is optional. Equally, the reason why such interlacing should be favoured with conatives is understandable, inasmuch as the distinctive matrix/dependent clausal boundary is independently obscured by the presence of the thematic subject of the embedded verb in the matrix subject position. However, we have seen that main verbs exhibit an analogous raising of the subject to the matrix in OC structures but fail to license clitic climbing:

(62) a.   *me   mecco   appaura 'e   'o mpacchià 'o lietto*
            pro$_i$ myself put.PRES.1SG fright   of [$_{CP}$ t$_i$ it$_j$ soil.INF   the bed$_j$]

      b. * *m'   'o mecco   appaura 'e   mpacchià 'o lietto*
            pro$_i$ myself it$_j$ put.PRES.1SG fright   of [$_{CP}$ t$_i$ t$_j$ soil.INF   the bed$_j$]
            'I am afraid of soiling (it) the bed'

In contrast to the example in (61b), raising of the clitic in (62b) entails movement through CP. Given our previous argument that in such structures the C position is filled by temporal features, namely R$_{INF}$, raising to the intermediate C position will not be a possible step, causing the clitic to move directly to the matrix T in violation of the MLC. It follows that the availability of clitic climbing falls out as a concomitant of the CP/TP distinction in a principled fashion.[15]

5.6. SUMMARY

From the preceding discussion have emerged a number of significant conclusions. We have demonstrated that the category of infinitive even within Neapolitan itself is not homogeneous. Besides the infinitival CP complements discussed in chapter 3, Neapolitan also has two other types of infinitival complement, characterized by a reduced clausal structure which has notable consequences for the properties of such clauses. In the case of TP infinitivals to conatives, the embedded subject is forced to raise to the matrix subject position, obscuring surface clausal boundaries. It follows from this single raising operation that a series of locally constrained phenomena (for example, binding of anaphors, passivizer *se* and clitic climbing) typical of simplex sentences are licensed, all of which give the superficial impression of a monoclausal structure.

  As for infinitival complements to modal-aspectuals, on the other hand, these lack any inflectional structure whatsoever. Consequently, such infinitives are essentially verbal roots that, like any canonical inflected verbal form, must raise to check their inflectional features under T. Such inflectional features are realized in the form of base-generated modal-aspectual auxiliaries that merge proclitically with their infinitival verbal root in a monoclausal structure.

184 COMPARATIVE SYNTAX OF DIALECTS OF SOUTHERN ITALY

To conclude, there remains one final point which merits some comment, namely the prepositional particles that occur in conjunction with many of the conative and modal-aspectual verbs, for example *avé 'a, incommenzare de, accummencià a, fernì 'e, cercà 'e, pruvà a*. There is apparently no available slot in the proposed structure for such an item, whatever its status may be. Yet, such particles cannot possibly be prepositions since the verbs in question never require such a preposition in their lexical uses, for example *avé/accummencià/fernì/cercà/ vedé/pruvà [caccosa]* 'to obtain/begin/finish/ask for/see/try something'. Moreover, as prepositions their function would be that of realizing Case on the infinitival complement. In chapter 3, we established that the element that requires Case in infinitives is the head of CP, a position not projected within the infinitival complements to conative and modal-aspectual verbs.

It is abundantly clear then that such particles are not prepositions. Nor are they amenable to an analysis that views them as prepositional non-finite complementizers, for the infinitival complements to such verbs, TPs and *v*Ps, lack the C position. We propose therefore that these particles form part of the lexical structure of conative and modal-auxiliary verbs, for example [$_V$ *avé* [$_P$*'a*]] and not *[$_V$ *avé*] + [$_P$ *'a*], for it is the presence of such particles that serves to differentiate the auxiliary or quasi-auxiliary conative functions of such verbs from their lexical uses, where the same particle is invariably absent, for example *avé* 'to receive' (lexical) versus *avé 'a* 'must; future marker' (AUX), *sapé* 'to know' (lexical) versus *sapé a* 'epistemic modal' (AUX), *pruvà* 'to sample' (lexical) versus *pruvà a* 'to try' (conative), *veré* 'to see' (lexical) versus *veré 'e* 'to try' (conative).

Indeed, in a number of cases such particles have been morphologically incorporated into the base verb, such that the latter displays a specialized auxiliary paradigm quite distinct from its lexical counterpart. One such case is provided by the contrast witnessed by the present tense paradigms of the modal-auxiliary *avé 'a* 'must; future marker' and the lexical *avé* 'to receive, obtain' (both < Latin HABERE) presented in table 5.2:

Table 5.2 Present tense paradigms of *avé 'a* and *avé*

	Avé 'a	Avé
1SG	*aggia* ['adʤa]	*aggio* ['adʤə]
2SG	*hêja* [eja]	*aje* ['ajə]
3SG	*hadda* ['adda]	*ave* ['avə]
1PL	*amma* ['amma]	*avimmo* [a'vimmə]
2PL	*(a(v))ita* [(a(v))'ita]	*avite* [a'vitə]
3PL	*hanna* ['anna]	*aveno* ['avənə]

6

AUXILIARY SELECTION

6.1. Introduction

Apart from a handful of poor and inadequate descriptions, the distribution of the perfective auxiliaries *avé(re)* 'have' and *esse(re)* 'be' in Neapolitan has attracted little attention from Romance linguists.[1] This proves all the more surprising when one considers that Neapolitan and its various diastratic, diamesic, diaphasic and diatopic varieties exhibit an unprecedented wealth of variation in this area, affording the linguist a unique opportunity to evaluate the full range of auxiliary alternations common to Romance within one dialect, as witnessed by the synopsis given in table 6.1:

Table 6.1 Perfective auxiliary distribution in the Neapolitan area

Verb class	Literary Neapolitan	Spoken Neapolitan		
		Urban	Peripheral	Procidano
Transitives/ unergatives	*avé*	*avé*		
Clitic-doubled transitives	*avé*	*avé* (or *essere* (1/2))		
Unaccusatives	*essere* (rarely *avé*)	*avé*		
Accusative pronominals	*essere*	*avé*	*essere* (1/2 pers) *avé* (3 pers)	*avé* (present) *essere* (past)
Dative pronominals	*essere* (rarely *avé*)	*avé*		
Pleonastic pronominals	*avé*	*avé*		
Inherent pronominals	*essere*	*avé* (rarely *essere*)		

As can be seen, literary Neapolitan is the more conservative variety, exhibiting the familiar Romance transitive/unergative-HAVE versus unaccusative-BE split (1a–b), whereas urban spoken Neapolitan proves more innovative, displaying a quasi-universal use of the HAVE auxiliary irrespective of verb class (2a–b). Among the more striking cases, we find HAVE/BE distributed according to grammatical person (peripheral varieties; 3a–b), according to tense (Procidano; 4a–b), and an apparently unique instance of HAVE/BE determined by a combination of grammatical person and clitic-doubling (obsolescent urban dialect; 5a–c):

(1) a. *aggiu   visto   a Ciro*
     have.PRES.1SG see.PART PA Ciro
     'I have seen Ciro' (transitive)

    b. *so'   arrevato*
     be.PRES.1SG arrive.PART
     'I have arrived' (unaccusative)

(2) a. *aggiu   visto   a Ciro*
     have.PRES.1SG see.PART PA Ciro
     'I have seen Ciro' (transitive)

    b. *aggiu   arrevato*
     have.PRES.1SG arrive.PART
     'I have arrived' (unaccusative)

(3) a. *so'   visto   a Ciro /arrevato*
     be.PRES.1SG see.PART PA Ciro /arrive.PART
     'I have seen Ciro / arrived' (1SG subject)

    b. *ha   visto   a Ciro /arrevato*
     have.PRES.3SG see.PART PA Ciro /arrive.PART
     'he has seen Ciro / arrived' (3SG subject)

(4) a. *hó   visto   a Ciro /arrevèto*
     have.PRES.1SG see.PART PA Ciro /arrive.PART
     'I have seen Ciro / arrived' (present perfect)

    b. *fove   visto   a Ciro /arrevèto*
     be.PAST.1SG see.PART PA Ciro /arrive.PART
     'I had seen Ciro / arrived' (pluperfect)

(5) a. *aggiu   visto   a Ciro*
     have.PRES.1SG see.PART PA Ciro
     'I have seen Ciro' (1SG subject, DP-object)

    b. *'o so'   visto   a Ciro*
     him be.PRES.1SG see.PART PA Ciro
     'I have seen (him) Ciro' (1SG subject, clitic-doubled DP-object)

    c. *(l') ha   visto   a Ciro*
     (him) have.PRES.3SG see.PART PA Ciro
     'he has seen (him) Ciro' (3SG subject, (clitic-doubled) DP-object)

In the present chapter we shall provide an account of such alternations based on a modified version of Kayne's (1993) modular analysis. According to his proposal, the structure attributed to the sequence auxiliary +

participle consists of a copula BE + participle, the latter headed by an abstract preposition which, when incorporated into BE, is spelt-out as HAVE: BE + P → HAVE (see Benveniste 1966; Freeze 1992). Evidence will be presented to demonstrate that the incorporation of P into BE, yielding HAVE, is driven by properties of the participial clause which, as an argument, finds itself subject to the same licensing conditions as those which characterize infinitival and tensed clauses.

On this view, there is no rule of auxiliary selection *per se*, in that the presence of HAVE or BE now falls out from independent principles on argument licensing. In short, there arise two possibilities by which the participial clause may be licensed:

- the participle incorporates into BE (see discussion of restructuring verbs in section 3.2.2.3); or
- endowed with a [+finite] specification, the participial clause bears an intrinsic structural Case feature (see discussion of tensed clause in section 3.2.1.2);

The distribution of HAVE/BE is now interpreted as the overt reflex of one of these two licensing mechanisms operative on the participial clause: HAVE obtains whenever the participle incorporates (through the abstract P) into BE, whereas BE is preserved whenever a structural Case feature is licensed by a [+finite] specification within the participial clause. In the latter case, we propose that the participial clause may be associated with such a [+finite] specification by virtue of one or more of its functional heads (T, v) being endowed with strong features. This requires then a particular interpretation of finiteness, a term which, though commonly adopted by linguists of many diverse theoretical persuasions, figures among one of the most poorly understood concepts of linguistic theory. Indeed, there appears to be no generally accepted view of how finiteness is manifested in natural languages, or to what precise entities or categories the terms *finite* and *non-finite* readily apply (for an overview, see Vincent 1998).

Traditionally, in the description of Indo-European languages finiteness has been interpreted in terms of verbal morphology and categorial features (Koptjevskaja-Tamm 1993: 256). Consequently, non-finite verb forms are taken to exhibit reduced morphology, manifested in the absence of both personal and objective inflections, and possibly a change of category, as in the case of infinitives interpreted as nominal forms. Finite verb forms, in contrast, are typically argued to bear rich inflectional morphology, variously marking such categories as person, number, tense, aspect and mood. As a direct consequence of such definitions, it follows that non-finite verbs cannot have full lexical subjects and that they generally occur as dependent verb forms, restrictions which do not apply to finite verb forms. In view of these distinctions and according to traditional practices, verb forms are typically classified in terms of a finite versus non-finite dichotomy.

However, such rigid definitions of finiteness prove inadequate, running into severe difficulties when a broader range of cases is examined. By way of example, consider the old Neapolitan inflected infinitival sentences in (6):

(6) a.   *determenaro. . . de   se repartireno*
       pro$_i$ determine.PAST.3PL of [t$_i$ re-leave.inf.3pl]
       'they decided. . .to leave again' (De Blasi 1986: 259, 18)

   b. *ave   plazuto   ai   nuostri Diey de **nuy** esseremo in*
       have.PRES.3SG please.PART to-the our   Gods of [we be.INF.1PL in
       questa parte
       this   part]
       'it has pleased our Gods for us to be here' (ibid., 69, 35)

Notwithstanding their infinitival status, the so-called non-finite embedded verb forms in (6) exhibit overt person/number marking, a possibility not envisaged by traditional definitions of finiteness (see section 3.5).

A further complication for the classical approach to finiteness concerns the correlation between person/number marking and the availability of full lexical subjects in the inflected infinitival examples in (6). Similar considerations hold of the so-called finite embedded clauses in (7) and the personal infinitive in (8):

(7) a. *Giuanne prummette   che Ø /*isso accatta   'e purtualle*
       Gianni$_i$ promise.PRES.3SG [that Ø$_i$ /he$_i$ buy.PRES.3SG the oranges]
       'Gianni promises that he will buy the oranges'

   b. *Giuanne se crereva   ca   Ø /isso venceva   'o premio*
       Gianni$_i$ believe.PAST.3SG [that Ø$_i$ /he$_i$ win.PAST.3SG the prize]
       'Gianni believed that he would win the prize'

(8) *pe esse **na città** ô   mare, ce aspettavamo tanta   risturante*
     [for be.INF a city   at-the sea] expect.PAST.1PL so-many   restaurants
     'e pesce
     of fish
     'being a coastal city, we expected to find lots of seafood restaurants'

Despite all four embedded verbs forms in (6) and (7) being inflected for person and number, only in the (b) examples does the verb license nominative and a full lexical subject. Conversely, the infinitive in (8) lacks all person/number marking whatsoever but still licenses a nominative subject (see discussion of OC/NOC distinction in sections 3.4 and 4.2.1). Such facts illustrate that so-called finite verbs do not invariably license nominative (7a) and, conversely, that so-called non-finite infinitival forms (6b, 8) may indeed license nominative. Finiteness cannot therefore be exhaustively reduced to the availability of person/number marking and its repercussions on nominative Case-licensing, as has been common practice within the generative tradition (see Ledgeway 1998b).

In a move which apparently departs from this approach, Rizzi (1998) takes finiteness to be a linguistic primitive. Within his split C-system, finiteness is identified with a distinct functional projection *FinP*, variously marking the core IP-related characteristics in accordance with parametric variation. On this view, person/number marking and nominative Case no longer bear directly on finiteness but follow from the properties of the IP-system. Instead, finiteness is taken to be a property of the C-system which may indirectly replicate information encoded in the IP-system. However, given this dependency between the CP and IP systems, even within Rizzi's model finiteness cannot be wholly divorced from person/number marking and nominative, inasmuch as finiteness may be correlatively marked on the verb (VP), at the level of the sentence (IP) and/or the clause (CP) (see also Vincent 1993: §7.6.1). It would appear then that, even within Rizzi's system, finiteness is not strictly a primitive reducible to any one category or structural position. Instead, it is a global property of the clause, spelling out the cumulative effect of the featural content of a collection of functional heads, notably C, T and *v*.

We therefore reject the traditional dichotomy between finite and non-finite verb forms, adopting instead a scalar interpretation of finiteness (Ledgeway 1998b: 58; Vincent 1998: §3.2) in terms of the properties of individual heads within the functional structure of the clause. Understood in this way, finiteness within the participial clause finds a natural interpretation in terms of Chomsky's (1995) feature system, in which functional heads are drawn from the numeration replete with particular feature specifications. Within such a framework, the empirical cases of auxiliary alternation observed in (1)–(5) above follow from the properties of T and *v* and, specifically, the strong/weak specification of particular features they carry. For instance, the presence of BE in (5b) induced by a [-3pers] subject and a doubling-clitic ensues from the combination of a strong person/number D-feature on T and a strong agreement D-feature on *v*, respectively. These strong features endow the participial clause with a [+finite] specification that licenses an intrinsic structural Case feature, thereby excluding the possibility of incorporation and hence HAVE.

Below it will be demonstrated how the entire range of auxiliary alterna-tions identified above, as well as those found in other dialects, can be accounted for by such an analysis. In particular, the presence/absence of overt morphological evidence will be evaluated to posit the relative strength of T and *v*, and which combinations thereof are (un)able to license an intrinsic [+finite] specification within the participial clause. Undeniably, such a proposed analysis makes some strong and illuminating predictions concerning the distribution of *avé* and *essere* in the Neapolitan area.[2]

The chapter is organized as follows: In section 6.2 we outline Kayne's (1993) original proposal, pointing out a number of difficulties with his analysis. This leads us in section 6.3.1 to propose a novel interpretation of the facts, deriving BE/HAVE selection in conjunction with transitives/unergatives from the finiteness specification of the participial clause. This same analysis is subsequently demonstrated in section 6.3.2 to extend to pronominal and unaccusative predicates.

6.2. KAYNE's (1993) MODULAR ANALYSIS

Kayne (1993) generalizes the analysis of possessive BE (for example, Hungarian *van*, Welsh *mae*) or HAVE (for example, French *avoir*) to that of auxiliary BE and HAVE. In particular, he argues that the basic structure to be attributed to possessive BE/HAVE and auxiliary BE/HAVE in Romance is that of a copula BE which takes a DP complement, headed by a covert prepositional D (labelled D/P), that contains an NP (possessive) or VP (auxiliary) substructure, plus any required layers of functional projections. The two types of BE/HAVE differ then minimally, specifically in whether the embedded D/P contains an NP or VP substructure. Under this analysis, HAVE is considered identical to BE but for the incorporation of the abstract preposition, namely D/P, into BE (Freeze 1992), triggered by properties of the participial clause.

6.2.1. *Transitives and unergatives:* HAVE-*dialects*

We begin by considering the behaviour of transitives and unergatives in urban Neapolitan which, providing that they are not used pronominally (see section 6.3.2.1), preserve HABERE > *avé* in all paradigms, witness the examples in (9) and (10), respectively:

(9) a. *parea*   *a lloro de may non avere*   *veduta femena de*
       seem.PAST.3SG to them of never not have.INF see.PART woman of
       semeglyante bellezze
       similar   beauty
       'it seemed to them to never have seen a lady of such beauty' (De Blasi 1986: 206, 13–14)

    b. *aggio*   *patuto*   *cchiù de no mbarazzo*
       have.PRES.1SG suffer.PART more of one embarrassment
       'I've suffered more than one embarrassment' (Stigliola 1784, in Capozzoli 1889)

    c. *aggio*   *vennute*   *tutt' 'e storne*
       have.PRES.1SG sell.PART all the tickets
       'I have sold all the lottery tickets' (De Filippo 1973: 132)

(10) a. *se ve pare*   *che eo aya*   *ben parlato*
       if you seem.PRES.3SG that I have.PRES.SUBJ.1SG well speak.PART
       'if you think that I have spoken well' (De Blasi 1986: 127)

b. *aggio   chiagnuto?*
have.PRES.ISG cry.PART
'have I cried?' (Spassatiempo 1875, in Capozzoli 1889)

c. *avite   capito*
have.PRES.2PL understand.PART
'you have understood' (Scarpetta 1992: 64)

Now, according to Kayne's analysis, the typical structure for copular BE followed by a transitive participial clause, including its substructure with relevant AgrS and AgrO projections, is as in (11):

(11) BE [$_{DP}$ Spec D/P. . . AgrS AgrO [$_{VP}$ Spec [$_{V'}$ V DP]]]

How then do we derive a typical transitive sentence like (12) from the structure in (11)?

(12) *i' aggiu   rott'   (*rutt')   'a butteglia*
I   have.PRES.ISG break.PART.F (break.PART.M) the bottle.F.SG
'I have broken the bottle'

The subject DP *i'* 'I', generated VP-internally, moves up to [Spec, AgrS], by-passing [Spec, AgrO] for independently motivated reasons (namely, accusative Case requirement for object in [V, DP]), and as demonstrated by the ungrammaticality of masculine (metaphonic) participial agreement with the subject in (12). From [Spec, AgrS], the subject then moves to [Spec, D/P]. From this position, however, the subject cannot straightforwardly move through to [Spec, BE], an A-position, because this would give rise to an improper movement violation since [Spec, DP] is presumably an A'-position (compare [Spec, CP]). Moreover, if the subject were to raise to [Spec, BE], this would incorrectly result in *essere* selection, a possibility not available in the urban dialect with transitives. In order for the subject to be able to raise to [Spec, BE], Kayne proposes that [Spec, DP] must become assimilated to an A-position, a possibility which is allowed if D/P incorporates into BE. As observed above, incorporation of D/P into BE, namely [BE +D/P], is spelt out as HAVE (Freeze 1992), yielding (12) as desired.

An analogous analysis can be proposed for unergatives like (13a):

(13) a. *i' aggiu   durmuto*
I   have.PRES.ISG sleep.PART
'I have slept'

b. *Nannina ha   parréto   /*parràta*
Annina   have.PRES.3SG speak.PART.M /speak.PART.F
'Annina has spoken' (Procida (NA))

The only difference between (13a) and (12) is that the direct object is phonetically unrealized in the former (see Hale and Keyser 1993). Thus, parallel to the transitive example (12), the unergative participle can never agree with its subject, as the Procidano example (13b) illustrates, where maximal metaphony clearly indicates the ungrammaticality of feminine participial agreement.

6.2.2. Transitives and unergatives: BE-dialects

A major divergence from the above pattern can be found in the peripheral Neapolitan varieties (for example, Torre del Greco, Torre Annunziata, Pompei, Sorrento; see Altamura 1961: 73), where *essere* has generalized as universal auxiliary even with transitives and unergatives. In these varieties, *avé* is increasingly more common with all verb classes to the detriment of *essere*, presumably due to the influence of the urban Neapolitan dialect and the growing influence of Italian. Consequently, auxiliary selection with transitives and unergatives may proceed here too in a parallel fashion to that of the urban dialect above. However, when *essere* does occur, it is restricted to the 1/2SG (14a), more rarely the 1/2PL (14b), but never obtains in the 3rd person which licenses *avé* (14c):

(14) a. *so'*   /*sî*   *rott'*   *'a butteglia*
       be.PRES.1SG /be.PRES.2SG break.PART the bottle
       'I have/you have broken the bottle'

   b. *avimmo*   /*avite*   *durmuto* (*simmo*   /*site*   *durmuto*)
       have.PRES.1PL /have.PRES.2PL sleep.PART be.PRES.1PL /be.PRES.2PL sleep.PART
       'we have/you have slept'

   c. *ha*   (**è*)   /*hanno*   (**so'*)   *pavato tutta cosa*
       have.PRES.3SG (be.PRES.3SG) /have.PRES.3PL (be.PRES.3PL) pay.PART all   thing
       'he has/they have paid for everything'

Similar, but often complex, patterns of auxiliary alternation according to person are found in a number of central-southern dialects (see Rohlfs 1969: §730; Tuttle 1986), in particular the southern Marche, southern Lazio, Abruzzo and northern Apulia.[3] For example, in the Lazio dialect of Marino (province of Rome) investigated by Tufi (1999), the 1st/2nd persons predominantly license BE (15a–d) and the 3rd person HAVE (15e–f) in the present perfect of transitives and unergatives:

(15) a. *so'*   *accompagnatu Gianni au*   *lavoru*
       be.PRES.1SG accompany.PART Gianni to-the work
       'I have accompanied Gianni to work'

   b. *'e   si'*   *pagate   'e bollette?*
       them be.PRES.2SG pay.PART the bills
       'have you paid the bills?'

c. *ieri   semo   datu 'na pulita 'a   cantina*
yesterday be.PRES.IPL give a   clean to-the cellar
'yesterday we gave the cellar a clean'

d. *'a sete   cotta   'a verdura?*
the be.PRES.2PL cook.PART the vegetables
'have you cooked the vegetables?'

e. *Maria, n' a   sentita più   nisunu*
Maria not have.PRES.3SG hear.PART anymore nobody
'As for Maria, nobody has since heard her'

f. *du' munielli   m' hanno buttato   pe' tera*
two lads   me have throw.PART for land
'two lads threw me on the floor'

Kayne claims that this sensitivity to person, whereby the 3rd person tends to prefer HAVE, suggests that AgrS has strong features in these varieties when BE is selected. In particular, these strong features of AgrS may be activated by a DP with the appropriate person/number features passing through its Spec. In the urban Neapolitan variety, by contrast, AgrS is weak and a DP passing through its Spec has no effect, leaving AgrS inert. On this view, only in the peripheral varieties do 1st/2nd person subjects, in particular the singular persons, have strong features able to activate AgrS when they pass through [Spec, AgrS]. Therefore in order for *essere* to be selected in (14a), AgrS, once activated and endowed with strong person/number features, can raise to D/P and convert [Spec, DP] into a position compatible with an A-position. This has the consequence that the subject DP can move legitimately through to [Spec, DP], now an A-position, and on up to [Spec, BE] without entailing an improper movement violation. As a result, D/P is not required to incorporate into BE and *essere* obtains.

In some apparently similar Italian dialects, Kayne (1993: 14ff.) observes that auxiliary selection may be affected by the presence of clitic climbing from the participial clause to the auxiliary verb. Consider the following examples from the Piedmontese dialect of Novara (see Turri 1973: 116–19):

(16) a. *mi i   son   mìa parlà*
I S.CL be.PRES.ISG not speak.PART
'I haven't spoken'

b. *lü l' à   durmì*
he S.CL have.PRES.3SG sleep.PART
'he has slept'

c. *mi i t' ò   mài parlà*
I S.CL you have.PRES.ISG never speak.PART
'I have never spoken to you'

Analogously to the peripheral Neapolitan varieties, BE in Novarese is the usual auxiliary in the 1st/2nd persons with transitives and unergatives (16a), while HAVE is preferred with the 3rd person (16b). However, this difference is neutralized when an object clitic climbs to the auxiliary clause, insofar as HAVE is invariably selected (16c). Drawing on previous analyses of clitic climbing (Kayne 1989; 1991), Kayne derives the presence of HAVE with clitic climbing in (16c) from the fact that the object clitic *t'* to you' must use D/P (by analogy with C) as an escape-hatch to climb into the matrix clause. Thus, if D/P incorporates into the auxiliary, yielding HAVE, the clitic can raise together with D/P.

The overt reflex of this proposed analysis can be clearly seen in the central Italian dialect of Martinsicuro (TE; see Mastrangelo Latini 1981), where BE is usual in the 1st/2nd persons and HAVE in the 3rd person. Kayne gives the following examples:

(17) a. *(a) l' à   ditte*
   (s.cl) it have.PRES.3SG say.PART
   'he has said it'

 b. *sillu   ditte*
   be.PRES.2SG-it say.PART
   'you have said it'

In (17a) HAVE in the 3rd person follows parallel to that of Novarese in (16b). However, in (17b) BE-selection obtains even in the presence of an object clitic, though in contrast to (17a), the object clitic *-lu* 'it' occurs enclitic to the auxiliary. This leads Kayne to maintain that the clitic adjoins to D/P together with AgrS, which has strong features as a result of the 1SG subject passing through its Spec. However, instead of incorporating together with D/P into BE to yield HAVE, as in (17a), the clitic can legitimately remain in D/P, as reflected by the surface linear order AUX + CL + PART, preserving auxiliary BE.

Now consider the effect of clitic climbing in the Neapolitan peripheral varieties in (18a):

(18) a. *'o so'   visto*
   him be.PRES.1SG see.PART
   'I have seen him' (Sorrento (NA))

 b. *ci só   visti*
   you be.PRES.1SG see.PART
   'I have seen you' (Cori (LT), Chiominto 1984: 157)

The clitic in (18a) has climbed to the matrix clause to adjoin to the auxiliary and BE is preserved. This situation is not unique and Kayne (1993: 26, n. 37) acknowledges that analogous facts hold of other dialects, such as Corese (18b) and even to some extent Martinsicurese. The analyses proposed for

(16c) and (17b) cannot therefore apply to (18), which must find an alternative explanation.

6.2.3. *Summary*

Leaving aside many of the technical aspects of the discussion above, let us briefly sum up the essentials of Kayne's (1993) analysis. Auxiliary + participle structures are uniformly analysed underlyingly as consisting of BE + participle. The latter is headed by an abstract preposition D/P (see 19a) which, if moved into BE, is spelt-out as HAVE (see 19b):

(19)   a.   BE + [D/P participle]

   b.   [BE + D/P$_i$] (= HAVE) + [t$_i$ participle]

Now, in order for the participial subject to move into the auxiliary clause, where it can be marked nominative, it must first pass through the specifier position of D/P, a sort of escape-hatch into the auxiliary clause. However, [Spec, D/P] is a position typically occupied by non-arguments (an A'-position). Therefore, if the subject is to pass though [Spec D/P], this position must be adapted to an A(rgument)-position, a possibility which arises if D/P incorporates into BE. Significantly, incorporation of D/P into BE yields HAVE (19b). This is what happens in conjunction with transitive/unergative participles in urban Neapolitan.

Alternatively, in dialects such as the peripheral Neapolitan varieties where transitives/unergatives license BE uniquely in the 1st/2nd persons, the subject Agr(eement) features of the participle are assumed to be strong in such instances. Consequently, the strong Agr features can adjoin to D/P and convert its associated specifier [Spec, D/P] into an A-position. As a result, the subject can pass through this position, precluding D/P from incorporating into BE and the possibility of HAVE.

In short then, the distribution of HAVE/BE under Kayne's account falls out as a reflex of one of two possible operations: D/P-incorporation into BE or incorporation of subject Agr into D/P, both of which legitimize movement of the subject to the auxiliary clause via the A'-bar position [Spec, D/P].

In addition, there arise cases where the presence/absence of clitic climbing in BE-dialects has repercussions on auxiliary distribution. In Novarese movement of an object clitic to the auxiliary clause with 1st/2nd person subjects results in HAVE, as opposed to BE in the absence of an object clitic. Given that clitic climbing entails movement through the intermediate D/P position, an escape-hatch into the auxiliary clause, D/P must incorporate into BE (yielding HAVE) so that the clitic can raise along with it to attach to the auxiliary (see 20a):

(20)   a.   [clitic$_i$+D/P]$_j$ + BE (= HAVE) + [t$_j$ . . .t$_i$ participle]

   b.   BE + [clitic$_i$+D/P . . .t$_i$ participle]

In dialects like Martinsicurese, in contrast, the clitic can climb all the way to the auxiliary clause with resultant HAVE, as in (20a), or stop in an intermediate position adjoined to D/P, preserving BE as in (20b).

Finally, we examined some apparently problematic cases from the Neapolitan peripheral varieties and Corese, where the clitic can climb to the auxiliary clause without any repercussions on the presence of BE. These are analysed below in section 6.3.1.2.1.

6.3. MODIFYING KAYNE'S ANALYSIS

Let us begin by repeating the structure proposed by Kayne for AUX + PART:

(21) BE [$_{DP}$ Spec D/P. . .AgrS AgrO [$_{VP}$ Spec [$_{V'}$ V DP]]]

Recurrent throughout Kayne's analysis (see in particular pages 7, 22 and footnotes 4, 12) is the correlation between the DP (complement of BE) in (21) and CP, as maintained by Szabolcsi (1981; 1983). Although labelling it throughout as DP, Kayne comes very close to straightforwardly treating DP as CP, attributing to DP the same properties as those generally attributed to CP: its Spec position is an A'-bar position and D/P functions as an escape-hatch for clitics, parallel to [Spec, CP] and C, respectively. In fact, Szabolcsi actually equates this D/P position (D in his analysis) to C. Following Ledgeway (1996b: ch. 3; 1998c), we shall take what Kayne labels as the DP (complement to BE) in (21) to be CP, headed by C/P.

Moreover, in Kayne's original proposal, the participial clause was held to contain subject and object agreement projections, namely AgrSP and AgrOP. In accordance with minimalist assumptions (Chomsky 1995; 1998), which advocate an Agr-less system, we replace these with T and *v*, respectively. The modified structure that we propose for AUX + PART is given in (22):

(22) BE [$_{CP}$ Spec C/P. . .T [$_{vP}$ Spec . . .*v* [$_{VP}$ V DP]]]

The structure in (22) captures in a highly natural way the similarities between participial clauses and infinitival/tensed CP clauses. As such, the CP participial clause in (22) is predicted to be a clausal argument and therefore subject to formal licensing conditions on a par with other CPs. Now in section 3.2.3 it was argued that Neapolitan clausal complements can be licensed by one of the three mechanisms in (23):

(23) a. Intrinsic structural Case feature licensed by [+finite] specification: tensed CPs (24a);

   b. Inherent Case: [-finite] infinitival CPs (24b);

   c. Incorporation (Baker's 'Case-indexing'): restructured infinitival CPs (24c);

(24) a. *nun te miette scuorno (*'e)   che num vonno   pavà?*
         not be-ashamed.PRES.2SG (of) [CP that not   want.PRES.3PL pay.INF]
         'are you not ashamed that they don't want to pay'

      b. *nun te miette scuorno *('e)   m' 'o dicere a me?*
         not be-ashamed.PRES.2SG (of) [CP me it tell.INF to me]
         'are you not ashamed of telling me?'

      c. *nun me vuo'   spiecà   stu fatto?*
         not me want.PRES.2SG explain.INF$_i$ [CP t$_i$ this fact]
         'don't you want to explain this matter to me?'

Following the essentials of Stowell (1981), we maintained that tensed CPs are licensed by their [+tensed], hence [+finite] specification, which endows them with an intrinsic structural Case feature at the head of CP. Consequently, finite CP complements prove incompatible with prepositional inherent Case-markers (compare *'e* 'of' in 24a). By the same token, infinitival CPs, as untensed and hence non-finite arguments, lack an intrinsic structural Case feature and must therefore be Case-marked like DPs (24b).[4] Finally, incorporation was demonstrated in section 3.2.2.3 to license the infinitival complements of restructuring verbs (24c), whereby adjunction-incorporation into the matrix predicate was argued to 'Case-index' (Baker 1988: 108ff.) the infinitival clause.

Returning to CP participial clauses, it is clear that they cannot be licensed by an inherent Case feature. In the modified structure in (22) the participial CP is the complement of the copula BE, which only checks structural (nominative) Case in subject position. BE will not then have a Case feature (Chomsky 1995: §4.5.3, though see Lasnik 1999: 30ff., 85ff.) to license the participle. Even if one accepts Belletti's (1988) proposal that BE checks partitive Case, this will not save the participial CP in (22) since partitive is an inherent Case and the participle does not enter into a thematic relation with BE.

By a process of elimination, it follows that participial CPs can only be licensed by an intrinsic structural Case feature or restructuring-incorporation, each correlating with a distinct auxiliary in accordance with empirical expectations:

- endowed with a [+finite] specification, the participial clause bears an intrinsic structural Case feature, therefore precluding C/P-incorporation and HAVE;
- the participle restructures into BE which, in accordance with the MLC, requires the infinitive to first adjoin to C/P with which it moves to incorporate into BE yielding HAVE.

The distribution of BE/HAVE is now understood as the surface manifestation of finiteness and restructuring-incorporation, respectively. In the general case, the latter will apply since participial CPs, unlike tensed CPs, are negatively specified for tense, as witnessed by the fact that the category of tense in the Romance HABERE/ESSE periphrases is invariably realized on the auxiliary, whereas aspect is realized in the participial desinence -TUM > -*to* (Vincent 1988: 56). Under particular conditions, though, we suggest that the participle may be associated with a [+finite] specification (and, by implication, an intrinsic structural Case feature) by virtue of one or more of its functional heads (T, v) being endowed with strong features. As we shall see, our proposed analysis of auxiliary distribution, now simply viewed as a concomitant of the independent licensing requirements on clausal arguments, makes some strong and illuminating predictions which are capable of deriving all the variations in Neapolitan auxiliary selection.

Moreover, the present analysis eliminates one of the more questionable premises of Kayne's original analysis. Within his account, the distribution of HAVE/BE rests on the exceptional assumption that the subject has to pass through [Spec, D/P] in order to raise to [Spec, BE].[5] Under general minimalist assumptions (in particular, the MLC), as well as within the Principles and Parameters framework (Rizzi 1990b), raising of the subject directly to [Spec, BE] proves a legitimate step. However, Kayne is forced to assume subject raising to [Spec, D/P], since only then can he derive HAVE by D/P-incorporation into BE in order to transform [Spec, D/P] into an A-position. If there were no raising to the intermediate position of [Spec, D/P], then HAVE would never obtain under his analysis.

The distribution of HAVE/BE then falls out as a stipulation: incorporation of D/P into BE (yielding HAVE) is necessary just in case the subject cannot raise from [Spec, D/P] to [Spec, BE]. Ideally, the incorporation or otherwise of D/P into BE, and hence the distribution of HAVE/BE, should follow in a principled fashion, independently of the need of the subject to raise to [Spec, BE]. Just such an approach, we believe, is offered by the licensing requirements of participial CPs proposed above. Now, the appearance of HAVE falls out independently as a concomitant of the licensing conditions on CPs, rather than constituting an unprincipled requirement to move the subject to [Spec, BE] via [Spec, D/P] in order to yield HAVE à la Kayne.

6.3.1. *Transitives and unergatives revisited*

6.3.1.1. HAVE-*dialects*

How then do we get HAVE out of the structure in (22) with transitives (25a) and unergatives (25b) in the Neapolitan urban dialect?

(25) a. *i' aggiu   rott'   'a butteglia*
      I   have.PRES.1SG   break.PART   the bottle

    b. *i' aggiu   durmuto*
      I   have.PRES.1SG   sleep.PART

The subject DP raises from its vP-internal base position through [Spec, T] and out of the participial clause to [Spec, BE]. Agr in T within the participial clause is inert and cannot be activated by a DP passing through [Spec, T]. In the absence of a degree of finiteness within the participial clause, the latter can only be licensed by the participle incorporating into BE, an operation spelt out as HAVE.

6.3.1.2. BE-*dialects*

Let us now return to BE-dialects and Kayne's proposal that in these dialects certain types of subject passing through [Spec, AgrS] can activate AgrS and endow it with appropriate person/number features. Retaining the essential idea underlying Kayne's proposal, we propose to interpret the appearance of BE in these dialects as a finiteness effect (see section 6.1). Specifically, we take the strong person/number features of Kayne's AgrS in BE-dialects, activated following movement of a 1st/2nd person subject to [Spec, AgrS], to be an indication of a certain degree of finiteness absent in HAVE-dialects. Adapting this idea within Chomsky's (1995) Agr-less feature checking-system, the appearance of BE in the 1st/2nd persons (26a), in contrast to HAVE in the 3rd persons (26b), finds a natural interpretation in terms of the D-feature on T and the strong/weak dimension.

(26) a. *so'   accattato nu chilo 'e fasule*
      be.PRES.1SG buy.PART a   kilo of beans
      'I have bought a kilo of beans' (Sorrento (NA))

   b. *ha   (*è)   accattato nu chilo 'e fasule*
      have.PRES.3SG (be.PRES.3SG) buy.PART a kilo of beans
      'he has bought a kilo of beans' (Sorrento (NA))

Assuming D to be the locus of ϕ-features (namely Agr), we propose that the D-feature of participial T encodes the ϕ-features of person and number.[6] Consequently, the presence of BE in (26a) is to be understood as the reflex of a strong participial T whose person/number D-feature (henceforth $D_{P/N}$-feature) has been activated by a 1SG subject raised to [Spec, T] within its checking domain.[7] It is this strong $D_{P/N}$-feature specification of T that we are equating with a certain degree of finiteness within the participial clause and which licenses an intrinsic structural Case feature in the head of CP (C/P), analogous to that argued for tensed CP clauses. It now follows that participial clauses of transitives/unergatives in BE-dialects are licensed by the strong finiteness specification of T, excluding the possibility of restructuring-incorporation, as in (26b), and concomitant incorporation of C/P into BE to yield HAVE.

6.3.1.2.1. *Clitic climbing*

Let us now return to the effects of clitic climbing to the auxiliary clause. Essentially, there arise three cases, as exemplified by the sentences in (27):

(27) a. *sillu   ditte*   (Martinsicuro (TE))
      be.PRES.2SG-it   say.PART

    b. *mi   i   t'   ò   mài   parlà*   (NO)
       I   S.CL   you   have.PRES.1SG   never speak.PART

    c. *o'   so'   visto*   (Sorrento (NA))
      him   be.PRES.1SG   see.PART

In the Martinsicurese example (27a), clitic climbing fails to obtain and the auxiliary surfaces as BE, whereas examples with 3rd person subjects and HAVE (see 17a) exhibit obligatory clitic climbing. In the latter case, obligatory clitic climbing falls out as a concomitant of restructuring-incorporation of the participle into BE, while in (27a) there is no restructuring-incorporation of the participle (compare presence of BE), hence no obligatory clitic climbing. The facts then are quite simple: in (27a) the object clitic *lu* 'it' remains in the participle clause within the Vb complex adjoined to T, with encliticization to the auxiliary *si* 'you-are' at PF. This is not such an odd outcome since the clitic is predicted to remain under T, the position standardly assumed for clitics. Under Kayne's analysis, however, the clitic *lu* is taken to be stranded under D/P, a position similar, if not identical, to C but which is not generally considered to be a position occupied by Romance clitics.

What then of Novarese examples like (27b)? Raising of the 1SG subject to [Spec, T] activates the strong $D_{P/N}$-feature on T, endowing the participial clause with a sufficient degree of finiteness to license a structural Case feature on C/P. Consequently, restructuring-incorporation into BE with resultant HAVE is excluded, yielding the (simplified) structure in (28a):

(28) a. **mi   i   son   mài   te   parlà*
      I   S.CL   be.PRES.1SG   never [$_{CP}$ C/P [$_T$ you speak.PART]]

    b. *mi   i   t'   ò   mài   parlà*
      I   S.CL   you$_i$ have.PRES.1SG   never [$_{CP}$ t$_i$ [$_T$ t$_i$ speak.PART]]

(28a) is however not an acceptable derivation in Novarese since the 2SG object clitic *te* 'to-you' must raise to attach to the auxiliary. This requires the clitic to use C/P as an escape-hatch into the matrix clause, from where it raises together with C/P to incorporate into BE (see 28b). As is by now familiar, C/P-incorporation into BE is spelt out as HAVE, producing (27b) as required.

One significant advantage of this analysis over that of Kayne's is that it predicts that, despite the presence of a clitic, BE nonetheless obtains, as is in examples like (16a) where there is no object clitic. This is to be expected since 1st/2nd person subjects license a strong $D_{P/N}$-feature on T in this dialect and its overt repercussions, namely BE-selection, should be expected to apply irrespective of any other factors. Only at a later stage in the derivation is canonical BE-selection overridden when the clitic is required to move through to BE for independently motivated reasons on clitic placement. Therefore, it is predicted that at some point in the derivation (27b) and (16a) are structurally identical.

Let us now turn to the examples of clitic climbing in the Neapolitan peripheral variety in (27c). In contrast to Novarese and Martinsicurese, the object clitic climbs and auxiliary BE still obtains. This indicates that the participle cannot have incorporated into BE with prior concomitant raising to C/P, for this would have yielded HAVE. Furthermore, the object clitic 'o 'him' cannot remain *in situ* within Vb under T, as in Martinsicurese, since clitics in these varieties must invariably procliticize to their auxiliary. We are forced to conclude therefore that after T has been endowed with a strong $D_{P/N}$-feature and hence finiteness, precluding restructuring-incorporation and HAVE, the clitic under T raises to auxiliary BE through C/P. However, in contrast to (27b), HAVE does not obtain since the clitic excorporates out of C/P,[8] a move independently motivated by Roberts (1991) as an option available to a number of languages (compare such phenomena as Italian clitic climbing, Dutch verb raising).

As a consequence, the differences between Novarese, Martinsicurese and the Neapolitan peripheral varieties reduce to differing dialect-internal conditions on clitic placement and the availability of excorporation, wholly independent of the distribution of HAVE/BE.[9]

6.3.1.2.2. *Alternation according to tense*

The Neapolitan variety spoken on Procida also presents evidence of the generalization of BE (*esse*) as a universal auxiliary. In contrast to the other Neapolitan peripheral varieties, however, BE in Procidano is not sensitive to grammatical person, BE with the 3rd person having legitimate status. Instead, it is determined by tense (see Parascandola 1976: 108). More precisely, the distribution of BE (*esse*) is strictly limited to the pluperfect (29), excluded in the present perfect (30) where HAVE (*avé*) obtains (following examples from Parascandola 1976):[10]

(29) a. *jé fovo   ritto   ca te fuve   puosto cu Nannina ca*
       I   be.PAST.1SG say.PART that you be.PAST.2SG put.PART with Annina   that
       fove   fetto   sciarra cu Satore ca se   fove
       be.PAST.3SG make.PART argument with Salvatore that himself be.PAST.3SG
       'mbarcheto
       join-up.PART
       'I had said that you had got engaged to Annina who had fallen out with Salvatore who had joined the navy'

   b. *comme nen lu fusse   visto*
      as-if   not him be.SUBJ.2SG see.PART
      'as if you had not seen him'

   c. *a primma lenza nen lu fovo   canisciuto*
     at first   look not him be.PAST.ISG know.PART
     'at first I had not recognised him'

   d. *jé nen sapevo   ca fuve   sturieto   la matafissa!*
     I not know.PAST.ISG that be.PAST.2SG study.PAST.2SG the metaphysics
     'I didn't know that you were so intelligent!'

   e. *fovene   parreto   peto e   peto*
     be.PAST.3PL speak.PART father and father
     'their respective fathers had spoken'

(30) a. *jé nun hó   (*so')   sturiéto, ma sòccio fa ri cunte*
     I not have.PRES.ISG (be.PRES.ISG) study.PART but. . .
     'I haven't studied but I can add up'

   b. *hé   (*si)   ritto   na cosa*
     have.PRES.2SG (be.PRES.2SG) say.PART a   thing
     'you have said something'

   c. *nen ha   (*è)   'uto   lu curieggio ra criatura*
     not have.PRES.3SG (be.PRES.3SG) have.PART the courage   as child
     'he was weak as a child'

   d. *amme   (*simme)   magneto allevrete*
     have.PRES.IPL (be.PRES.IPL) eat.PART in-haste
     'we have eaten in a hurry'

This type of alternation according to tense is also found elsewhere in Campania. For example, in the dialect of San Leucio del Sannio (BN) studied by Iannace (1983 :§119), HAVE (*avé*) has generalized in the present perfect to all verb classes, the passive excluded:

(31) a. *eggio   (*so')   fatto   tutto quello ch' eggio*
     have.PRES.ISG (be.PRES.ISG) do.PART all   which that have.PRES.ISG
     pututo
     be-able.PART
     'I have done all that I could'

   b. *iti   (*siti)   venuto   priesto?*
     have.PRES.2PL (be.PRES.2PL) come.PART early
     'did you arrive early?'

   c. *nun ino   (*so')   state   loro*
     not have.PRES.3PL (be.PRES.3PL) be.PART they
     'it was not them'

   d. *eggi'   (*so')   auta   parte*
     have.PRES.ISG (be.PRES.ISG) must.PART leave.INF
     'I have had to leave'

In the pluperfect, in contrast, *esse* is the universal auxiliary with all verb classes:

(32) a. *erem'*   *(*avevamo) auta   dice quello che   diceveno   loro*
be.PAST.1PL (have.PAST.1PL) must.PART say   that   which say.PAST.3PL they
'we had had to say what they said'

b. *illu era   (*aveva)   venuto   priesto*
he be.PAST.3SG (have.PAST.3SG) come.PART early
'he had come early'

c. *s'   era   (*aveva)   truatu   nu bellu postu*
himself be.PAST.3SG (have.PAST.3SG) find.PART a   nice   job
'he had found himself a nice job'

d. *iéri   (*avivi)   jut'   a ccasata*
be.PAST.2SG (have.PAST.2SG) go.PART to house.POSS.2SG
'you had gone home'

To account for the distribution of HAVE in the present perfect and BE in the pluperfect of these varieties, we assume that the head of TP within the participial substructure is co-indexed with the head of TP under BE, with which it forms a T(emporal)-chain. Without entering into the precise mechanisms of T-chains, let us simply assume that the temporal specification of the matrix T is copied into the subordinate participle T, presumably via C/P.[11] What is of prime importance is that BE is only licensed in Procidano and the dialect of San Leucio del Sannio when the auxiliary is specified as [+Past]. Interpreting this within the scalar approach to finiteness outlined in section 6.1, we take past tense verb forms, following Vincent (1990) and Ledgeway (1996b: ch. 1, 3), to be specified as more finite than those marked [-Past], a conclusion substantiated by Giorgi and Pianesi's (1997: §2.2) claim that present tense is zero, hence weak.

What this means for the pluperfect examples (29) and (32) is that participial T inherits via its T-chain with the matrix clause a strong, hence finite, T(ense)-feature. Assimilating this strong T-feature to the previous examples of a strong $D_{P/N}$-feature on T, let us assume that this strong finiteness specification within the participial clause licenses an intrinsic structural Case feature at the head of C/P. It follows, as with the previously studied examples, that BE will obtain since restructuring (= BE-incorporation) cannot take place. In the present perfect (30, 31), on the other hand, the participial T will inherit a weak T-feature, necessitating restructuring-incorporation and yielding HAVE.

Clearly, the present analysis of Procidano and the dialect of San Leucio del Sannio can be straightforwardly extended to account for the similar examples discussed by Kayne (1993: 17–18). Citing Paola Benincà, he notes that an impersonal *se* subject in the Veneto dialect of Padua licenses HAVE, and not BE (see 33a). However, if a reflexive *se* '-self' clitic is added, then the status of auxiliary BE in conjunction with impersonal *se* marginally improves (see 33b). Significantly, though, if the tense of the auxiliary in (33c) is changed from present to imperfect (see 33c), conditional or future, auxiliary BE becomes almost perfect:

(33) a. *se ga   /*ze   balà   tuta la   note*
          se have.PRES.3SG / be.PRES.3SG dance.PART all   the night
          'one has danced all night'

      b. ?? *se se   ze   visti*
             se -self be.PRES.3SG see.PART
             'one has seen oneself'

      c. *se se   gera   visti*
          se -self be.PAST.3SG see.PART
          'one had seen oneself'

Other representative examples come from the Lazio dialect of Cori (LT; see Chiominto 1984: 178–80) and the Abruzzese dialect of Martinsicuro (TE; see Mastrangelo Latini 1981: 242), where 3PL subjects in the present perfect require HAVE with all verb classes, contrary to other persons which generally license BE. Yet, when the auxiliary is [-present], BE is equally licensed with the 3PL. Also of interest is the dialect of Servigliano (AP; see Camilli 1929: 230). Here the distribution of BE excludes 3rd person subjects in the present perfect, where a transitive/unergative-HAVE versus unaccusative-BE split (see 34a–b) uniquely persists, but not in other tenses (see 34c):

(34) a. *quanno ha   parturito la 'acca*
          when   have.PRES.3SG calve.PART the cow
          'when the cow has calved' (Servigliano (AP), Camilli 1929: 244)

      b. *issu è   vvinutu*
          he   be.PRES.3SG come.PART
          'he has come' (ibid., 230)

      c. *quilli de   sagneneso . . . èra   mmazzato lu pettè* (ibid., 238)
          those from Sanginesio   be.PAST.3PL kill.PART the robin
          'those from Sanginesio had killed the robin'

A not too dissimilar case is presented by Altamurano (BA; see Loporcaro 1988: 278ff., 290,;1998: 65) where HAVE/BE occur in free variation in the 1st/2nd persons with all verb classes (see 35a–b). In the 3rd person, by contrast, HAVE/BE occur in complementary distribution with certain verb classes: 3SG subjects with unaccusatives license exclusively BE (see 35c) and 3PL subjects with transitives/unergatives only allow HAVE (see 35d):

(35) a. *'agːjə   man'dʒɛit /sɔ   mːan'dʒɛit*
          have.PRES.ISG eat.PART /be.PRES.ISG eat.PART
          'I have eaten' (Loporcaro 1988: 278)

b. a   mwert   /sə   mːwert
have.PRES.2SG die.PART / be.PRES.2SG die.PART
'you have died' (ibid.)

c. e   /*a   rːʊ'mwɛsə 'sʊul (but awɔnː   rʊ'mwɛsə
be.PRES.3SG / have.PRES.3SG remain.PART alone   (have.PRES.3PL remain.PART
/sɔ   rːʊ'mwɛsə
/be.PRES.3PL remain.PART)
'he has remained alone' (but 'they have remained') (ibid., 281)

d. nan a'wɔnːə   /*ʤɔ   'skrɪtːə mɛ[i] (but nan a
not   have.PRES.3PL /be.PRES.3PL write.PART never   (not have.PRES.3SG
/e   'skrɪtːə mɛ[i])
/be.PRES.3SG write.PART never)
'they have never written' (but 'he has never written') (ibid.)

Yet, in the pluperfect indicative (though not subjunctive) these restrictions disappear, with both 3SG (36a) and 3PL (36b) subjects occurring freely with either auxiliary with all verb classes:

(36) a. a'vaj   /'jerə   man'ʤɛi̯t /mwert
have.PAST.3SG /be.PAST.3SG eat.PART   /die.PART
'he had eaten/died' (Loporcaro 1988: 285)

    b. a'vainə /'jernə   man'ʤɛi̯t /mwert
have.PAST.3PL /be.PAST.3PL eat.PART   /die.PART
'they had eaten/died' (ibid.)

The general conclusion to be drawn from such dialects and the examples in (34)–(36) is that in the present perfect BE obtains invariably with the 1st/ 2nd persons, whereas the 3rd person (more frequently 3PL) licenses HAVE. When the auxiliary is specified as [-present], in contrast, BE obtains uniformly in all persons, 3rd person (plural) included. This suggests that the presence of HAVE in the 3rd person present perfect results from a weak $D_{P/N}$-feature on T, forcing restructuring-incorporation, in contrast to the 1st/2nd persons which license a strong $D_{P/N}$-feature on T and concomitant BE. It follows that the presence of BE in the 3rd person pluperfect be interpreted as the result of the strong T-feature on T, which of course has no effect on the 1st/2nd persons which independently take BE on account of a strong $D_{P/N}$-feature on T.

The category of tense (together with mood) is also reported by Voci (1994: XV) to have repercussions on auxiliary choice in the central Calabrian dialect of Sant'Andrea (CZ). In line with other dialects of the province of Catanzaro and the Extreme South in general (see Rohlfs 1969: §729; Lombardi 1997: ch. 1, 1998b: §3.3), HAVE (*avira*) is generalized to all verb classes irrespective of grammatical person:

(37) a. *avìa statu prima*
    have.PAST.ISG be.PART before
    'I had been before' (Voci 1994: XV)

   b. *avìa accattatu /vindutu*
    have.PAST.ISG buy.PART /sell.PART
    'I had bought/sold' (Voci 1994: XVI)

   c. *àiu statu fora*
    have.PRES.ISG be.PART outside
    'I have been out (a lot recently)' (ibid.: XV)

   d. *àiu jutu /venutu /fattu*
    have.PRES.ISG go.PART /come.PART /do.PART
    'I have been going/coming/doing (recently)' (ibid.)

Exceptionally, however, BE (*essira*) is (optionally) employed in past counter-factuals (at least with unaccusatives):

(38) a. *si fussa statu io. . .*
    if be.SUBJ.ISG be.PART I
    'if I had been. . .' (Voci 1994: XVII)

   b. *si fussa jutu iddu. . .*
    if be.SUBJ.3SG go.PART he
    'if he had gone. . .' (ibid.)

Although these data clearly require further investigation, the restricted use of BE in past counterfactuals, as opposed to generalized HAVE in all other contexts, points to a degree of finiteness within the participial clause licensed by the combination of strong T- and M(ood)-features on T. If this turns out to be the correct interpretation of the facts, then the presence of BE in (38) follows straightforwardly.

6.3.1.2.3. *Clitic-doubling*
Carlo Iandolo (personal communication) points out that in Naples itself the use of a mixed paradigm according to grammatical person characteristic of the peripheral varieties (see section 6.2.2) is rare. This is further supported by the literary medium where such examples prove extremely infrequent:

(39) *ammore perduto, i' t' ero truvato* (De Curtis 1989: 55)
    love lost I you be.PAST.ISG find.PART
    'lost love, I had found you'

However, there is one instance in which *avé* in modern urban Neapolitan alternates with *essere*, namely when a full DP object is doubled by an accusative clitic. This auxiliary alternation obtains on condition that the verb is in the 1/2SG (40a–e), less commonly in the 1/2PL (40f–g), but never obtains when the verb is 3rd person (40h).

(40) a. *'o so'*   *pigliato*   *'o*   *bicchiere*
     it   be.PRES.1SG take.PART the glass
     'I have taken (it) the glass' (Iandolo 1994: 260)

    b. *'a so'*   *vista*   *'a*   *guagliona*
       her be.PRES.1SG see.PART PA-the girl
       'I have seen (her) the girl' (ibid., 258)

    c. *'o*   *songo*   *visto*   *a*   *Ciccio*
       him be.PRES.1SG see.PART PA Ciccio
       'I have seen (him) Ciccio' (ibid., 247)

    d. *'a sî*   *accattata*   *'na casa?*
       it   be.PRES.2SG buy.PART   a   house
       'have you bought (it) a house?'

    e. *'a sî*   *vippeta*   *tutt'*   *'a birra*
       it   be.PRES.2SG drink.PART all   the beer
       'you have drunk (it) all the beer'

    f. *'a simmo*   *astutat'*   *'a radio*
       it   be.PRES.1PL   switch-off.PART the radio
       'we have switched (it) off the radio'

    g. *'a site*   *cuffiata*   *a Rosa*
       her be.PRES.2PL mock.PART PA Rosa
       'you made fun of (her) Rosa'

    h. *l' ha*   *(*è)*   *pigliat'*   *'o bicchiere*
       it   have.PRES.3SG (be.PRES.3SG) take.PART the glass
       'he has taken (it) the glass'

Though in such cases there appears to be a mixed paradigm superficially parallel to that of the peripheral varieties discussed above, the two are very different. Whereas the auxiliary alternation found in the peripheral varieties hinges solely on either grammatical person and/or tense, that found with clitic-doubling in the urban dialect is determined by both grammatical person and the presence of a doubling object clitic. Iandolo (1994: 247, 258, 260), the only grammar of Neapolitan to discuss the phenomenon, observes that such auxiliary alternation is always optional – compare (40a) with (41a) – and increasingly less frequent in the modern dialect. In essence, it tends to be restricted to the speech of older generations. As a result, *avé* is now predominantly used in clitic-doubled constructions in all grammatical persons, especially by younger speakers (see 41b–d):

(41) a. *ll' aggiu*   *pigliato*   *'o bicchiere* (Iandolo 1994: 260)
     it   have.PRES.1SG take.PART the glass

    b. *l' hê*   *accattata*   *'na casa?*
       it   have.PRES.2SG buy.PART   a   house

c. *l'   ammo   astutat'   'a   radio*
   it   have.PRES.1PL   switch-off.PART   the   radio

d. *l'   avite   cuffiat'   a   Rosa*
   her   have.PRES.2PL   mock.PART   PA   Rosa

As is generally the case with auxiliary alternation in Neapolitan, it receives little attention from existing grammars and is barely reflected in the literary language. From the diachronic corpus of texts analysed, only one such example (see 42) of *essere* determined by clitic doubling and grammatical person was found. We are therefore led to conclude that this use of *essere* is restricted to the spoken medium.

(42) *se vuy non avisse   maniate l'   arme non furo-ve*
    if you not have.PAST.SUBJ.2PL use.PART the arms not be.COND.1SG-you

    canesuto né vuy né vustra condicione
    know.PART nor you nor your   condition
    'if you had not used weapons I would not have met you or come to know of your state' (McArthur n.d., 50)

How then do we account for the occurrence of BE in these cases? In the preceding sections we established how strong $D_{P/N}$-, T- and M-feature specifications on T, which we have equated with a certain degree of finiteness, can license an intrinsic structural Case feature in C/P. Under this analysis we should also expect to find examples of the other remaining functional head, namely *v*, triggering BE, if it too can be endowed with the necessary strong (hence finite) features to license an intrinsic structural Case feature. Such a case, we suggest, is represented by the examples in (40a–g). As the contrast between (43a) and (43b) illustrates, it is the doubling clitic which triggers BE, or rather prevents HAVE from obtaining:

(43) a. *'a   so'   chiammat' a   Maria*
      her   be.PRES.1SG call.PART   PA   Maria
      'I have called (her) Maria'

    b. *l'   aggiu   /*'a so'   chiammata*
      her$_i$ have.PRES.1SG /her$_i$ be.PRES.1SG call.PART   pro$_i$
      'I have called her'

In contrast to (43a) where the object clitic references an overt DP object, the object clitic in (43b) licenses and identifies pro and HAVE obtains. An explanation for the occurrence of BE in (43a) therefore presents itself in terms of the status of the doubling clitic. Following Ledgeway (1995: M.I. §6.3; 1996b: ch. 1), we maintain that modern Neapolitan object clitics be treated as verb-object agreement. This conclusion is substantiated by the extremely frequent occurrence of clitic doubling constructions,[12] in some cases quasi-obligatory, where the clitic cannot be interpreted synchronically as a pronominal merged in object position and subsequently raised by head-movement to adjoin to v. Rather, as argued in section 2.3, Neapolitan clitics represent the overt realization of a D-feature on v.

It becomes immediately clear then how we can account for the occurrence of BE in examples such as (43a): by virtue of hosting an object clitic agreeing with an overt DP object, v is endowed with strong Agr features. In other words, v carries a strong D-feature (henceforth D_{Agr}-feature). On the uncontroversial assumption that Agr is one of the exponents of finiteness, we interpret the strong D_{Agr}-feature borne by v in (43a) as an indicator of a certain degree of finiteness within the participial clause which, in turn, licenses an intrinsic structural Case feature in the head of C/P. Consequently, BE-incorporation and resultant HAVE are ruled out.

Finally, however, we must note that BE is excluded in clitic doubling constructions if the subject is 3rd person (see 40h). This implies that a strong D_{Agr}-feature alone on the participial v is not sufficient to license an intrinsic Case feature. In addition to a strong D_{Agr}-feature on v, the participial clause must also be endowed with a strong $D_{P/N}$-feature on T, activated by a 1st/2nd person subject passing through its Spec. Significantly, parallel to the other BE-dialects above, urban spoken Neapolitan exhibits the widespread failure of 3rd person subjects to license a strong $D_{P/N}$-feature on T. The relevant generalization for BE-licensing in urban spoken Neapolitan is therefore the combination of a strong D-feature on T and on v,[13] which together can produce the requisite degree of finiteness necessary to license a structural Case feature in C/P.

6.3.1.3. *Summary*

Keeping technical details to a minimum, we summarize below the results of the preceding discussion. Like other clausal arguments (for example, infinitives, tensed clauses), participial clauses must be licensed. Two possibilities present themselves: either the participle incorporates into the matrix (auxiliary) verb via C/P yielding HAVE (44a), as happens with infinitival complements to restructuring verbs (44b), or the participial clause is marked with a degree of finiteness which licenses an intrinsic Case feature (44c), as with tensed clauses (44d), and BE is preserved:

(44) a. BE + C/P$_i$ (= HAVE) + PART$_j$ [t$_i$ t$_j$]

    b. '*o   voglio   chiammà*
        him$_i$ want.PRES.1SG call.INF$_j$ [$_{CP}$ t$_i$ t$_j$]
        'I want to call him'

    c. BE + [C/P PART [+finite]]

    d. *voglio   che 'o chiammano*
        want.PRES.1SG [$_{CP}$ that him call.PRES.3PL]
        'I want them to call him'

Given this approach, the occurrence of BE licensed by 1st/2nd subjects (peripheral Neapolitan varieties), [-present] tense (Procidano), a combination of [-present] tense and subjunctive mood (Sant'Andrea), and a combination of 1st/2nd subjects and clitic doubling (obsolescent urban Neapolitan), can be simply interpreted as the reflex of a strong (hence finite) feature borne by one or more functional heads of the participial clause, namely strong subject Agr features, T features, T and M features, and subject and object Agr features, respectively.

6.3.2. *Pronominal verbs*

In considering the distribution of the auxiliaries with pronominal verbs,[14] we distinguish four subclasses of pronominal verb:

1. Accusative pronominals: the verb selects as its direct object complement a clitic co-referential with its subject, for example *lavarse* 'to wash (oneself)', *guardarse* 'to look at one self', *menarse* 'to throw oneself, leap';

2. Dative pronominals: the clitic co-referential with the subject corresponds to a genuine indirect object complement subcategorized by the verb, for example *metterse scuorno* 'to be ashamed' (literally 'put shame to oneself'), *muzzecarse 'a lengua* 'to bite one's tongue', *farse male* 'to hurt oneself';

3. Pleonastic pronominals: the verb co-occurs with a dative clitic co-referential with its subject. This clitic is a dative of interest or benefit which heightens the subject's involvement, an extremely common and productive phenomenon of Neapolitan (and other southern Italian dialects) which applies freely to many transitives/unergatives, for example *magnarse na pizza* 'to eat a pizza', *sunnarse caccosa* 'to dream something', *crererse* 'to believe';

4. Inherent pronominals: the clitic co-referential with the subject does not correspond to a verbal argument but is part of the verb's inherent lexico-morphological structure, for example *addunarse* 'to realize', *jirsenne* 'to go away', *affeziunarse* 'to become fond of', *appiccecarse* 'to fall out';

As with unaccusative verbs (see section 6.3.2.4), in the following discussion it will frequently prove necessary to draw a distinction between two varieties of Neapolitan, a literary and a spoken variety. The former is more conservative, patterning more like standard Italian, whereas the latter is of a more innovative nature, characterized by the generalization of *avé*. As with all such generalized distinctions, there is inevitably a degree of overlap with features of the spoken variety sometimes seeping into the literary variety and *vice versa*. For the present analysis, however, we shall treat the two varieties as two quite distinct complementary systems in order to facilitate the discussion. It should be borne in mind, nonetheless, that this is merely an artificial segmentation which in reality proves a lot more complex, determined by a whole range of varying sociolinguistic factors (Sornicola 1977).

6.3.2.1. *Accusative and dative pronominals*

Accusative pronominals in both literary and spoken Neapolitan varieties agree in admitting either *avé* or *essere* (see 45a/f, 45e/j, 45g), although in early texts and present-day spoken Neapolitan *avé* is clearly preferred (Altamura 1961: 73; Radtke 1988: 657). Below follow examples from literary sources with *essere* (45a–e) and *avé* (45f–j) and examples from present-day Neapolitan speakers (46):

(45) a. *se   foy   bene dellongato*
     himself be.PAST.3SG well   distance.PART
     'he had gone far away' (De Blasi 1986: 301, 3)

   b. *te   sei   amirato*
     yourself be.PRES.2SG admire.PART
     'you have admired yourself' (Formentin 1987: LXX)

   c. *me   so   acciso e   mme so   strutto*
     myself be.PRES.1SG kill.PART and myself be.PRES.1SG destroy.PART
     'I have exhausted and destroyed myself' (Lombardi 1783, in Capozzoli 1889)

   d. *nce   simme   assettate e   nce   simme   mise   a*
     ourselves be.PRES.1PL seat.PART and ourselves be.PRES.1PL put.PART to
     mangià
     eat.INF
     'we have sat down and have begun to eat' (Scarpetta 1994: 85)

   e. *chille 'e panne se   so'   'nfracetate*
     those the clothes themselves be.PRES.3PL soak.PART
     'the clothes have got soaked' (Terzigno (NA), De Simone 1994: 764)

   f. *non se   avendo troppo dellongato da   lloro*
     not themselves have.GER too-much distance.PART from them
     'not having moved away too far from them' (De Blasi 1986: 73, 36)

   g. *ma ben me   sono   lamentato . . . me   ho*
     but well myself be.PRES.1SG complain.PART   myself have.PRES.1SG
     lamentato e   lamento
     complain.PART and complain.PRES.1SG
     'however I have complained . . . I have complained and I (continue to) complain' (Formentin 1987: LXIV)

   h. *t'   è   portato da chi compune*
     yourself have.PRES.2SG carry.PART to who compose.PRES.3SG
     'you have gone to the house of he who makes it' (Cortese 1783, in Capozzoli 1889)

i. *v'   avite   fatto   aspettà nu poco*
yourself have.PRES.2PL make.PART wait.INF a little
'you have made them wait for you for a while' (Scarpetta 1994: 79)

j. *quanno s'   hanno   'nfracetate 'e panne*
when themselves have.PRES.3PL soak.PART the clothes
'when the clothes got soaked' (Terzigno (NA), De Simone 1994: 762)

(46) a. *ce   simmo   /ammo   susuto   priesto*
ourselves be.PRES.1PL / have.PRES.1PL get-up.PART early
'we got up early'

b. *s'   ha   menato 'ncuollo a chella llà*
himself have.PRES.3SG throw.PART in-neck to that-one there
'he has thrown himself at her'

c. *v'   'ite   arricriato*
yourself have.PRES.2PL console.PART
'you have consoled yourself'

d. *ma 'o bbello è   ca nun s'   aveva   vestuta*
but the beautiful be.PRES.3SG that not herself have.PAST.3SG dress.PART
ancora
yet
'but the funniest part is that she hadn't yet got dressed'

e. *chille   s'   hanno   vasate sott'   ô   purtone*
those-ones themselves have.PRES.3PL kiss.PART under to-the doorway
'they have kissed each other under the doorway'

Dative pronominal verbs pattern rather like the previous class in that they predominantly select *avé*, although *essere* is found, especially in the literary dialect. Examples with *avé*, the preferred auxiliary, are given in (47a–f) and examples with *essere* in (47g–j):

(47) a. *se   avea   yà   bagnato lo piecto e la face*
herself have.PAST.3SG already wet.PART the chest and the face. . .
'she had already bathed her chest and beautiful face' (De Blasi 1986: 103, 38–104, 1)

b. *me   ayo   ayuncta fatica e pinsiere*
myself have.PRES.1SG add.PART hardship and thoughts
'I have given myself hardship and worries' (ibid., 201, 32–3)

c. *n' autro ppoco lo cuollo m'   aggio   romputo*
an other little the neck myself have.PRES.1SG break.PART
'I almost broke my neck' (Federico 1728, in Capozzoli 1889)

d. *jettaje   na mano de scute ricce, che s'   aveva*
   throw.PAST.3SG a hand of coins   which himself have.PAST.3SG
   fatto   dare   pe chesto effetto
   make.PART give.INF for this   purpose
   'he threw a handful of coins which he had somebody give him for
   this purpose' (Basile 1788, in Capozzoli 1889)

e. *e gamme s'   ha   tirate   e s'   ha*
   the legs   himself have.PRES.3SG pull.PART and himself have.PRES.3SG
   tenute   tutt' arrugnate
   keep.PART all   curled-up
   'he stretched out his legs and then kept them curled up into his
   body' (De Filippo 1975: 189)

f. *vì   che belli   complimenti che s'   hanno   fatto!*
   see.IMP what beautiful compliments   that themselves have.PRES.3PL make.PART
   'what fine compliments they have paid each other' (Scarpetta 1992: 9)

g. *non essendome concessa   una minima bona o per contrario*
   not be.GER-myself concede.PART a   minimal good or for contrary
   resposta
   reply
   'not having given myself a reply, not even a small one' (Formentin
   1987: XXXII)

h. *li rre de Napole se   songo   dato lo titolo de rre de*
   the kings of Naples themselves be.PRES.3PL give the title of king of
   Gierusalemme
   Jerusalem
   'the kings of Naples have given themselves the title of King of
   Jerusalem' (Spassatiempo 1875, in Capozzoli 1889)

i. *io nun me   so'   misa   maie appaura d' 'e muorte*
   I not myself be.PRES.1SG put.PART never fright   of the dead
   'I have never been frightened of ghosts' (De Filippo 1973: 270)

j. *ce   fossemo   parlato 'e niente*
   ourselves be.SUBJ.1PL speak.PART of nothing
   'we had spoken to each other about nothing' (Di Giacomo 1991a: 48)

We begin then by considering how we derive *avé*, the preferred auxiliary in
the spoken dialect with accusative (48a) and dative (48b) pronominals:

(48) a. *m'   aggiu   lavato*
        myself have.PRES.1SG wash.PART
        'I have washed (myself)'

     b. *m'   aggiu   lavato   'e capille*
        myself have.PRES.1SG wash.PART the hairs
        'I have washed my hair'

As with the clitic doubling examples above, we take the 1SG clitic *me* in (48) to be merged on *v*, since, as argued in chapter 2, this is the head responsible for checking accusative in monotransitive structures (48a) and structural dative in ditransitive structures (48b). The derivation proceeds straightforwardly with the participial verb first raising from within VP to *v*, where it adjoins with the clitic *me*. Subsequently the Vb complex, containing the clitic and participle, raises to T where the clitic *me* enters into a Spec-head checking configuration with the coreferential subject, now raised to the intermediate [Spec, T] position *en route* to [Spec, BE]. However, the participial clause lacks an intrinsic structural Case feature, since in the Neapolitan urban dialect a 1st/2nd person subject passing through [Spec, T] is not sufficient in itself to license a requisite degree of finiteness. As we saw in relation to clitic-doubling structures, a strong D_{Agr}-feature on *v* is required in addition. However, this can only obtain on condition that the object clitic doubles an *overt* DP, and not pro as in (48). Consequently, the participle undergoes restructuring-incorporation into BE yielding HAVE.

We now turn to the corresponding examples from the literary variety (49a–b), which preferably licenses BE:

(49) a. *me   so'   lavato*
         myself be.PRES.1SG wash.PART

      b. *me   so'   lavato   'e capille*
         myself be.PRES.1SG wash.PART the hairs

      c. *se è   /so'   lavato   ('e capille)*
         -self be.PRES.3SG /be.PRES.3PL wash.PART (the hairs)
         'he has/they have washed (his/their hair)'

To account for BE in (49a–b), one cannot maintain that, in contrast to the spoken variety, the $D_{P/N}$-feature on T can be activated by a DP subject passing through its Spec, since BE equally obtains with 3rd person subjects (see 49c). Given the widespread failure of the 3rd person to license BE in the Neapolitan peripheral varieties, as well as many central-southern dialects, it would be counterintuitive to suggest that BE in (49) is licensed by a strong $D_{P/N}$-feature on T.

We must therefore find an alternative account which does not rely on the inherent ability of particular grammatical persons to activate the $D_{P/N}$-feature of T. The solution we propose is that in the literary dialect *v* can be activated, namely endowed with a strong D_{Agr}-feature, simply by a clitic merged in an adjoined position, irrespective of whether it references an overt DP or pro. This, however, in itself is not sufficiently strong to trigger BE, since it would incorrectly predict BE with all verb classes when a clitic is present (50):

(50) a. *l' aggiu   /*'o so'   fatto*
         it have.PRES.1SG /it be.PRES.1SG do.PART
         'I have done it'

b. *nce aggiu /*nce so' scritto 'na lettera*
   him.DAT have.PRES.1SG /him.DAT be.PRES.1SG write.PART a letter
   'I have written him a letter'

Rather, in order for BE to be triggered with transitive and dative pronominals in the literary dialect, the D_{Agr}-feature on T must also be activated, an operation made possible when the clitic (together with participle in the Vb complex) raises to adjoin to T. The clitic now adjoined to T enters into a Spec-head checking relation with the coreferential subject raised to [Spec, T], as schematized in (51):

(51) BE + [C/P [$_{TP}$ subj$_i$ *me*$_i$+T [$_{vP}$ t(subj$_i$) t(*me*$_i$). . .]]]

It is this co-indexation between the subject DP and the clitic now adjoined under T that we suggest activates T, endowing it with strong Agr features. Consequently, in conjunction with one another, a strong D_{Agr}-feature on T and on *v* contrive to produce a sufficient degree of finiteness within the participial clause which licenses a structural Case feature in C/P. Therefore, restructuring-incorporation and HAVE are precluded.[15]

6.3.2.1.1. *D-feature strength: some predictions*

The preceding analysis of BE/HAVE distribution in the literary and spoken varieties with accusative/dative pronominals yields some significant results, since it predicts that the spoken and literary varieties are only minimally distinct. In both varieties BE can only be triggered by a combination of a strong D-feature on T and on *v*. In the spoken variety the D-feature on T is activated by a 1st/2nd person subject in its Spec, whereas in the literary variety it is activated by a clitic raised into a Spec-head relation with the coreferential subject in [Spec, T]. On the other hand, the D_{Agr}-feature on *v* is activated in both varieties in a parallel fashion by the presence of a clitic merged under *v*. Yet, the two varieties differ in that the D_{Agr}-feature (hence clitic) on *v* is only activated in the spoken dialect when it agrees with an *overt* full DP object, not pro. In the literary variety, by contrast, the strong D-feature on *v* is activated whether the DP object is overt or pro.

Summarizing, the specific environments in which strong $D_{P/N}$-features on T and strong D_{Agr}-features on *v* obtain in literary Neapolitan (LN) and spoken Neapolitan (SN) are presented in table 6.2:

Table 6.2 D-feature strength in literary and spoken Neapolitan

	T		*v*	
	1/2 pers subject in [Spec, T]	Co-referential clitic in T	Clitic-doubled lexical DP	Clitic-identified pro-DP
LN	–	+	+	+
SN	+	–	+	–

It is thus predicted that BE in conjunction with clitic-doubling constructions and with accusative/dative pronominals is only permitted in the spoken and literary varieties, respectively, and not *vice versa*. BE cannot obtain with clitic-doubling constructions in the literary dialect despite a strong D_{Agr}-feature on v induced by the merged clitic which it hosts, since the D_{Agr}-feature on T is not activated by a subject passing through its Spec as in the spoken variety. This further predicts that BE can only obtain with clitic-doubling constructions in the literary variety if the D_{Agr}-feature on T can be simultaneously activated by an adjoined clitic co-indexed with the subject in its Spec. This prediction is indeed borne out (see 52a):

(52) a. *m'   'e   so'   lavate   'e   capille*
        myself   them   be.PRES.1SG   wash.PART   the   hairs
        'I have washed (it) my hair'

    b. *se   l'   ha   /hanno   lavate   'e   capille*
        -self   them   have.PRES.3SG   /have.PRES.3PL   wash.PART   the   hairs
        'he has/they have washed (it) his/their hair'

Equally, the reverse holds. BE can only obtain with accusative/dative pronominals in the spoken variety if the (in)direct object clitic doubles an overt DP complement, giving rise to a strong D_{Agr}-feature on v. Consequently, example (52a) is also representative of the spoken variety. Examples such as (52a) thus constitute an area of overlap where both the spoken and the literary dialects converge, insofar as their differing conditions on activating the D-features on T and v are simultaneously met.

In addition, this analysis predicts that in the spoken variety HAVE, not BE, will be triggered in (52a) if the subject is not 1st/2nd person because 3rd person subjects cannot activate the $D_{P/N}$-feature on T, and a strong D_{Agr}-feature on v alone is insufficient. Consequently, restructuring-incorporation into BE yielding HAVE is forced to apply. Once again this prediction is borne out (see 52b).

Nevertheless, we observed above that clitic-doubling constructions triggering BE in the spoken dialect are representative only of the speech of older speakers, younger speakers preferring HAVE. This means that in the speech of younger generations the D_{Agr}-feature of v cannot be activated by a clitic agreeing with an overt DP complement. It remains therefore to explain why in the spoken variety a clitic agreeing with an overt DP complement is sufficient to activate the D_{Agr}-feature on v only in the grammar of older speakers, but insufficient in the grammar of younger speakers.

One possible solution that presents itself lies in the progressive increase of clitic-doubling constructions in the dialect over a period of time. Initially, clitic-doubling was a marked option carrying an emphatic interpretation of the object complement (53a), absent from non-doubling structures (53b):[16]

(53) a. *te veco a te*

you see.PRES.1SG PA you

'I see YOU'

b. *veco a te*

see.PRES.1SG PA you

'I see you'

Thus the particular emphasis attained by a clitic doubling an overt DP endowed v with a strong D_{Agr}-feature. However, in the modern dialect doubling structures like (53a) have lost their original emphatic status and now constitute the norm. Indeed, in certain circumstances doubling structures are quasi-obligatory, such that in the modern dialect (53b) is frequently replaced by (53a) without any detectable interpretative difference. We can logically correlate this loss in emphasis of a doubling clitic in the modern dialect with a parallel loss in the strong D_{Agr}-feature on v. As a result, it is predicted that only amongst older speakers can the former emphasis attained by a clitic doubling an overt DP complement still persist and engender a strong D_{Agr}-feature on v. As a consequence, a sentence such as (52a) in the speech of younger generations usually triggers HAVE even in the 1st/2nd persons (see 54), since a strong $D_{P/N}$-feature on T alone is not sufficient to license the requisite degree of finiteness:

(54) *me l' aggiu /te l' hê lavat' 'e capille*

myself it have.PRES.1SG /yourself it have.PRES.2SG wash.PART the hairs

'I/you have washed (it) my/your hair'

To conclude, the relevant generalization to be made about the differences with respect to HAVE/BE alternation in the spoken and literary varieties of Neapolitan is in terms of how the D-features on T and v can be respectively activated. More recently, in the speech of the younger generations the D_{Agr}-feature on v can no longer be activated following the widespread generalization of clitic-doubling, such that BE-incorporation is forced to apply, invariably yielding HAVE.

6.3.2.2. *Pleonastic pronominals*

Pleonastic pronominal verbs invariably select *avé* in both literary and spoken Neapolitan and have done so since earliest texts:

(55) a. *se l' ave perduto*

himself it have.PRES.3SG lose.PART

'he has lost it' (De Blasi 1986: 166, 12)

b. *ve avite aduto novella de chillo che più*

yourself have.PRES.2PL hear.PART news of that-one who most

amo a lo mundo

love.PRES.1SG to the world

'you have heard news of the one I love most in this world'
(McArthur n.d., 52)

    c. *non s'   averria   creduto   maje che lo frate*
       not himself have.COND.3SG believe.PART never that the brother
       fosse   dato   a sti   saute
       be.PAST.SUBJ.3SG give.PART to these jumps
       'he never would have believed that his brother was given to these
       mood swings' (Basile 1788, in Capozzoli 1889)

    d. *lo bello   è   che ncè   avimmo   spise   tutte li*
       the beautiful be.PRES.3SG that ourselves have.PRES.1PL spend.PART all the
       denare
       money
       'the best of it is that we have spent all the money' (Scarpetta 1994:
       187)

    e. *s'   ha   nchiavato ncuorpo cchiù de duje litre de vino*
       himself have.PRES.3SG lock.PART in-body more of two litres of wine
       'he has knocked back more than two litres of wine' (Scarpetta 1992:
       23)

    f. *ce   ammo   affittato na casa ô   mare*
       ourselves have.PRES.1PL rent.PART a house at-the sea
       'we have rented a house at the sea'

    g. *che t'   hê   cucinato 'e bello?*
       what yourself have.PRES.2SG cook.PART of nice
       'what have you cooked, anything nice?'

Very rarely does one find examples of *essere* with these verbs, and then only in literary Neapolitan, presumably due to Italian influence:

(56) a. *te   si   ppigliato collera?*
        yourself be.PRES.2SG take.PART anger
        'have you got angry?' (Spassatiempo 1875, in Capozzoli 1889)

     b. *me   so'   visto 'a morte cu ll'uocchie*
        myself be.PRES.1SG see.PART the death with the-eyes
        'I have seen death with my own eyes' (Di Giacomo 1991a: 60)

As noted above, pleonastic pronominals are heavily utilized in the dialect as a means of heightening the subject's participation in the activity expressed by the verb (see Rohlfs 1969: §640, Tuttle 1986: 277–9, Iandolo 1994: 259, 253–4). However, the pleonastic clitic does not license and identify an argument pro but, rather, references an adjunct pro which functions as a benefactive/ethic dative. It can therefore be omitted without affecting the grammatical status of the sentence, as witnessed in (57):[17]

(57) a. *(s')   avevano   scurdat'   'e chiave â   casa*
        (themselves) have.PAST.3PL forget.PART the keys at-the house
        'they had left the keys at home'

b. *ma stasera (t') hê leggiut' 'o giurnale?*
but this-evening yourself have.PRES.2SG read.PART the newspaper
'have you read the newspaper?'

c. *(ce) amm' accattata na cucina nova*
(ourselves) have.PRES.1PL buy.PART a cooker new
'we have bought a new cooker'

Examples such as (57) are then structurally identical to the sentences in (58), where the benefactive/ethic dative clitic identifies an adjunct pro distinct in reference from the sentential subject and HAVE invariably obtains. It is thus natural to expect HAVE to be licensed even when the benefactive/ethic clitic is co-referential with the sentential subject as in (57).

(58) a. *m' avevano scurdat' 'e chiave â casa*
me have.PAST.3PL forget.PART the keys at-the house
'they left my keys at home'

b. *m' hê leggiut' 'o giurnale*
me have.PRES.2SG read.PART the newspaper
'you read (for) me the newspaper'

c. *t' amm' accattata na cucina nova*
you have.PRES.1PL buy.PART a cooker new
'we have bought you a new cooker'

How then do we account for HAVE in conjunction with pleonastic pronominals? Being associated with a (covert or overt) adjunct DP, and not an argument DP, the pleonastic clitic in (57) will not have a corresponding functional projection within the participial clause. This entails that an adjunct benefactive/ethic clitic cannot activate a functional head, as subjects and complements can. We assume then that the pleonastic clitic is merged under T since it serves to heighten subject participation. Therefore, when the subject passes through [Spec, T], it will also enter into a Spec-head checking relation with the coreferential pleonastic clitic under T. Though this checking relation may activate the D_{Agr}-feature on T in the literary variety (but not the spoken variety), as was the case with transitive and dative pronominal verbs above, a strong D_{Agr}-feature on T alone will not suffice to license BE without a corresponding strong D_{Agr}-feature on v. Restructuring-incorporation of the participle is then forced to apply both in the spoken and literary varieties, yielding HAVE.[18]

6.3.2.3. *Summary*

Let us recap on the results reached in the preceding sections. Beginning with accusative and dative pronominals (for example, *lavarse ('e capille)* 'to wash oneself (one's hair)'), we noted that these license predominantly HAVE and BE in spoken and literary Neapolitan, respectively. In both varieties a strong finiteness feature, and hence BE, can only obtain if both the subject Agr features on T and the object Agr features on *v* can be simultaneously activated. Concretely, in the spoken dialect of older speakers this requires a 1st/2nd person subject and an object clitic doubling an overt DP object, otherwise HAVE obtains. In the speech of younger generations, on the other hand, clitic-doubling cannot activate *v*, thereby precluding BE. In the literary dialect, by contrast, the object Agr features on *v* can be activated by a clitic referencing either an overt DP object or pro, and the subject Agr features on T activated by the accusative/dative clitic raised to T. Consequently, restructuring-incorporation with concomitant HAVE is excluded in the literary dialect.

As for pleonastic pronominals (for example, *crererse* 'to believe'), these were shown to have no effect on auxiliary distribution, with HAVE obtaining in both literary and spoken varieties in accordance with the expected behaviour of transitives/unergatives. Interpreting the pleonastic clitic as an emphatic marker of subject Agr in T, since it serves to highlight subject participation, it alone will not be sufficient to license a degree of finiteness within the participial clause and concomitant BE.

6.3.2.4. *Inherent pronominals and unaccusatives*

6.3.2.4.1. *Inherent pronominals*

Inherently pronominal verbs may take either auxiliary. Nonetheless, the literary dialect clearly prefers *essere* in most instances (see 59), although *avé* is occasionally found with verbs of motion, for example *chesta soa figlyola non se nde **averia** fuyuta con Iasone* (De Blasi 1986: 57, 24) 'this daughter of his would not have run away with Jason.' The modern spoken dialect, by contrast, uses both auxiliaries interchangeably, although there is a notice-able tendency (Carlo Iandolo, personal communication) for *avé* to win out in most cases (see 60):

(59) a. *se   nd'   era   stato   fuyuto*
   himself from-there be.PAST.3SG be.PART flee.PART
   'he had fled' (De Blasi 1986: 267, 3)[19]

   b. *se   nn'   era   ncrapicciato*
   himself of-her be.PAST.3SG fall-for.PART
   'he had fallen for her' (Sarnelli 1788, in Capozzoli 1889)

   c. *se   nn'   era   addonato*
   himself of-it be.PAST.3SG realize.PART
   'he had realized it' (Lombardi 1783, ibid.)

   d. *se   n'   è   caduto*
   himself from-there be.PRES.3SG fall.PART
   'he has fallen down' (Di Giacomo 1991a: 77)

   e. *te   si   contrastato cu   Beatrice, certo?*
   yourself be.PRES.2SG argue.PART with Beatrice certain
   'you have fallen out with Beatrice, haven't you?' (Scarpetta 1994: 64)

f. *s'   era   già   pentuto   'e lassà   'e figlie*
   himself be.PAST.3SG already repent.PART of leave.INF the children
   'he had already repented leaving his children' (Terzigno (NA), De
   Simone 1994: 764)

(60) a. *me   n'   aggio   /me   ne   so'   pentuto*
        myself of-it have.PRES.1SG /myself of-it be.PRES.1SG repent.PART
        'I have repented'

   b. *s'   hann'   /se   so'   appiccecate*
      themselves have.PRES.3PL /themselves be.PRES.3PL fall-out.PART
      'they have fallen out'

   c. *lloro nun s'   avevan'   addunate dô   tubo rutto*
      they   not themselves have.PRES.3PL notice.PART of-the pipe broken
      'they hadn't noticed the broken pipe'

   d. *ce   n'   avevamo   venute   c'   'a lettera ca*
      ourselves from-there have.PAST.1PL come.PART with the letter that
      vulìveve
      want.PAST.2PL
      'we had come with the letter you wanted'

   e. *se   n'   ha   sciso   'a   'ncopp' ô   palazzo*
      himself from-there have.PRES.3SG descend.PART from on   to-the building
      'he came down from the roof of the building'

   f *me   ne   aggiu   fujut'   â   casa*
     myself from-there have.PRES.1SG flee.PART to-the house
     'I have run home'

Neapolitan inherent pronominals are generally descendants of Latin deponents, for example MOVERI 'to move'. Yet, in the passage from Latin to Romance many original (semi-)deponents increasingly became to be marked analytically, used in the active form in conjunction with the anaphor SE '-self', for example SE MOVERE. This made it possible to disambiguate between a true passive reading and an active reading (Tuttle 1986: 250–4) in such pairs as MOVETUR 'he is moved' versus SE MOVET 'he moves' (namely, 'he moves himself'). Thus the Neapolitan equivalent of Classical Latin MOVERI is the pronominal *moverse* 'move.INF-self', arguably a synchronic deponent construction. Other such inherent pronominals in Neapolitan include, among others, *addunarse* 'to realize', *appiccecarse/cuntrastarse* 'to fall out', *pentirse* 'to repent', *nnammurarse* 'to fall in love', *fidanzarse* 'to get engaged', *jirsenne* 'to leave', *turnarsenne* 'to return', *venirsenne* 'to come (away)'. Of significance is the fact that the clitic proform of such inherent pronominal verbs constitutes part of the verb's lexical structure and is not co-indexed with some complement position. This is demonstrated by the fact that the clitic cannot be substituted by a tonic pronoun:

(61) a. *Maria se   pente*   ⇒ **Maria pente   a   se stessa*
Maria   herself repent.PRES.3SG   Maria repent.PRES.3SG PA her self
'Maria repents'

b. *me   n'   adduno*   ⇒ **n' adduno   a   me*
myself of-it realize.PRES.1SG   of-it realize.PRES.1SG PA me
'I realize it'

These are clearly then monovalent verbs. As for their status, we shall take them to be unaccusatives, as is generally assumed to be the case for many of the descendants of Latin (semi-)deponents (Vincent 1982: 85–6). Treating inherent pronominals as unaccusatives is also supported by the fact that they pattern in a parallel fashion to canonical unaccusatives (see section 6.3.2.4.2) with respect to BE/HAVE selection. Moreover, most inherent pronominals share semantic properties with unaccusatives. For instance, many are verbs of motion which independently occur as unaccusatives in their bare pronominal-less form, for example, *jirsenne/jì, turnarsenne/turnà, venirsenne/venì*. Others, by contrast, are verbs of change of state, both physically and metaphorically, for example, *pentirse, nnamurarse, fidanzarse*.

Finally, analysing such verbs as unaccusatives has the advantage of straightforwardly accounting for the impossibility of replacing the pronominal clitic with a tonic pronoun in (61). Under the unaccusative hypothesis, the surface subjects of inherently pronominal verbs are merged as complements in [V, DP], a position which cannot be simultaneously occupied by a tonic object pronoun. For this reason, we take the inherent clitic to be merged under *v*, the canonical licensing head of object clitics, co-indexed with the complement position (here the merger position of the subject). From its adjoined position under *v*, the clitic then enters into a Spec-head checking relation with the sentential subject when the latter is moved through to [Spec, *v*][20] and [Spec, T]. Accordingly, the derivation for a simple inherently pronominal like (61a) will be as in (62):

(62)   *Maria   se   pente*
[$_{SpecT}$ Maria$_i$ [$_T$ {herself$_j$ repent.PRES.3SG$_k$}$_l$ [$_{Specv}$ t$_i$ [$_v$ t$_l$ [$_{VP}$ t$_k$ t$_i$]]]]]

To conclude, under the present analysis inherently pronominal unaccusatives are in fact treated as instances of inherent clitic-doubling constructions, in which the clitic merged on *v* clitic-doubles the subject DP merged in [V, DP].

6.3.2.4.2. *Unaccusatives*

The principal variation in auxiliary selection in the urban dialect occurs with unaccusative verbs. Most grammars of Neapolitan (Oliva 1970, Bichelli 1974; Cicala 1983; Fierro 1989; Imperatore n.d.) do not recognize such variation and simply describe the distribution of the two auxiliaries as identical to that of Italian in terms of a transitive/unaccusative split. The only exceptions to this generalization are Capozzoli (1889: 217–19), Rohlfs (1969: §729) and, in particular, Iandolo (1994: 258–9), who shed some light on the matter.[21] Once again, however, this alternation, in many cases free variation, is seldom reflected in the literary dialect which essentially follows the same pattern as found in modern Italian, namely *essere* with unaccusatives. However, there are some frequent aberrations in the literary dialect which reflect the distribution of *essere* and *avé* in the spoken medium. We must therefore be sure to recognize two distinct varieties of Neapolitan for the purposes of discussing unaccusatives, as proved necessary in the discussion of clitic-doubling structures and pronominal verbs above. In the literary dialect, unaccusatives have since earliest texts generally licensed *essere*:

(63) a. *io non seo   venuto   i' canpo per audire prediche*
        I   not be.PRES.1SG come.PART in field for hear.INF sermons
        'I have not come into battle to listen to sermons' (McArthur n.d., 36)

    b. *chello poco che era   romaso*
        that little that be.PAST.3SG remain.PART
        'the little that had remained' (De Blasi 1986: 61, 5)

    c. *quann' è   cresciuta*
        when be.PRES.3SG grow.PART
        'when it has risen' (Cavalcanti 1837: 80)

    d. *l'   è   ssautato lo grillo de volé   ascì*
        him.DAT be.PRES.3SG jump.PART the caprice of want.INF go-out.INF
        'he has got it into his head that he wants to go out' (Federico 1728, in Capozzoli 1889)

    e. *so   muorto nfra le braccia de l' ammore*
        be.PRES.1SG die.PART in the arms   of the love
        'I have died in the arms of love' (Spassatiempo 1875, ibid.)

    f. *è   trasuto llà dinto*
        be.PRES.3SG enter.PART there inside
        'he has gone inside there' (Di Giacomo 1991a: 116)

    g. *i' songo   nato tunno, ch' aggia   fà?*
        I be.PRES.1SG born round, what must.PRES.1SG do.INF
        'I was born fat, what can I do about it?' (De Filippo 1975: 53)

Spoken Neapolitan, on the other hand, is not so conservative in that unaccusatives may also license *avé*:

(64) a. *sempe aggiu   stato 'n nu negozio 'e pazzielle*
        always have.PRES.1SG be.PART in a shop   of toys
        'I have always been in a toy shop'

b. *a Napole hann' accumminciato 'e frutt' 'e mare ca nu*
at Naples have.PRES.3PL begin.PART the fruits of sea that a
Napulitano va pazzo
Neapolitan go.PRES.3SG crazy
'in Naples the sea food (season) has begun, which Neapolitans go crazy for'

c. *ha schuóppeto*
have.PRES.3SG stop-raining.PART
'it has stopped raining'

d. *aveva sciso mamma a se piglià l' acqua*
have.PAST.3SG descend.PART mum to fetch.INF the water
'mum had gone down to fetch the water'

e. *aggiu turnato ogge*
have.PRES.1SG return.PART today
'I have come back today'

f. *hanno venut' 'e spuse?*
have.PRES.3PL come.PART the newly-weds
'have the newly weds arrived?'

g. *un ce ammo juto cchiù*
not there have.PRES.1PL go.PART anymore
'we haven't gone there since'

It must be noted, though, that this does not mean that a speaker who uses *avé* with unaccusatives, for example, never uses *essere*. Rather, it appears that the two are used interchangeably by all speakers. Particularly pertinent are Capozzoli's (1889: 217) remarks with regard to the free variation of the two:

> In quanto all'ausiliario che accompagna il verbo, francamente confessiamo essere cosa difficilissima dar regole certe, tanto più che, nell'adoperarli [*sic.*], così la plebe, come gli scrittori si avvalgono di una grandissima libertà.

> (As for the auxiliary which accompanies the verb, frankly we confess that it proves very difficult to give any precise rules, so much so that both the masses and writers alike display considerable freedom in their choice of auxiliary.)

Just over a century later, similar claims are echoed in Iandolo's (1994: 258–9) treatment of auxiliary selection in conjunction with unaccusatives:

> Alcuni << Attivi intransitivi >> fanno ricorso – nei tempi composti – all'aiuto contemporaneo e indifferente di << *avere* ed *essere* >> . . . Ess. aggio venuto/so' vvenuto = sono venuto; aggio sagliuto/so' ssagliuto = son salito; aggio turnato/so' tturnato = sono ritornato ecc.

(Some 'active intransitives' [= unaccusatives] in compound tenses can be used interchangeably with *avere* and *essere* . . . e.g. aggio venuto/so' vvenuto 'I have/am come'; aggio sagliuto/so' ssagliuto = 'I have/am gone up'; aggio turnato/so' tturnato = 'I have/am returned', etc.)

The only identifiable limitations of *avé* with unaccusatives seem to be more relevant to sociolinguistic factors than to either syntactic or semantic factors. From discussions with informants, it emerges that the less familiar a speaker is with Italian, the greater use s/he makes of *avé* with unaccusatives. Those speakers that have a greater knowledge of Italian and contact with Italian tend to be more conservative. Thus, for example, speakers of the latter group, broadly speaking, tend to use *avé* with unaccusative verbs of motion, position and change-of-state such as *jì* 'to go', *venì* 'to come', *rummané* 'to stay', *cagnà* 'to change', but not with *essere* 'to be' (and hence the passive) and verbs such as *nascere* 'to be born', *murì* 'to die' (see also Cennamo 1998: 208). Speakers of the first group, in contrast, find *avé* perfectly acceptable with all unaccusatives, *essere* (though not the passive), *nascere* and *murì* included.

A similar situation would appear to obtain in many Campanian dialects, where unaccusatives license both *essere* (65) and *avé* (66), as witnessed by the following contrasts:

(65) a. *nu figlio che è   ghjuto 'nfunno 'e torre*
     a   son   who be.PRES.3SG go.PART in-bottom of tower
     'a son who ended up in the tower' (AV, De Simone 1994: 216)

   b. *la gatta nostra è   morta!*
     the cat   our   be.PRES.3SG die.PART
     'our cat has died' (Serino (AV), ibid., 256)

   c. *Giuvanniello era   muorto comm' a ll' ate*
     Giovanni   be.PAST.3SG die.PART like to the others
     'Giovanni had died like the others' (Guardia Sanframondi (BN), ibid., 320)

   d. *chello che è   stato è   stato!*
     that   which be.PRES.3SG be.PART be.PRES.3SG be.PART
     'what has happened has happened and you can't change it!' (Castellammare di Stabia (NA), ibid., 342)

   e. *so'   sagliuto   ncoppa*
     be.PRES.1SG ascend.PART up
     'I went up' (Ferrari (AV), ibid., 358)

   f. *nun site   jute   addu Su' Maestà?*
     not be.PRES.2PL go.PART to   his majesty
     'did you not go to his Majesty?' (Pomigliano d'Arco (NA), ibid., 448)

g. *era   asciuta   incinta*
be.PAST.3SG go-out.PART pregnant
'she had fell pregnant' (Valle dei Maddaloni (CE), ibid., 532)

h. *c'   erano   juti   rignati, avvocati, studenti*
there be.PAST.3PL go.PART rulers   lawyers   students
'rulers, lawyers and students had gone there' (Baselice (BN), ibid., 728)

(66) a. *sti   parole hanno   asciute   sulo d'   'a vocca d' 'o*
these words have.PRES.3PL come-out.PART only from   the mouth of the
viecchio!
old-one
'these words only came out of the old man's mouth!' (AV, De Simone 1994: 218)

b. *mò âte   venuto   ccà?*
now have.PRES.2PL come.PART here
'now you've come here?' (Serino (AV), ibid., 254)

c. *llà   hanno   muorte 'e paura tanti   crestiani*
there have.PRES.3PL die.PART of fright   so-many men
'there many men died of fright' (Guardia Sanframondi (BN), ibid., 320)

d. *truva' a uno ch' êsse   stato   'e guardia*
find.INF PA one who have.SUBJ.3SG be.PART of guard
'to find someone who had been on guard'(Castellammare di Stabia (NA), ibid., 338)

e. *aggiu   sciso   rint' 'o cellaro*
have.PRES.1SG descend.PART into   the cellar
'I went down into the cellar' (Ferrari (AV), ibid., 358)

f. *chiste   hanno   nate   ccà*
these-ones have.PRES.3PL born.PART here
'they were born here' (Pomigliano d'Arco (NA), ibid., 446)

g. *quanno hanno   arrivate   llòco*
when   have.PRES.3PL arrive.PART there
'when they arrived there' (Valle dei Maddaloni (CE), ibid., 530)

h. *nce n'   hanno   juti   tanti!*
there of-them have.PRES.3PL go.PART many
'many of them have gone there! (Baselice (BN), ibid., 728)

Precisely how long *avé* has been used in Neapolitan with unaccusatives is a rather difficult question to answer satisfactorily without a certain degree of speculation, since literary Neapolitan has remained faithful to the complementary distribution of the two auxiliaries found in early Romance, thus not reflecting spoken practices. Nonetheless, there is good reason to

assume that the use of *avé* goes back at least six centuries, if we are willing
to accept that the occasional use of *avé* with unaccusatives in early written
texts betrays the already growing use of this auxiliary in the spoken dialect
(Cennamo 1998: §2).[22] Below follows a representative sample of such
examples that may plausibly betray spoken usage, as well as some more
recent literary examples:

(67) a. *qualunca   homo   nce   avarria   potuto   morire*
          any   man   thereby have.COND.3SG be-able.PART die.INF
          'any man could have died in this endeavour' (De Blasi 1986: 50, 26)

      b. *se illo avesse   arrivato in Grecia, averriamole*
          if he   have.PAST.SUBJ.3SG arrive.PART in Greece   have.COND.1PL-him.DAT
          facto   plu   honore
          make.PART   more   honour
          'if he had come to Greece, we would have treated him more
          honourably' (ibid., 54, 36–7)

      c. *avessemo   andato a asseyare Troya*
          have.COND.1PL go.PART to siege.INF Troy
          'we would have gone to siege Troy' (ibid., 140, 23)

      d. *ben che avessero   puro foyuto   per luongo spacio de via*
          well that have.PAST.SUBJ.3PL even flee.PART for long   space of road
          'although they had even fled afar' (ibid., 238, 29–30)

      e. *cquanno appe   trasuto a la dereto cammara*
          when   have.PAST.3SG enter.PART to the back room
          'when he had entered into the back room' (Cortese 1783, in
          Capozzoli 1889)

      f. *avite   arrivato*
          have.PRES.2PL arrive.PART
          'you have arrived' (Lombardi 1783, ibid.)

      g. *comme si avesse   iuto   truvanno a quaccheduno*
          as   if have.SUBJ.3SG go.PART find.GER PA someone
          'as if he had been looking for someone' (De Filippo 1973: 127)

      h. *nun saccio   comm' aggio   arrivato   a passà*
          not know.PRES.1SG how   have.PRES.1SG arrive.PART to pass.INF
          'I don't know how I have managed to get through' (Scarpetta 1994:
          186)

The number of examples grows considerably if we also consider raising
and impersonal verbs which can conceivably be analysed as unaccusatives in
most cases. Meteorological verbs are also frequently constructed with *avé* in
early texts and are exclusively constructed with *avé* in present-day Neapolitan:

(68) a. *per che avesse   a lloro paruto   inlicita cosa a crederello*
     for that have.PAST.SUBJ.3SG to them seem.PART . . .
     'because it would have seemed to them illicit to believe him' (De
     Blasi 1986: 58, 4)

   b. *parea quase che   may non avesse   tanto   pyovuto*
     . . .   never not have.PAST.SUBJ.3SG so-much rain.PART
     'it seemed almost as if it had never rained as much' (ibid., 176, 34)

   c. *poi che non te ha   piaciuto . . . reallentare queste mei*
     then that not you have.PRES.3SG please.PART . . .
     fiamme
     'since it has not pleased you . . . to slow my flames' (Formentin
     1987: VIII)

   d. *poco ha   mancato che non fosse   stato*
     little have.PRES.3SG lack.PART that not be.PAST.SUBJ.3SG be.PART
     arzo   a lo ffuoco
     burn.PART at the fire
     'it was almost burnt in the fire' (Basile 1788, in Capozzoli 1889)

   e. *l' autre bellizze avarriano   parzeto   scarpune scarcagnate*
     the other beauties have.COND.3PL seem.PART boots   shabby
     'the other beauties would have seemed like a pair of shabby old
     boots' (Basile 1788, ibid.)

   f. *m' ha   piaciuto   de stare sciuoveto*
     me have.PRES.3SG please.PART of be.INF free
     'it has pleased me to be free' (Cerlone 1825, ibid.)

In view of the large number of such literary examples, it would not appear rash to conclude that the use of *avé* with unaccusatives dates back to at least the fourteenth century. Nonetheless, in the literary language *essere* is the auxiliary *par excellence*. In spoken Neapolitan, in contrast, unaccusatives license either *essere* or *avé*, with the proviso that more conservative speakers tend to avoid *avé* with those verbs which represent the last bastion of residual *essere* territory, namely *essere, nascere, murì*.[23]

6.3.2.4.3. *Adjectival and verbal participles*
Discussing the distribution of BE/HAVE in conjunction with unaccusatives, Kayne (1993: 19) maintains that a clausal projection headed by AgrS 'can never function as an argument to a higher predicate'. Hence if AgrS is present in a participial projection, it must, by implication, be embedded under C/P (= his D/P). Now, for languages like literary Neapolitan which have BE with unaccusatives, Kayne argues that AgrS is absent from the participial clause because movement of the sole argument from [Spec, AgrO] to [Spec, AgrS] would result in a violation of Chomsky's (1991) Last Resort Condition. Consequently, if AgrS is absent, CP (= his DP) need not be

associated with the participial clause. The relevant structure for unaccusatives with BE is then as in (69a):

(69) a. ... BE AgrO [$_{VP}$ [$_{V'}$ V DP]]

   b. ... BE v [$_{VP}$ [$_{V'}$ V DP]]

What the structure in (69a) amounts to saying is that unaccusative participles that license BE are IPs, not CPs. Translated into Chomsky's (1995) T-model, it is not immediately obvious how the results of Kayne's proposed analysis are to be captured, given that there are no exact equivalents of AgrS and AgrO. However, assuming (the outer) [Spec, v] and [Spec, T] to be the positions in which the features of the object and subject are overtly checked, hence intuitively, if not formally, equivalent in this respect to [Spec, AgrO] and [Spec, AgrS], respectively, the structure for unaccusatives with BE in an Agr-less model will be as illustrated in (69b). In short, unaccusative participles with BE are simple vP constituents which fail to project the T and C/P functional layers.

At this point it remains to determine what evidence there is to support the reduced clausal vP structure in (69b) for unaccusative participles with BE in literary Neapolitan. Significant in this respect is Kayne's (1993: 19) observation that, given the structure in (69a) (= our 69b), subject agreement exhibited by unaccusative participles with BE now reduces to a straightforward case of copula-adjective agreement. In short, the bare vP structure in (69b) amounts to treating the participle as a simple adjective. Indeed, this is exactly what we find in Neapolitan (and many other upper southern dialects) which provides evidence of a formal distinction between adjectival and verbal unaccusative participles used with BE and HAVE, respectively.

In particular, it is a striking feature of Neapolitan that since early times participles have presented a multiplicity of forms (see Capozzoli 1889: 138–60; Ledgeway 1995: M.II.§ 2.1.7). With the exception of six verbs, all verbs with an inherited irregular participle have also developed an innovative morphologically regular pendant in -*uto*, giving rise to such irregular/regular pairs as *apierto/araputo* 'open(ed)', *(j)arzo/arduto* 'burnt/burned', *chiuso/chiuduto* 'closed', *cuotto/cociuto* 'cooked', *cuovete/cogliuto* 'collected', *ditto/diciuto* 'said', *lietto/leggiuto* 'read', *rutto/rumputo* 'broken', *scivete/scegliuto* 'chosen', *scritto/scrivuto* 'written', *spaso/spannuto* 'hung out'.[24] Rather than constituting simple free variants, these irregular/regular participial pairs have been morphologically specialized to mark a new and productive formal aspectual distinction between a durative and a punctual participle, respectively. The distinction is not however fully established or invariably respected with all verbs (see Ledgeway 1995: M.II.§2.1.7.4).[25] In particular, the irregular participle is underspecified for the feature [±punctual], which allows it still to be used with punctual value, though there is an increasing tendency for the morphologically regular participle to be preferred in such cases.

230 COMPARATIVE SYNTAX OF DIALECTS OF SOUTHERN ITALY

In general, the aspectual distinction marked by these two participial forms is highlighted by their distribution in conjunction with particular auxiliaries. Specifically, the dynamic aspectual value of the perfective/ passive auxiliaries *avé* 'to have' and *esse* 'to be' calls for the regular [+punctual] participial pendant (see (a) and (b) examples below) or, in some cases, the underspecified irregular pendant (see 70a–b and 71a–b). On the other hand, the resultative aspectual value of the perfective/passive auxiliaries *tené* 'to have, keep' and *stà* 'to stand' (Rohlfs 1969: §733; Ledgeway 1995: S.II.§2.3) renders them compatible only with the irregular [+durative] pendant (see (c) and (d) examples below), providing of course such pairs are available:[26]

(70) a. *sorata   ha   rutt'   /rumput'   'o telefuno*
   sister.POSS.2SG have.PRES.3SG break.PART.IRREG /break.PART.REG the telephone
   'your sister has broken the telephone'

   b. *'o telefuno fuje   rutto   /rumputo*
   the telephone be.PAST.3SG break.PART.IRREG /break.PART.REG
   'the telephone was broken'

   c. *sorata   tene   rutt'   /*rumput'   'o telefuno*
   sister.POSS.2SG have.PRES.3SG break.PART.IRREG / break.PART.REG the telephone
   'your sister has got the telephone broken'

   d. *'o telefuno steva   rutto   /*rumputo*
   the telephone be.PAST.3SG break.PART.IRREG / break.PART.REG
   'the telephone was broken'

(71) a. *'a vecchiarella ha   spase   /spannuto   'e ffiche*
   the old-lady   have.PRES.3SG lay-out.PART.IRREG /lay-out.PART.REG the figs
   ô   sole
   to-the sun
   'the old lady has laid out the figs (to dry) in the sun'

   b. *'e ffiche fujeno   spase   /spannute   ô   sole*
   the figs   be.PAST.3PL lay-out.PART.IRREG /lay-out.PART.REG to-the sun
   ra 'a vecchiarella
   by the old-lady
   'the figs were laid out (to dry) in the sun by the old lady'

   c. *'a vecchiarella tene   spase   /*spannute   'e*
   the old-lady   have.PRES.3SG lay-out.PART.IRREG /lay-out.PART.REG the
   ffiche ô   sule
   figs   to-the sun
   'the old lady has got the figs laid out (to dry) in the sun'

   d. *'e fiche stevano   spase   /*spannute   ô   sule*
   the figs   be.PAST.3PL lay-out.PART.IRREG /lay-out.PART.REG to-the sun
   'the figs were laid out (to dry) in the sun'

(72) a. *aveva   *nfuse   /nfunnuto   'e panne 'nzaccheriate*
have.PAST.ISG soak.PART.IRREG /soak.PART.REG the clothes muddy
'I had soaked the muddy clothes'

b. *'e panne 'nzaccheriate nun erano   state *nfuse*
the clothes muddy   not   be.PAST.3PL be.PART soak.PART.IRREG
/nfunnute
/soak.PART.REG
'the muddy clothes had not been soaked'

c. *teneva   nfuse   /*nfunnute   'e panne 'nzaccheriate*
have.PAST.ISG soak.PART.IRREG /soak.PART.REG the clothes   muddy
rint' a ll' aqua
in   to the water
'I had the muddy clothes soaking in the water'

d. *'e panne 'nzaccheriate stevano   nfuse   /*nfunnute*
the clothes muddy   be.PAST.3PL soak.PART.IRREG /soak.PART.REG
rint' a ll' acqua
in   to the water
'the muddy clothes were soaking in the water'

The aspectual distinctions evidenced in (70)–(72) find a close parallel in
the distribution of the limited Italian distinction between [+durative]
deverbal adjectives and [+punctual] verbal participles in such pairs as
carico/caricato 'laden/loaded', *colmo/colmato* 'full/filled', *fermo/fermato*
'still/stopped', *gonfio/gonfiato* 'swollen/swelled', *guasto/guastato* 'spoilt/
spoiled', *logoro/logorato* 'worn-out/consumed', *scalzo/scalzato* 'bare-foot/
removed (socks and shoes)', *stanco/stancato* 'tired', *sveglio/desto* 'awake,
alert' versus *svegliato/destato* 'woken' (Rohlfs 1968: 376). Given this parallel,
we might therefore conclude that the Neapolitan irregular participle is
ambivalently adjectival and verbal in nature, hence underspecified for the
feature [±N],[27] whereas its regular pendant is strictly verbal, hence marked
[−N]. Indeed, this conclusion is substantiated by the fact that adjectival
participles and canonical adjectives display a parallel distribution (see 73a–
b), whereas verbal participles and canonical adjectives are in complementary
distribution (74a–b):

(73) a. *tengo   scritta   /pronta   chella lettera*
have.PRES.ISG write.PART.IRREG /ready   that   letter
'I have that letter written/ready'

b. *'e vruoccole stevano   ggià   fritte   /pronte*
the broccoli   be.PAST.3PL already fry.PART.IRREG /ready
'the broccoli were already fried/ready'

(74) a. *aggiu   screvuta   /*pronta chella lettera*
have.PRES.ISG write.PART.REG /ready   that   letter
'I have written/ready that letter'

    b. *'a porta fuje   araputa   /*granne*
       the door be.PAST.3SG open.PART.REG /big
      'the door was opened/big'

The (optionally) adjectival nature of irregular participles is further confirmed by the behaviour of agreement. Whereas (desinential) participial agreement in regular participles has tended to progressively disappear in Romance in line with the increasingly verbal function of the participle, (metaphonic) participle agreement in inherited irregular participles has proved remarkably resilient (Ledgeway 1995: M.II. §2.1.7.6; Loporcaro 1998: 24, n. 46, 11ff.).[28] For instance, in examples (70) and (72) above the regular participles display default agreement, namely [-ə], whereas the irregular participles exhibit metaphonic agreement in all cases with their associated DP. Analysing irregular and regular participles as adjectives and verbs, respectively, such agreement patterns find a natural explanation, since only adjectives, but not verbs, typically exhibit agreement with their complements in Romance.

Returning to unaccusatives, we note a similar pattern: the regular participle, marked unambiguously [-N] and hence verbal, only co-occurs with HAVE (see (a) examples below), whereas its irregular pendant, under-specified for [N] and hence ambiguously verbal/adjectival, may occur with either HAVE (verbal function; see (a) examples) or BE (adjectival function; see (b) examples), provided such participial pairs exist (see also Leone 1995: §35 for Sicilian):

(75) a. *ha   scennuto   /sciso   abbascio*
          have.PRES.3SG descend.PART.REG /descend.PART.IRREG down

      b. *è   *scennuto   /sciso   abbascio*
          be.PRES.3SG descend.PART.REG /descend.PART.IRREG down
        'he has come down'

(76) a. *ha   curruto   /curzo   addu Carmela*
          have.PRES.3SG run.PART.REG /run.PART.IRREG to   Carmela

      b. *è   *curruto   /curzo   addu Carmela*
          be.PRES.3SG run.PART.REG /run.PART.IRREG to   Carmela
        'he has run to Carmela's'

(77) a. *aggiu   rimmanuto   /rimasto   senza niente*
          have.PRES.1SG remain.PART.REG /remain.PART.IRREG without anything

      b. *so'   *rimmanuto /rimasto   senza niente*
          be.PRES.1SG remain.PART.REG /remain.PART.IRREG without anything
        'I was left without anything'

The irregular/regular participle dichotomy also correlates with a discrete stative/punctual aspectual distinction in some cases:[29]

(78) a. *ha*   *muruto*   */?muorto*
      have.PRES.3SG die.PART.REG /die.PART.IRREG
      'he has died/?dead'

    b. *è*   *muorto*   */*muruto*
      be.PRES.3SG die.PART.IRREG /die.PART.REG
      'he is dead/*died'

Interpreting the irregular unaccusative participles as adjectives/verbs and their regular pendants as verbs, the appearance of BE/HAVE with the former and HAVE with the latter follows straightforwardly, since copula HAVE is independently excluded with canonical adjectives (compare *stu vino èl/*ha doce* 'this wine is/*has sweet').

In what follows therefore, we interpret the Neapolitan evidence of a formal distinction between adjectival and verbal unaccusative participles in conjunction with BE and HAVE, respectively, to correlate with two distinct participial structures. In particular, we propose in line with Kayne (1993) that unaccusative participles with BE lack the T and C/P functional layers, headed instead by a (light) *a(djective)* as in (79a),[30] whereas unaccusative participles with HAVE project a full CP clause structure (see 79b):

(79) a. . . . BE *a* [$_{AP}$ [$_{A'}$ A DP]] (unaccusatives with BE)

    b. . . . BE C/P T *v* [$_{VP}$ [$_{V'}$ V DP]] (unaccusatives with HAVE)

6.3.2.4.4. *Unaccusatives with* BE

Given the structure in (79a), let us now see how canonical unaccusatives (80a) and inherently pronominal unaccusatives (80b) with BE are derived in the literary dialect.

(80) a. *Maria è*   *scesa*
      Maria be.PRES.3SG descend.PART.F
      'Maria has come down'

    b. *Maria s'*   *è*   *pentuta*
      Maria herself be.PRES.3SG repent.PART
      'Maria has repented'

Beginning with (80a), the sole argument *Maria* is merged as the complement of *scesa* in [V, DP], from which it raises to [Spec, BE] before Spell-Out, as witnessed by the surface order in (80a). Yet, the obligatory feminine agreement on the participle *scesa* (compare metaphonic masculine *sciso*) indicates that *Maria* first raises to [Spec, *a*] within the checking domain of the participle where it checks the latter's strong D-feature and feminine agreement. To all intents and purposes, the derivation of (80a) is therefore identical to that of canonical copula + adjective structures. It follows without further stipulation that C/P-incorporation into BE with resultant HAVE (= restructuring) is not possible, since there is no T or C/P in the relevant structure in (80a).[31] The derivation of the inherent pronominal unaccusative example in (80b) proceeds essentially as for (80a), except that the inherent clitic merged under light *a* raises to adjoin to BE, in accordance with independent conditions on clitics which require them to attach to verbs, and not (participial) adjectives.

6.3.2.4.5. *Unaccusatives with* HAVE
Returning to unaccusatives in the spoken dialect, these predominantly take HAVE, witness (81a–b):

(81) a. *Maria   ha   scennuto   /sciso*
   Maria   have.PRES.3SG descend.PART.REG /descend.PART.IRREG.M
   'Maria has come down'

   b. *Maria   s'   ha   pentuta*
   Maria   herself   have.PRES.3SG repent.PART
   'Maria has repented'

The presence of HAVE in these structures is a sure indication that, contrary to the examples in (80), the participial clause contains a T projection, and by implication C/P in order for BE-incorporation (= restructuring) to take place. Another factor which points to the necessity of a T projection (and hence C/P) in (81) is the fact that *Maria* does not raise to [Spec, *v*], as witnessed by the impossibility of metaphonic participle agreement in (81a), namely *sciso* (M) versus **scesa* (F). In fact, given the impossibility of participial agreement, it is natural to assume that [Spec, *v*] is not projected with unaccusative participles with HAVE. It follows by a process of elimination that the φ-features of the subject *Maria* are checked in [Spec, T]. For unaccusatives with HAVE we propose then the structure in (79b).

   The structures in (81) are now derived as follows: the participle undergoes head-movement first adjoining to *v* (and the inherent clitic in the case of (81b)), and then raises to adjoin to T (where the inherent clitic in (81b) enters into a Spec-head checking relation with the subject now raised to [Spec, T]). However, neither the D-feature on *v* or T has been activated. Therefore, BE cannot obtain and the participle (together with the inherent clitic in the case of (81b)) must incorporate via C/P into BE, yielding HAVE.

6.3.2.4.6. *Summary*
Inherent pronominals (for example, *penterse* 'to repent') were demonstrated to pattern with unaccusatives, both licensing HAVE in the spoken dialect and BE in the literary variety. This led us to propose that inherent pronominals be treated as pronominal unaccusatives, a conclusion substantiated by their similar semantic characteristics (verbs of motion, state and change) and frequent formal similarity (for example, *turnà/turnaresenne* 'to return') with canonical unaccusatives. Furthermore, the proposed unaccusative status of inherent pronominals straightforwardly accounts for the impossibility of

realizing the inherent clitic as a tonic pronoun, since the latter would be competing for the merger position of the subject.

In light of this unified treatment of unaccusatives and inherent pronominals, their distribution with HAVE/BE in the spoken and literary dialects, respectively, was interpreted in terms of two distinct participial structures. In the literary dialect unaccusative participles require BE since they are adjectives and adjectives always license BE. In support of this analysis, a number of cases were noted where Neapolitan formally distinguishes between verbal and adjectival participial pairs. Significantly, only the adjectival pendant of such pairs is compatible with BE, a fact which further explains why participial agreement is restricted to unaccusatives with BE (compare copula-adjective agreement). In the spoken dialect, by contrast, unaccusative participles with HAVE are verbal and can only be licensed by restructuring-incorporation into BE, thereby yielding HAVE.

7

WANT-PASSIVES

7.1. INTRODUCTION

In the present chapter the various uses of VOLERE 'to want' (+ ESSERE 'to be')
+ participle will be examined,[1] a passive periphrasis indigenous to numerous
southern Italian dialects and, to a lesser extent, Italian and several other
Italo-Romance varieties. Save a handful of scant observations, such passive
constructions have remained hitherto essentially unexplored, such that the
geographical distribution and semantic and morphosyntactic properties of
the constructions in question still await in-depth investigation. As an initial
characterization of such structures, we note that VOLERE variously occurs in
three distinct, albeit related, constructions, as witnessed by the Neapolitan
paradigm in (1):

1 a. *Mario vô   mannata   chella   lettera*
      Mario   want.PRES.3SG [send.PART.F.SG that letter.F.SG]
      'Mario wants that letter (to be) sent'

   b. *Mario vô   esse mannata   chella lettera*
      Mario   want.PRES.3SG [be.INF send.PART.F.SG that   letter.F.SG]
      'Mario wants to be sent that letter'

   c. *vô   esse   mannata   chella lettera*
      want.PRES.3SG [be.INF send.PART.F.SG that   letter.F.SG]
      'that letter must be sent/needs sending'

As indicated by their English glosses, all three uses of the VOLERE
periphrasis have a clearly passive value, representing complex complementation structures in which the embedded participial clause represents a non-
finite canonical passive. Notwithstanding such functional affinity, each of
the three sentences in (1a–c) is marked by its own semantic and morphosyntactic characteristics. In sentences (1a–b) VOLERE clearly has a volitional
reading, whereas in (1c) it acquires a distinctly deontic interpretation, in this
respect analogous to the Italian periphrasis *andare* 'to go' + participle (see
Benincà and Poletto 1997: §3.2).

Related to these semantic differences is the interpretation of the passivized
subject. By way of example, consider the Cosentino sentences in (2a–c),
semantically analogous to those in (1a–c), respectively:

(2) a. *Mariu vo   mannata   chira littera*
       Mario   want.PRES.3SG [send.PART.F.SG that   letter.F.SG

b. *Mariu* *vo*   *mannatu*   *chira littera*
   Mario   want.PRES.3SG [send.PART.M.SG that   letter.F.SG]

c. *vo*   *mannata*   *chira littera*
   want.PRES.3SG [send.PART.F.SG that   letter]

As evidenced by participial agreement, the passivized subject in (2a–c) is variously interpreted as the underlying direct object *chira littera* 'that letter' (2a), the underlying indirect object *Mariu* (2b), and the underlying direct object *chira littera* 'that letter' (2c).

When considered in relation to the core properties exhibited by southern Italian dialects, the syntax of the various VOLERE periphrases proves quite exceptional, raising a number of issues of interest to both Romance and theoretical linguists alike. In particular, one of the most salient features of the dialects of southern Italy is the general unpopularity of the canonical passive marked by the auxiliary ESSERE + participle (Cennamo 1997: 146–53).[2] While it emerges that canonical passives are limitedly attested (see 3), particularly in formal and learned registers, they tend to prove less felicitous when the subjectized argument and, if present, the by-phrase AGENT are specified as [+hum.] or [+an.]:

(3) a. la 'kasa a   'ʃtati   'fœttə di 'pokə
       the house have.PRES.3SG be.PART do.PART of little
       'the house has been built recently' (Tollo (CH), Cennamo 1997: 149)

   b. lʊ 'pwɛnə nan ɛ   'stɛtə ta'gːjɛit
       the bread   not be.PRES.3SG be.PART cut.PART
       'the bread has not been cut' (Altamura (BA), Loporcaro 1988: 291)

   c. *'a coscia d' 'o malato fuie*   *tagliato*
       the thigh   of the patient   be.PAST.3SG cut.PART
       'the patient's leg was amputated'   (NA, Iandolo 1994: 259)

   d. *i ficu su*   *stati*   *coti*
       the figs be.PRES.3PL be.PART harvest.PART
       'the figs have been harvested' (CS)

   e *ssa varca fu*   *arrubbata*
       this boat   be.PAST.3SG steal.PART
       'this boat was stolen' (TP, Pitré 1875: IV, 3)

In their place are generally preferred active structures, frequently involving left-dislocation of the topicalized argument and referencing of the latter on the verb with a clitic proform:

(4) a. *'hanu*   *muzzicatu i*   *cani*
       him-have.PRES.3PL bite.PART   the dogs
       'he was bitten by the dogs' (Castrovillari (CS), Battipede 1987: 256)

b. a mːai mə rə'spetːənə
PA me   me respect.PRES.3PL
'I am respected' (Altamura (BA), Loporcaro 1988: 291)

c. *'a varca, se   l' hanno   arrubbata   'e   mariuole*
the boat   themselves it have.PRES.3PL steal.PART the thieves
'the boat was stolen by the thieves' (NA)

d. *a   piekura, si   l' ha   mangiata u   lupu*
the sheep   itself it have.PRES.3SG eat.PART   the wolf
'the sheep was eaten by the wolf' (Cetrara (CS), Forestiero 1985: 39)

e. *a   casa n' incendiu a bruciàu*
the house a fire   it burn.PAST.3SG
'the house was burnt down in a fire' (RC, Meliadò 1994: 145)

f. *Pippinu, comu lu   víttiru,   u   chiamaru*
Peppino when him see.PAST.3PL him call.PAST.3PL
'Peppino, as soon as he was seen, was called over' (Sicily, Varvaro 1988: 725)

Analogously, in parts of southern Italy, particularly Calabria and Sicily, the canonical passive is frequently rivalled by an active periphrasis consisting of HABERE + HABITU + participle:[3]

(5) a. *essa ha   'vuto   rialata   'na bicicletta*
she have.PRES.3SG have.PART give.PART a   bicycle
'she was given a bicycle (as a present)' (NA)

b. *amu   avutu   aggiustat' 'a machina*
have.PRES.1PL have.PART repair.PART the car
'our car was repaired' (CS)

c. *nun aju   avutu   regalatu mancu 'nu sordu*
not have.PRES.1SG have.PART give.PART not-even a   penny
'I've never been given a penny' (Aprigliano (CS), Accattatis 1895: §224)

d. *na nobbili signura di   Guascogna . . . appi   fatta   da alcuni*
a noble   lady   from Guascon   have.PAST.3SG do.PART by some
omini na vriugnusa offisa
men   a shameful insult
'a noble lady from Guascon . . . had received a disgraceful insult from some men' (Sicily, Rohlfs 1969: 131, n. 3)

e. *li dui armali ca avèvinu   avutu   libbràta la vita d' iddu*
the two animals that have.PAST.3PL have.PART free.PART the life by him
'the two animals which had been freed by him' (Acireale (CT), Pitrè 1875: II, 287)

f. *stu iocu, l' aiu   avutu   'nsignatu di me patri*
   this game it have.PRES.ISG have.PART teach.PART by my father
   'I had this game taught to me by my father' (Sicily, La Fauci 1984:
   124, footnote 53)

g. *sta cosa,   l' aiu   avutu/a   ditta   di iddu*
   this thing.F.SG it have.PRES.ISG have.PART.M.SG/F.SG tell.PART.F.SG by him
   'I had this thing told to me by my father' (ibid.)

By contrast, we have seen that the want-passive construction, which in
all respects can be considered to comprise an embedded canonical passive,
is a frequently employed structure in the dialects of southern Italy, despite
the frequent [+an., + hum.] specification of the subjectized non-AGENT
argument.

Even more striking in this respect is the range of arguments which can be
subjectized in want-passives. In section 2.2.2.2 we noted that, besides direct
objects, some indirect objects of monotransitive verbs can, though often
with somewhat marginal results, be passivized. In ditransitive structures, on
the other hand, dative passivization invariably produces unacceptable
results, witness the Neapolitan examples in (6):

(6) a. *te ha   turnato   arreto 'e sorde* ⇒ **sî   stato*
       you have.PRES.3SG return.PART back   the money   be.PRES.2SG be.PART
       turnato   arreto 'e   sorde ('a isso)
       return.PART back   the money (by him)
       'he returned the money to you' ⇒ 'you were returned the money (by
       him)'

   b. *nce mannaieno 'na lettera* ⇒ **fuje   mannato 'na littera ('a*
      him send.PAST.3PL a   letter   be.PAST.3SG send.PART a   letter   (by
      lloro)
      them)
      'they sent him a letter' ⇒ 'he was sent a letter'

With the exception of Altamurano, which freely allows dative passivization
for independent historical reasons arising out of a variable pattern of
auxiliary selection (Loporcaro 1988: 292–3), the equivalent sentences of
(6a–b) prove ungrammatical in all southern Italian dialects.[4] Nonetheless,
dative passivization with ditransitive participles embedded under VOLERE
proves perfectly acceptable (see 1b, 2b).

Related to this latter point is the contrast between southern Italian
dialects on the one hand and northern Italian varieties, including Italian,
on the other. Whereas dative passivization under VOLERE proves grammatical in the former (see 1b, 2b), it is entirely excluded in the latter, witness the
ungrammatical Turinese and Italian examples in (7):

(7) a. *'marjo a vøl   'ese   man'dɒ   la 'lɛtra (TO)

   b. *Mario vuole   essere mandatola la lettera (Italian)
      Mario   want.PRES.3SG be.INF send.PART   the letter
     'Mario wants to be sent the letter'

Finally, we need to establish the precise pragmatico-semantic function of want-passives and, in particular, the contrast which arises between the choice of a participial complement (see 1a–b, 2a–b) and a finite *che/chi-*complement (see 8a–b) following VOLERE:

(8) a. *Mario vuleva*   *che mannasseno 'a lettera*
      Mario want.PAST.3SG that send.SUBJ.3PL the letter
     'Mario wanted that they send the letter' (NA)

   b. *Mario vuleva*   *che ce mannasseno 'a lettera*
      Mario$_i$ want.PAST.3SG that him$_i$ send.SUBJ.3PL the letter
     'Mario wanted that they send him the letter' (NA)

The chapter is organized as follows. In section 7.2 we lay bare the essentials facts on the syntax of want-passives, concentrating, in particular, on their distribution, participial agreement, the occurrence of the ESSERE auxiliary and the availability of dative passivization. This is followed in sections 7.3–7.5 by a theoretical interpretation of such facts, demonstrating the importance of the MLC in constraining dative passivization, participial agreement and the presence of the auxiliary ESSERE. Finally, in section 7.6 an explanation is proposed to account for the availability of dative passivization in the South and its absence in the North, drawing on the analysis of structural and inherent dative Case outlined in chapter 2.

7.2. FUNDAMENTAL PROPERTIES

7.2.1. Complement type

We begin by considering the three Italian infinitival structures in (9):

(9) a. *vedo*   *Gianni scrivere la lettera* (ECM)
      see.PRES.1SG [Gianni write.INF the letter]
     'I see Gianni write the letter'

   b. *Gianni promette*   *di*   *scrivere la lettera* (OC)
      Gianni$_i$ promise.PRES.3SG [of t$_i$ write.INF the letter]
     'Gianni promises to write the letter'

   c. *la lettera deve*   *essere scritta*   (SR)
      the letter$_i$ must.PRES.3SG [t$_i$ be.INF write.PART t$_i$]
     'the letter must be written'

Although the infinitival subjects *Gianni* in (9a–b) and *la lettera* in (9c) are θ-marked in the embedded infinitival clause, they check their Case feature in the matrix clause. In the exceptional Case-marking (ECM) example (9a), *Gianni* raises to the matrix verb *vedo* 'I see' at LF to check accusative, as witnessed by the accusative clitic in (10a) and its ability to undergo passivization in (10b):

(10) a. *lo vedo   scrivere la lettera*
           him$_i$ see.PRES.1SG [t$_i$ write.INF the letter]
           'I see him write the letter'

     b. *Gianni fu   visto   scrivere la lettera*
           Gianni$_i$ be.PAST.3SG see.PART [t$_i$ write.INF the letter]
           'Gianni was seen to write the letter'

In the subject control (OC) and subject raising (SR) examples in (9b–c), by contrast, *Gianni* and *la lettera* raise overtly to the matrix subject position to check nominative. However, they differ minimally from one another in that *Gianni* in (9b) checks, in addition, the external θ-role of *promette* 'promises' (see discussion in section 3.3.2.1). In (9c), on the other hand, *deve* 'must' is athematic and as such does not assign an external θ-role. Thus, subject-raising targets a θ-position in (9b), but not (9c).

Parallel complementation structures are licensed by the three VOLERE participial constructions, witness the following Neapolitan examples:

(11) a. *('a) voglio   scritt'   'a lettera* (ECM)
           (it) want.PRES.1SG [write.PART the letter]
           'I want (it) the letter written'

     b. *Giuanne vô   essere scritt'   'a lettera* (OC)
           Gianni$_i$ want.PRES.3SG [t$_i$ be.INF write.PART the letter]
           'Gianni wants to be written the letter'

     c. *'a lettera vô   essere scritta* (SR)
           the letter$_i$ want.PRES.3SG [t$_i$ be.INF write.PART t$_i$]
           'the letter must be written'

In the ECM construction (11a) the participial THEME *'a lettera* 'the letter' is marked accusative by the matrix verb *voglio* 'I want', as demonstrated by the doubling accusative clitic *'a* 'it' given in parentheses. In the OC and SR constructions in (11b–c), in contrast, the subjectized arguments *Giuanne* and *'a lettera*, respectively, raise to the matrix clause to check nominative. Furthermore, the differing thematic properties of volitional (ECM/OC) VOLERE in (11a–b) versus deontic (SR) VOLERE in (11c) are demonstrated by the fact that in the former VOLERE imposes a specific thematic interpretation on its subject, assigning to it the EXPERIENCER θ-role. By virtue of being thematically interpreted as an EXPERIENCER, the subject of ECM VOLERE (12) and OC VOLERE (13) must be [+an.]:

(12) a. *màmmeta   te   vo'   morta*
mum.POSS.2SG you want.PRES.3SG die.PART
'your mother wants you dead' (Valle dei Maddaloni (CE), De Simone 1994: 526)

b. *i ssa stòria a vòglio   fənita*
I this story it want.PRES.1SG finish.PART
'I want this episode finished' (San Leucio del Sannio (BN), Iannace 1983: §152)

c. *Santu vo   appicciatu   'u fuornu pi cocia u pane*
Santo want.PRES.3SG switch-on.PART the oven   . . .
'Santo wants the oven switched on to bake the bread' (Belsito (CS))

d. *mi cce vuliti   assittatu ccu bbue supra 'ssi vanchi?*
me there want.PRES.2PL seat.PART with you on   these benches
'do you want me seated next to you on this bench?' (Conflenti (CZ), Butera 1978: 36)

e. *u voliti   diciutu in lingua 'taliana?*
it want.PRES.2PL say.PART in language Italian
'do you want it said in Italian?' (Delianuova (RC), Coloprisco 1986: 70)

f. *vosi   cantata chidda d' u   pulici*
want.PAST.3SG sing.PART that-one of the flea
'she wanted sung the one about the flea' (Belpasso (CT), Martoglio 1978a)

g. *lu Re vulìa   sbarratu lu magazè di sterru*
the king want.PAST.3SG clear.PART the warehouse of rubble
'the King wanted the warehouse cleared of rubble' (Casteltermini (AG), Pitrè 1875: I, 147)

h. *vogghiu   fatta   n' àutra cosa: vogghiu   nutricatu un*
want.PRES.1SG do.PART an other thing want.PRES.1SG nourish.PART a
cagnulinu
dog
'I want another thing done: I want a puppy raised' (Borgetto (PA), Pitré 1875: I, 397)

(13) a. *lo 'rano lo 'ɔʎʎo   'ɛsse pa'ɣatu adde'ma*
the wheat it want.PRES.1SG be.INF pay.PART tomorrow
'I want to be paid for the wheat tomorrow' (Ascrea (Lazio), Cennamo 1997: 151)

b. *chella vuleva   essere affittata na casa*
that-one want.PAST.3SG be.INF rent.PART a house
'she wanted to be rented a house' (NA, Scarpetta 1994: 24)

c. *mmò voglio   essere pagato 'o danno*
   now want.PRES.1SG be.INF pay.PART the damage
   'now I want to be paid for the damage' (Calitri (AV), De Simone
   1994: 362)

d. *nun vuleva   essere sbruvignata nnanze a tutti*
   not want.PAST.3SG be.INF shame.PART before to all
   'she didn't want to be shamed in front of everybody' (Basilice (BN),
   ibid., 734)

e. *sempre lui vuol   essere passato il pallone*
   always he want.PRES.3SG be.INF pass.PART the ball
   'he always wants to be passed the ball' (reg. Italian, Anzi (PZ),
   Ruggieri and Batinti 1992: 86)

f. pə'pːinə   wol   'esːə tələfu'nɛit
   Peppino want.PRES.3SG be.INF telephone.PART
   'Peppino wants to be telephoned' (Altamura (BA), Loporcaro
   1988: 305)

g. nam 'bʷogːj   esː   mbru'gɛi̯t
   not want.PRES.1SG be.INF trick.PART
   'I don't want to be tricked' (ibid., 208, n. 17)

h. *vò   chiamatə*
   want.PRES.3SG call.PART
   'he wants to be called' (Salento, Rohlfs 1956–61: II, 847)

i. *vulera   aiutatu   a tija*
   want.COND.1SG help.PART by you
   'I'd like to be helped by you' (Castrovillari (CS), Battipede 1987:
   218)

j. *nu piacire oje . . . de tia vorra   fattu*
   a favour today by you want.COND.1SG do.PART
   'a favour today . . . I'd like granted of you' (CS, Chiappetta 1899:
   92)

k. *vo'   circata   scusa!*
   want.PRES.3SG ask-for.PART forgiveness
   'she wants to be asked for forgiveness!' (CZ, Butera 1978: 75)

l. *vônnu   chiusi   menzura cu la figghia*
   want.PRES.3PL close.PART half-hour with the daughter
   'they want to be left alone with their daughter for half an hour'
   (VV, Satriani 1953: 186)

m. *non vulimu   essiri scunzati*
   not want.PRES.1PL be.INF bother.PART
   'we don't want to be bothered' (Gallina (RC), Zolea 1986: 32)

n. *Maria vosi   essiri ccattata a casa*
Maria want.PAST be.INF buy.PART the house
'Maria wanted to be bought the house' (Sicily, Leone 1995: 72)

o. *vuogliu   essiri assittata a lu giru di mà niputi*
want.PRES.1SG be.INF seat.PART to the round of my nephew
'I want to be seated next to my nephew' (Casteltermini (AG), Pitrè 1875: II, 280)

In its deontic function, on the other hand, VOLERE is an athematic predicate which imposes no such thematic restrictions on its subject, witness its incompatibility with the EXPERIENCER-oriented adverb *persunalmente* 'personally' in (14a). Consequently, the subject can be, and most frequently is, specified [-an.], as in (14b-j):

(14) a. (**persunalmente**) i   milungiane vonnu   girate*
(personally)   the aubergines want.PRES.3PL turn.PART
'(*personally) the aubergines must be turned over' (CS)

b. *la çhosse la   ul   fate*
the thing.F.SG S.CL.F.SG want.PRES.3SG do.PART
'the thing must be done' (Friulian, Salvioni 1912: 379)

c. *questo sonetto vuol   copiato su cartoncino bianco*
this   sonnet want.PRES.3SG copy.PART on card   white
'this sonnet must be copied onto white card' (Sardinian reg. Italian, ibid., 380)

d. *chella machina da   soja vuleva   esse aggiustata*
that   car   of-the his want.PAST.3SG be.INF repair.PART
'that car of his had to be repaired' (Boscotrecase (NA))

e. *'kɛsa kʊ'wɛrt wol   'esːə la'vɛit*
this blanket want.PRES.3SG be.INF wash.PART
'this blanket must be washed' (Altamura (BA), Loporcaro 1988: 306)

f. *lu pisce ulia   mangiatu stammane*
the fish want.PAST.3SG eat.PART this-morning
'the fish had to be eaten this morning' (Maglie (LE), Salvioni 1912: 379)

g. *vuenu   lavati i piatti e vò   jettatu u brodu*
want.PRES.3PL wash.PART the dishes and want.PRES.3SG throw.PART the broth
languidu
languid
'the dishes have to be washed up and that weak broth needs to be thrown away' (Mendicino (CS), Barca 1996: 110)

h. *l'   apunioni . . . vau   rispettate!*
the opinions   want.PRES.3PL respect.PART
'opinions . . . must be respected' (Savelli (CZ), Gentile 1992: 121)

i. *tutti li rosi vonnu   mbiverati*
all   the roses want.PRES.3PL water.PART
'all the roses must be watered' (Casignana (RC), Convitto 1894: 28)

j. *il   muro vuole   aggiustato*
the wall   want.PRES.3SG repair.PART
'the wall must be repaired' (reg. Sicilian Italian, Alfieri 1992: 848)

7.2.2. *Participial agreement*

In ECM structures participial agreement is invariably controlled by the embedded THEME argument, as evidenced by the following examples:

(15) a. *voglio   fatta   giustizia*
want.PRES.1SG do.PART.F.SG justice.F.SG
'I want justice to be done' (Italian, Rohlfs 1969: 131)

b. *maritoma   vuleva   cott'   /*cuott'   'a torta*
husband.POSS.1SG want.PAST.3SG cook.PART.F / cook.PART.M the cake
'my husband wanted the cake cooked' (NA)

c. *le   vuâgghju   fatti   cumu i   vuastri*
them.M.PL want.PRES.1SG do.PART.M.PL like   the yours
'I want them done just like yours' (Longobucco (CS), Parrilla 1990: 264)

d. *ngi dumandáu pecchí avía   volutu   minata   chija*
him ask.PAST.3SG why   have.PAST.3SG want.PART deal.PART.F.SG that
fandalata
slap.F.SG
'he asked him why he had wanted that slap dealt' (Pizzo (CZ), Cosco 1987: 114)

e. *vogghiu   annullat'   u   mathrimonio!!!*
want.PRES.1SG cancel.PART.M.SG the marriage.M.SG
'I want the wedding called off' (Zagarise (CZ), Gallelli 1987: 21)

f. *no la   vogghiu   maniata   la testa*
not it.F.SG want.PRES.1SG handle.PART.F.SG the head
'I don't want my head touched' (RC, Satriani 1953: 177)

g. *illa vulìa   accattata   chilla terra*
she want.PAST.3SG buy.PART.F.SG that   land.F.SG
'she wanted that land to be bought' (Gioiosa Ionica (RC))

h. *vogghiu   mannatu   nu paccu*
   want.PRES.1SG send.PART.M.SG a   package.M.SG
   'I want a package to be sent' (Sicily, Varvaro 1988: 725)

i. *iddu voli   fattu   nu palazzu aguali di lu sò*
   he   want.PRES.3SG make.PART.M.SG a   palace.M.SG equal of the theirs
   'he wants a palace built identical to theirs' (Casteltermini (AG),
   Pitrè 1875: I, 146)

j. *vulía   fattu   un siggiuni   magnificu*
   want.PAST.3SG make.PART.M.SG a   pack-saddle.M.SG magnificent
   'he wanted made a magnificent pack-saddle' (Polizzi-Generosa
   (PA), Pitrè 1875: III, 226)

In OC and SR sentences, by contrast, participial agreement shows
considerable cross-dialectal variation in accordance with the nature of the
subjectized argument. In dialects of northern Calabria (CS/CZ) and Salento,
henceforth group 1 dialects, participial agreement is invariably controlled by
the subjectized argument, be it the underlying THEME (16) or GOAL of a
monotransitive (17) or ditransitive (18) participle:

(16) a. *sta situazione vò   aggiustata*
         this situation.F.SG want.PRES.3SG sort-out.PART.F.SG
         'this situation must be sorted out' (Mendicino (CS), Barca 1996: 96)

      b.   *vo   fattu   cunziglieri*
         pro.3SG.M want.PRES.3SG make.PART.M.SG councillor
         'he wants to be made a councillor' (Rogliano (CS), Falbo 1991: 144)

      c.   *vonnu   misi   a moddhu*
         pro.3PL.M want.PRES.3PL put.PART.M.PL to soak
         'they must be soaked' (CZ, Gemelli 1990: 16)

      d.   *ha   bbulutu   accumpagnata*
         pro.3SG.F have.PRES.3SG want.PART accompany.PART.F.SG
         'she wanted to be accompanied' (Conflenti (CZ), Butera 1978: 90)

      e.   *uéi   jutatu*
         pro.2SG.M want.PRES.2.SG help.PART.M.SG
         'you want to be helped' (Salento, Rohlfs 1956–61: II, 785)

(17) a. *tu, Signuri, lu sai,   non vue   'mparatu*
         you Lord   it know.PRES.2SG not want.PRES.2SG teach.PART.2.M.SG
         'Lord you know, you don't need to be taught' (Serra San Bruno
         (CZ), Carlino 1981: 58)

      b.   *vonnu   telefunati   /parrati*
         pro.3PL.M want.PRES.3PL telephone.PART.M.PL /speak-to.PART.3.M.PL
         /rispusi   /cucinati   /sparati
         /reply-to.PART.3.M.PL /cook-for.PART.M.PL /shoot-at.PART.M.PL
         'they want to/must be telephoned/spoken to/replied to/cooked for/
         shot at' (CS)

(18) a. *nne*   *vuegliu*   *data*   *e*   *vue!*
of-it   pro.1SG.F   want.PRES.1SG   give.PART.F.SG   by you
'I want to be given some by you' (CS, Ciardullo 1984: 289)

b.   *vò*   *rennuta*   *a*   *dota*
pro.3SG.F   want.PRES.3SG   return.PART.F.SG   the   dowry.F.SG
'she wants to be given back her dowry' (CS, De Marco 1986a: 71)

c. *tu*   *vu*   *dittu*   *e*   *mia cumu stai?*
you.M.SG   want.PRES.2SG   tell.PART.M.SG   by me   how   be.PRES.2SG
'you want to be told by me how you are?' (ibid., 92)

d. *idda vo*   *lavata*   *sti*   *capiddi*   *fitusi*
she   want.PART.F.SG   wash.PART.F.SG   these   hairs.M.PL   dirty
'she wants her hair washed' (CS)

e. *vonnu*   *cuotti*   *nu piattu*   '*i pasta* '*i*   *guagliuni*
want.PRES.3PL   cook.PART.3.M.PL   a   plate.M.SG   of   pasta   the   boys
'the boys want to be cooked a bowl of pasta' (CS)

f. *se*   *fimmine vulissinu*   *ammaccate a*   *capu*
these   women   want.COND.3PL   dent.PART.F.PL   the   head.F.SG
'these women need their heads banged together' (Mendicino (CS), Barca 1996: 119)

g. *l'*   *auture*   *vogliu*   *dittu!*
the   author.M.SG   pro.1SG.M   want.PRES.1SG   tell.PART.M.SG
'I want to be told who the author is' (Rogliano (CS), Falbo 1991: 69)

h. *la gallina sua*   *volìa*   *votata*
the hen   her   pro.3SG.F   want.PAST.3SG   return.PART.F.SG
'she wanted to be returned the hen' (Calabria, Gliozzi, n.d., 16)

i.   *volarrissavu misi*   *i*   *ferra!*
pro.2PL.M   want.COND.2PL   put.PART.M.PL   the   irons.F.PL
'you ought to be handcuffed' (Nicotera (CZ), Carè 1984: 103)

In all other dialects, henceforth group 2 dialects, participial agreement is invariably controlled by the THEME argument (19), including ditransitive structures (20) where the GOAL argument has been subjectized:

(19) a.   *chère*   *castigada*
pro.3SG.F   want.PRES.3SG   castigate.PART.3SG
'she must be punished' (NU, Salvioni 1912: 380)

b. *Su' Maistà,* '*e Rigginelle voste vonno*   *essere spusate*
your majesty   the princesses   your   want.PRES.3PL   be.INF   marry.PART.F.PL
tutt' e   *ttre*
all   the three
'Your Majesty, your princesses ought to be married all three of them' (Valle dei Maddaloni (CE), De Simone 1994: 1064)

c.   *vonno   essere pagati*
pro.3PL.M want.PRES.3PL be.INF pay.PART.M.PL
'they want to be paid' (NA, Scarpetta 1992: 221)

d. *si   vuo'   essere libberato*
if pro.2SG.M want.PRES.2SG be.INF free.PART.M.SG
'if you want to be freed' (Ferrari (AV), De Simone 1994: 402)

e. pə'pːinə wol   esː   a'tʃːɪis
Peppino want.PRES.3SG be.INF kill.PART.M
'Peppino wants to/must be killed' (Altamura (BA), Loporcaro 1988: 305)

f.   *volia   essari tenuta   di la vecchia*
pro.3SG.F want.PAST.3SG be.INF keep.PART.F.SG by the old-lady
'she wanted to be looked after by the old lady' (RC, Satriani 1953: 179)

g. *ora   vogghiu   essiri ammazzatu*
now pro.1SG.M want.PRES.1SG be.INF kill.PART.M.SG
'now I want to be killed' (Mélito Porto-Salvo (CZ), Mandalari 1881–3: 235)

h. *comu   vuliti   essiri pagata . . . a pugnè o a*
how pro.2SG.F want.PRES.2PL be.INF pay.PART.F.SG to punches or to
pizzichè?
pinches
'how do you want to be paid . . . in punches or pinches?' (PA, Pitrè 1875: II, 24)

i.   *voli   essiri jittata   di lu finistruni appinninu*
pro.3SG.F want.PRES.3SG be.INF throw.PART.F.SG from the window down
'she wants to be thrown out of the window' (Casteltermini (AG), ibid., II, 281)

(20) a. *sapite   che piacere   voleva   essere*
know.PRES.2PL what pleasure.M.SG pro.3SG.F want.PAST.3SG be.INF
fatto?
do.PART.M.SG
'do you know what favour she wanted to be granted?' (NA, Scarpetta 1994: 138)

b.   *vo   essere tornate   li denare*
pro.3SG.M want.PRES.3SG be.INF return.PART.M.PL the money.M.PL
'he wants to be given back his money' (ibid., 203)

c.   *voglio   essere imbucata   questa lettera*
pro.1SG.M want.PRES.1SG be.INF post.PART.F.SG this letter.F.SG
'I want this letter to be posted for me' (Scarpetta 1992: 179)

d. *si   vuo'   essere fatte   'e servizie,   te miette*
   if   pro.2SG.M want.PRES.2SG be.INF   do.PART.M.PL the services.M.PL   . . .
   na serva!
   'if you want your chores done for you, get yourself a maid!' (Torella
   dei Lombardi (AV), De Simone 1994: 1086)

e.   *voglio   esser fatto   un servizio   di te*
   pro.1SG.M want.PRES.1SG be.INF   do.PART.M.SG a   service.M.SG by you
   'I want to be granted a favour of you' (reg. Italian, Anzi (PZ),
   Ruggieri and Batinti 1992: 86)

f. *illu voli   essiri spiegata   'a lezioni*
   he   want.PRES.3SG be.INF   explain.PART.F.SG the lesson.PART.F.SG
   'he wants to be explained the lesson' (Roccella Ionica (RC))

g.   *voglio   esser ripetuta   la lezione*
   pro.1SG.M want.PRES.1SG be.INF   repeat.PART.F.SG the lesson.F.SG
   'I want the lesson to be gone over again for me' (Sicily, Leone 1982:
   §106)

h. *vulimu   essiri cucinata   na torta*
   want.PRES.1PL be.INF   cook.PART.F.SG a   cake.F.SG
   'we want to be cooked a cake' (PA)

If there is no THEME, as in monotransitive structures with a GOAL
complement, the participle manifests default M.SG agreement and not
GOAL-controlled agreement:

(21) a. *Maria vulesse   essere rispuosto   /*risposta*
        Maria want.COND.3SG be.INF   reply.PART.M.SG /reply.PART.F.SG
        'Maria would like to be replied to' (NA)

    b. *vonnu   essiri parratu   /rispunnutu   /cucinatu*
       want.PRES.3PL be.INF   speak.PART.M.SG /reply.PART.M.SG /cook-for.PART.M.SG
       'they want to be spoken to/replied to/cooked for' (Roccella Ionica
       (RC))

As we shall see below in section 7.5.2, these cross-dialectal differences with
respect to participial agreement are intimately linked to the presence/absence
of the auxiliary ESSERE. In group 1 dialects ESSERE is invariably excluded in
OC and SR structures (22a–b). In group 2 dialects, by contrast, ESSERE
proves obligatory (23a–b):

(22) a. *Cicciu e   Ida vulissaru   (*essa) salutati*
        Ciccio and Ida want.COND.3PL (be.INF)   greet.PART.M.PL
        'Ciccio and Ida would like to be greeted' (CS)

    b. *Maurizio vo   (*essa) spiegatu   chira lezione*
       Maurizio want.PRES.3SG (be.INF) explain.PART.M.SG that   lesson.F.SG
       'Maurizio wants that lesson to be explained to him' (CS)

(23) a. *'e bicchiere nu monno   *(essere) rutte*
      the glasses.M.PL not want.PRES.3PL (be.INF)   break.PART.M
      'the glasses mustn't be broken' (NA)

   b. *Ciro vulesse   *(essere) scritta   na lettera*
      Ciro want.COND.3SG (be.INF)   write.PART.F.SG a letter.F.SG
      'Ciro would like to be written a letter' (NA)

It emerges then that the role of ESSERE in group 2 dialects is analogous to that of participial agreement in group 1 dialects, in that its presence marks raising of the participial THEME/GOAL argument to the matrix subject position. By way of further illustration, consider the Cosentino and Neapolitan minimal pairs in (24) and (25), respectively:

(24) a. *Giuvanni vo   scritta   na littera* (ECM)
      Giovanni want.PRES.3SG write.PART.F.SG a letter.F.SG
      'Giovanni wants a letter written'

   b. *Giuvanni vo   scrittu   na littera* (OC)
      Giovanni want.PRES.3SG write.PART.M.SG a letter.F.SG
      'Giovanni wants to be written a letter'

(25) a. *Giuanne vô   scritta   na lettera* (ECM)
      Gianni want.PRES.3SG write.PART.F.SG a letter
      'Gianni wants a letter written'

   b. *Giuanne vô   **essere** scritta   na lettera* (OC)
      Gianni want.PRES.3SG be.INF write.PART.F.SG a letter
      'Ganni wants to be written a letter'

The participle in the Cosentino sentence (24a) displays F.SG concord with the THEME argument *na littera* 'a letter', an agreement relation which signals the subjectization of the latter and hence the ECM interpretation of the sentence. In (24b), on the other hand, M.SG participial agreement marks subjectization of the GOAL *Giuvanni*, which has been raised to the matrix subject position to yield the OC reading. In the corresponding Neapolitan examples (25a–b), on the other hand, where participial agreement is invariably controlled by the THEME, the same contrast is marked purely by the absence (= ECM) versus presence (= OC) of ESSERE.[5]

7.2.3. *Dative passivization*

At this point we shall briefly consider some of the restrictions on dative passivization in the OC and SR constructions. In group 1 dialects, these restrictions reduce to the question of which type of underlying dative DP may qualify as the licit controller of participial agreement. This is demonstrated by the following Cosentino examples:

(26) a. *zia   Isa   vo*   *accattatu*   (ECM) /*accattata* (OC) '*u*
        aunt Isa want.PRES.3SG buy.PART.M.SG   /buy.PART.F.SG   the
        café
        coffee.M.SG
        'aunt Isa wants the coffee bought / to be bought the coffee'

     b. *Robertu   vulissa*   *stirata*   (ECM) /**stiratu*   (OC) '*a*
        Roberto   want.COND.3SG iron.PART.F.SG   /iron.PART.M.SG   the
        cammisa
        shirt.F.SG
        'Roberto would like the shirt ironed / his shirt to be ironed for
        him'

In conjunction with *accattà* 'to buy' in (26a), both subjectization of the
THEME argument '*u café* 'the coffee', with concomitant M.SG participial
agreement (ECM reading), and subjectization of the GOAL argument *zia
Isa* 'aunt Isa', with concomitant F.SG participial agreement (OC reading), are
possible. With *stirà* 'to iron' in (26b), by contrast, dative passivization is
excluded, witness the ungrammaticality of the M.SG participial agreement
with *Roberto*. Instead, only the ECM interpretation with subjectization of
the THEME '*a cammisa* 'the shirt' produces grammatical results.

    Identical contrasts obtain in group 2 dialects but with the difference that
dative passivization is marked here by the presence of ESSERE, witness the
following Neapolitan examples:

(27) a. *fratema*   *vulesse*   *scesa*   (ECM) /*essere*
        brother.POSS.1SG want.COND.3SG bring-down.PART.F   /be.INF
        scesa   (OC) '*a balicia*
        bring-down.PART.F   the suitcase
        'my brother would like the suitcase brought down / to be brought
        down the suitcase'

     b. *Gianfranco   vo*   *appesa* (ECM) /**essere appesa* (OC)
        Gianfranco   want.PRES.3SG hang.PART.F   /be.INF   hang.PART
        '*a   giacca*
        the   jacket
        'Gianfranco wants the jacket hung up / his jacket to be hung up for
        him'

While subjectization of the GOAL argument *fratema* 'my brother' in conjunction with *scennere* 'to bring down' in (27a) proves acceptable, dative
passivization of *Gianfranco* in (27b) in conjunction with *appennere* 'to
hang up' is excluded. Essentially, it appears that affectedness is the crucial
parameter which excludes or licenses dative passivization, variously manifested in participial agreement (group 1 dialects) or the presence of ESSERE
(group 2 dialects).

    In line with Larson's (1990) explanation of the constraints operating on

English dative shift, it appears necessary to draw two distinctions: on the one hand a semantic distinction between dative DPs which bear the BENEFACTIVE and RECIPIENT roles, and a related syntactic distinction between argument and adjunct dative DPs on the other. Significantly, only a restricted set of dative DPs bearing the BENEFACTIVE role (traditionally termed ethic datives) can be advanced to passive subject, as demonstrated by the following Cosentino (28) and (29) and Neapolitan (30) and (31) sentences:

(28) a. *Giginu vo   piscatu   'i surici*
       Gigino want.PRES.3SG fish.PART.M.SG the scallops.M.PL
       'Gigino wants to be fished some scallops'

     b. *Peppinu vulissa   cacciatu   sti struogli du*
        Peppino want.COND.3SG remove.PART.M.SG this junk.M.PL from-the
        magazzinu sua
        warehouse his
        'Peppino would like this rubbish to be removed from his warehouse for him'

(29) a. *Antonella vo   pulizzatu/*-a   'u fuornu*
        Antonella want.PRES.3SG clean.PART.M.SG/F.SG the oven.M.SG
        'Antonella wants the oven cleaned'

     b. *papà vo   cunzata/*-u   'a Cinquecento 'i*
        dad want.PRES.3SG repair.PART.F.SG/M.SG the Cinquecento.F.SG of
        mammata
        mum.POSS.2SG
        'dad wants your mum's Cinquecento (car) repaired'

(30) a. *Michele vuleva   essere cotta   na torta*
        Michele want.PAST.3SG be.INF cook.PART.F.SG a cake.F.SG
        'Michele wanted to be cooked a cake'

     b. *'On Gennà vô   essere appriperata   na tazza 'i café*
        Don Gennaro want.PRES.3SG be.INF prepare.PART.F.SG a cup.F.SG of coffee
        'Don Gennaro wanted to be prepared a cup of coffee'

(31) a. *zia Tersilla vô   (*essere) lavat'   'e piatte*
        aunt Tersilla want.PRES.3SG (be.INF) wash.PART the dishes
        'aunt Tersilla wants the washing up done'

     b. *Alfredo vuleva   (*essere) apppicciat' 'a sicaretta*
        Alfredo want.PAST.3SG (be.INF) light.PART the cigarette
        'Alfredo wanted his cigarette lit'

In examples (28) and (30) the participial predicates select a THEME argument (for example, 'the scallops', 'a cake') and a dative argument (for example, Peppino, Michele) assigned the BENEFACTIVE role. Crucially, in these examples the BENEFACTIVE is invariably interpreted as the RECIPIENT of the THEME and therefore qualifies in some sense as the affected participant. Consequently, it is amenable to dative passivization. In examples (29) and (31), on the other hand, the participial predicates select a THEME argument (for example, 'the oven', 'the plates') and an implicit dative DP co-referential with the matrix subject bearing the BENEFACTIVE role. In contrast to examples (28) and (30), however, the BENEFACTIVE cannot in any sense be understood as the RECIPIENT of the THEME. As a result, dative passivization is ruled out. Instead, an ECM complement must be used in which the desired event is interpreted as taking pace to the advantage of the understood BENEFACTIVE co-referential with the matrix subject.

Similar considerations appear to operate in the following sentences:

(32) a. *Valentina vo   fasciata   'i   vrazza*
        Valentina   want.PRES.3SG bandage.PART.F.SG the   arms.F.PL
        'Valentina wants her arms to be bandaged up' (CS)

    b. *Carla vô   essere scippato   nu dente cariato*
       Carla   want.PRES.3SG be.INF   pull.PART   a   tooth   decayed
       'Carlo wants his decayed tooth to be pulled out' (NA)

(33) a. *'a signora Pagnotta num vo   rutti/*-a   sti*
        the signora   Pagnotta   not   want.PRES.3SG break.PART.M.PL/F.SG these
        bicchieri
        glasses.M.PL
        'Signora Pagnotta doesn't want these glasses broken' (CS)

    b. *vulimmo   (*essere) cunzat'   'a   televisione*
       want.PRES.1PL (be.INF)   repair.PART the television
       'we want the television repaired' (NA)

The crucial contrast between sentences (32) and (33) is one of inalienable versus alienable possession, respectively. In (32a–b) the relation of possession between the understood BENEFACTIVE (Valentina, Carla) and the THEME ('the arms', 'a tooth') is seen as a permanent and necessary relationship to its possessor. Consequently, the BENEFACTIVE is naturally interpreted as the affected participant and the RECIPIENT of the desired event, and hence amenable to subjectization.[6] In (33a–b), on the other hand, the THEME ('these glasses', 'the television') only enters into a temporary and non-essential dependency on the understood possessor, namely the BENEFACTIVE ('Signora Pagnotta', 'we'). Thus, the latter cannot be readily perceived as the affected participant and is only interpreted as the beneficiary of the desired event, hence the obligatory use of the ECM construction with THEME-controlled participial agreement.

The relevant parameter operative in such sentences constraining dative passivization appears therefore to relate to the possibility of the BENEFACTIVE dative DP being construed as the RECIPIENT of the THEME and hence an argument of the verb. Indeed, this conclusion lends itself most naturally to

Larson's (1990: 615) observation that subjectization of BENEFACTIVES only proves licit with those verbs which 'denote events of preparation and creation' in which 'the created or prepared objects must be intended for the benefit of the beneficiary.'

Turning now to those verbs that occur with dative DPs bearing the RECIPIENT role, these too do not invariably allow subjectization of the dative argument:

(34) a. *lassa   stà   a Cuncetta ca un bo   circata*
      let.IMP.2SG be.INF PA Concetta that not want.PRES.3SG ask-for.PART.F.SG
    sordi
    money.M.PL
    'leave Concetta alone, she doesn't want to be asked for money' (CS)

   b. *vulianu   prumisi   sta casa*
     want.PAST.3PL promise.PART.M.PL this house.F.SG
    'they wanted to be promised this house' (CS)

   c. *a Natale Carmela vo   essere rialato nu rologio*
     to Christmas Carmela want.PRES.3SG be.INF give.PART a watch
    'for Christmas Carmela wants to be given a watch' (NA)

   d. *'o piccerillo vo   essere letta   na fiabba*
     the little-one want.PRES.3SG be.INF read.PART a fairy-table
    'the little one wants to be read a fairy tale' (NA)

(35) a. *Maria un bo   fricatu/*-a   'u guagliune sua* (CS)
     Maria not want.PRES.3SG steal.PART.M.SG/F.SG the boy   her

   a′. *Maria un bo   (*essere) fricat'   'o guaglione suojo* (NA)
     Maria not want.PRES.3SG (be.INF) steal.PART the boy   her
    'Maria doesn't want her boyfriend to be stolen from her'

   b. *un bulimu   ammucciata/*-i 'a verità* (CS)
     not want.PRES.1PL hide.PART.F.SG/M.PL the truth.F.SG

   b′. *um mulimmo   (*essere) annascost' 'a verità* (NA)
     not want.PRES.1PL (be.INF) hide.PART.F the truth.F.SG
    'we don't want the truth to be hidden (from us)'

As argued by Larson (1990: 615), the relevant factor which determines the availability of dative passivization in (34) and (35) hinges on whether the THEME can be understood as being set in motion along a trajectory by the (understood) AGENT. Whereas in (34) the participial predicates denote an event of motion in which the understood AGENT imparts a trajectory to the THEME, the same does not hold of the participles in (35) and their respective THEMES. Rather, we suggest that the predicates *fricatu/fricato* 'stolen' and *ammucciata/annascosta* 'hidden' are 2–place verbs which select for an AGENT and a THEME, the understood RECIPIENT representing an adjunct. More specifically, we adopt the two lexical rules of argument augmentation proposed by Larson (1990: 616) for English presented in (36) and (37):

(36) *Benefactive Augmentation (Optional)*: Add θ_{BENEF} to the θ-grid of α:
      Condition: α denotes an event of creation or preparation.
      Result: the THEME is for the benefit of the beneficiary.

(37) *Recipient Augmentation (Optional)*: Add $\theta_{\text{RECIPIENT}}$ to the θ-grid of α:
      Condition: α denotes an event of motion in which the AGENT imparts a trajectory to the THEME.

Now, sentences (29), (31) and (33) are predicted to exclude dative passivization, for such predicates do not denote an event of creation or preparation in which the THEME is for the benefit of the beneficiary in accordance with (36). Consequently, the BENEFACTIVE DP in such sentences does not qualify as an argument of the verb, thereby ruling out dative passivization, since verbal selection is required in order for dative shift to apply. Analogously, in examples (35a–b′) the participial predicates fail to satisfy the conditioning clause of (37), thereby excluding argument augmentation and dative passivization.

7.2.4. *Distribution*

We close our discussion with some comments on the distribution of the various want-passive constructions in Italo-Romance. Beginning with the ECM construction, this appears to be predominantly limited to dialects and varieties of Italian spoken in southern Italy.[7] For instance, Telmon (1993: 122, 126) traces its distribution to an area south of an isogloss running from Naples to Bari, with two epicentres in Campania and Sicily. Additional representative examples from various southern varieties are given below:

(38) a. *me vuói   muórto*
         me want.PRES.2SG die.PART
         'you want me dead' (San Leucio del Sannio (BN), Iannace 1983: §152)

      b. *'i rape 'i   vu   purtati?*
         the greens them want.PRES.2SG carry.PART
         'do you want the greens to be carried?' (Fiumefreddo (CS))

      c. *volarrì   acconzatu puru u   mattunatu*
         want.COND.1SG repair.PART also the tiling
         'I would like the tiling repaired as well' (Nicotera (CZ), Carè 1992: 31)

      d. *non la vorzi   mancu masurata*
         not it want.PAST.3SG not-eve measure.PART
         'he didn't even want it measured' (Siderno (RC), Filocamo 1984: 60)

e. *tuttu chiddu chi vosi   accattatu custava   chiú assai*
all which that want.PAST.ISG buy.PART cost.PAST.3SG more much
'everything that I wanted bought cost too much' (Belpasso (CT), Martoglio 1978b)

f. *vulia   fattu   'nfurnari   ddu pitittu*
want.PAST.3SG make.PART put-in-oven.INF that loaf
'she wanted to have that small loaf put in the oven' (PA, Pitrè 1875: I, 384)

g. *voli   fattu   un anieddu cuomu lu miu*
want.PRES.3SG make.PART a ring like the mine
'she wants a ring made like mine' (Casteltermini (AG), Pitrè 1875: II, 281)

h. *iu a mè figghia nun la vogghiu   mossa*
I PA my daughter not her want.PRES.ISG move.PART
'I don't want my daughter touched' (Polizzi-Generosa (PA), Pitrè 1875: IV, 201)

In Italian the construction is infrequent and predominantly restricted to literary registers (see Ambrosini 1982: 67–71; Salvi 1988: 166; Serianni 1991: VIV, §65). Indeed, Salvioni (1912: 378) characterizes the Italian construction as more marked and restricted than its southern Italian analogue and 'in certa misura proprio . . . della lingua letteraria' ('to a certain extent characteristic . . . of the literary language'). Some Italian examples are given below:

(39) a. *volle   eretto   un tempio*
want.PAST.3SG erect.PART a temple
'he wanted erected a temple' (Salvioni 1912: 378)

b. *volle   raccomandata la sua memoria a una buona opera*
want.PAST.3SG commend.PART the his memory to a good cause
'he wanted his memory to be associated with a good cause' (ibid.)

c. *vorrò   rispettate allo scrupolo tutte le apparenze*
want.FUT.ISG respect.PART to-the scruple all the appearances
'I will want all appearances respected scrupulously' (Pirandello, cited in Serianni 1991: XIV, §155)

d. *voglio   copiato   quel progetto in un' ora*
want.PRES.ISG copy.PART that project in an hour
'I want that project copied in an hour' (Ambrosini 1982: 70)

Indeed, from discussions with informants it emerges that sentences like (39) prove most, if not exclusively, acceptable to southern Italian speakers.
As for OC VOLERE, all Italo-Romance varieties would appear to allow

such a structure when the subjectized argument is the underlying direct object, as in the following Turinese and Italian examples:

(40) a. ma'rjo a vøl   'ese   man'dɒ (TO)

   b. *Mario   vuol   essere mandato* (Italian)
      Mario   want.PRES.3SG be.INF send.PART
      'Mario wants to be sent'

In contrast to all other varieties, though, southern Italian dialects of group 1 do not use ESSERE in such structures (see Salvioni 1912: 379):

(41) a. *aviamu   vulutu   mmitati*
        have.PAST.1PL want.PART invite.PART
        'we had wanted to be invited' (CS)

   b. *ulianu   cunsulate*
      want.PAST.3PL   console.PART
      'they wanted to be consoled' (LE, Salvioni 1912: 379)

Subjectization of an underlying GOAL, on the other hand, is strictly limited to southern varieties (Pasquali 1942: 112; De Mauro 1976: 401), witness the ungrammaticality of the Italian sentences in (42), in contrast to the grammatical southern Italian examples in (43):

(42) a. **voglio   essere fatto   un favore*
        want.PRES.1SG be.INF do.PART a favour
        'I want to be done a favour'

   b. **vorrebbero essere parlati*
      want.COND.3PL be.INF speak.PART
      'they would like to be spoken to'

(43) a. *voglio   essere cuntato tutto*
        want.PRES.1SG be.INF tell.PART everything
        'I want to be told everything' (NA, Scarpetta 1994: 145)

   b. *vò   essere fatto   cerimonie, complimenti, congratulazioni*
      want.PRES.3SG be.INF do.PART ceremonies compliments congratulations
      'he wants to be showered with pompous comments, compliments and good wishes' (ibid., 1992: 221)

   c. *voglio   esser fatto   un servizio di te*
      want.PRES.1SG be.INF do.PART a service by you
      'I want to be granted a favour by you' (reg. Italian, Anzi (PZ), Ruggieri and Batinti 1992: 86)

   d. pə'pːɪnə wol   'esːə   'dɛtə   nʊ ʃkwafː
      Peppino want.PRES.3SG be.INF give.PART a slap
      'Peppino wants to/must be given a slap' (Altamura (BA), Loporcaro 1988: 305)

e. *vu   offertu   nguna cosa?*
want.PRES.2SG offer.PART some   thing
'do you want to be offered something?' (CS)

f. *vozza   fattu   'u cicerona*
want.PAST.3SG do.PART the guide
'he wanted to be given a personal guide' (CZ, Colacino 1994: 70)

g. *e chi piaciri vôi   fattu?*
what pleasure want.PRES.2SG do.PART
'and what favour do you want granted?' (S.Costantino Briatico (CZ), Satriani 1953: 215)

h. *Marco vuol   essere comprato il trenino*
Marco want.PRES.3SG be.INF buy.PART the little-train
'Marco wants to be bought the toy train' (reg. Sicilian Italian, Alfieri 1992: 848)

i. *voglio   essere ripetuta la geografia*
want.PRES.1SG be.INF repeat.PART the geography
'I want the geography lesson to be gone over again for me' (ibid.)

j. *vuogghiu   èssiri spiegatu   comu fu*
want.PRES.1SG be.INF explain.PART how   be.PAST.3SG
'I want to be explained how it happened' (Sicily, Leone 1995: 72)

Turning finally to the deontic use of VOLERE, this would appear to enjoy a wider distribution (Cennamo 1997: 151). In northern Italy, it is found in the Veneto (44a–b) and Friuli (44c–d):

(44) a. *el   vole   magnà*
S.CL.3SG want.PRES.3SG eat.PART
'it must be eaten' (Basso Polesano (PD), Benincà and Poletto 1997: 102)

b. *el   li   vole   petenà*
S.CL.3SG.M /S.CL.3PL want.PRES.3 comb.PART
'his/their hair must be combed' (ibid., 103)

c. *vuein   metûz i muel*
want.PRES.3PL put.PART of soak
'they need to be soaked'

d. *al   û   savût*
S.CL.3SG want.PRES.3SG know.PART
'it must be known'

In Italian, by contrast, its distribution is much more limited, often producing very marginal results for speakers outside of southern Italy. Ambrosini (1982: 68) observes that the deontic value of *volere* only proves pragmatically felicitous under certain conditions and, consequently, is marked in comparison to the analogous southern construction:

(45) a. *la verità vuol   esser detta   da Cesare*
the truth   want.PRES.3SG be.INF say.PART by Cesare
'the truth should be told by Cesare' (Ambrosini 1982: 68)

  b. *questo libro vuol   esser letto   con attenzione dai   ragazzi*
this   book want.PRES.3SG be.INF read.PART with attention   by-the children
'this book must be read carefully by the children' (ibid.)

  c. *questa destruzione indiscriminata si   vorrebbe   condotta   in*
this   destruction   indiscriminate   one want.COND.3SG carry-out.PART in
termini rapidi
terms   quick
'this indiscriminate destruction ought to be carried out quickly' (*La Stampa* 13/8/99)

Sardinian dialects are equally reported (Salvioni 1912: 379–80; Jones 1988: 340; 1993: 125, 290–1) to make use of a deontic want-passive in conjunction with *kérrere* (< QUAERERE) 'to want', witness the following examples:

(46) a. *chere   frittu*
want.PRES.3SG fry.PART
'it must be fried' (NU, Salvioni 1912: 379)

  b. *ghere   saludada*
want.PRES.3SG greet.PART.F.SG
'she must be greeted' (id, 380)

  c. *cussas faínas keren   fattas   prima de nos corcare*
these   chores want.PRES.3PL do.PART   . . .
'these chores must be done before we go to bed' (Jones 1993: 125)

  d. *cussa dzente keret   tímita*
this   people want.PRES.3SG fear.PART
'these people should be feared' (ibid.)

  e. *sa màkkina keret   accontzata dae unu meccànicu*
the car   want.PRES.3SG repair.PART by a   mechanic
'the car needs to be repaired by a mechanic' (ibid.)

As for southern Italy, Cennamo (1997: 51) reports the deontic use of VOLERE to be widespread in Lazio, Apulia, Salento and Calabria. In addition, it is found in Campania. Examples are given below:

(47) a. *vô   essere scupato   nterra*
want.PRES.3SG be.INF sweep.PART in-floor
'the floor needs sweeping' (NA)

b. *'a mozzarella vo esse magnata fresca*
the mozzarella want.PRES.3SG be.INF eat.PART fresh
'the mozzarella must be eaten fresh' (NA)

c. *'ʧakːə wol 'esːə fatː?*
what want.PRES.3SG be.INF do.PART
'what needs to be done?' (Altamura (BA), Loporcaro 1988: 306)

d. *'wolə ʃʊt a fːɛ nʊ srʊ'widzːj*
want.PRES.3SG go.PART to do.INF a service
'an errand needs running' (ibid.)

e. *ci vo pruvatu /ghiutu*
to-it want.PRES.3SG try.PART /go.PART
'it must be tried / one must go there' (CS)

Observe furthermore that in Calabrian (48a–c) and Apulian (48d), as well as in Sardinian (48e–g), deontic VOLERE is equally employed with adjectives:

(48) a. *a scarpa vole forte*
the shoe want.PRES.3SG strong
'shoes must be hard-wearing' (Calabria, Rohlfs 1969: 131, n. 1)

b. *u vinu buonu vòle viecchiu*
the wine good want.PRES.3SG old
'good wine should be old' (ibid.)

c. *'i priccoche vonnu toste*
the peaches want.PRES.3PL hard
'peaches ought to be firm' (CS)

d. *ʊ dɪawʊ'lɪkːjə 'wolə fʷort*
the chilli want.PRES.3SG strong
'chillies should be hot' (Altamura (BA), Loporcaro 1988: 306)

e. *la gonnella vuole corta*
the skirt want.PRES.3SG short
'the skirt ought to be short' (reg. Sardinian Italian, Salvioni 1912: 380)

f. *l' abito di nozze vuol bianco*
the dress of wedding want.PRES.3SG white
'wedding dresses ought to be white' (ibid.)

g. *la vernaccia, perchè sia buona, vuol molto*
the white-wine in-order-that be.PRES.SUBJ.3SG good want.PRES.3SG very
vecchia
old
'white wine, for it to be good, must be very old' (ibid.)

Moreover, in Calabrian dialects deontic VOLERE can also take adverbial (49a–b) and prepositional complements (49c–c):

(49) a. *la   virgola   voleva   prima*
      the comma   want.PAST.3SG before
      'the comma should have been placed in front' (Salvioni 1912: 380,
      n. 1)

   b. *questo   tavolino   non   voleva   qui*
      this   coffee-table not   want.PRES.3SG here
      'this coffee table shouldn't have been placed here' (ibid.)

   c. *questo   sonetto   vuol   dopo la   canzone*
      this   sonnet   want.PRES.3SG after the song
      'this sonnet must be executed after the song' (ibid.)

   d. *'u   petrusinu   un   bo   intr 'a   grasta   da   menta*
      the parsley   not want.PRES.3SG in   the pot   of-the mint
      'the parsley should not be put in the pot with the mint' (San Biase
      (CS))

   e. *'sta pasta   vo   cu   ru   sugu*
      this pasta   want.PRES.3SG with the sauce
      'this pasta should be eaten with tomato sauce' (CS)

The picture for Sicilian dialects, on the other hand, is far from clear.
Salvioni (1912: 379) argues that the deontic use of VOLERE is unknown in
Sicilian varieties, a conclusion not entirely supported by the present author's
Sicilian informants who accept examples such as those in (50):

(50) a. *'a   cammisa voli   essiri lavata*
      the shirt   want.PRES.3SG be.INF wash.PART
      'the shirt needs to be washed'

   b. *'a   pasta vulia   essiri mangiata cauda*
      the pasta   want.PAST.3SG be.INF eat.PART   hot
      'the pasta had to be eaten warm'

Moreover, Alfieri (1992: 844, 848) cites the following two examples of
deontic VOLERE:[8]

(51) a. *in cucina vuol   esser rifatto   il   focolare*
      in kitchen want.PRES.3SG be.INF re-do.PART the fireplace
      'in the kitchen the fireplace needs to be replaced' (Verga, cited in
      Alfieri 1992: 844)

   b. *il   muro   vuol essere   aggiustato*
      the   wall   want.PRES.3SG   be.INF repair.PART
      'the wall needs repairing' (Alfieri 1992: 848)

7.2.5. *Summary*

Below we summarize the results of the preceding discussion:

- There are three distinct want-passive constructions, in which VOLERE variously behaves as an ECM, OC and SR predicate;

- In the ECM construction, participial agreement is invariably controlled by the embedded THEME argument, whereas in the OC and SR constructions there arise two patterns:
  - (i) Group 1 dialects: participial agreement is controlled by the subjectized argument, be it a THEME or GOAL;
  - (ii) Group 2 dialects: participial agreement is controlled by the THEME argument, when present, or displays the default M.SG form;

- The ESSERE auxiliary is invariably excluded in the ECM construction and the OC and SR constructions of group 1 dialects, but is obligatory in the OC and SR constructions of group 2 dialects;

- Dative passivization is limited to southern Italian dialects and to the following two cases:
  - (i) the BENEFACTIVE dative argument must be understood as the RECIPIENT of the THEME;
  - (ii) the dative argument must be understood as the RECIPIENT of a THEME set in motion along a trajectory by the AGENT;

- Want-passives are distributed as follows:
  - (i) ECM VOLERE is widespread in southern Italy and is occasionally found in literary Italian;
  - (ii) OC VOLERE with THEME subjectization is common to all varieties, though GOAL subjectization is limited to southern Italy;
  - (iii) SR VOLERE is widespread throughout the South and limitedly found in some northern varieties and in Sardinian.

7.3. PARTICIPLE STRUCTURE

We now turn to ascertain the precise structure to be attributed to the participial complement in the three want-passive constructions. Theoretically, the participle could instantiate one of three clausal types, namely CP, TP or vP. A straightforward test to determine whether the participle is a CP is to ascertain whether it can be *wh*-extracted by the pro-CP interrogative *che/cchi* 'what'. Relevant Neapolitan and Cosentino examples are given in (52) and (53), respectively:

(52) a. *Roberto vô*   *scesa*   *'a canoa 'a   llà   ncoppa*
Roberto   want.PRES.3SG [xP bring-down.PART the canoe from there up]
(ECM)
'Roberto wants brought down the canoe from up there'

a'. **che vô*   *Roberto?*   *– scesa*   *'a canoa 'a*
what₁ want.PRES.3SG Roberto [xP t₁] [xP bring-down.PART the canoe from
llà   ncoppa
there up]
'what does Roberto want? – the canoe brought down from up there'

b. *Roberto vô*   *esse   turnate   arreto 'e sorde* (OC)
Roberto   want.PRES.3SG [xP be.INF return.PART back   the money]
'Roberto wants to be returned the money'

b'. *che   vô*   *Roberto?*   *– essere   turnate   arreto 'e*
what₁ want.PRES.3SG Roberto [xP t₁] [xP be.INF   return.PART back   the
sorde
money]
'what does Roberto want? – to be returned the money'

c. *'e sorde vonno*   *essere turnate   arrreto* (SR)
the money want.PRES.3PL [xP be.INF return.PART back]
'the money must be returned'

c'. **che vonno*   *'e sorde?*   *– essere   turnate   arreto*
what₁ want.PRES.3PL the money [xP t₁] [xP be.INF   return.PART back]
'what must the money? – be returned'

(53) a. *Paoletto vulia*   *cunzata   'a vespa* (ECM)
Paoletto   want.PAST.3SG [xP repair.PART the vespa]
'Paoletto wanted his vespa repaired'

a'. **cchi vulia*   *Paoletto?*   *– cunzata   'a vespa*
what₁ want.PAST.3SG Paoletto [xP t₁] [xP repair.PART the vespa]
'what did Paoletto want? – his vespa repaired'

b. *Paoletto vulia*   *rigalatu na vespa* (OC)
Paoletto   want.PAST.3SG [xP give.PART a   vespa]
'Paoletto wanted to be given a vespa as a present'

b'. *cchi vulia*   *Paoletto?*   *– rigalatu na vespa*
what₁ want.PAST.3SG Paoletto [xP t₁] [xP give.PART a   vespa]
'what did Paoletto want? – to be given a vespa'

c. *'a vespa vulia*   *cunzata*   (SR)
the vespa want.PAST.3SG [xP repair.PART]
'the vespa had to be repaired'

c'. **cchi vulia*   *ra vespa?*   *– cunzata*
what₁ want.PAST.3SG the vespa [xP t₁] [xP repair.PART]
'what did the vespa have to? – be repaired'

As the (b') examples indicate, only the participial complement of OC VOLERE can be *wh*-extracted, confirming its CP status.

A further indication of a functional layer above *v*P within the participial clause is provided by the presence of the auxiliary ESSERE. Taking the latter to be merged under T (see further section 7.5.2.2), its presence can be interpreted as an overt marker of a TP projection within the participle clause. As we have already seen, ESSERE is invariably excluded in all dialects in the ECM construction (54a). In dialects of group 2, in contrast, ESSERE is obligatory in OC (54b) and SR (54c) structures:

(54) a. *lu vuliti   livatu?*
         it want.PRES.2PL remove.PART
         'do you want it removed' (Borgetto (PA), Pitrè 1875: III, 253)

      b *Maria vosi   **essiri** ccattata a   casa*
         Maria   want.PAST.3SG be.INF   buy.PART the house
         'Maria wanted to be bought the house' (Sicily, Leone 1995: 72)

      c. *vulissi   **essiri** accattata 'a cainne*
         want.COND.3SG   be.INF   buy.PART   the meat
         'the meat needs to be bought' (PA)

These sentences demonstrate two facts: (i) ECM participial complements only project to *v*P; and (ii) OC and SR participial complements project to at least TP.

The evidence reviewed so far suggests then that OC, SR and ECM participial complements are CPs, TPs and *v*Ps, respectively. Another fact which lends supports to this conclusion comes from participial morphology. In section 6.3.2.4.3 we provided evidence to demonstrate that many dialects of the Upper South distinguish between an adjectival and a verbal participle in conjunction with a number of verbs that present both irregular and regular participial pendants. In such cases, the irregular participle is under-specified for the feature [N] and may be used as a pure adjective (hence [+N]) with a reduced vP (or *a*P) structure, or as a verbal predicate (hence [-N]) projecting to CP or TP. The regular participle in such pairs, on the other hand, is exclusively verbal (hence [+N]), projecting at least to TP, if not CP.

It is predicted then that ECM participial complements should only be compatible with the irregular pendant, as they select a *v*P complement, while OC and SR participial complements should prove compatible with either participial pendant. Indeed, this prediction is borne out:

(55) a. *mamma vo   spas'   /*spannut'   'i   panni*
         mum   want.PRES.3SG hang-out.PART.IRREG /hang-out.PART.REG the clothes
         'mum wants the clothes hung out' (CS; ECM)

      b. *Isabella vulissa   letta   /lejuta   'u   giurnale*
         Isabella   want.COND.3SG read.PART.IRREG /read.PART.REG the newspaper
         'Isabella would like to be read the newspaper' (CS; OC)

   c. *'a balicia vulia   scisa   /scinnuta   prima*
      the suitcase want.PAST.3SG bring-down.PART.IRREG /bring-down.PART.REG before
      'the suitcase should have been brought down before' (CS; SR)

(56) a. *essa aveva   vuluto   fritte   /*frijute'e vruoccole*
      she   have.PAST.3SG want.PART fry.PART.IRREG /fry.PART.REG the broccoli
      'she had wanted the broccoli fried' (NA; ECM)

    b. *vulesse   essere scritta   /scrivuta   na lettera accussì*
      want.COND.1SG be.INF   write.PART.IRREG /write.PART.REG a letter   thus
      'I would like to be written a letter like that' (NA; OC)

    c. *'o vino vô   essere vippeto   /vevuto   frisco*
      the wine want.PRES.3SG be.INF drink.PART.IRREG /drink.PART.REG fresh
      'the wine should be drunk cooled' (NA; OC)

Identical results, at least for OC and SR participial complements, are obtained by examining the behaviour of floating quantifiers. Consider the following Cosentino sentences:

(57) a. *(tutti₄) iddi vonnu   (tutti₃) fatti   (tutti₂)   buonu*
      (all)   they want.PRES.3PL (all)   do.PART [TP (all)   [vP well
      (tutti₁) 'a lezione (OC)
      (all)   the lesson]]
      'they (all) want to be (all) taught (all) properly (all) the lesson'

    b. *(tutti₄) 'i piatti vonnu   (tutti₃) priperati   (tutti₂) buonu*
      (all)   the dishes want.PRES.3PL (all)   prepare.PART [TP (all) [vPwell
      (tutti₁) (SR)
      (all)]]
      '(all) the dishes must be (all) prepared (all) properly (all)'

Leaving aside movement of the participle into the matrix clause (see section 7.4 below), we take the manner adverb *buonu* 'well' in (57a–b) to mark the left-edge of *v*P, presumably occurring in an outer specifier of *v* (see discussion in section 4.6.2). Interpreting the possible positions of the quantifier *tutti* 'all' in examples (57a–b) as traces left by the subject successively raised to the matrix subject position, it follows that the participle clause must project to at least TP: in addition to occurring in various intermediate positions within the matrix clause ($tutti_{3/4}$) and its base position ($tutti_1$), the quantifier may equally occur between the participle and the adverb *buonu* 'well' (namely $tutti_2$). Given that the participle marks the right-edge of the matrix clause and *buonu* marks the left-edge of *v*P, it follows that $tutti_2$ must occupy [Spec, T].

In light of the preceding evidence we conclude therefore that participial complements to ECM, OC and SR VOLERE are *v*P, CP and TP constituents, respectively.

7.4. PARTICIPLE MOVEMENT

Although VOLERE + participle appear superficially to yield a biclausal structure along the lines of (58a), there is good reason to prefer a monoclausal analysis (see 58b), in which the participle raises to the matrix clause dominated by VOLERE to form a single verbal complex:

(58) a. [VOLERE] + [PART]   (biclausal structure)

      b. [VOLERE + PART$_i$] [t$_i$]   (monoclausal structure)

We begin by examining the position of the participle in relation to manner adverbs, which, as noted above, mark the left periphery of vP. Consider first the Neapolitan sentences in (59):

(59) a. *voglio   scritta   buono 'a lettera* (ECM)
      want.PRES.1SG write.PART [$_{vP}$ well   the letter]
      'I want the letter written correctly'

      b. *voglio   essere scritta   buono 'a lettera* (OC)
      want.PRES.1SG be.INF   write.PART [$_{vP}$ well   the letter]
      'I want to be written the letter correctly'

      c. *'a lettera vô   essere scritta   buono* (SR)
      the letter   want.PRES.3SG be.INF   write.PART [$_{vP}$ well]
      'the letter must be written correctly'

Above we saw that ECM participial complements are vP constituents. Therefore, the order participle + adverb in (59a) incontrovertibly demonstrates that the participle has raised to the matrix clause. On the other hand, the order ESSERE + participle + adverb in the OC and SR examples (59b–c) is inconclusive, in that it only indicates raising of the participle out of vP. We cannot therefore be sure that the participle is not under T within the participle clause. However, if we combine these results with those of quantifier floating considered above, then the facts become clearer.

In discussing quantifier floating in the Cosentino examples in (57), we ascertained that *tutti$_2$* occupies [Spec, T] of the participle clause, in turn preceded by the participle. The order participle + *tutti$_2$* indicates therefore that the participle has raised to the matrix clause. Moreover, the fact that the participle may also be preceded by *tutti$_3$*, presumably marking the matrix [Spec, v], demonstrates that the participle raises to adjoin to v, before the latter raises alone to T.

Similar results obtain in the corresponding Neapolitan sentences in (60a–b), where the order [*essere* + participle] + *tutte$_2$* clearly marks raising of the verbal complex [*essere* + participle] to the matrix v:

(60) a. *(tutte₄)* *lloro* *vonno*   *(tutte₃)* *essere fatte*   *(tutte₂)* *buono*
      (all)   they want.PRES.3PL (all)   be.INF do.PART [TP (all)   [vP well
      (tutte₂) *'a* *lezione* (OC)
      (all)   the lesson]]
      'they (all) want (all) to be taught (all) properly (all) the lesson'

   b. *(tutte₄)* *chilli* *vine* *vulevano*   *(tutte₃)* *essere vippete*   *(tutte₂)*
      (all)   those wines want.PAST.3PL (all)   be.INF drink.PART [TP (all)
      frische *(tutte₁)* (SR)
      [vP fresh   (all)]]
      '(all) those wines had (all) to be drunk (all) cooled (all)'

Another piece of evidence which yields identical results concerns the behaviour of negation. Consider first the Italian sentences in (61):

(61) a. *non* *pensavo*   *mai*   *di* *vincere il premio*
         not think.PAST.1SG [NegP never . . . [CP of win.INF the prize]]
         'I never thought I would win the prize'

   b. **non* *pensavo*   *di* *vincere mai*   *il premio*
         not think.PAST.1SG [NegP [of win.INF]ᵢ never . . . [CP tᵢ the prize]]

   c. *non* *pensavo*   *di* *vincere MAI il   premio*
         not think.PAST.1SG [NegP . . . [CP of win.INF never the prize]]
         'I NEVER thought that I would win the prize'

In line with standard assumptions about negation, we take the negative clitic *non* 'not' and its associated negative modifier *mai* 'never' in (61) to be merged under Neg and [Spec, Neg], respectively, in turn embedded under TP. The surface order in (61a) is thus derived by moving the matrix verb *pensavo* 'I thought' through Neg, where it adjoins to *non*, to raise to T where it precedes *mai* in [Spec, Neg]. The order infinitive + *mai* in (61b), by contrast, is ruled out since the infinitive cannot raise out of the embedded clause to reach the matrix T. Observe that the grammatical (61c) is only an apparent counter-example, since in this case *MAI* 'NEVER' has an emphatic reading, absent from (61b), and must be analysed differently.

We can therefore adopt the position of the negative specifier *mai* as a further diagnostic to ascertain verb raising to the matrix clause. By way of illustration consider the following Cosentino sentences:

(62) a. *um* *bo*   ***mai*** *tuccata* *'a machina du   meccanicu*
         not want.PRES.3SG [NegP never touch.PART the car   by-the mechanic]
         (ECM)

   b. *um* *bo*   *tuccata*   ***mai***   *'a machina du*
         not want.PRES.3SG touch.PART [NegP never . . . [vP the car   by-the
         meccanicu (ECM)
         mechanic]]
         'he never wants his car touched by the mechanic'

(63) a. *um bo*   ***mai*** *dittu*   *bugìe* (OC)

      not   want.PRES.3SG [$_{\text{NegP}}$ never tell.PART lies]

   b. *um bo*   *dittu*   ***mai***   *bugìe*]] (OC)

      not   want.PRES.3SG tell.PART [$_{\text{NegP}}$ never . . . [$_{\text{CP}}$ . . . lies]]

      'he never wants to be told lies'

(64) a. *'a machina um bo*   ***mai*** *cunzata*   (SR)

      the car   not want.PRES.3SG [$_{\text{NegP}}$ never repair.PART]

   b. *'a machina um bo*   *cunzata*   ***mai***   (SR)

      the car   not want.PRES.3SG repair.PART [$_{\text{NegP}}$ never . . . [$_{\text{TP}}$ . . .]]

      'the car never must be repaired'

Under the unmarked non-emphatic reading, the negative specifier *mai* 'never' in examples (62)–(64) can freely precede or follow the participle, thereby providing us with an indication of the position of the participle. In the (a) examples, the order *mai* + participle yields ambiguous results since the participle could either be under Neg, the matrix *v* or within the participle clause under *v* (62) or T (63 and 64). The (b) examples, in contrast, are quite conclusive: the order participle + *mai* clearly shows that the participle has moved out of the participle clause to raise to the matrix T together with VOLERE. By the same token, the participle in the (a) examples must also be within the matrix clause, presumably stranded under *v* following raising of VOLERE to T. We conclude therefore that in all three want-passive constructions the participle raises to the matrix clause, either remaining under the matrix *v* or adjoining to T together with VOLERE.[9]

Observe furthermore that incorporation of (ESSERE+) participle into OC VOLERE is also independently supported by our analysis of restructuring verbs in section 3.2.2.3. There it was established that incorporation of infinitival CP complements into VOLERE is necessary in order to license the non-finite complement. It follows that the participial CP complement to OC VOLERE will be subject to an analogous incorporation process.

7.4.1. *Causative status of volitional* VOLERE

Significantly, the observed raising of (ESSERE +) participle in conjunction with the ECM and OC want-passive constructions finds further support in their pragmatico-semantic characterization. Consider, for instance, the following ECM (65a) and OC (66a) examples and their corresponding finite paraphrases in (65b) and (66b):

(65) a. *'a parocchia vuleva*   *detta*   *'a messa ('a Padre Luigge)*

      the parish   want.PAST say.PART the mass   (by Father Luigi)

      'the parish wanted mass celebrated (by Father Luigi)' (NA; ECM)

b. *'a   parocchia   vuleva   che Padre Luigge dicesse   'a   messa*
   the parish   want.PAST.3SG that Father Luigi   say.SUBJ.3SG the mass
   'the parish wanted that Father Luigi celebrate mass' (NA)

(66) a. *Luca vo   quadiatu 'a minestra (da   mamma)*
        Luca want.PRES.3SG warm.PART the soup   (by-the mum)
        'Luca wants warmed up the soup (by his mum)' (CS; OC)

     b. *Luca vo   c' a mamma cci quadiassa   ra minestra*
        Luca want.PRES.3SG that the mum him warm.SUBJ.3SG the soup
        'Luca wants that mum warm up the soup' (CS)

What then is the pragmatico-semantic function of the ECM and OC want-
passives and, in particular, the precise contrast engendered by the choice of a
participial versus finite complement following volitional VOLERE? Essentially,
the choice between the use of a participial and a finite complement in (65)
and (66) relates to the intended informational content of the desired state/
event predicated by VOLERE. In the (b) examples the AGENT (Father Luigi,
mum) is foregrounded and presented as a key participant in the activity,
whereas in the (a) examples the AGENT is backgrounded, as evidenced by its
optional adjunct status. Such a contrast finds an immediate parallel in the
Romance causative construction, where identical pragmatico-semantic
considerations determine the choice of a *Faire-Par* (FP) versus *Faire-Infinitif*
(FI) construction (Kayne 1975).

By way of example, consider the corresponding causative sentences:

(67) a. *'a parocchia facette   dicere 'a messa ('a Padre Luigge)* (FP)
        the parish   make.PAST.3SG say.INF the mass   (by Father Luigi)
        'the parish had mass celebrated (by Father Luigi)'

     b. *'a parocchia facette   dicere 'a messa a Padre Luigge* (FI)
        the parish   make.PAST.3SG say.INF the mass   to Father Luigi
        'the parish made Father Luigi celebrate mass'

(68) a. *Luca fa   quadià 'a minestra (da   mamma)* (FP)
        Luca make.PRES.3SG warm.INF the soup   (by-the mum)
        'Luca has the soup warmed up (by his mum)'

     b. *Luca fa   quadià 'a minestra a ra mamma* (FI)
        Luca make.PRES.3SG warm.INF the soup   to the mum
        'Luca makes his mum warm up the soup'

The semantic contrast between a FP versus FI causative in (67)–(68) is
parallel to that between a participial and finite complement in (65) and (66).
Specifically, in the (a) examples in (65) and (68) we have a 2-place complex
predicate (namely, [VOLERE+participle] and [FARE+infinitive]) which selects
for a desirer/causer (the parish/Luca) and a desired/caused event (celebration
of mass/warming of the soup), in which the AGENT (Father Luigi/mum) is

interpreted as instrumental to the activity, and hence an optional by-phrase. In the (a) examples, by contrast, we have a 3–place predicate which selects for a desirer/causer, a desired/caused event and a desiree/causee (Father Luigi/mum) which, in contrast to the (b) examples, is fore-grounded and interpreted as the RECIPIENT of the desired/caused event.

In view of such similarities, we suggest that volitional VOLERE is a causative predicate, only differing from the canonical causative FARE in that it predicates an unrealized state or event of causation. The parallels with the canonical causative construction are clear. As often claimed with the FP construction (67a, 68a), the embedded infinitive has a passive reading and is often argued to be a type of passive, but without the passive morphology. Significantly, the corresponding VOLERE construction (65a, 66a) is indeed a passive, endowed with typical passive morphology. Thus, as in the canonical FP causative construction, a want-passive is used when the desired event is presented as uppermost and the AGENT is defocalized, essentially viewed as instrumental to the desired event. A finite tensed clause (65b, 66b), by contrast, is employed, as with the canonical FI causative construction (67b, 68b), when the AGENT is thrown into relief and interpreted as a crucial participant in the desired event.

In light of our proposed causative interpretation of volitional VOLERE in the ECM and OC constructions, the observed cohesion between VOLERE and participle follows. On a par with the canonical Romance causative construction (see Guasti 1993; Ledgeway 1996b: ch. 4), we have seen that such cohesion is the reflex of a process of incorporation of the participle (+ESSERE) into VOLERE, identical to the incorporation of the infinitive into causative FARE.

7.5. DP-MOVEMENT

7.5.1. *ECM*

We begin by considering the ECM construction and the Neapolitan sentences in (69):

(69) a. *'e   voglio   astutate   buono   'e luce*
       them want.PRES.1SG extinguish.PART$_i$ [$_{vP}$ well   t$_i$ the lights]
       'I want (them) the lights switched off properly'

   b. *voglio   astutate   buono   (tutte$_2$) 'e luce (*tutte$_1$)*
       want.PRES.1SG extinguish.PART$_i$ [$_{vP}$ well   t$_i$ (all)   the lights (all)]
       'I want switched off properly (all) the lights (all)'

   c. *'e   voglio   cazziate   buono   a lloro*
       them want.PRES.1SG tell-off.PART$_i$ [$_{vP}$ well   t$_i$ PA them]
       'I want them told off properly'

d. *'e voglio cazziate buono a (tutte₂) lloro (tutte₁)*
them want.PRES.1SG tell-off.PARTᵢ [ᵥₚ well tᵢ PA (all) them (all)]
'I want (all) them (all) told off properly'

The manner adverb *buono* 'well' in (69) marks the left-edge of the participial *v*-VP, demonstrating that the participial THEME *'e luce/lloro* 'the lights/them' remains with the participial clause. The distribution of floating quantifiers demonstrates that DPs in the UA (69b) remain *in situ* within the embedded VP, whereas DPs in the PA (69d) raise overtly to [Spec, *v*]: only in the latter case can the DP THEME be followed by the stranded quantifier *tutte₁*. We conclude then that in the ECM construction overt raising of the THEME DP to the matrix outer [Spec, *v*] is not possible. Rather, the relevant features of the DP are checked at LF when its accusative Case and D-features adjoin to the matrix *v*.

As for participial agreement, which we have seen is always controlled by the THEME DP, this can be checked both covertly and overtly. In (69a) the DP occurs in the UA and checks agreement on the participle when its φ- and D-features raise to the participial *v* at LF. In the case of (69c), on the other hand, the THEME DP occurs in the PA and raises overtly to the participial [Spec, *v*] to check the strong D-feature on *v*, its φ-features checked against the participle as 'free riders'.

7.5.2. *OC and SR*

7.5.2.1. *Participial agreement*

We have just seen that in the ECM construction participial agreement is invariably controlled by the THEME argument, regardless of whether its φ-features are checked covertly against the participle at LF or overtly before Spell-Out. In configurational terms this means that the agreement features of the passive participle are controlled either by a DP merged in [V, DP] (DPs in the UA; see 69a) or by a DP raised to [Spec, *v*] (DPs in the PA; see 69c).[10] Consequently, whenever a THEME is subjectized in OC/SR constructions in dialects of group 1 and 2, the participle will invariably manifest agreement determined by the THEME in its merger position [V, DP]. This is illustrated by the following example from the dialect of San Biase (CS), which we have seen (see n. 5) behaves both like a group 1 and a group 2 dialect:

(70) *'u piccirillu vulerra (essere) cummegliatu*
the child.M.SG want.COND.3SG (be.INF) cover.PART.M.SG
'the child would like/ought to be wrapped up'

On the other hand, subjectization of a GOAL argument is only registered by participial agreement in group 1 dialects (see 71a–b). In group 2 dialects, in contrast, participial agreement is controlled by the THEME when present (see

72a), or otherwise presents the default M.SG form (see 72b). These facts are illustrated by the following San Biasese examples:

(71) a. *nua vulimu scritti n' assegnu*
we want.PRES.1PL write.PART.1PL a cheque.M.SG
'we want to be written a cheque'

b. *nua vulimu scritti*
we want.PRES.1PL write.PART.1PL
'we want to be written to'

(72) a. *nua vulimu essere scrittu n' assegnu*
we want.PRES.1PL be.INF write.PART.M.SG a cheque.M.SG
'we want to be written a cheque'

b. *nua vulimu essere scrittu*
we want.PRES.1PL be.INF write.PART.M.SG
'we want to be written to'

These facts find a natural explanation in terms of the intermediate positions reached by DP-movement. In group 1 dialects, A-movement of the subjectized GOAL passes through [Spec, v] within the checking domain of the participle triggering agreement. In group 2 dialects, on the other hand, the GOAL raises directly from its merger position to the embedded [Spec, T], therefore failing to trigger participial agreement. DP-movement of the GOAL argument in (71) and (72) will then be as in (73a–b), where we omit raising of (ESSERE+) participle to the matrix clause for expository reasons:

(73) a. *nua vulimu scritti (n' assegnu)*
we$_i$ want.PRES.1PL [$_{CP}$ [$_{TP}$ t$_i$ write.PART.M.PL$_j$ [$_{vP}$ t$_i$ t$_j$ [$_{VP}$ t$_i$ t$_j$ (a cheque.M.SG)]]]]

b. *nua vulimu essere scrittu*
we$_i$ want.PRES.1PL [$_{CP}$ [$_{TP}$ t$_i$ be.INF write.PART.M.SG$_j$ [$_{vP}$ t$_j$ [$_{VP}$ t$_i$ t$_j$
(n' assegnu)
(a cheque.M.SG)]]]]

Observe that in group 1 dialects (see 73a) movement of the GOAL DP through [Spec, v] invariably triggers participle agreement, overriding any potential agreement relation in ditransitive structures (see 71a) between the participial and the THEME DP *in situ*. In the absence of overt DP-raising to [Spec, v] in group 2 dialects (see 73b), the agreement features of the participle can only be controlled, if present, by a THEME DP *in situ* (see 72a).

Our proposed account of the differences in participial agreement between group 1 and group 2 dialects in terms of movement or otherwise through [Spec, v] is substantiated by another piece of evidence relating to adverb agreement. In contrast to the Western Romance languages and Italian, there never arose in the dialects of southern Italy a distinct manner adverb category. Instead, adverbial functions are marked by the corresponding adjective. Below follow some representative examples from Rohlfs (1969: 243):

(74) a. *può   mannà libbər' a ppascə lə pècchər' a la mundagnə*
         can.PRES.2SG send.INF free   to graze.INF the sheep   to the mountain
         'you can freely send the sheep to graze on the mountain' (Abruzzo)

    b. *la fegliola cossí bella   vestuta*
        the girl   so   beautiful.F.SG dress.PART
        'the girl so beautifully dressed' (NA)

    c. *jamə   buonə*
        go.PRES.1PL.M   good.M
        'we're getting on well' (Apulia)

    d. *àrdənə   bbònə*
        burn.PRES.3PL good.F
        'they burn well' (Apulia)

    e. *segretu   parlàamu*
        secret.M.SG speak.PRES.1PL
        'we talk secretly' (Salento)

    f. *tu   sa'   lèggiri bonu*
        you know.PRES.2SG read.INF good.M.SG
        'you can read well' (Sicily)

    g. *càntanu   biellu*
        sing.PRES.3PL beautiful.M.SG
        'they sing beautifully' (Sicily)

Even when used adverbially, the adjective frequently agrees in number and gender with its associated DP (see examples 74b–d). Nonetheless, agreement with such forms in their adverbial function is not unconstrained, in that it can only be controlled by nominals which occupy specific syntactic positions, in particular [V, DP], the canonical merger position of direct objects, or the outer [Spec, *v*] position targeted by DP complements in the PA (see section 2.3). Simplifying somewhat, the syntactic constraints on adverbial adjective agreement thus parallel those of participial agreement. In particular, the agreement features of the adjective can only be controlled by an object complement (UA or PA; see 75a–c) or the subject of an (inherent pronominal) unaccusative (see 75d–e), but not by the subject of a transitive or unergative predicate (see 75f). We illustrate these facts with the adverbial adjective *buonu* 'good' (= well) in the following Cosentino sentences:

(75) a. *Nicola, misca   bone   chiri carte!*
        Nicola shuffle.IMP.2SG good.F.PL those cards.F.PL
        'Nicola, shuffle those cards well!'

b. *Maria unn' ha   crisciutu buoni   a ri figli*
   Maria not have.PRES.3SG raise.PART good.M.PL PA the children.M.PL
   'Maria has not brought the children up well'

c. *l' he   sempe cucinata   bona   a Maria*
   her have.PRES.1SG always cook-for.PART good.F.SG PA Maria
   'I've always cooked well for Maria'

d. *'a criatura sta   bona*
   the child.F   be.PRES.3SG good.F.SG
   'the child is well'

e. *Maria s'   era   liticata   bona   ccu ra   suoru*
   Maria herself be.PAST.3SG argue.PART good.F.SG with the   sister
   'Maria had argued fiercely with her sister'

f. *amu   studiatu buonu   /*buoni ('a lezione)*
   have.PRES.1PL study.PART good.M.SG /good.M.PL (the lesson)
   'we studied (the lesson) well'

Within a multiple specifier model (Chomsky 1995: §4.9) these facts can be straightforwardly accounted for on our previous assumption that manner adverbs like *buonu* mark the left periphery of the *v*-VP complex, for they follow the verb raised to T and precede any complements of the verb, including DPs in the PA raised to the outer [Spec, *v*] (Alexiadou 1997: §5.2; Laenzlinger 1998: 101–2; Cinque 1999: §4.2.4). In particular, we take adverbial adjectives of manner to be merged in the outermost specifier position of *v*, as illustrated schematically in (76):

(76)

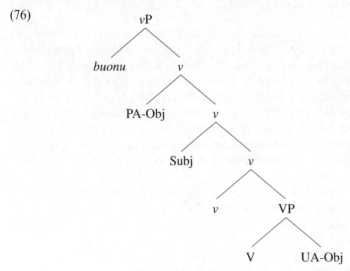

The agreement facts now follow naturally: agreement on the adjective can be checked covertly by LF feature raising of the DP merged in [V, DP]

(see 75a) or by overt DP-raising before Spell-out to the first outer [Spec, *v*] (see 75b–e), where it and the adjectival adverb both occur within the checking domain of *v*.

Assuming this analysis to be correct, in OC/SR want-passives we should expect a subjectized GOAL to license adjective agreement in group 1 dialects, since it passes through [Spec, *v*], but not in group 2 dialects where the subjectized GOAL raises directly to the embedded [Spec, T]. Indeed, these predictions are confirmed by the following contrasts between group 1 (77) and group 2 (78) dialects:

(77) a. *Rosa vulerra   parrata   bona*
      Rosa   want.COND.3SG speak.PART.FSG good.F.SG
      'Rosa would like to be spoken to properly' (San Biase (CS))

    b. *vulimu   cuntati   buoni   stu fattu*
      want.PRES.1PL tell.PART.M.PL good.M.PL this fact
      'we want to be told this story correctly' (CS)

(78) a. *Rosa vulerra   essere parratu   buonu   /*bona*
      Rosa   want.COND.3SG be.INF   speak.PART.M.SG good.M.SG /good.F.SG
      'Rosa would like to be spoken to properly' (San Biase (CS))

    b. *Filumena vô   essere cuntato buono   /*bona   sto fatto*
      Filomena want.PRES.3SG be.INF tell.INF   good.M.SG /good.F.SG this fact
      'Filomena wants to be told this story correctly' (NA)

7.5.2.2. *Movement and the MLC*

In the preceding section the differences in participial agreement were demonstrated to follow from whether the GOAL argument can be object-shifted via [Spec, *v*], where it can control the agreement features of the participle. Thus, in group 1 dialects the GOAL argument must first be advanced to direct object via [Spec, *v*] in order to raise through the embedded [Spec, T] and subsequently into the matrix clause. In group 2 dialects, on the other hand, the GOAL argument raises directly to the embedded [Spec, T]. As it stands, however, the failure of the GOAL argument to raise through [Spec, *v*] in group 2 dialects lacks a principled explanation. Consider the participial structure for the San Biase (CS) examples (79a–b) given in (80a–b), respectively:

(79) a. *Carla um bulerra   circata   sordi*   (group 1)
      Carla not want.COND.3SG ask-for.PART.F.SG money.M.PL

    b. *Carla um bulerra   essere circati   sordi*   (group 2)
      Carla not want.COND.3SG be.INF ask-for.PART.M.PL money.M.PL
      'Carla would not like to be asked for money'

(80)

a.

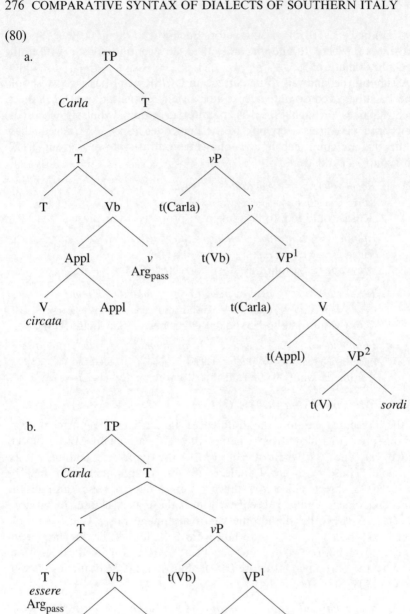

b.

Assuming in accordance with general minimalist principles, and in particular the MLC, that movement operations proceed by the shortest steps possible (Chomsky 1995: §4.5.5), there emerges an apparent conflict between group 1 and group 2 dialects. In the former (see 80a), raising of the GOAL argument *Carla* merged in [Spec, Appl] involves two 'short' steps, namely [Spec, Appl] → [Spec, v] → [Spec, T], whereas in group 2 dialects (see 80b) raising involves one 'long' step, namely [Spec, Appl] → [Spec, T]. Within a global approach to economy (Chomsky 1995: §4.5.5), the derivation in (80b) should apparently be excluded, since it proves more costly than that in (80a). However, the two derivations cannot be compared since they have different numerations. In particular, the numeration for (80b) contains the passive auxiliary ESSERE, absent from that for (80a).

It would appear then that it is the presence of the passive auxiliary which licenses long movement in group 2 dialects or, to put it another way, its absence in group 1 dialects which renders a two-step derivation necessary. How then can we formalize this intuition? Let us assume, following Baker, Johnson and Roberts (1989), that the passive morphology is an argument which receives the verb's external θ-role and structural Case (henceforth referred to as Arg_{pass}). More specifically, in group 2 dialects the external θ-role is assigned to the passive auxiliary ESSERE under T, while in group 1 dialects, where ESSERE is invariably absent, the external θ-role is assigned to the passive participle morpheme -TU(M) under v.

Let us now return to the derivations in (80). The target of movement, namely [Spec, T], has a strong D-feature which must be checked before Spell-Out. Besides the DP-theme merged under VP^2, there are two closer candidates in (80a) with a D-feature which can check that on T, namely Arg_{pass} under v and the GOAL argument merged in [Spec, Appl]. Following Chomsky (1995: 356), the notion of 'closeness' is defined as in (81) (see also section 1.3.6):

(81)   If β c-commands α and τ is the target of raising, then β is closer to K than α unless β is in the same minimal domain as (a) τ or (b) α.

In (80a) Arg_{pass} c-commands *Carla* in [Spec, Appl] and occurs in the minimal domain of v. In contrast, *Carla* and the target [Spec, T] occur in the minimal domains of Appl and T, respectively. Consequently, Arg_{pass} qualifies as a closer candidate. However, in (80a) it is *Carla* which raises and not Arg_{pass}. In order then for *Carla* to raise, Arg_{pass} and *Carla* must be equidistant from [Spec, T], as defined in (82):[11]

(82)   γ and β are equidistant from α if γ and β are in the same minimal domain.

(82) entails then that *Carla* must first move to [Spec, v], where it will be in the same minimal domain as Arg_{pass} and hence equidistant from [Spec, T]. From this position *Carla* can then legitimately raise to [Spec, T] and subsequently

through to the matrix subject position. DP-movement through [Spec, v] with concomitant participial agreement in group 1 dialects thus falls out directly from the definition of the MLC.

Finally, let us turn to the derivation in (80b) representative of group 2 dialects. Recall that in group 2 dialects Arg$_{pass}$ is assigned to the auxiliary ESSERE under T. Consequently, the target of raising [Spec, T] and Arg$_{pass}$ are both in the minimal domain of T and, hence by (82), equidistant from *Carla* in [Spec, Appl]. According to our definition of closeness in (81), and in particular case (a), this means that Arg$_{pass}$ is not closer to [Spec, T] than *Carla*. Therefore, raising of *Carla* from [Spec, Appl] directly to [Spec, T] in (80b) follows once again from the definition of the MLC.

7.6. DATIVE PASSIVIZATION: NORTH VERSUS SOUTH

In northern dialects and Italian we have seen that the OC/SR constructions only license THEME-subjectization, whereas in southern varieties both THEMES and GOALS may be freely subjectized:

(83) a. *Mario   vuole   essere mandato* (Italian)

a′. *Mariu   voli   essiri mannatu* (Sicily)

  Mario   want.PRES.3SG be.INF send.PART

  'Mario wants to be sent'

b. **Mario vuole   essere mandata una lettera* (Italian)

b′. *Mariu   voli   essiri mannata na   littra* (Sicily)

  Mario   want.PRES.3SG be.INF send.PART a   letter

  'Mario wants to be sent a letter'

Clearly, this difference between northern and southern varieties cannot derive from the structural analysis proposed above, inasmuch as northern varieties equally license an OC/SR construction (83a) to all intents and purposes identical to that of southern varieties (83a′). Rather, the relative grammaticality judgements of the Italian and Sicilian examples in (83b–b′) must follow from a more general difference between the grammars of these two varieties, wholly independent of the VOLERE OC/SR construction. The relevant difference, we suggest, hinges on the availability or otherwise of the prepositional accusative, the distribution of which largely coincides with that of GOAL-passivization in the OC/SR constructions.

In common with Italian, northern dialects are virtually unanimous in their failure to make use of the prepositional accusative (Rohlfs 1969: §632). In chapter 2 we established how the widespread phenomenon of the prepositional accusative in southern Italian dialects has had significant consequences on the structural/inherent Case dichotomy and, in particular, on the syntax of dative objects. Specifically, extensive evidence was presented to demonstrate that dative Case in southern dialects may be structural or inherent, the former checked by the verb on DP objects bearing the GOAL role and the latter realized by the preposition *a* 'to' on objects of various thematic interpretations. In Italian and northern dialects, on the other hand, dative Case is invariably an oblique inherent Case realized by the true preposition *a* 'to'. The distinction between dative-marked GOAL arguments in southern dialects on the one hand and Italian and northern dialects on the other reduces therefore to one of structural versus inherent Case, as represented schematically in (84a–b):

(84) a. V + [_DP *a* + NP]   (southern dialects)

b. V + [_PP *a* [_DP NP]]   (Italian and northern dialects)

The contrast between (83b–b′) now follows in a principled fashion. In accordance with Burzio's Generalization, passivization of the embedded participial clause in (83) entails suppression of the external θ-role and the verb's structural Case. In the Italian examples this will leave the THEME arguments *Mario* in (83a) and *una lettera* 'a letter' in (83b) without an appropriate Case-checker within the participial clause. Consequently, raising to the matrix subject position to check nominative on T, as in (83a), is forced for convergence. The ungrammaticality of (83b), in contrast, falls out as violation of the Last Resort Condition, since raising of the GOAL argument *Mario* to the matrix subject position will result in it illicitly bearing two Case features, for its inherent dative Case is not suppressed under passivization. *Mario* is therefore frozen in place in (83b), the only convergent derivation being that in (85) where the THEME argument raises to check nominative in the matrix [Spec, T]:[12]

(85) *una lettera vuole   essere mandata a Mario*
      a   letter want.PRES.3SG be.INF send.PART to Mario
      'a letter must be sent to Mario'

In contrast, raising of the GOAL argument *Mariu* to the matrix [Spec, T] in the Sicilian example (83b′) proves a legitimate step, since the verb's structural Case, be it accusative or dative, is suppressed under passivization. Unable to check Case within the participial clause, *Mariu* is therefore forced to raise to the matrix clause where it can check the nominative Case feature on T. Significantly, suppression of the participle's structural Case in (83b′) will equally entail that the THEME argument *na littra* 'a letter' cannot check structural accusative. Indeed, this conclusion is borne out by the examples in (86a–b):

(86) a. *Mariu (*'a) vo   mannatu   'a littera*
         Mario (it) want.PRES.3SG send.PART.M.SG the letter.F.SG
         'Mario wants to be sent (it) the letter' (CS)

b. *Mariu (*'a) voli   essiri mannata   'a littra*
   Mario (it)   want.PRES.3SG be.INF send.PART.F.SG the letter.F.SG
   'Mario wants to be sent (it) the letter' (Sicily)

c. *a   Mario, 'o   (*'a) scrivo   'a lettera*
   PA Mario_i him_i (it_j) write.PRES.1SG the letter_j
   'Mario, I'll write him (it) a letter' (NA)

In both group 1 (86a) and group 2 (86b) dialects, the THEME argument *'a litteral/littra* 'the letter' cannot be referenced with a corresponding structural accusative clitic *'a* 'it', whenever the GOAL argument is subjectized. Similar cases of the GOAL argument being shifted to [Spec, v], usurping the verb's structural Case in active structures, were discussed in section 2.4. For example, in (86c) the THEME argument *'a lettera* 'the letter' was argued to be marked with a default inherent accusative Case *in situ*. Identical considerations carry over to the THEME argument in (83b′) and (86a–b), thereby accounting for the ungrammaticality of referencing the THEME argument with a structural accusative clitic.[13] This is further confirmed by the ungrammaticality of marking the THEME *Luca* in (87) with the PA, which as a structural Case, proves incompatible with the (default) inherent accusative Case borne by *Luca*.

(87) a. *Pina vulesse   essere purtato   (*a) Luca* (NA)
        Pina want.COND.3SG be.INF bring.PART (PA) Luca

     b. *Pina vulissa   purtata   (*a) Luca* (CS)
        Pina want.COND.3SG bring.PART.F.SG (PA) Luca
        'Pina would like Luca to be brought to her

7.7. SUMMARY

We have established that participle complements to ECM, SR and OC VOLERE are vP, TP and CP constituents, respectively. Despite such differences, evidence was presented to demonstrate that in every case the participle incorporates into the matrix verb, giving rise to a monoclausal structure. In the case of the ECM and OC constructions, it was observed that incorporation of the participle into VOLERE parallels the incorporation of the infinitive into causative FARE, a conclusion further substantiated by the analogous causative interpretation of volitional VOLERE in these constructions.

As for A-movement, the THEME argument of the ECM construction was demonstrated to remain *in situ*, its accusative Case and φ-features checked against [VOLERE + participle] at LF. In OC and SR constructions, in contrast, movement of the subjectized THEME/GOAL argument occurs before Spell-Out. In the latter case, the facts on the distribution of auxiliary ESSERE and participial agreement follow from the MLC. Specifically, in group 1 dialects the subjectized DP must move through the intermediate outer [Spec, v] position, where it triggers participial agreement, to preclude the passive argument (Arg$_{pass}$) in v from qualifying as a closer candidate for movement. In group 2 dialects, in contrast, Arg$_{pass}$ is assigned to ESSERE under T and not therefore closer to the target of movement than the subjectized argument in its merger position. Consequently, the subjectized argument can move directly to [Spec, T], bypassing [Spec, v] and thereby failing to control participial agreement.

Finally, we established that the ungrammaticality of dative passivization in the North, as opposed to its grammaticality in the South, follows from the nature of dative Case. In northern varieties, GOAL arguments are marked with inherent dative Case realized by a true preposition. Consequently, suppression of structural Case under passivization has no effect on the inherent Case borne by GOAL arguments. Consequently, GOAL-subjectization cannot obtain in accordance with the last resort nature of movement. In southern dialects, in contrast, GOAL arguments are marked with structural dative Case which is suppressed under passivization. Therefore, GOAL-subjectization is forced for convergence, otherwise the GOAL would remain in a Caseless position. Moreover, this analysis accounts for the default inherent accusative Case assumed by THEME arguments in GOAL passives.

NOTES

1 Introduction

1 See Pellegrini (1975), Bruni (1984: 290ff.), Cortelazzo (1988), Savoia (1997).
2 The uninterpretable nature of Case is evidenced particularly strongly by the virtually synonymous sentences in (i.a-b):

(i) a. *I believe [that **he** is a liar]*
    b. *I believe [**him** to be a liar]*

In (i.a) *believe* selects for a finite complement in which the embedded 3M.SG subject is marked nominative. In (i.b), on the other hand, *believe* takes an Exceptional Case Marking (ECM) infinitival complement, whose embedded 3M.SG subject is marked accusative by the matrix verb. Significantly, the difference in Case-marking between *he* and *him* in (i.a–b) does not correlate with any discernible interpretative difference.

3 In what follows we shall refer to *Attract/Attraction* with the more familiar terminology *Move/Movement*.
4 However, in the following chapters the familiar X-bar terminology and notation is often employed for ease of exposition.
5 We follow traditional practice in representing the position(s) occupied by a moved category with the abbreviation t(race).
6 Essentially, once a nominal category has checked its Case feature, it is 'frozen' in place and cannot, in accordance with the 'last resort' nature of movement, raise to further Case-checking positions.

2 Case-marking

1 See Torrego (1998a) for similar proposals with regard to Spanish.
2 This interpretation of object clitics extends equally to subject clitics in northern Italian varieties, where the clitic can be considered the spell-out of a D-feature on T, variously encoding person, number, gender and nominative (see Goria in progress).
3 Although we adopt the traditional label 'prepositional accusative', we argue below that AD > *a* in such sequences is not a preposition.
4 Far from being a unique claim or property of Neapolitan and southern Italian dialects more generally, the existence of a structural dative Case in Romance has been argued elsewhere in the literature (see Chomsky 1981: 171–2, n. 6; and Torrego 1998a: 8–9; also Holmberg and Platzack 1995 for Scandinavian).
5 For some interesting observations on the factors which determine the distribution of the PA in early Sicilian and Neapolitan texts, see Sornicola (1997b).
6 See Jaeggli (1981; 1986), Demonte (1987; 1988), Chomsky (1988: 104–6), Suñer (1988), Brancadell (1992), Torrego (1998a). For Italian and Catalan, see Rizzi (1988) and Badia (1998), respectively.
7 See Rohlfs (1969: §632; 1971), Jones (1993: 65ff; 1995), Trumper (1996: 354–5), Green (1988: 106). Also of interest is the southern Calabrian *dativo greco* (Greek-style dative) discussed in Rohlfs (1969: §639) and Vincent (1997b: 209).
8 The so-called articulated forms are also represented in orthography as *ô*, *â* and *ê*. As

indicated by the circumflex accent, in slow speech or when pronounced in isolation, these can be realized with a longer vowel, namely [oː], [aː] and [eː], respectively, in order to distinguish them from the forms of the definite article with an invariably [-long] vowel: [o], [a] and [e]. However, in practice, the lengthening of such vowels in the articulated forms is generally obscured and not detectable, as maintained by Pring (1950: 118) who observes that '[the dialect] is spoken very fast, with much obscuration and running together of sounds' and processes such as '[e]lision, assimilation . . . are frequent'. Moreover, the reality of such ambiguity and morphophonemic weakening of the articulated forms is directly reflected by the emergence and subsequent widespread usage of innovative periphrastic dative markers such as *vicino a* (literally 'close to'), which unambiguously mark structural dative Case (see below).

 9 See Rohlfs (1969: §633), Ledgeway (1995: S.II.§1.2.2), Sornicola (1997a: 335–37), Loporcaro (1986: 268ff.; 1997b: 346; 1998: 129–30, 174–6).

10 These analytic markers of structural dative are discussed in Rohlfs (1969: 638), Bichelli (1974: §326), Fierro (1989: 178–9), Ledgeway (1995: S.II.§1.2.3).

11 Altamurano proves an exception, which for independent historical reasons arising out of a variable pattern of auxiliary alternation (see Loporcaro 1988: §235), freely allows all types of indirect object passives.

12 For further discussion of participial agreement in Neapolitan, see sections 6.3.2.4 and 7.5.2.1, and Ledgeway (1995: S.III.§1.1.1).

13 Within a more articulated structure, we could represent the PA/SD Case-marker *a* 'to' as a separate K(ase) head which takes a DP complement (see Giusti 1993; Lyons 1995; 1999: 294–302).

14 Light *v* is the same head identified variously as Tr(ansitivity) in Johnson (1991), Bowers (1993), Collins and Thráinsson (1993), Collins (1997: 15ff.), Basilico (1998: 545, 590–1), and as Voi(ce) in Kratzer (1994) and Jones (1998).

15 See Capozzoli (1889: 214), Bichelli (1974: §188), Radtke (1988: 657), Iandolo (1994: 258, 260), Ledgeway (1995: M.I.§6.3).

16 See, among others, Savini (1881: 86), Finamore (1893: 22), Rohlfs (1968: §468), Vaccaro (1969: 41), Mennonna (1997: 116), Gioscio (1985: 64), Marinucci (1988: 647), Ruggieri and Batinti (1992: 46), Meliadò (1994: 18) and Leone (1995: §30).

17 For discussion, see Diesing (1988, 1992), Diesing and Jelinek (1995), Enç (1991a), Mahajan (1992), Demonte (1995), Rapoport (1995), Alexiadou and Anagnostopoulou (1998a), Basilico (1998), Ordóñez (1998) and Torrego (1998a).

18 A similar proposal is maintained by Basilico (1998) who argues that the distinction between thetic (= non-affected) and categorical (= affected) predications correlates with the VP-internal and VP-external positions of the object, respectively.

19 Further evidence relating to the position of objects in the PA with respect to infinitival subjects reviewed in section 4.6.2 demonstrates that such objects raise overtly to an outer [Spec, *v*].

20 See also Alexiadou and Anagnostopoulou (1998a: n. 44; 1998c: n. 31), Torrego (1998a: 161); for an alternative approach to inherent Case we refer the reader to Lasnik (1999).

21 A small number of the present author's Neapolitan informants also accepted the sentences in (52), where the indirect object is overt and follows the direct object. At present, we have no explanation to offer for such structures.

22 See Granatiero (1987: 55).

23 For further discussion of these data, see Scerbo (1886: 63) and Lombardi (1997: 55–6) for Calabrian and Leone (1995: §51) for Sicilian.

24 Spanish behaves differently in this respect (see Torrego 1998a: 131ff. and references cited there).

25 See also Trumper (1996: 354–5; 1997: 363) for Calabrian and Loporcaro (1988: 273) for Altamurano.

26 On a par with the parameters identified above as responsible for the restriction of the PA-marking of indirect objects in Neapolitan, the underlying indirect object of the English dative shift construction is also widely reported to be restricted by such parameters as animacy, specificity and the obligatory agentive interpretation of the subject. For further discussion, we refer the reader to Larson (1988, 1990), Pinker (1989), Jackendoff (1990), Pesetsky (1995), Torrego (1998a) and references cited there.

27 Spanish, another language where AD > a marks structural Case, has also recently been argued by Demonte (1995) to exhibit a double-object construction in structures in which the indirect object is doubled by a dative clitic.

28 See also Aoun and Li (1989), Speas (1990), Demonte (1995) and Torrego (1998a).

29 Similar analyses regarding the position of the indirect and direct object positions have also been made in a number of other recent analyses, for example, Collins and Thráinsson (1993), Chomsky (1995b: 305, 333ff.), Demonte (1995) and Torrego (1998a).

30 Analogous proposals have been made by Demonte (1995) and Torrego (1998a) who argue that the indirect object is generated in the specifier position of DClP (Doubled Clitic Phrase) and a (light) p projection, respectively. In what follows we shall continue to refer to this head as Appl, although nothing of our present analysis rests on this assumption which could be stated equally well in Demonte's or Torrego's system.

31 For similar proposals regarding the assignment of inherent accusative within VP, see Belletti (1990) and n. 20 above.

32 In the discussion of want-passives in chapter 7, however, evidence will be provided to demonstrate that under quite different circumstances all southern Italian dialects license inherent accusative Case (see section 7.6).

3 Finite and infinitival complementation

1 For discussion of the problems associated with the PRO Theorem, see Manzini (1983), Bouchard (1984), Koster (1984), Borer (1986) and Huang (1989).

2 Dialects of the Extreme South, namely southern Calabria, Salentino peninsula and north-western Sicily (province of Messina), present an even more restricted use of the infinitive, generally employing in its place clauses headed by the complementizer *ca/chi* or a reflex of (QUO)MODO (see Rohlfs 1969: §717; Trumper and Rizzi 1985; Calabrese 1993; Lombardi 1997, 1998a). The problems raised by these dialects are discussed in Ledgeway (1998b).

3 Analogous considerations apply to the other Romance languages, with the notable exception of Romanian (see Dobrovie-Sorin 1993: ch. 4).

4 Frequently spelt *cha* in early texts.

5 Some dialects of southern Lazio equally display a dual complementizer system (see examples 13).

6 In some dialects where *ca* has now generalized, the *che/chi* complementizer has been retained as an optional variant to introduce non-propositional complements. Interestingly, where this is the case, the *che/chi* complementizer invariably requires the verb in the (imperfect) subjunctive (i.a), whereas both the (imperfect) subjunctive and indicative are possible following the *ca* complementizer (i.b; see also note 37 below). This is demonstrated by the following Cosentino examples:

(i) a. *vulite chi ci jissa /*vaju   iu?*
   want.PRES.2PL that there go.SUBJ.1SG /go.PRES.INDIC.1SG I

 b. *vuliti ca ci jissa /vaju   iu?*
   want.PRES.2PL that there go.SUBJ.1SG /go.PRES.INDIC.1SG I
  'do you want me to go?'

7 Savini (1881: 80) reports for the Abruzzese dialect of Teramo a similar distinction in the complementizer system based on a modification of the declarative/epistemic complementizer *che*, to which *o* (< *voglio* 'I want') is prefixed, as exemplified in (i):

(i) *ha dette ocche te n' avisse jite*
 have.PRES.3SG say.PART that yourself from-there have.SUBJ.2SG go.PART
 'he ordered that you leave'

In many Abruzzese and Molisano dialects the sequence *o* + *chi/che* [ɔ kki/kkə] appears to serve also as an exhortative marker:

(ii) a. ɔ kki vve
   want that come.PRES.3SG
  'may he come!' (Hastings 1999: 2)

b. *ò   cchə lə mannə*   */mannèssə*
   want that it send.PRES.INDIC.3SG /send.SUBJ.3SG
   'would that he send it!' (Giammarco 1968–85: 1370)

8   Tollese examples from Robert Hastings (personal communication).
9   See however Leone (1995: 66, n. 157).
10   See Bošković (1995) for evidence that clauses bear Case features.
11   This does not mean that infinitival complements to structural Case-checkers are not to be found in written texts, witness the examples below:

(i) a. *si ve credite   'e me sfrocolià 'o pasticciotto avite   sbagliato*
        if believe.PRES.2PL of [me wind-up.INF]   have.PRES.2PL mistake.PART
        palazzo
        building
        'if you think you can wind me up, you've picked on the wrong person' (De Filippo 1973: 24)

   b. *se   permette   'e se   mettere cu' na figliola 'e vintiduie!*
      himself allow.PRES.3SG of [himself put.INF with a young-girl of twenty-two]
      'he allows himself to get together with a young girl of twenty-two!' (ibid., 315)

   c. *ha   deciso   de non volerse   cchiù   nzurà*
      have.PRES.3SG decide.PART of [not want.INF-himself any-more marry.INF]
      'he's decided to no longer want to get married' (Scarpetta 1994: 206)

   d. *ve raccomanno però   de non ve   scordà mai de Papele vuosto*
      you ask.PRES.1SG though of [not yourself forget.INF never of Papele your]
      'I ask you though to never forget your Papele' (Scarpetta 1992: 15)

These and similar examples are to be ascribed to influence from the corresponding Italian infinitival structures, a conclusion confirmed by the present authors' informants who characterized such structures as 'Italianized' and alien to the spoken dialect where a finite complement would be readily used. This view is reinforced by the results of a questionnaire, in which informants consistently translated such Italian infinitivals with a finite complement. Some examples are given in (ii):

(ii) a. *so   di aver   sbagliato* (Italian)
        know.PRES.1SG [of have.INF   err.PART]
        sacciu   c' aggiu   sgarrato (NA)
        know.PRES.1SG [that have.PRES.1SG err.PART]
        'I know that I have made a mistake'

    b. *Ciro aveva   deciso   di nascondere i   soldi*   (Italian)
       Ciro have.PAST.3SG decide.PART [of hide.INF   the money]
       Ciro aveva   deciruto   c' avev'   ânnosconnere 'e sorde (NA)
       Ciro have.PAST.3SG decide.PART [that must.PAST.3SG hide.INF   the money]
       'Ciro had decided to hide/that he would hide the money'

    c. *non crediamo   di vincere la lotteria* (Italian)
       not believe.PRES.1PL [of win.INF the lottery]
       nun credimmo   ca vencimmo 'a lotteria (NA)
       not believe.PRES.1PL [that win.PRES.1PL the lottery]
       'we don't believe that we'll win the lottery'

12   For Campanian varieties, see Bichelli (1974: 201), Ledgeway (1995: M.I.§6.1.1.3) and Sornicola (1996). Expletives in southern Calabrian and Sicilian dialects are discussed in Accattatis (1895: §181), Rohlfs (1968: §449), Meliadò (1994: 100) and Leone (1995: §70, §77).
13   The inability of the infinitive to check nominative in such structures may well follow from economy conditions, insofar as merger of a covert/overt expletive in [Spec, T] represents a more economical way of satisfying the EPP than the more costly alternative of raising the infinitive to [Spec, T] (see Bošković 1995).
14   Conceivably, the albeit rare use of infinitival clauses in Tollese may be attributed to influence from the equivalent Italian infinitival structures.
15   Our account of Neapolitan structural Case-checkers like *decirere* 'to decide', which lack an

appropriate structural Case feature whenever they subcategorize for a sentential complement, goes against the spirit of *Burzio's Generalization*: though transitive verbs which assign
an external θ-role, they fail however to check structural (accusative) Case. For further
discussion, see Chomsky (1995: 313–16, n. 90) and Lasnik (1999: 124–5, 132, 147, n. 18).

16	In other Romance varieties, Italian and Occitan for instance, restructuring also occasions
the generalization of the perfective auxiliary appropriate to the dependent infinitive.
Neapolitan restructuring, in contrast, invariably triggers the *avé(re)* 'have' auxiliary,
irrespective of the semantico-syntactic class of the dependent infinitive (see Ledgeway
1996b: §3.4.6 for discussion).

17	Restructuring verbs do not include modal and aspectual auxiliaries such as *puté* 'can' and
accummencià 'to begin', since, as will be demonstrated in chapter 5, the properties of
infinitival constructions in conjunction with such auxiliaries are quite different.

18	Recall from the discussion in chapter 2 that inherent Case-checkers only license the
invariable clitic *(n)ce*, whereas predicates that check SD license a full array of clitics
variously marked for person, number and gender.

19	See among others Accattatis (1895: §194), Rohlfs (1969: §470), Meliadò (1994: 95), Ruggieri
and Batinti (1992: 87) and Leone (1995: §66).

20	Further consequences of the present analysis of restructuring are discussed in Ledgeway
(1998a).

21	The present outline of Martin's (1992) analysis of PRO is based on the discussion presented
in Watanabe (1996: ch. 2) and Bošković (1997: ch. 2). See also Lasnik (1999: 63ff.).

22	Hornstein (1999: 91, n. 36) also suggests that Martin's (1992) proposal restricting OC PRO
to [+tense] non-finite T is compatible with his movement-based account.

23	Observe that Hornstein's proposed analysis of the complementation structures with *try* and
seem strikingly parallels in many respects the LFG treatment of such structures (see
Bresnan 1982, Vincent forthcoming).

24	See also Bouchard (1984), Sportiche (1982) and Koster (1984).

25	See, among others, Anderson (1982), Giorgi (1983–4), Picallo (1984–5), Raposo (1985–6),
Manzini and Wexler (1987).

26	A not too dissimilar approach is proposed by Holmberg and Platzack (1995: 90ff.) who
derive long-distance binding from the finiteness features of the embedded clause.

27	Similar claims are made in Guéron and Hoekstra (1994) and Hoekstra, Hyams and Becker
(1999: 255–9).

28	Giorgi (1983–4: 339) also demonstrates that the effects of long-distance binding observable
in Italian subjunctive clauses (see 59a) carry over to control infinitival clauses, both marked
by a [+dep] INFL. By way of illustration, compare the possible antecedents of the anaphor
propria in the following infinitival (i.a) and finite (i.b) clauses:

(i)	a.	*Gianni$_j$ costrinse Osvaldo$_i$ ad* [PRO$_i$ *ammettere di* [PRO$_i$ *essere entrato nottetempo
nella propria$_{i/j}$ casa*]]
'Gianni$_j$ forced Osvaldo$_i$ [PRO$_i$ to admit [PRO$_i$ to have gone during the night into
self's$_{i/j}$ house]]'

	b.	*Gianni$_j$ mi ha detto che* [*Osvaldo$_i$ ti$_k$ costrinse ad* [PRO$_k$ *entrare nottetempo nella
propria$_{i/?*j}$ casa*]]
'Gianni$_j$ told me that [Osvaldo$_i$ forced you$_k$ [PRO$_k$ to enter during the night in
self's$_{i/?*j}$ house]]'

29	Similar ideas regarding the role of Tense in licensing *wh*-movement are discussed in
Simpson (1999).

30	See also Giorgi and Pianesi (1997: ch. 4).

31	For a detailed survey of the relationship between the habitual and non-habitual readings of
the present in a wide range of Romance varieties, see Giorgi and Pianesi (1997: ch. 4) and
Posner (1999).

32	The popularity of the *stà* + gerund periphrasis is such that it may even encroach upon the
simple present in its generic reading, as evidenced in (i):

(i)	*cchiú a famiglia se sta perdenno e cchiú 'o pate 'e famiglia ha da piglià 'a responsabilità*
(De Filippo 1973: 250)
'the more the family loses (literally 'is losing') its sense of direction, the more the father
of the family must take charge'

33   For individual dialects, similar observations are not lacking either. Finamore (1893: 24) in his survey of Abruzzese reports the wide-spread use of periphrastic paradigms in the present and imperfect in conjunction with the auxiliary *tené* 'to have', the synthetic forms rarely being used (see also Bertoni 1916: §120). Some of his examples are given in (i):

(i) a. *ji' téngo'*   *a   ffa'*
      I   have.PRES.1SG   to do.INF
      'I am doing' (Finamore 1893: 24)

   b. *cullù   té'*   *a   mmagná*
      that-one have.PRES.3SG to eat.INF
      'he is eating' (ibid.)

   c. *nu' teném'*   *a   ccandá*
      we have.PRES.1PL to   sing.INF
      'we are singing' (ibid.)

   d. *tè*   *a   vestì*
      have.PRES.3SG   to dress.INF
      'he is dressing' (Bertoni 1916: §120)

Mennonna's (1977: 128) study of the Lucanian dialect of Muro Lucano (PZ) also highlights the fact that the *stà* 'be' + gerund periphrasis is the preferred means of expressing 'azione *in fieri*' ('action in progress'), as illustrated in (ii):

(ii) *pàtrim'*   *stài'*   *parlànn' e   r' sòr   mi' stànn'   cusénn'*
     father.POSS.1SG   be.PRES.3SG speak.GER and the sisters my be.PRES.3PL sew.GER
     'my father is speaking and my sisters are sewing'

Calabrian dialects present a similar picture. Trumper (1997: 363) reports in the dialects of northern Calabria a 'clear, much-used aspectual contrast ['staju 'jiennu] 'I'm going' vs ['vaju] 'I go', though its precise nature requires further study.' From the present author's own investigations, such dialects appear to pattern with Neapolitan in that the simple present is generally restricted to expressing the habitual/generic value, whereas the periphrastic paradigm is the predominant form employed to mark continuous present time, witness (iii):

(iii) *ccà   ste*   *stannu bona*
      here   be.PRES.1SG   be.GER good
      'I am comfortable here' (CS)

Southern Calabrian dialects behave in a similar fashion, as confirmed by Meliadò's (1994:146) remarks about the high frequency of the *stari* + gerund periphrasis in Reggio Calabria to mark continuous action.

   Dialects of Apulia and the Salentino peninsula equally favour periphrastic means of expressing present time, witness Loporcaro (1997b: 347–8) who observes that the '[s]imple present and imperfect are strictly limited to non-progressive use' whereas 'invariable [sta / ʃta] (< coordinated STAT (AC)), is preposed to indicative present or imperfect to convey progressive meaning: Otranto (LE) ['tutti sta 'spɛttene] 'everybody is waiting', Cellino Sano Marco (BR) [ʃta b'bɛɲɲu] 'I am coming".'

   Similar conclusions emerge from Stehl's (1988: §5.3.4) survey of Apulian and Salentino dialects, which he notes make very frequent use of a continuous periphrasis both with conjugated (iv.a–b) and non-conjugated (iv.c) auxiliary:

(iv) a. *stóne*   *ffákənə*
       be.PRES.3PL   do.PRES.3PL
       'they are doing' (Ostuni (BR), Stehl 1988: §5.3.4)

   b. *no stók*   *a   kkúdə*
      not be.PRES.1SG   to close.PRES.1SG
      'I am not closing' (TA, ibid.)

   c. *sta   ttráse*   *lu   súle*
      be   enter.INF   the sun
      'the sun is going in' (LE, ibid.)

Greater use of such forms over the simple present (and the simple imperfect) are also reported by Stehl (1988: 712) to characterize the non-standard Italian varieties of the region:

(v) a. *sta*   *a*   *mangiare*
    be.PRES.3SG to   eat.INF
    'he is eating'

    b. *mi*   *stava*   *piacendo tanto*
    me.DAT   be.PAST.3SG please.GER a-lot
    'I liked it a lot'

Sicilian dialects are also characterized by an extremely frequent use of the *stari* + gerund periphrasis (see Varvaro 1988: §8.9). This view is echoed by Leone (1995: §45) who reports the periphrasis to be frequently employed where the simple present would suffice in Italian:

(vi) a. *la mamma frigge*   *il   pesce* (Italian)
    the mum   fry.PRES.3SG the fish

    b. *'a   mamma sta*   *friennu 'u   pisci* (Sicily)
    the mum   be.PRES.3SG fry.GER   the fish
    'mum is frying the fish'

34 For similar arguments, see Bertoni (1916: §119), Maiden (1995: 156–7), Cordin (1997: 96) and Posner (1999: 133, n. 26).

35 For further discussion, see Vikner (1995: §3.4), Watanabe (1996: §2.3.2) and Zwart (1997: 212ff.).

36 The distribution of the subjunctive in individual dialects is discussed in Capozzoli (1889: 221–2), Finamore (1893: 25), Accattatis (1895: §209a, §211e), Gentili (1897: §140), Bichelli (1974: 165), Mennonna (1977: 123), Gioscio (1985: 77–8), Ruggieri and Batinti (1992: 85), Villa (1992: 95ff.), Iandolo (1994: 205), Ledgeway (1995: M.II.§2.2.7), Leone (1995: §40) and Cordin (1997: 90–1).

37 Although the question requires further investigation, the distribution of the present/past indicative versus the (imperfect) subjunctive in these contexts does appear to be subject to some restrictions. For instance, in Cosentino there are verbs which, in contrast to their Italian congeners, always take an indicative complement (i) and others which always require a subjunctive complement (ii):

(i) a. *criju*   *ca* *vena*   /*venissa*   *Elio*
    believe.PRES.1SG that come.PRES.INDIC.3SG /come.SUBJ.3SG   Elio
    'I believe that Elio is coming/will come'

    b. *cridia*   *ca* *venia*   /*venissa*   *Elio*
    believe.PAST.1SG that come.PAST.INDIC3SG /come.SUBJ.3SG   Elio
    'I thought that Elio was coming/would come'

(ii) a. *pregu*   *a Diu ca* *mi mannassa*   /*manna*   *ri   sordi*
    pray.PRES.1SG to God that me send.SUBJ.3SG /send.PRES.INDIC.3SG the money
    'I pray to God that he send me the money'

    b. *pregava*   *a Diu ca* *mi mannassa*   /*mannava*   *ri   sordi*
    pray.PAST.1SG to God that me send.SUBJ.3SG /send.PAST.INDIC.3SG the money
    'I prayed to God that he send me the money'

In addition, there are verbs which allow either an indicative (iii.a) or subjunctive (iii.b) complement:

(iii) a. *Alessandra vo*   *ca Luca si*   *mangia*   *nu milu*
    Alessandra want.PRES.3SG that Luca himself eat.PRES.INDIC.3SG an apple
    ogni ghjuornu
    every day

    b. *Alessandra vo*   *ca Luca si*   *mangiassa nu milu ogni*
    Alessandra want.PRES.3SG that Luca himself eat.SUBJ.3SG   an apple every
    ghjuornu
    day
    'Alessandra wants that Luca eat an apple everyday'

The choice of mood in (iii.a–b) correlates with two distinct readings. The use of the indicative in (iii.a) forces a jussive interpretation of *vulire* 'to want' > 'to order', and implies that Luca will definitely eat an apple every day whilst in somebody else's care. The subjunctive in (iii.b), by contrast, expresses an attenuated wish or desire on Alessandra's part, *vulire* 'to want' now being interpreted as 'to wish'. The implication here is that Luca may eat an apple or something entirely different everyday, the choice being determined by the person left in charge of him.

In short, then, the use of the indicative in these examples marks the expected realization of the denoted condition, while the subjunctive expresses the result of a presently unfulfilled condition. This distinction may be related to a similar aspectual contrast between the imperfect and pluperfect subjunctive paradigms in past time contexts (see n. 38 below).

38 As pointed out by Martin Maiden (personal communication), the choice of an imperfect or pluperfect subjunctive in these cases appears not to be free. Following a questionnaire and the examination of a small number of Neapolitan and Calabrian texts, the choice between the two paradigms in past time contexts is subject to an aspectual distinction. In particular, the interpretation of the imperfect subjunctive is neutral with respect to the realization of the denoted event or state, although the most natural reading is that in which the event/ state is assumed to have taken place:

(i) a. *io me   metteva   appaura che muglierema nun turnasse*
     I myself put.PAST.ISG fear   that wife.POSS.ISG not return.SUBJ.3SG
     'and to think that I was afraid that my wife would not come back' (NA)

    b. *iddu avia   cunzigliatu ca   ni   stipassimu   a ra casa*
     he have.PAST.3SG advise.PART that ourselves keep.SUBJ.IPL at the home
     'he had advised that we should stay at home' (CS)

In contrast, a pluperfect subjunctive in the embedded clause signals that the denoted event/state never occurred:

(ii) a. *vuleva   che avesse   fatto   na parlata al   pubblico*
     want.PAST.3SG that have.SUBJ.3SG do.PART a speech to-the audience
     fora   lo   siparo . . . Nun voglia maje lo cielo, io sarria muorto de lo scuorno
     outside the   curtain
     'he wanted that I should have spoken to the audience out on the stage. God forbid, I would have died of embarrassment' (NA, Scarpetta 1992: 192)

    b. *Maria Carla avia   telefunatu   pi mi   di   ca*
     Maria Carla have.PAST.3SG telephone.PART for me.DAT say.INF that
     avissa   calatu   'a   pasta
     have.SUBJ.ISG lower.PART the   pasta
     'Maria Carla rang to tell me to that I should have put the pasta into boiling water' (San Biase (CS))

Particularly exemplary in this respect are the following minimal pairs, where the choice of imperfect/pluperfect subjunctive marks the realization/non-realization of the event:

(iii) a. *vuleva   che io me   nzurasse   /me   fosse   nzurato*
     want.PAST.3SG that I myself marry.SUBJ.ISG /myself be.SUBJ.ISG marry.PART
     'he wanted that I should marry' (= and I did/but I didn't)' (NA)

    b. *mamma aveva   scritto   ca cunzassa   /avissa*
     mum have.PAST.3SG write.PART that arrange.SUBJ.ISG /have.SUBJ.ISG
     cunzatu   'i lietti
     arrange.PART the beds
     'mum had written that I should prepare the beds' (= and I did/but I didn't)' (CS)

39 According to the definition of Romance infinitivehood proposed in Ledgeway (1998b), verb forms embedded under *che/chi* should be considered inflected infinitival forms (specified as [−T, +Agr]), much like southern Calabrian MODO-clauses.

40 See also Ingria (1981) and Felix (1989) for Greek, and Farkas (1984), Grosu and Horvath (1984), Rivero (1989), Motapanyane (1994) and Watanabe (1996: 39ff.) for Romanian.

41 We are not claiming that verbs embedded under *che/chi* never check nominative. Rather, nominative cannot be checked in OC *che/chi*-structures. When OC fails to obtain, however, the embedded verb does check nominative, witness the contrast in the Neapolitan examples in (i.a–b):

(i) a. *Ciro   prummette   che   vene*
   Ciro$_i$ promise.PRES.3SG [that t$_i$ come.PRES.3SG] (embedded T [-NOM])
   'Ciro promises to come'

   b. *Ciro   prummette   che   Maria vene*
   Ciro   promise.PRES.3SG [that Maria come.PRES.3SG] (embedded T [+NOM])
   'Ciro promises that Maria will come'

42 Similar arguments regarding the distribution of pro and PRO in relation to the OC/NOC distinction have been independently proposed for Italian infinitivals (see Mereu 1986; Chierchia 1989; Vincent 1996: 394, n. 10; Ippolito 1999: 56–8). For instance, Ippolito (1999: 57–8) notes that when embedded under *promettere* 'to promise', the finite complement in (i.a) displays the same OC properties as its infinitival counterpart in (i.b):

  (i) a. *(tu$_i$) mi$_j$ hai promesso che* [ec] *partivi$_i$/*partivo$_j$ prima delle 8*
   'you$_i$ promised me$_j$ that [ec] would leave$_{i/*j}$ before 8 o'clock'

    b. *(tu$_i$) mi$_j$ hai promesso di* [ec]$_{i/*j}$ *partire prima delle 8*
   'you$_i$ promised me$_j$ [ec]$_{i/*j}$ to leave before 8 o'clock'

43 For a fuller discussion of the old Neapolitan inflected infinitive, see Loporcaro (1986), Ledgeway (1996: ch. 1) and Vincent (1996).

4 The personal infinitive

1 See also the discussion in section 6.1.
2 Indeed, it has been claimed (Emonds 1976; Koster 1978; Torrego 1998b: 230) that subject sentences in general do not exist.
3 Sardinian dialects prove an exception to the generalization restricting the personal infinitive to non-argument positions (Jones 1988: 344; 1992; 1993: 268–9, 281–2, 1999; Blasco Ferrer 1986: 159). In addition to adverbial (i.a–b) and subject clauses (i.c), the personal infinitive equally occurs in complement clauses (i.d–e):

  (i) a. *Juanne at   tuncatu   su barcone pro non s'istrempare* **sa janna**
   Juanne have.PRES.3SG   close.PART   the window [for not slam.INF   the door]
   'Juanne shut the window so the door wouldn't slam' (Jones 1992: 295)

    b. *su postinu est   colatu   prima de arrivare* **jeo**
   the postman be.PRES.3SG pass.PART [before of arrive.INF I]
   'the postman came by before I arrived' (ibid.)

    c. *bisonzat   a   l'   ochiere* **tue**
   be.-necessary.PRES.3SG to [him kill.INF you]
   'it is necessary for you to kill him' (Blasco Ferrer 1986: 159)

    d. *non bollu   a   ddu scì*   **nisciunus**
   not want.PRES.1SG to [it know.INF nobody]
   'I don't want anybody to know' (ibid.)

    e. *kredo   de éssere andatu* **isse**
   believe.PRES.1SG [of be.INF go.PART he]
   'I believe him to have gone' (Jones 1988: 344)

The greater distributional freedom exhibited by the Sardinian personal infinitive, together with facts relating to the position of the infinitival subject (see Jones 1992: 308, n. 4), mark it off as a distinct species of personal infinitive, quite distinct from that found in other Romance varieties. Indeed, Jones (1992: 303–5; 1993: 281–2) argues that the so-called Sardinian personal infinitive is more felicitously analysed as a variant of the Sardinian inflected infinitive endowed with abstract agreement. The principal reason for this conclusion is based on the fact that the syntax of the so-called personal infinitive is identical to that of the overtly inflected infinitive and that the two are apparently in free variation (see Ledgeway 1998b: 15, n. 5). We shall not discuss the Sardinian data any further here.

4 In what follows we limit examples to a few exemplary cases, referring the interested reader to the cited authors for more examples.

5 See, among others, Hernanz-Carbó (1982), Fernández-Lagunilla (1987), Körner (1983), Piera (1987), Yoon and Bonet-Farran (1991), Fernández-Lagunilla and Anula (1994), Rigau (1995), De Miguel (1996), Pérez-Vázquez (1997) and Torrego (1998b).

6 See Hernanz-Carbó (1982: 351–3), Fernández-Lagunilla (1987: §1.1), Morales (1988: 90), Yoon and Bonet-Farran (1991: 357), De Miguel (1996: 45–6, n. 17), Pérez-Vázquez (1997: 128) and Torrego (1998b: 209).

7 See Joan Solà (1973: 45–60), Körner (1983: 80), Hualde (1992: 38, 251), Rigau (1995), Torrego (1998b) and Wheeler, Yates and Dols (1999: 399).

8 For Occitan, see Ronjat (1937: 595), Alibèrt (1976: 306), Wheeler (1988: 270). The Romanian construction is discussed in Sandfeld and Olsen (1936: 269–70), Lombard (1974: 294), Körner (1983: 80–1) and Dobrovie-Sorin (1993: 89–90).

9 The same point is made by Hernanz-Carbó (1982: 351–2):

> Las subordinadas adverbiales se diferencian de las completivas en que mantienen una relación mucho más laxa con la principal que estas últimas. En otras palabras, no van 'regidas' por el verbo dominante, pues dependen en el árbol de un nóduo superior a FV. Por lo tanto, su presencia dentro de un enunciado se halla siempre desvinculada de la naturaleza semántica del predicado, así como de las propiedades de correferencia que se puden derivar del mismo. Ello determina que el sujeto incrustado no se vea constreñido en estos casos por dependencia semántica ninguna que le viniera impuesta por una proposición situada en un punto más elevado dentro del indicador.'

> (Adverbial clauses differ from complement clauses in that they enter into a much looser relation with the matrix clause than the latter. In other words, they are not "governed" by the matrix verb, since within the tree structure they are projected from a node above VP. Therefore, their presence in a sentence is not constrained by the semantics or by any relations of coreferentiality with the matrix predicate. This has the effect that in these cases the embedded subject does not enter into any semantic dependence with a category in a clause higher up in the structure.)

10 Significant in this respect is Torrego's (1998b: 213) observation that 'the distribution of [obligatory; AL] control clauses does not overlap with the distribution of infinitival clauses with overt subjects.'

11 See Fernández-Lagunilla (1987: 135) who maintains that 'la presencia del sujeto léxico no depende sólo de que el infinitivo no esté regido, sino también de que no haya correferencia.' ('the presence of a lexical subject does not require only that the infinitive not be governed, but also that there be no coreference.')

12 The exceptional status of the examples in (17) is further highlighted by the presence of the non-finite complementizer *di* 'of' which introduces the personal infinitive. Typically, the personal infinitive in such contexts does not function as the complement of the matrix verb. Instead, it generally occurs in a non-subcategorized adjunct clause introduced by the (prepositional) adverb *p(r)i* 'for', witness (i):

(i) *cci   dicinu   pi   jittari   li   vanii*
     him.DAT$_i$ tell.PRES.3PL [for pro$_i$ throw.INF the bands]
     'they tell him to announce the marriage' (Cianciana (AG), Pitré 1875: II, 186)

13 See Keniston (1937b: 234–5, 237), Gili y Gaya (1955: 169), Hernanz-Carbó (1982: 339), Suñer (1986: 190), Fernández-Lagunilla (1987: 127), Morales (1988: 85), Yoon and Bonet-Farran (1991: 355), Hualde (1992: 38), Dobrovie-Sorin (1993: 89), Cresti (1994: §4.3), Rigau (1995: 281, n. 4), De Miguel (1996: 45–6, n. 17), Cuneo (1997: 108–10), Ledgeway (1998b: 5–6).

14 In our corpus totalling 171 examples of the Sicilian personal infinitive, 61 examples of infinitives with overt subjects were found. Of these examples, 30 had nominal subjects and only two of these had a preverbal subject (see section 4.7.1 for discussion). Of the remaining 31 examples with pronominal subjects, 13 were in postverbal position and 18 in preverbal position.

15 Leone (1995: §67) claims that postverbal (pronominal) subjects are more frequent than preverbal (pronominal) subjects in modern Sicilian. Delia Bentley (personal commun-

ication), in contrast, reports that pronominal subjects may occur in either position without any interpretative difference (see also Bentley 1997: 216, who argues that the preverbal position represents a 'well-established tendency').

16 See Suñer (1986: 20, n. 1), Fernández-Lagunilla (1987: 127, n. 3), Pérez-Vázquez (1997: §1.4), Torrego (1998b: 207, n. 3).

17 Torrego (1998b: 207, n. 3) notes furthermore that the personal infinitive preferably precedes the matrix clause whenever the subject occurs before the personal infinitive.

18 According to Lipski (1991: 201; 1994: 61), preverbal subjects occur most frequently in Caribbean dialects of Spanish, including Cuban, Puerto Rican, Dominican, Venezuelan, Panamanian and coastal Colombian (see also Kany 1951: 126).

19 For further discussion, see Henríquez Ureña (1940: 230), Flórez (1946: 377), Padrón (1949: 164), Kany (1951: 126, 159), Mateus (1953: 68), Jiménez Sabater (1975: 169), Suñer (1986), Morales (1988), Lipski (1991; 1994: 61).

20 In addition, Keniston (1937a: 550) observes that sixteenth-century Spanish displays 'a fairly strong tendency to place the subject before the infinitive', as in (i.a). Judging from his examples (see pages 543ff.), the preverbal position seems once again restricted to pronominal subjects, nominal subjects occurring solely in postverbal position (i.b).

(i) a. *se   habían   movido   sin   él habérselo*
        themselves have.PAST.3PL   move.PART   [without he have.INF-them.DAT-it
        mandado
        order.PART]
        'they had moved without his ordering them to' (Keniston 1951: 550)

   b. *no es   buena manera de saludar   un hombre a otro*
       not be.PRES.3SG good manner of [greet.INF one man   PA other]
       'it is not good manners for one man to greet another' (ibid., 547)

Together with other factors, Lipski (1991: 206–7; 1994: 61) suggests that the preference for preverbal pronominal subjects in Latin-American Spanish may reflect a form of conservatism.

21 Lipski (1994: 242) reports, however, that in Dominican Spanish the preverbal subject position can be occupied by 'long noun phrases and not merely subject pronouns.' (see also Henríquez Ureña 1940: 230, Jiménez Sabater 1975: 169). Furthermore, Suñer (1986: 194) observes in Caribbean varieties that 'although pronominal subjects predominate heavily in the sequence under study, it is possible to hear occurrences with non-pronominal subjects in preverbal position . . . in colloquial speech':

(i) a. *para el gobernador tomar   eso en consideración debe*
        [for the governor   take.INF that in consideration] must.PRES.3SG
        ser   presentado   por escrito
        be.INF   present.PART by writing]
        'for the governor to take that into account, it must be presented in writing' (Suñer 1986:194)

   b. *pasó   toda la tarde   sin   Daniel devolverse a su casa*
       pass.PAST.3SG   all the afternoon [without Daniel return.INF to his home]
       'the whole afternoon went by without Daniel returning home' (ibid.)

   c. *antes   de Juan conocerte   a ti, se la pasaba   vagando*
       [before of Juan know.INF-you PA you] himself it spend.PAST.3SG idle.GER]
       'before Juan knew you, he used to waste his time' (ibid.)

However, even Suñer's comments suggest that such examples are at best marginal and rare in comparison to pronominal preverbal subjects. Indeed, a more cautious approach is adopted by Morales (1988: 92) in her discussion of Puerto Rican Spanish: 'Lo que no parece tan claro, por falta de datos adecuados, es que la aparición de sujeto antepuesto se extienda a todo tipo de sujeto (pronominal y frase nominal).' ('What does not appear very clear, due to an absence of adequate data, is whether the preverbal position extends to all types of subject (pronominal and nominal).')

Given the questionable status of examples such as (i.a–c) and their apparent restriction to colloquial speech, as well as their relative infrequency even in these registers, we shall not discuss these examples further.

22 See Fernández-Lagunilla (1987: 127), Loporcaro (1988: 261), Dobrovie-Sorin (1993: 89), Cresti (1994: 41), Rigau (1995: 287), Ledgeway (1998b: 6) and Torrego (1998b: 207).

23 That the infinitival verb does effectively raise to C is also maintained, though for a variety of reasons, by Fernández-Lagunilla (1987: 142–4), Ledgeway (1996b: ch. 1; 1998b: 12–18), Yoon and Bonet-Farran (1991: 356), Elordieta (1993), and De Miguel (1996: 45–6, n. 17). For a survey of the various proposals underlying V-2, see Vikner (1995: §3.4).

24 Note that desemanticized 'grammatical' prepositions (namely reflexes of DE, AD) introducing the personal infinitive in NOC contexts are not prepositional complementizers but, rather, the realization of inherent Case on the infinitival CP (see discussion in section 3.2.2). In other cases where the personal infinitive is introduced by a lexical (prepositional) adverb (for example, equivalents of 'for/in order to', 'without', 'before', 'after'), the latter cannot be analyzed as a complementizer since it always precedes the overt complementizer in the corresponding finite clauses (Pérez-Vázquez 1997: §3.1):

(i) a. *aju*   *gridatu*   *pi*   *mi*   *senta*   *Giginu*
        have.PRES.1SG   shout.PART [PP for [CP me hear.INF$_i$ [TP t$_i$ Gigino]]]
        'I shouted in order for Gigino to hear me' (CS)

    b. *aju*   *gridatu*   *pi*   *cchì*   *Giginu* *mi* *sintissa*
        have.PRES.1SG   shout.PART [PP for [CP that [TP Gigino me hear.SUBJ.3SG]]]
        'I shouted so that Gigino would hear me' (CS)

(ii) a. *avevano*   *sciso*   *senza*   *'e*   *manco*   *ce*   *ne*
        have.PAST.3PL   descend.PART [PP without of [CP not-even ourselves it
        addunà
        realize.INF$_i$ [TP t$_i$]]]

    b. *avevano*   *sciso*   *senza*   *che*   *manco*   *ce*   *ne*
        have.PAST.3PL   descend.PART [PP without [CP that [TP not-even ourselves it
        addunassemo
        realize.SUBJ.1PL]]]
        'they had gone down without our realizing it' (NA)

25 Recall that Sicilian examples like (17a–b) where the personal infinitive occurs as the complement of the matrix verb introduced by the non-finite complementizer *di* 'of' are exceptions. Typically in such contexts, the personal infinitive appears in an adjunct clause introduced by the prepositional adverb *p(r)i* 'for' (see also n. 12 above).

26 Delia Bentley (personal communication) also confirms that the preverbal position of pronominal subjects is incompatible with a focused or topicalized interpretation.

27 The Sicilian examples in (36a–b) are from Delia Bentely (personal communication).

28 The 2SG pronoun *tu* in this example is not to be construed as a focused infinitival subject with concomitant transitive use of *ascì* 'to get/take out'. Instead, it functions as a *tema sospeso* ('suspended theme'; see Benincà 1988: §1.2.2) with concomitant unaccusative reading of *ascì* 'to come out', occurring in the CP-field above FinP.

29 Another possibility is that the subject is not in either of these positions but has been raised to [Spec, Foc] with remanant TP-raising (see Rizzi 1998; Zubizarreta 1998: ch. 3). However, this analysis is not supported by the interpretation of the infinitival subject, which lacks the rhematic/constrastive interpretation and characteristic focal stress of right-focused elements (see also Cuneo 1997: 109–10).

30 See Cardinaletti (1997: §2) for extensive evidence that pro always raises out of [Spec, *v*].

31 For a different analysis, see Zanuttini (1997: ch. 3).

32 In addition to occurring in *v*P-initial position, such adverbs may equally occur in VP-final position. In the latter position, however, such adverbs receive an emphatic reading (and are also frequently doubled, for example *BUONO BUONO*), not relevant in examples (41a–b). Moreover, when in sentence-final position, the adverb always occurs in the default M.SG form. As can be seen in the Boschese example (41a), the adverb *bona* (compare M.SG *buono*) shows F.SG agreement with the infinitival subject, therefore excluding the sentence-final position. For discussion of adverb agreement, see futher section 7.5.2.1 and Ledgeway (in preparation).

33 Irrelevant here is the interpretation in (45b) where *Marco* has narrow focus, as in (i) below:

(i) *pe essere prufessore MARCO*. . .
[for be.INF [sc t$_i$ teacher]] Marco$_j$. . .
'for MARCO to be a teacher. . .'

In such cases, the word order is obtained by moving the small clause subject (*MARCO*) to [Spec, Foc] with remanant TP-raising (see Rizzi 1998; Zubizarreta 1998: ch. 3). Such an analysis must also be adopted for the following Ligurian example:

(ii) *egnî*   *padrùn lê, sajà   in pô   difìsile*
[become.INF [sc t$_i$ boss]   he$_i$ be.FUT.3SG a   little difficult
'for him to become boss will be rather unlikely' (Cicagna (GE), Cuneo 1997: 107)

Being a pro-drop dialect, the marked use of the 3SG pronoun *lê* rather than pro in (ii) necessarily entails a focused interpretation of the pronoun in such contexts.

34 Spanish and Romanian apparently violate the SIG, in that they allow VSO orders in finite clauses. However, as argued by Alexiadou and Anagnostopoulou (1998c), both the subject and object may licitly remain *v*P-internal since in these languages the nominative Case feature of the subject is always checked before Spell-Out by overt verb-raising to T. It follows that in Spanish (i.a) and Romanian (i.b) personal infinitival constructions full lexical objects are always grammatical:

(i) a. *antes de cruzar los niños la calle, siempre miran   hacia   los*
        [before of cross.INF the kids the street] always look.PRES.3PL towards the
        lados
        sides
        'before the kids cross the road, they always look both ways' (Torrego 1998b: 209)

   b. *înainte de a-i   fi   trimis   mama   cartea*
        [before of to-him be.INF send.PART mum-the book-the]
        'before his mum sent him the book' (Dobrovie-Sorin 1993: 41)

35 Although the identity of the infinitival subject in this example coincides with that of the matrix verb, the structure nonetheless instantiates a personal infinitive construction since the reference of the infinitival subject is not constrained (obligatorily controlled) by the matrix verb.

36 Unlike Spanish and Romanian which freely allow VSO in finite clauses, thereby apparently violating the SIG (see note 34 above), Catalan is reported, like Italian and southern Italian dialects, not to allow VSO in finite clauses (Jaume Solà 1992; Alexiadou and Anagnosto-poulou 1998c). We should therefore expect Catalan to obey the SIG in personal infinitival clauses, just like southern Italian dialects. Indeed, this prediction would appear to be borne out by the contrast in grammaticality judgements evidenced in the near minimal pairs (i.a–b) from Hualde (1992: 28):

(i) a. ?*fer vosaltres l' examen ara presentaria   problemes*
        [do.INF you   the exam   now] present.COND.3SG problems
        'for you to do the exam now would prove problematic'

   b. *cantare nosaltres ara no seria   mala idea*
        [sing.INF we   now] not be.COND.3SG bad idea
        'for us to sing now wouldn't be a bad idea'

Whereas (i.a) contains a transitive infinitive and is judged to be marginal, the use of an unergative infinitive (see i.b) in an otherwise structurally identical context produces entirely grammatical results. Moreover, apart from (i.a), there was only one other example of a transitive infinitive with a full DP object in our corpus of Catalan examples, as illustrated in (ii):

(ii) *dir   tu això no té   sentit*
       [say.INF you this] not have.PRES.3SG sense
       'for you to say this has no sense' (Benucci and Poletto 1992, cited in Cuneo 1997: 104)

Presumably, the grammaticality of (ii) is to be understood in the context of the complement *això* 'this' having raised out of *v*-VP to [Spec, Foc] with concomitant right-focus reading.

37 This analysis also explains the fact noted by Benincà (1988: 125) that postverbal subjects of

transitive verbs (i.a) prove better in Italian when the object is pronominalized (i.b) or *wh*-extracted (i.c):

(i) a. *?ha   mangiato la   torta la   mamma*
        have.PRES.3SG eat.PART the cake the mother
        'mum has eaten the cake'

    b. *l' ha   mangiata la   mamma*
        it have.PRES.3SG eat.PART   the mother
        'mum has eaten it'

    c. *cosa ha   mangiato la   mamma?*
        what have.PRES.3SG eat.PART   the mother
        'what has mum eaten?'

38 In contrast, Cardinaletti (1994) argues that (strong) personal pronouns are underlyingly nouns, which raise overtly to D, while Lyons (1999: §8.3.2) claims that personal pronouns are DPs without an NP complement. Our analysis is compatible with either of these proposals, since in both cases personal pronouns are predicted to be $X^{max/min}$ categories under D.

39 Analogous arguments carry over to bare quantifiers which, we saw in examples (36), can also occur in the preverbal position. Like pronominals, these too are both Q^{max} and Q^{min}, hence suitable candidates for head-adjunction to the infinitive under T.

40 This raises the question why the subject, be it pronominal or nominal, cannot raise to check the EPP in [Spec, T], the canonical derived position of subjects. A simple answer is that [Spec, T] in personal infinitives is simply not projected, as confirmed by the evidence reviewed in section 4.6.2 where overt (pro)nominal postverbal subjects were demonstrated to always occur in [Spec, v]. In contrast to OC infinitivals (see sections 3.2.2.1 and 3.3.2.2.2), the unavailability of [Spec, T] in the personal infinitive may follow from economy considerations and the infinitive's 'weak' Tense specification discussed in section 4.4.2: only by moving to C can the infinitival Tense be given content and license nominative. Therefore, while overt raising of a (pro)nominal subject to [Spec, T] would satisfy the EPP, nominative Case would still have to be checked by covert raising of F[NOM] to T (in C) at LF. Consequently, a more economical derivation is that in which the EPP is satisfied by a merged expletive with a single covert raising operation of F[NOM] to T (in C) at LF.

41 Identical facts hold of dialects of the Upper South, where again only kinship terms raise overtly to D and prove incompatible with the definite article (see section 1.3.5). In contrast to Sicilian and dialects of southern Calabria, however, the possessive determiner in these varieties is enclitic, namely *-mo* (1SG), *-to* (2SG) and, less commonly, *-so* (3SG), *-no* (1PL) and *-vo* (2PL).

42 It is therefore not coincidental then that in sixteenth-century Spanish prose preverbal pronominal subjects can be found to break up the sequence object clitic + infinitive (Keniston 1937a: 101), as demonstrated in (i):

(i) *sin   lo él entender*
    without it he understand.INF
    'without his understanding it' (Keniston 1937a: 101)

43 The present analysis begs the question why overt pronominal subjects cannot adjoin to T under C in these varieties, as in Sicilian and Latin-American Spanish. The answer, we suggest, is that while an expletive clitic pro is optional in the latter, hence accounting for the optionality of the preverbal position of pronominals, the numeration for a personal infinitive in other varieties always draws an expletive pro from the lexicon, thereby excluding preverbal pronominal clitics. One exception to this generalization, however, are referential null subjects (namely pro) discussed below, whose particular licensing requirements override the more economical option of merging an expletive clitic pro.

44 The present analysis of the personal infinitive would appear to also carry over to the Italian AUX-to-COMP infinitival construction (see Rizzi 1982: ch. 3; Skytte and Salvi 1991: 529–31), characteristic of formal Italian registers. The latter shares many properties in common with the personal infinitive. For instance, it is restricted to NOC environments as the infinitival complement of VERBA DICENDI and PUTANDI (i.a); the infinitive raises overtly to C

(Rizzi 1982: 86–7), witness its incompatibility with the infinitival complementiser *di* 'of' that introduces OC infinitival complements to these verbs (i.b) and *wh*-operators (i.c); the subject is invariably postverbal, occurring either between or after an auxiliary (i.d), presumably in [Spec, *v*] as witnessed by its order with respect to negative modifiers (i.e) and the fact that pronominalized objects prove more acceptable than full DP objects (compare SIG) when the subject does not raise to the auxiliary clause (i.f):

(i) a. *il   presidente ritiva   essere lei /*PRO responsabile della*
    the president$_i$ believe.PAST.3SG [be.INF she /PRO$_i$ responsible of-the
    crisi economica
    crisis economic]
    'the president believed that she/he was responsible for the economic crisis'

  b. *affermava   (*di) essere lui il   colpevole*
    maintain.PAST.3SG [(of) be.INF he the guilty-one]
    'he maintained that he was the guilty one'

  c. *sappiamo   (*come) aver   i   nostri alleati reagito   a quest'*
    know.PRES.1PL [(how) have.INF the our   allies react.PART to this
    offensiva
    offensive]
    'we know (how) our allies reacted to this offensive'

  d. *credeva   essersi   (la regina) spenta   (la regina)*
    believe.PAST.3SG [be.INF-herself (the queen) pass-away.PART (the queen)]
    'he believed the queen to have passed away'

  e. *sostennero   non esistere più   la moneta (*più*
    maintain.PAST.3PL [not exist.INF anymore the currency (anymore
    /PIÙ)
    /ANYMORE)]
    'they maintained that the currency no longer exists'

  f. *ribadiva   non poterlo   sopportare Ugo /?non poter*
    confirm.PAST.3SG [not be-able.INF-it bear.INF Ugo /not be-able.INF
    sopportare Ugo il sole
    bear.INF   Ugo the sun]
    'he confirmed that Ugo cannot bear it / Ugo cannot bear the sun'

In addition, the temporal properties of the infinitive are characteristic of NOC (personal) infinitivals, lacking the obligatory irrealis interpretation of OC structures, as witnessed by the contrast in (ii.a–b):

(ii) a. *spero   di essere cosciente dei miei limiti* (OC)
    hope.PRES.1SG [of be.INF aware   of-the my limits]
    'I hope I know/will know my limits'

  b. *spero   essere lui cosciente dei suoi limiti* (AUX-to-COMP)
    hope.PRES.1SG [be.INF he aware   of-the his limits]
    'I hope he knows/*will know his limits'

Skytte and Salvi (1991: 528) argue that the only predicates which can occur as the infinitival in the AUX-to-COMP construction are *essere* 'to be' (copula/AUX), *avere* 'to have' (copula/AUX), *dovere* 'must', *potere* 'can', *trattarsi* 'to be a matter of', *esistere* 'to exist' and *spettare* 'to be due', all other verbs only occuring in conjunction with one of the auxiliaries. In actual fact, it would appear that the correct generalization is that stative, but not eventive predicates, can occur in this construction. The latter are excluded since the infinitival clause lacks an internally organized Tense to bind the eventive predicate's temporal argument (see Enç 1991b, and discussion in section 3.3.2.2.2). Hence, a stative predicate such as *conoscere* 'to know' can occur in the infinitival complement (see iii.a), but not on the eventive reading 'to meet' (see iii.b).

(iii) a. *credono   conoscerla   Gianni*
    believe.PRES.3PL [know.INF-her Gianni]
    'they believe Gianni to know her'

b. *credono   conoscerla   Gianni   a   Firenze
   believe.PRES.3PL [meet.INF-her Gianni at Florence]
   'they believe Gianni will meet her in Florence'

In this respect, infinitival complements in the AUX-to-COMP construction are just like ECM and raising predicates, which only prove compatible with eventive predicates if there is an aspectual auxiliary to bind the temporal argument of the eventive predicate (iv.a). On the other hand, when used as OC predicates, these same verbs freely allow eventive infinitival predicates, for infinitival C hosts an internally organized Tense able to bind the temporal argument of the eventive predicate (iv.b).

(iv) a. credono   averla   Gianni conosciuta a Firenze
        believe.PRES.3PL [have.INF-her   Gianni know.PART   at Florence]
        'they believe Gianni to have met her in Florence'

     b. credono   di PRO conoscerla   a Firenze   quando ci
        believe.PRES.3PLᵢ [of PROᵢ know.INF-her at Florence] when   there
        vanno   la   settimana prossima
        go.PRES.3PL the week   next
        'they believe they will meet her in Florence when they go there next week'

As with the personal infinitive, the infinitive in the AUX-to-COMP construction has a 'weak' Tense which must raise to C in order to enter into a T-chain with the matrix verb, which will determine its temporal reference and enable it to license nominative. This means then that in Italian too, at least in formal registers, the EPP of the infinitive in the AUX-to-COMP construction must be checked by merger of an expletive clitic pro on T (raised to C). Importantly, though, there is one major exception with respect to the personal infinitive construction, in that AUX-to-COMP does not license referential pro (v) (see Torrego 1998b: §4.2).

(v) dubito   poter   loro /*pro ripagare il   debito
    doubt.PRES.1SG [be-able.INF they /pro repay.INF the debt]
    'I doubt they/pro will be able to repay the debt'

Significantly, however, we have overt evidence that AUX-to-COMP licenses expletive pro, since impersonal and meteorological verbs freely occur in the construction:

(vi) a. affermò   non convenire   prendere la metropolitana
        maintain.PAST.3SG [not be-worthwhile.INF take.INF the subway]
        'he maintained that it wasn't worth taking the subway'

     b. credevamo   essere piovuto tutto il   pomeriggio ieri
        believe.PAST.1PL [be.INF rain.PART all   the afternoon   yesterday]
        'we thought it had rained the whole afternoon yesterday'

The contrast between (v) and (vi) is then immediately accounted for under our analysis of the AUX-to-COMP construction: Italian only has expletive, and not referential, clitic pro in infinitival contexts. Consequently, the grammaticality of expletive pro in (iv.a–b) is expected, since expletive clitic pro independently occurs as the EPP checker in examples like (i.a–f) where the logical infinitival subject remains in situ.

5   Auxiliary infinitival constructions

1 See Ledgeway (1995: M.II.§2.3.5, S.III.§3.1).
2 This instance of se is presumably analogous to the [+arg] si of Italian proposed by Cinque (1988).
3 Rohlfs (1969: 83–4) notes that the occurrence of temporal/aspectual distinctions on the modal-aspectual verb, rather than on the dependent infinitive, is quite common in a number of Italian dialects. Significantly, he considers that this pattern 'si spiega grazie allo strettissimo nesso sintattico tra verbo servile e verbo principale, che fa sì che il rapporto temporale venga trasferito al primo verbo' ('can be explained as a consequence of the very tight syntactic cohesion between auxiliary and lexical (infinitival) verb, such that the

temporal properties are transferred to the auxiliary'). Indeed, it will be argued below that the infinitival verb in southern Italian modal-aspectual constructions enters into a strictly local relation with the modal-aspectual verb.

4 By way of further illustration, consider the following Neapolitan epistemic examples and their Italian equivalents:

   (i) a. *nce* **ha**   **avuta da**   *essere*   *na*   *ragione?* (Scarpetta 1992: 40)
          there have.PRES.3SG must.PART [be.INF a reason]
      b. *ci*   *dev'*   **essere**   **stata**   *una ragione?* (Italian)
          there must.PRES.3SG [be.INF be.PART a reason]
      'must there have been a reason?'

   (ii) a. *chisto certamente* **ha**   **avuta**   *essere*   *nu*   *sbaglio* (Scarpetta, 142)
          this certainly have.PRES.3SG must.PART [be.PART an error]
      b. *questo certamente dev'*   **essere**   **stato**   *uno sbaglio*
          this certainly must.PRES.3SG [be.INF be.PART an error]
      'this surely must have been an error'

In the Neapolitan examples the aspectual auxiliary occurs on the modal, whereas in the corresponding Italian sentences the auxiliary occurs in the infinitival clause (for the question of auxiliary selection in conjunction with modal-aspectuals, see Ledgeway 1996b: §3.4.6).

5 See Skytte and Salvi (1991: §3.3.4.3).

6 Lombardi (1997: 148–9, 1998a: 623–4) reports that aspectual predicates like *ncignà* 'to begin' and *finiscia* 'to finish' in Cosentino present a somewhat ambiguous behaviour, allowing both biclausal and monoclausal structures. However, in the modern dialect such verbs predominantly yield a monoclausal structure, as witnessed by the preference for clitic climbing in (i):

   (i) *l' aju*   *ncignatu*   *a*   */finisciutu*   *'i*   *pulizzà*
       it have.PRES.1SG begin.PART to /finish.PART of clean.INF
      'I have begun/finished (to) clean(ing) it' (Lombardi 1998a: 623)

7 Equally, Robert Hastings (personal communication) reports that in Tollese (CH) aspectual auxiliaries never appear on the infinitive, witness (i.a–b):

   (i) a. *l a*   *pʊ'tutə*   *fa*
          it have.PRES.3SG be-able.PART do.INF
      'he could do it'

      b. *l a*   *vuta*   *pa'ɣa*
          it have.PRES.3SG must.PART pay.INF
      'he had to pay'

8 Interestingly, such dialects also present the possibility of a 'doubled' clitic structure in conjunction with conatives, an overt copy of the raised clitic appearing in the embedded clause:

   (i) *l' amu*   *pruvatu*   *a*   **ru**   *leja*
       it have.PRES.1PL try.PART to [it read.INF]
      'we tried to read it'

We leave the significance of such examples for future research.

9 See the discussion of the interaction between periphrasis and inflection in Vincent (1987).

10 This essentially derives Baker's (1988: 104) Stray Affix Filter.

11 Particularly relevant in this respect are the loss of the present subjunctive and the overwhelming use of the past subjunctive as a conditional (see discussion in section 3.4 and Ledgeway 1995: M.II.§2.2.7–8).

12 A similar argument is proposed by Plank (1984) to account for the genesis of the English modal auxiliaries.

13 Mereu (1986) reaches a similar conclusion within a LFG framework for equivalent Italian conative complementation structures. In particular, she observes that infinitival complements to Italian conative verbs sit astride the COMP/XCOMP distinction, exhibiting properties of both.

14 Observe that the behaviour of conatives provides independent evidence against Watanabe's (1996) Layered Case Checking approach to PRO (see section 3.3.1.1). Under his approach, PRO could not be licensed in the embedded infinitival clause in (i.a) since there is no available C position to check the null Case feature on the embedded T. One would therefore be forced to analyse conatives as subject-raising verbs (see i.b), a possibility excluded under his assumptions which preclude raising from one θ-position to another:

(i)   Ciro   prova   a   parlà
    a. *Ciro   try.PRES.3SG   to   [TP PRO speak.INF]
    b. Ciroᵢ try.PRES.3SG   to   [TP tᵢ   speak.INF]
        'Ciro tries to talk'

Observe furthermore that our proposed subject-raising analysis of conatives, on a par with OC infinitivals, is further supported by the intrinsic irrealis temporal interpretation they impose on their infinitival complement (see section 3.3.2.2.1). In other words, conative verbs s-select for a [+tense] infinitival T.

15 Our analysis of Neapolitan conative infinitival structures is further supported by comparative evidence from Italian control and raising structures in conjunction with verbs like *sembrare* 'to seem'. In its OC function, *sembrare* subcategorizes for a CP infinitival complement and clitic climbing to the matrix clause is blocked by the infinitival complementizer *di* (see i.a). However, as a raising predicate *sembrare* subcategorizes for a TP infinitival complement and clitic climbing proves optional (see i.b) as in Neapolitan conative structures, highlighting a greater degree of integration between matrix and embedded clauses than in (i.a):

(i) a. mi   (*lo)   sembra   di   capirlo
       me   (itᵢ)   seem.PRES.3SG [CP of   understand.INF-itᵢ]
       'it seems that I understand it'

    b. Ciro   (lo)   sembra   capir(lo)
       Ciroᵢ (itⱼ)   seem.PRES.3SG [TP tᵢ understand.INF(-itⱼ)]
       'Ciro seems to understand it'

6   Auxiliary selection

1 Except in cases of enclisis (for example, *chiammarlo* 'to call him'), the final *-r(e)* desinence of original paroxytone infinitives has since the nineteenth century been systematically dropped, for example *avére* > *avé* 'to have'. In contrast, proparoxytone infinitives generally retain final *-re*, although apocope is also sometimes encountered here, especially with *ESSERE* > *èsse(re)* 'to be', for example *scénnere (?scénne)* 'to descend' (see Ledgeway 1995: M.II.§1.1, 1997: §2). In some of the peripheral varieties (for example, Procidano, Ischitano), however, apocope of final *-re* is systematic even with proparoxytones, namely *scénne(*re), mètte(*re)* 'to put'. In what follows, we shall refer to the Neapolitan HAVE/BE auxiliaries as *avé* and *essere*, irrespective of diachronic and areal variation.

2 Space limitations force us to restrict the number of examples provided in the text. A larger selection of examples can be found in Ledgeway (1995: S.III.§1.1.2; 1996: ch. 3; 1998c).

3 We refer the reader to the discussion in Savini (1881: 64, 94), Finamore (1893: 25–6), Rohlfs (1969: §730), Tuttle (1986), Loporcaro (1988: 276ff.; 1997b: 347), Stehl (1988: §5.2.6), Villa (1992: 99–100), Cocchi (1995; 1998), Cordin (1997: 93ff.), Hastings (1997: 329) and Tufi (1999).

4 For reasons discussed in section 3.2.2.2., infinitival CPs can only be licensed by inherent Case-checkers. Consequently, infinitival CPs in structural Case-checking positions prove ungrammatical and are substituted by a tensed complement.

5 Kayne (1993: §2.3) assumes movement to [Spec, D/P] by analogy with the overt Hungarian cases discussed in Szabolcsi (1981; 1983).

6 Observe that this essentially derives Chomsky's (1992) AgrS from properties of the D-feature on T (see further Chomsky 1995: §4.10.1).

7 Our proposed analysis finds a more natural interpretation in the checking theory of Chomsky (1998), according to which functional heads enter the derivation with under-

specified feature templates which are 'filled in' only when they enter into a checking relation with a substantive category. On this view, a strong (hence finite) T in BE-dialects can be understood as the reflex of a 1st/2nd person subject passing through its specifier and endowing it with the appropriate features.

8   This possibility is also suggested by Kayne (1993: 26, n. 37).

9   In contrast, the application or otherwise of clitic climbing under Kayne's analysis is driven by auxiliary alternation: for the clitic to climb, D/P has to incorporate into BE (= HAVE), but not if the clitic is to remain within the participial clause.

10 The imperfect indicative of *esse* in Procidano is derived from the Latin pluperfect indicative, namely FUERA(M) > *fora* > *fovo*, and not the Latin imperfect ERA(M)>*era*, as in urban Neapolitan.

11 See discussion of T-chains in sections 3.3.2.2 and 4.4.2. Observe, moreover, that under the analysis of A-movement in OC structures outlined in section 3.3.2.2.1, the construction of a T-chain between the auxiliary and participial clauses is independently required to license subject-raising to the auxiliary clause.

12 See Capozzoli (1889: 214), Bichelli (1974: §188), Radtke (1988: 657), Iandolo (1994: 258, 260) and Ledgeway (1995: M.I.§6.3). A similar situation is reported for southern dialects more generally in Rohlfs (1968: 169).

13 In particular, in the spoken dialect a clitic merged on *v* can only activate *v*, namely endow it with strong Agr features, when it doubles an *overt* direct object, not pro.

14 The evidence to be reviewed below does not support Rohlfs' (1969: 125) claim that *essere* is the only auxiliary used with reflexives in Neapolitan.

15 This means then that the object clitic *me* in (49a–b) must excorporate from T to move through C/P to reach BE, as in (27c) above.

16 For further discussion, see Ledgeway (1995: M.I.§6.3).

17 Under specific circumstances pleonastic pronominals are however excluded. For instance, in generic statements (see i.b) pleonastic pronominals generally prove ungrammatical:

(i) a. *num *(me)   magno   'o pane*
       not (myself) eat.PRES.1SG the loaf
       'I won't eat the loaf'

    b. *num (*me)   magno   'o ppane*
       not (myself) eat.PRES.1SG the bread
       'I don't eat bread (as a rule)'

In (i.a) the verb refers to a particular act of eating and the pleonastic 1SG clitic proves obligatory. In (i.b), by contrast, the clitic is excluded since the verb refers to the speaker's custom of never eating bread, as witnessed by the generic reading of *ppane* 'bread' marked by the so-called neuter article '*o* (with concomitant syntactic doubling; see Rohlfs 1966: 175; 1968: §419; Ledgeway 1995: F.III.§2.3; Loporcaro 1997b: 48). Clearly, the use and distribution of pleonastic clitics merits further investigation.

18 Our proposed analysis predicts therefore that the presence of the pleonastic pronominal has no effect on the distribution of BE/HAVE. The evidence of many other southern Italian dialects supports this conclusion. For instance, in Cosentino (see Lombardi 1997: §1.3.1.2, §1.5.1.2.3; 1998b: 152) accusative (i.a), dative (i.b) and inherent (i.c) pronominal verbs invariably license BE (*essa*), whereas pleonastic pronominals (i.d) always require HAVE (*avire*):

(i) a. *doppu ca vi   erati   chiamati*
       after that yourself be.PAST.2PL call.PART
       'after you had called each other' (Lombardi 1997: 107)

    b. *ni   simu   parrati   ped ure e   ure*
       ourselves be.PRES.1PL speak.PART for hours and hours
       'we have spoken to one another for hours on end' (ibid.)

    c. *ti   si   ammusciata*
       yourself be.PRES.2SG shrivel.PART
       'you have shrivelled up' (ibid., 109)

    d. *s'   a   cacciatu i   cavuzuna*
       himself have.PRES.3SG remove.PART the trousers
       'he has taken off his trousers' (ibid., 112)

19 On the distribution and genesis of *tempi sovraccomposti* (double compound tenses) in early texts in conjunction with unaccusative predicates, as in example (59a), see Ledgeway (1996b: ch. 3).

20 Interpreting the *v*-VP configuration as the expression of the causative/agentive θ-role of the external argument (see section 1.3.5), Chomsky (1995: 315–16, 352) argues that, lacking an external argument, unaccusatives equally lack the *v*-shell. Following Collins (1997: §2.2), we assume instead the *v*-shell to be present even in unaccusative structures (see also n. 30 below).

21 See also Sornicola (1996: 329, n. 9), Cennamo (1998: 203–8).

22 Significantly, most of the earliest examples of HAVE with unaccusatives (see 67a-d) occur in the conditional or subjunctive, a fact which *a priori* suggests a link with the examples from Sant'Andrea (CZ) considered in section 6.3.1.2.2.

23 In some cases semantico-syntactic factors can also influence auxiliary choice. For instance, a number of unaccusative verbs (see i.a-e) have developed a transitive pendant, a distinction which many speakers show a tendency, though in no way absolute, to mark by auxiliary choice with *essere* in the former case and *avé* in the latter (see also Iandolo 1994: 259; on the choice of participle in (i.c–d), see section 6.3.2.4.3):

(i) a. *aggiu   turnato   arreto 'o rialo   /so'   turnato*
       have.PRES.1SG return.PART   back   the present /be.PRES.1SG   return.PART
       'I have returned the present / I have returned'

   b. *t'   aggio   arrevato   /so'   arrevato*
      you   have.PRES.1SG arrive.PART   /be.PRES.1SG   arrive.PART
      'I have caught up with you / I have arrived'

   c. *ha   rimmanuto   'e libbre ccà /è   rimasto*
      have.PRES.3SG remain.PART   the books   here /be.PRES.3SG remain.PART
      'he has left the books here / has remained'

   d. *ammo   scennuto   'e prezze /simmo   scise*
      have.PRES.1PL descend.PART   the prices   /be.PRES.1PL   descend.PART
      'we have lowered the prices / have come down'

   e. *hanno   sagliut'   'e mobbile /so'   sagliute*
      have.PRES.3PL ascend.PART   the furniture /be.PRES.3PL ascend.PART
      'they have carried up the furniture / have gone up'

In other cases the use of *essere* with unaccusatives tends to mark resultant state, whereas *avé* highlights activity. For instance, Parascandola (1976: 74–5) distinguishes between (ii.a) and (ii.b) in Procidano:

(ii) a. *ha   chiuóppeto*
        have.PRES.3SG rain.PART
        'it has rained'

    b. *è   schiuóppeto*
       be.PRES.3SG stop-raining.PART
       'it has stopped-raining'

    c. *ha   schiuóppeto*
       have.PRES.3SG stop-raining.PART
       'it has stopped-raining'

    d. *?*è   chiuóppeto*
       be.PRES.3SG rain.PART
       'it has rained'

Whereas (ii.a) reports the event of it having rained, (ii.b) reports the resultant state and consequently requires *esse*. Such distinctions are however rather far from systematic in practice. For example, the present author's informants also accepted (ii.c) with *avé*, alongside of (ii.b), without apparently distinguishing between the two (though expressing a preference for the former). However, they only accepted (ii.a), considering the variant with *essere* in (ii.d), at best, marginal.

24 For a list of the major verbs with a dual participial form, see Ledgeway (1995: M.II.§2.1.7.2).

25 Rather than being simply ousted by their regular pendants, the inherited irregular participles have therefore been pressed into service to mark an innovative formal aspectual distinction *vis-à-vis* their regular counterparts. This looks like a *prima facie* case of what Lass (1990) has termed 'exaptation'.

26 Similar aspectual distinctions in the participle are common to many southern dialects, besides Neapolitan (see Leone 1980: 48, 126ff.; Loporcaro 1988: §227; 1998: 157, n. 167, 238, n. 12; Gioscio 1985: §2–73; Trumper and Lombardi 1996: 92–4). In Cosentino, for instance, regular [+punctual] participles are found exclusively in conjunction with the perfective/passive auxiliaries *avi(re)* 'to have'/ *essa(re)* 'to be' (see (a) and (b) examples below), whereas only irregular [+durative] participles are found in resultative structures with *tena* 'to have' and *essa(re)* 'to be' (see (c) and (d) examples below):

(i) a. *mamma   ha   spas'   /spannut'   'i   panni   fora 'u*
        mum   have.PRES.3SG hang.PART.IRREG /hang.PART.REG the clothes out   the
        barcune
        balcony
        'mum has hung the washing out on the balcony'

   b. *'i   panni   su   stati   spasi   /spannuti   fora 'u*
       the clothes be.PRES.3PL be.PART hang.PART.IRREG /hang.PART.REG out   the
       barcune
       balcony
       'the washing has been hung out on the balcony'

   c. *mamma   tena   i   panni   spasi   /*spannuti   fora 'u*
       mum   have.PRES.3SG the clothes hang.PART.IRREG /hang.PART.REG out   the
       barcune
       balcony
       'mum has got the washing hung out on the balcony'

   d. *'i   panni   su'   spasi   /*spannuti   fora 'u barcune*
       the clothes be.PRES.3PL hang.PART.IRREG /hang.PART.REG out   the balcony
       'the washing is hung out on the balcony'

(ii) a. *avia   (?)mbusu   /mbunnutu   'u pane ccu ll' acqua*
         have.PAST.1SG moisten.PART.IRREG /moisten.PART.REG the bread with the water
         'I had moistened the bread with water'

   b. *'u pane era   statu (?)mbusu   /mbunnutu   ccu ll' acqua*
       the bread be.PAST.3SG be.PART moisten.PART.IRREG /moisten.PART.REG with the water
       'the bread had been moistened with water'

   c. *tenia   'u pane mbusu   /*mbunnutu   ccu ll' acqua*
       have.PAST.1SG the bread moisten.PART.IRREG /moisten.PART.REG with   the water
       'I had got the bread moistened with water'

   d. *'u pane era   mbusu   /*mbunnutu   ccu ll' acqua*
       the bread be.PAST.3SG moisten.PART.IRREG /moisten.PART.REG with the water
       'the bread was moistened with water'

(iii) a. *aju   rutt'   /rumput'   'a cammisa*
          have.PRES.1SG break.PART.IRREG /break.PART.REG the shirt
          'I have torn my shirt'

   b. *'a cammisa è   stata   rutta   /rumputa*
       the shirt be.PRES.3SG be.PART break.PART.IRREG /break.PART.REG
       'the shirt has been torn'

   c. *tiegnu   'a cammisa rutta   /*rumputa*
       have.PRES.1SG the shirt   break.PART.IRREG /break.PART.REG
       'I have got my shirt torn'

   d. *'a cammisa è   rutta   /*rumputa*
       the shirt be.PRES.3SG break.PART.IRREG /break.PART.REG
       'the shirt is torn '

(Note that, in addition to lacking a distinct resultative copula (compare Neapolitan *stà* 'to stand'), Cosentino also lacks a fully grammaticalized resultative periphrasis with *tena*, comparable to that of Neapolitan *tené* + PART. Thus in the (c) examples above, there is no requirement that the implied AGENT of the participle be understood as coreferent with the LOC(ative) of *tena* (see discussion of HABERE + PART in Vincent (1982: §4), and TENERE + PART in Haare (1991)), and the object complement typically precedes the participle.)

The further South one moves, the more infrequent such participial pairs become (Trumper and Lombardi 1996: 93), such that in the Extreme South the original irregular participle has generally been ousted by its regular pendant. Significantly, it is precisely in this same area of the South that a punctual/durative distinction with HAVE (*aviri*) and BE (*essiri*) never arose, in contrast to the Upper South where the two aspectual values are distinguished by reflexes of HABERE/ESSE (punctual) and TENERE/STARE (durative). The two phenomena would appear then to be interrelated, as further evidenced by Spanish and Portuguese which draw a similar aspectual distinction with HAVE/BE and a number of participial pairs (see Willis 1971: 62–4; Butt and Benjamin 1988: §19.2, Parkinson 1988: 162–3; De Bruyne and Pountain 1995: §1.1.7.6).

27 Recall that the irregular participles continue the Latin passive participle which was adjectival in nature. Perhaps for this reason, the irregular participles were felt to be unsuited to the verbal nature of the participle in conjunction with the perfective *avé* and passive *essere* auxiliaries, leading ultimately to the emergence of a series of regular participles of a strictly verbal character (see also Ledgeway 1995: M.II.§2.1.7.3, §2.1.7.5).

28 A notable exception is Procidano (Rohlfs 1966: §22; Maiden 1991; Ledgeway 1995: P.II.§1.3) which exhibits maximal metaphony, with raising of [a] > [ɛ] triggered by original final -ŭ and -ī. Consequently, regular verbs of the first conjugation systematically display a masculine (*-ètə*) / feminine (*-àtə*) gender distinction (Parascandola 1976).

29 Some speakers report a parallel stative/puctual distinction to that in (78a–b) in conjunction with the unaccusative participial pairs *nato* (regular) and *nasciuto* (irregular) 'born'.

Note furthermore that even those dialects of the Extreme South, where the regular participle has generally ousted the original irregular pendant (see also note 26 above), a durative/punctual aspectual distinction between *m(u)ortu* 'dead' versus *murutu* 'died' persists in conjunction with BE/HAVE, witness the Sicilian examples from Casteltermini (AG) in (i.a-b) (see also Leone 1995: 35):

(i) a. *si'*   *muortu!*
         be.PRES.2SG   die.PART.IRREG
         'you are dead!' (Casteltermini (AG), Pitré 1875: III, 60)

     b. *tutti chiddi chi   nun avianu   murutu   nni li   quarant'   anni*
         all   those   who   not have.PAST.3PL die.PART.REG in   the forty   years
         'all those who had not died in the forty years' (ibid., 61)

30 Given their adjectival status, we maintain unaccusative participles with BE contain a (light) functional projection *a*P, equivalent to (light) *v*P in conjunction with verbal predicates (see also Radford 1997: §10.8), in which the agreement features of the adjective and its associated DP are checked.

Within his Agr-less system, Chomsky (1995: 353–4), argues however that copula + adjective structures have the derivation in (i.a)

(i) a. *John*ᵢ *is* [$_{AP}$ tᵢ [$_{A'}$ tᵢ *intelligent*]]

     b. *John*ᵢ *is* [$_{aP}$ tᵢ [$_{AP}$ tᵢ *intelligent*]]

As it is drawn from the derivation, the adjective is assigned a strong D-feature which is checked by [Subj, Adj] (= *John*) raising to the outer [Spec, A] within the checking domain of Adj, thus parallel to the cases of overt object raising to [Spec, *v*]. Yet, as Chomsky (1995: 393, n. 133) points out, this analysis entails assigning a strong D-feature to a substantive category, namely Adj, contrary to general minimalist principles. It would appear then that an analysis along the lines of the present one with a functional projection above Adj (see i.b) is independently required. Similarly, Collins (1997: §2.2) provides independent evidence for a functional projection (his TrP, here equivalent to *v*P) above VP in unaccusative structures (*pace* Chomsky 1995: 352). Collins's proposal would, by implication, lead also us to assume a parallel functional projection (*a*P) above AP in copular-adjectival structures, as in (79a) and (i.b).

31 Furthermore, the participle clause is not an argument since it fails to project to CP. Therefore it will not be subject to any of the licensing requirements (restructuring, finiteness feature) under which participial CPs fall.

7 Want-passives

1 Henceforth we adopt VOLERE and ESSERE as cover terms for the various Italo-Romance reflexes of VELLE > *VOLERE 'to want' and ESSE > *ESSERE 'to be', respectively.
2 For remarks on individual dialects, see Bichellli (1974: 155), Ruggieri and Batinti (1992: 87), Loporcaro (1988: §235), Battipede (1987: 256), Forestiero (1985: 39), Falcone (1983: 48), Meliadò (1994: 145), Ledgeway (1995: M.II §2.3.3–2.3.5, S.III.§3).
3 See Accattatis (1895: §224), Rohlfs (1969: 131, n. 3), Ambrosini (1982: §5), La Fauci (1984: 124, n. 53), La Fauci and Loporcaro (1989), Loporcaro (1998: 194–6, 239, n. 13).
4 Subjectization of the indirect object with ditransitives embedded under VOLERE cannot be derived from a previous active structure in which the indirect object has been promoted to direct object, as in the Neapolitan example in (i):

(i) *'o   mannajeno   'na lettera*
    him.ACC send.PAST.3PL a   letter
    'they sent him a letter'

In section 2.4 we noted that the possibility of ditransitive structures like (i) proves the exception, rather than the norm, among southern Italian dialects. Consequently, in most southern dialects (for example, Calabrian and Sicilian) there are no active structures like (i) from which indirect object passives under VOLERE can be derived. Moreover, it will be demonstrated in section 7.5.2.2 that even in Neapolitan such passives under VOLERE cannot be derived from structures analogous to (i), in that the indirect object is never a direct object at any point in the derivation.
5 The correlation between participial agreement and the presence/absence of ESSERE is further supported by evidence from the Calabrian dialect of San Biase (CS), which allows both strategies. For instance, in the absence of ESSERE (see i.a–b) subjectization of a GOAL argument triggers participial agreement but when ESSERE is present (see ii.a–b), default M.SG agreement obtains:

(i) a. *Maria Carla vulerra   parrata/*-u*
        Maria Carla want.COND.3SG speak-to.PART.F.SG/M.SG
        'Maria Carla would like to be spoken to'

    b. *Maria Carla vulerra   cuntata/*-u   stu fattu*
        Maria Carla want.COND.3SG tell.PART.F.SG/M.SG this fact
        'Maria Carla would like to be told this story'

(ii) a. *Maria Carla vulerra   essa parratu/*-a*
        Maria Carla want.COND.3SG be.INF speak-to.PART.M.SG/F.SG
        'Maria Carla would like to be spoken to'

    b. *Maria Carla vulerra   essa cuntatu/*-a   stu   fattu*
        Maria Carla want.COND.3SG be.INF tell.PART.M.SG/F.SG this fact
        'Maria Carla would like to be told this story'

6 The contrast in participial agreement which obtains in such Cosentino pairs as (i.a–b) would suggest a parallel with the so-called phenomenon of possessor ascension (see Blake 1991: §4.3.2) invoked within the Relational Grammar framework to account for such related pairs as the French sentences in (ii.a–b):

(i) a. *voglio   lavati   sti   capiddi fitusi*
        want.PRES.1SG wash.PART.M.PL these hairs   filthy

    b. *voglio   lavatu   sti   capiddi fitusi*
        want.PRES.1SG wash.PART.M.SG these hairs   filthy
        'I want this dirty hair of mine washed'

(ii) a. *la tête lui   tourne*
      the head him.DAT turn.PRES.3SG

    b. *sa tête tourne*
      his head turn.PRES.3SG
      'his head is spinning'

7   See Salvioni (1912: 378–80), Rohlfs (1969: §738), De Mauro (1976: 401), Lepschy and Lepschy (1988: 76), Sobrero (1988: 735) and Maiden (1995: 264–5). References to individual dialects include: Iannace (1983: §152) and Bianchi, De Blasi and Librandi (1992: 676) for Campania; Ruggieri and Batinti (1992: 86) for Basilicata; Accattatis (1895: XXII), Meliadò (1994: 109, 145), Forestiero (1985: 42) and Voci (1994: XVIII) for Calabria; Loporcaro (1988: §239; 1997b: 348) for Apulia; Meyer-Lübke (1900: III, §311), Leone (1982: 137, 1995: 71–72), Varvaro (1988: 725), Alfieri (1992: 844, 848) and Bentley (1997: 215) for Sicilian.

8   Interestingly, Alfieri (1992: 820) also cites a deontic use of VOLERE where the passive embedded complement occurs in the infinitival form in conjunction with passive *si*:

(i) a. *i figliuol vogliono   ammaestrarsi*
      the children want.PRES.3PL educate.INF-si
      'the children must be educated'

    b. *si voli   lassari*
      si want.PRES.3SG leave.INF
      'it must be left'

Analogous examples are also found in the dialect of Pantelleria (TP) cited by Tropea (1988: II, 339):

(ii) a. *si voli   nnikilíri*
      si want.PRES.3SG become-small.INF
      'it must be made smaller'

    b. *si rrumpíu e ssi voli   ggiustari*
      -self break.PAST.3SG and si want.PRES.3SG repair.INF
      'it broke and must be repaired'

    c. *a kuadára si voli   priunciri*
      the cauldron si want.PRES.3SG fill.INF
      'the (contents of the) cauldron must reach the required quantity'

    d. *si voli   kumpríri um-pok-i zzúkkiru*
      si want.PRES.3SG add.INF a-little-of sugar
      'a little sugar must be added'

9   In group 2 dialects like Neapolitan, the participle may only raise as far as *v*. The auxiliary ESSERE, in contrast, may raise out from *v* (stranding the participle) to adjoin to T together with VOLERE. This is shown by quantifier floating and negation. In the Neapolitan example (i.a), ESSERE remains under *v* together with the participle, as witnessed by the fact that it is preceded by *mmaje* 'never' and *tutte₃* in [Spec, *v*]. In (i.b), on the other hand, ESSERE raises to T with VOLERE and precedes *mmaje* 'never'. Note, however, that now *tutte₃* can now only follow ESSERE, as expected

(i) a. *(tutte₄) lloro um monno   mmaje (tutte₃) essere fatte   (tutte₂)*
      (all)   they not want.PRES.3PL never (all)   be.INF do.PART [TP (all)
         buono (tutte₁) 'a lezione
      [vP well (all)   the lesson]]
      'they (all) don't want ever (all) to be taught [(all) properly (all) the lesson'

    b. *(tutte₄) lloro um monno   (*tutte₃) essere mmaje (tutte₃) fatte*
      (all)   they not want.PRES.3PL (all)   be.INF never (all)   do.PART
       (tutte₂) buono (tutte₁) 'a lezione
      [TP (all)   [vP well (all)   the lesson]]
      'they (all) don't want (all) to be ever (all) taught (all) properly (all) the lesson'

10   In contrast to Loporcaro (1998) who argues for a unified analysis of participial agreement in active and passive structures, we draw a distinction between active and passive participial agreement. The need for such a distinction stems from the fact that in the want-passives of

all dialects under consideration the passive participle always shows full agreement with a nominal in [V, DP] or [Spec, *v*], irrespective of participial morphology. In the HAVE periphrasis, in contrast, agreement of the active participle is not consistently controlled by a nominal in such positions. For instance, in many dialects of the Upper South active participial agreement with a nominal in [V, DP] or [Spec, *v*] in the HAVE periphrasis is exclusively restricted to irregular participles with metaphonic agreement:

(i) a. *aggiu   rutt'   /*rott'   'o tubo*
     have.PRES.ISG break.PART.M /break.PART.F the pipe.M.SG
     'I have broken the pipe' (NA)

  b. *avevano   cott'/   *cuott'   'a pasta*
     have.PAST.3PL cook.PART.F /cook.PART.M the pasta.F.SG
     'they had cooked the pasta' (NA)

  c. *ha   moppeta   /*muoppeto a gamma*
     have.PRES.3SG move.PART.F /move.PART.M the leg.F.SG
     'he has moved his leg' (NA)

  d. *Maria Carla ha   cotta   /*cuottu   na torta*
     Maria Carla have.PRES.3SG cook.F.SG /cook.PART.M.SG a cake.F.SG
     'Maria has cooked a cake' (San Biase (CS))

  e *avia   rapiert'   /*rapert'   'u cassettu*
     have.PAST.ISG open.PART.M /open.PART.F the drawer.M.SG
     'I had opened the drawer' (San Biase (CS))

  f. *hê   letta   /*liettu   chira carta*
     have.PRES.2SG read.PART.F.SG /read.PART.M.SG that paper.F.SG
     'you have read that piece of paper' (San Biase (CS))

Regular active participles, in contrast, never manifest (desinential) agreement with a full DP object (see ii.a–b), only with a (doubling) clitic pronoun (see ii.c–d), as witnessed by those dialects where final vowels retain a distinct articulation:

(ii) a. *avia   cucinatu/*-a   na torta*
     have.PAST.3SG cook.PART.M.SG/F.SG a cake.F.SG
     'he had cooked a cake' (CS)

  b. *aju   fumatu/*-e   tria sigarette*
     have.PRES.ISG smoke.PART.M.SG/F.PL three cigarettes.F.PL
     'I have smoked three cigarettes' (CS)

  c. *('a torta)   l'   avia   cucinata/*-u*
     (the cake.F.SG) it.F.SG have.PAST.ISG cook.PART.F.SG/M.SG
     '(the cake) I had cooked it' (CS)

  d. *(i sigarette)   l'   aju   fumate/*-u*
     (the cigarettes.F.PL) them.F.PL have.PRES.ISG smoke.PART.F.PL/M.SG
     '(the cigarettes) I have smoked them' (CS)

It would appear then, as argued in section 6.3.2.4.3, that the otherwise exceptional agreement phenomena displayed by irregular participles like those in (i) are probably best analysed as simple adjectival agreement.

    Other dialects, on the other hand, such as those spoken in the Extreme South have generally lost all active participial agreement whatsoever (see Leone 1995: §68, Lombardi 1997: ch. 1; Lombardi 1998b: 152–3; Loporcaro 1998: §10.2):

(iii) a. *l' hava   portatu   cca 'nu saccu 'i voti*
     her have.PRES.3SG bring.PART.M.SG here a lot of times
     'he has brought her here many times' (CZ, Lombardi 1997: 93)

  b. *nci domandau cu l' avia   ferutu*
     her ask.PAST.3SG who her have.PAST.3SG injure.PART.M.SG
     'he asked her who had injured her' (RC, ibid., 95)

c. *(sta porta)*   *l'*   *onu*   *pittatu*   *propia mo'*
(this door.F.SG) it.F.SG have.PRES.3PL paint.PART.M.SG just   now
'(as for this door) they have painted it' (San Giorgio Jonico (TA), Loporcaro 1998: 169)

d. *(st' amici)*   *un ti*   *l'*   *ai*   *rispittatu*
(these friends.M.PL) not yourself them.M.PL have.PRES.2SG respect.PART.M.SG
'(as for these friends) you haven't respected them' (Sicily, ibid., 162)

Nonetheless, these same dialects invariably display full participial agreement in the want-passive construction:

(iv) a. *vógghiu*   *accattati:*   *na balla 'i farina, cendu*   *ova e*   *nu*
want.PRES.1SG buy.PART.M.PL a   lot   of flour   one-hundred eggs and a
guttazzu 'i meli
jar   of honey
'I want bought: a lot of flour, 100 eggs and a jar of honey' (Pizzo (CZ), Cosco 1987: 100)

b. *no*   *la*   *vogghiu*   *maniata*   *la testa*
not   it.F.SG want.PRES.1SG touch.PART.F.SG the head.F.SG
'I don't want my head touched' (RC, Satriani 1953: 177)

c. *la Corte te*   *'ole*   *castiato*
the Court you.M.SG want.PRES.3SG castigate.PART.M.SG
'the Court wants you punished' (LE, Salvioni 1912: 379)

d. *Mandruna vosi*   *fatta*   *'na carta*
Mandruna want.PAST.3SG do.PART.F.SG a   document.F.SG
'Mandruna wanted a document written up' (PA, Pitré 1875: I, 131)

Such considerations lead us to conclude that the structural configurations in which active and passive participial agreement are licensed are quite distinct.

11 See section 1.3.6 and Chomsky (1995: 356).

12 Recall from section 7.2.4 that the deontic use of VOLERE is stylistically more restricted in Italian than in other Italo-Romance varieties (see Ambrosini 1982). Consequently, the less than perfect status of (85) for some (northern) speakers is due to diamesic and diaphasic factors, and not a result of syntactic ill-formedness.

13 Our proposal that the THEME argument in such structures bears inherent accusative Case is echoed in Pasquali's (1942: 112) observation that in southern Italian sentences such as (i) *questo teorema* 'this theorem' functions as a 'specie di accusativo di estensione, di accusativo alla greca' ('type of extended accusative, Greek-style accusative').

(i) *voglio*   *essere spiegato*   *questo teorema*
want.PRES.1SG be.INF explain.PART this   theorem
'I want to be explained this theorem'

REFERENCES

Accattatis, Luigi, 1895. *Vocabolario del dialetto calabrese.* Castrovillari: Patitucci.

Acquaviva, Paolo, 1989. *Aspetti della complementazione frasale.* Degree thesis, Università di Pisa.

Alexiadou, Artemis, 1997. *Adverb placement. A case study in antisymmetric syntax.* Amsterdam: John Benjamins.

Alexiadou, Artemis and Anagnostopoulou, Elena, 1998a. Parametrizing AGR: word order, verb-movement and EPP checking. *Natural Languages and Linguistic Theory* **16**, 491–539.

Alexiadou, Artemis and Anagnostopoulou, Elena, 1998b. Covert feature movement and the placement of arguments. Ms., ZAS, Berlin and MIT/Tilburg.

Alexiadou, Artemis and Anagnostopoulou, Elena, 1998c. The subject in-situ generalization, and the role of Case in driving computations. Ms., ZAS, Berlin and University of Crete.

Alfieri, G., 1992. La sicilia. In Francesco Bruni (ed.), *L'italiano nelle regioni. Lingua nazionale e identità regionali.* Turin: UTET, 798–860.

Alibèrt, Loïs, 1976. *Gramatica occitana segon los parlars lengadocians,* 2nd ed. Montpellier: Centre d'Estudis Occitans.

Altamura, Antonio, 1961. *Il dialetto napoletano.* Naples: Fiorentino.

Ambrosini, R., 1982. *Negatività e senso: accettabilità e non-accettabilità nel passivo dell'italiano attuale.* Pisa: Pacini.

Anderson, Stephen, 1982. Types of dependency in anaphors: Icelandic (and other) reflexives. *Journal of Linguistic Research* **2**, 1–22.

Aoun, Joseph and Li, Jen-hui Audrey, 1989. Some aspects of wide scope quantification. *Journal of Linguistic Research* **1**, 69–95.

Badia, Toni, 1998. Prepositions in Catalan. In Sergio Balari and Luca Dini (eds), *Romance in HPSG.* Standford: CSLI Publications, 109–49.

Bagaglia, Daniela, 1997. *An insight into bilingualism: a study of the language used by a speaker of English as a second language.* A-level language project.

Baker, Mark, 1988. *Incorporation. A theory of grammatical function changing.* Chicago: University of Chicago Press.

Baker, Mark, Johnson, Kyle, and Roberts, Ian, 1989. Passive arguments raised. *Linguistic Inquiry* **20**, 219–51.

Barca, Franco, 1996. *Teatro dialettale. Commedie.* Mendicino: Edizioni Santelli.

Barss, Andrew and Lasnik, Howard, 1986. A note on anaphora and double objects. *Linguistic Inquiry* **17**, 347–54.

Basilico, David, 1998. Object position and predication forms. *Natural Language and Linguistic Theory* **16**, 541–95.

Battipede, Benedetto, 1987. *Studio linguistico tra Calabria e Lucania.* Castrovillari: Il Coscile.

Battisti, Carlo, 1921. *Testi dialettali in trascrizione fonetica. Parte seconda. Italia centrale e meridionale.* Halle: Niemayer (Beihefte füer Zeitschrift der Romanische Philologie LVI).

Belletti, Adriana, 1988. The Case of unaccusatives. *Linguistic Inquiry* **19**, 1–34.

Belletti, Adriana, 1990. *Generalized verb movement: aspects of verb syntax.* Turin: Rosenberg and Sellier.

Belletti, Adriana, 1994. Verb positions: evidence from Italian. In David Lightfoot and Norbert Hornstein (eds), *Verb movement.* Cambridge: Cambridge University Press, 19–40.

Benincà, Paola, 1988. L'ordine degli elementi della frase e le costruzioni marcate. In Lorenzo Renzi (ed.), *La grande grammatica italiana di consultazione. Volume 1: la frase. I sintagmi nominale e preposizionale,* Bologna: Il Mulino, 115–94.

Benincà, Paola and Poletto, Cecilia, 1997. The diachronic development of a modal verb of necessity. In Ans van Kemenade and Nigel Vincent (eds), *Parameters of morphosyntactic change.* Cambridge: Cambridge University Press, 94–118.

Bentley, Delia, 1997 [1999]. Language and dialect in modern Sicily. *The Italianist* **17**, 204–30.

Benucci, F. and Poletto, Cecilia, 1992. Inflected infinitives and the C projection. Paper presented at the 18° Incontro di Grammatica Generativa, Ferrara.

Benveniste, Emile, 1966. *Problèmes de linguistique générale*. Paris: Gallimard.

Bertinetto, Pier-Marco, 1991. Il verbo. In Lorenzo Renzi and Giampaolo Salvi (eds), *Grande grammatica italiana di consultazione. Vol. II: i sintagmi verbale, aggettivale, avverbiale. La subordinazione*. Bologna: Il Mulino, 13–161.

Bertoni, Giulio, 1916. *Italia dialettale*. Milan: Hoepli.

Bertuccelli Papi, Marcella, 1991. Frasi avverbiali finali. In Lorenzo Renzi and Giampaolo Salvi (eds), *Grande grammatica italiana di consultazione. Vol. II: i sintagmi verbale, aggettivale, avverbiale. La subordinazione*. Bologna: Il Mulino, 818–32.

Besten, Hans den, 1983. On the interaction of root transformations and lexical deletive rules. In Werner Abraham (ed.), *On the formal syntax of the Westgermania*. Amsterdam: John Benjamins, 47–131.

Bianchi, Patrizia, De Blasi, Nicola, and Librandi, Rita, 1992. La Campania. In Francesco Bruni (ed.), *L'italiano nelle regioni. Lingua nazionale e identità regionali*. Turin: UTET, 629–84.

Bichelli, Pirro, 1974. *Grammatica del dialetto napoletano*. Bari: Pégaso.

Blake, Barry, 1991. *Relational grammar*. London: Routledge.

Blasco Ferrer, Eduardo, 1986. *La lingua sarda contemporanea*. Cagliari: Della Torre.

Borer, Hagit, 1984. *Parametric syntax: case studies in Semitic and Romance languages*. Dordrecht: Foris.

Borer, Hagit, 1986. I-subjects. *Linguistic Inquiry* **17**, 375–416.

Bošković, Željko, 1995. Case properties of clauses and the Greed Principle. *Studia Linguistica* **49**, 32–53.

Bošković, Željko, 1997. *The syntax of nonfinite complementation. An economy approach*. Cambridge, Mass.: MIT Press.

Bouchard, Denis, 1984. *On the content of empty categories*. Dordrecht: Foris.

Bowers, John, 1993. The syntax of predication. *Linguistic Inquiry* **24**, 591–656.

Brancadell, Albert, 1992. *A study of lexical and non-lexical datives*. Doctoral thesis, Universitat Autònoma de Barcelona.

Bresnan, Joan, 1982. *The mental representation of grammatical relations*. Cambridge, Mass.: MIT Press.

Bruni, Francesco, 1984. *L'italiano. Elementi di storia della lingua e della cultura*. Turin: UTET.

Burzio, Luigi, 1986. *Italian syntax: a Government-Binding approach*. Dordrecht: Reidel.

Butera, Vittorio, 1978. *Prima cantu. . .e ddopu contu*. Cosenza: MIT.

Butt, John and Benjamin, Carmen, 1988. *A new reference grammar of modern Spanish*, 2nd edn. London: Edward Arnold.

Bybee, Joan and Dahl, Östen, 1989. The creation of tense and aspect systems in the languages of the world. *Studies in Language* **13**, 51–103.

Calabrese, Andrea, 1993. The sentential complementation of Salentino: a study of a language without infinitival clauses. In Adriana Belletti (ed.), *Syntactic theory and the dialects of Italy*. Turin: Rosenberg and Sellier, 29–98.

Camilli, Amerindo, 1929. Il dialetto di Servigliano. *Archivio Romanzo* **13**, 220–71.

Capozzoli, Raffaele, 1889. *Grammatica del dialetto napoletano*. Naples: Chiurazzi.

Cardinaletti, Anna, 1994. On the internal structure of pronominal DPs. *Linguistic Review* **11**, 195–219.

Cardinaletti, Anna, 1997. Subjects and clause structure. In Liliane Haegeman (ed.), *The new comparative syntax*. London: Longman, 31–63.

Cardinaletti, Anna and Starke, Michal, 1994. The typology of structural deficiency. On the three grammatical classes. *University of Venice Working Papers in Linguistics* **4**, 41–109.

Carè, Placido, 1982. *Ju matrimoniu*. Oppido Maritimo: Barbaro.

Carè, Placido, 1984. *Tre atti unici scritti in vernacolo calabrese e tradotti in lingua italiana*. Nicotera: Lambda Editrice.

Carè, Placido, 1992. *'A malatia 'I 'ndo Petru (commedia in tre atti). Natali 'nta 'na grutta (atto unico). Due favole in vernacolo calabrese*. Nicotera: Lambda Editrice.

Carlino, Carlo, 1981. *Re, poeti e contadini. La poesia dialettale calabrese dell'Ottocento*. Oppido Mamertina: Barbaro Editore.

Cavalcanti, Ippolito, 1837. *Cucina casareccia in dialetto napoletano*. Naples: Tommaso Marotta Editore.

Cennamo, Michela, 1997. Passive and impersonal constructions. In Martin Maiden and Mair Parry (eds), *The dialects of Italy*. London: Routledge, 145–61.

Cennamo, Michela, 1998. Transitività e inaccusatività in testi antichi abruzzesi e napoletani. In Paolo Ramat and Elisa Roma (eds), *Sintassi storica. Atti del XXX congresso internazionale della Società di linguistica italiana*. Rome: Bulzoni, 197–213.

Chiappetta, Antonio, 1899. *Jugale*. Cosenza: Chiappetta.

Chierchia, Gennaro, 1989. Anaphora and attitudes *de se*. In R. Bartsch et al. (eds), *Languages and contextual expressions*. Dordrecht: Foris.

Chiominto, Cesare, 1984. *Lo parlà forte della pora ggente*. Rome: Bulzoni.

Chomsky, Noam, 1980. On binding. *Linguistic Inquiry* 11, 1–46.

Chomsky, Noam, 1981. *Lectures on Government and Binding: the Pisa lectures*. Dordrecht: Foris.

Chomsky, Noam, 1986a. *Barriers*. Cambridge, Mass.: MIT Press.

Chomsky, Noam, 1986b. *Knowledge of language: its nature, origin, and use*. New York: Praeger.

Chomsky, Noam, 1988. *Language and problems of knowledge. The Managua lectures*. Cambridge, Mass.: MIT Press.

Chomsky, Noam, 1991. Some notes on economy of derivation and representation. In R. Freidin (ed.), *Principles and parameters in comparative grammar*. Cambridge, Mass.: MIT Press, 417–54. (Reprinted in Chomsky, Noam, 1995. *The minimalist program*. Cambridge, Mass.: MIT Press, 129–66.)

Chomsky, Noam, 1993. A minimalist program for linguistic theory. In K. Hale and S. J. Keyser (eds), *The view from Building 20: essays in linguistics in honor of Sylvain Bromberger*. Cambridge, Mass.: MIT Press, 167–217.

Chomsky, Noam and Lasnik, Howard, 1993. The theory of principles and parameters. In J. Jacobs, A. von Stechow, W. Sternefeld and T. Vennemann (eds), *Syntax: an international handbook of contemporary research*. Berlin: Walter de Gruter, 506–69. (Reprinted in Chomsky, Noam, 1995. *The minimalist program*. Cambridge Mass.: MIT Press, 13–127.)

Chomsky, Noam, 1995. *The minimalist program*. Cambridge Mass: MIT Press, 219–394.

Chomsky, Noam, 1998. Minimalist inquiries: the framework. Ms., MIT.

Ciardullo, Michele, 1984. *Il teatro*. Lorica: Mide.

Cicala, Giuseppe, 1983. *Grammatica napoletana*. Naples: Istituto Etnografico Meridionale.

Cinque, Guglielmo, 1998. On *si* constructions and the theory of *arb*. *Linguistic Inquiry* 19, 521–81.

Cinque, Guglielmo, 1999. *Adverbs and functional heads. A cross-linguistic perspective*. Oxford: Oxford University Press.

Cocchi, Gloria, 1995. *La selezione dell'ausiliare*. Padua: Unipress.

Cocchi, Gloria, 1998. Ergativity in Romance languages. In Olga Fullana and Francesc Roca (eds), *Studies on the syntax of central Romance languages*. University of Girona, 83–99.

Colacino, Enzo, 1994. *E cchi ni manca?*. Reggio Calabria: VIP Comunicazione.

Collins, Chris, 1997. *Local economy*. Cambridge, Mass.: MIT Press.

Collins, Chris, and Thráinsson, Höskuldur, 1993. Object shift in double object constructions and the theory of Case. *MIT Working Papers in Linguistics* 19, 131–174.

Coloprisco, Aldo, 1986. *Maschere. Tre opere teatrali in dialetto calabrese*. Reggio Calabria: Laruffa Editore.

Convitto Nazionale 'T.Campanella', 1894. *Fiori Selvatici. Poesie popolari calabresi*. (Reprinted 1977, Arnaldo Forni Editore: Bologna).

Cordin, Patrizia, 1997. Tense, mood and aspect in the verb. In Martin Maiden and Mair Parry (eds), *The dialects of Italy*. London: Routledge, 87–98.

Cortelazzo, Manlio, 1988. Ripartizione dialettale. In Günter Holtus, Michael Metzeltin and Christian Schitt (eds), *Lexikon der romanistischen Linguistik* 4, 445–453.

Cosco, Giuseppe, 1987. *Fiabe in Calabria*. Chiaravalle Centrale: Frama Sud.

Cresti, Arianna, 1994. La flessione personale dell'infinito nel repertorio italiano. *Rivista italiana di dialettologia* 18, 31–50.

Croft, William, 1990. *Typology and universals*. Cambridge: Cambridge University Press.

Cuneo, Marco, 1997. L'uso dell'infinito nei dialetti liguri: infinito con soggetto espresso e infinito flesso nel dialetto di Cicagna (GE). *Rivista italiana di dialettologia* 21, 99–132.

De Blasi, Nicola, 1986. *Libro de la destructione de Troya. Volgarizzamento napoletano trecentesco da Guido delle Colonne*. Rome: Bonacci.

De Bruyne, Jacques and Pountain, Christopher, 1995. *A comprehensive Spanish grammar*. Oxford: Blackwell.

De Curtis, Antonio, 1989. *'A livella*. Naples: Fausto Fiorentino Editrice.

De Filippo, Eduardo, 1973. *I capolavori di Eduardo*. Turin: Einaudi.

De Filippo, Eduardo, 1975. *Le poesie di Eduardo*. Turin: Einaudi.

De Marco, Ciccio, 1986a. *Teatro 1. Fegato gruppo C. . .poste e telegrafi*. Soveria Mannelli: Calabria Letteraria Editrice.

De Marco, Ciccio, 1986b. *Teatro 3. Processo a porte chiuse. Duv'è? Uno qualunque*. Soveria Mannelli: Calabria Letteraria Editrice.

De Marco, Ciccio, 1991. *Teatro 4. Palumba*. Soveria Mannelli: Calabria Letteraria Editrice.

De Mauro, Tullio, 1976. *Storia linguistica dell'Italia unita*. Bari: Laterza.

De Miguel, Elena, 1996. Nominal infinitives in Spanish: an aspectual constraint. *Canadian Journal of Linguistics* **41**, 29–53.

De Simone, Roberto (ed.), 1994. *Fiabe campane. I novantanove racconti delle dieci notti*, 2 vols. Turin: Einaudi.

De Vicentis, D., 1872. *Vocabolario del dialetto Tarantino*. Bologna: Arnaldo Forni Editore.

Demonte, Violeta, 1987. C-command, prepositions, and predication. *Linguistic Inquiry* **18**, 147–57.

Demonte Violeta, 1988. Remarks on secondary predicates: c-command, extraction and reanalysis. *Linguistic Review* **6**, 1–39.

Demonte, Violeta, 1995. Dative alternation in Spanish. *Probus* **7**, 5–30.

Diesing, Molly, 1988. Bare plurals and the stage/individual contrast. In M. Krifka (ed.), *Genericity in natural language: Proceedings of the 1988 Tübingen Conference*, SNS-Bericht 88–42, Seminar für natürlich-sprachliche Systeme. Universität Tübingen, 107–54.

Diesing, Molly, 1992. *Indefinites*. Cambridge, Mass.: MIT Press.

Diesing, Molly and Jelinek, Eloise, 1995. Distributing arguments. *Natural Language Semantics* **3**, 123–76.

Di Giacomo, Salvatore, 1991a. *Di Giacomo: tutto il teatro*. Rome: Grandi Tascabili Newton.

Di Giacomo, Salvatore, 1991b. *Di Giacomo: tutte le poesie*. Rome: Grandi Tascabili Newton.

Dobrovie-Sorin, Carmen, 1993. *The syntax of Romanian*. Berlin and New York: Mouton de Gruyter.

Dobrovie-Sorin, Carmen, 1998. Impersonal *se* constructions in Romance and the passivization of unergatives. *Linguistic Inquiry* **29**, 399–437.

Elordieta, Gorka, 1993. Lexical subjects in Spanish infinitival adjuncts. Ms., University of Southern California.

Emonds, Joseph, 1976. *A transformational approach to English syntax*. New York: Academic Press.

Enç, Mürvet, 1987. Anchoring conditions for Tense. *Linguistic Inquiry* **18**, 633–57.

Enç, Mürvet, 1991a. The semantics of specificity. *Linguistic Inquiry* **25**, 327–35.

Enç, Mürvet, 1991b. On the absence of the present tense morpheme in English. Ms., University of Wisconsin, Madison.

Falbo, Leonardo, 1991. *Vincenzo Gallo 'u chitarraru*. Cosenza: Editoriale Progetto 2000.

Falcone, Giuseppe, 1979. *Racconti popolari calabresi con prolegomeni linguistici*. Reggio Calabria: Casa del Libro.

Falcone, Giuseppe, 1983. *Lingua e dialetto nella società, nella scuola e nella narrativa*. Soveria Mannelli: Rubbettino Editore.

Farkas, Donka, 1984. Subjunctive complements in Rumanian. In Philip Baldi (ed.), *Papers from the XIIth Linguistic Symposium on Romance Languages*. Amsterdam: John Benjamins, 355–72.

Felix, Sascha, 1989. Finite infinitives in Modern Greek. In Christa Bhatt, Elisabeth Löbel and Claudia Schmidt (eds), *Syntactic phrase structure phenomena*. Amsterdam: John Benjamins, 113–32.

Fernández-Lagunilla, Marina, 1987. Los infinitivos con sujetos léxicos en español. In Violeta Demonte and Marina Fernández-Lagunilla (eds), *Sintaxis de las lenguas románicas*. Madrid: El Arquero, 125–47.

Fernández-Lagunilla, Marina and Anula, Alberto, 1994. Proceso de filtrado de rasgos categoriales en la sintaxis: los infinitivos y la legitimación del caso nominativo. In Violeta Demonte (ed.), *Estudios gramaticales de la lengua española*. Mexico: El Colegio de México, 471–530.

Fierro, Aurelio, 1989. *Grammatica della lingua napoletana*. Milan: Rusconi.

Filocamo, Salvatore, 1984. *Farse carnevalesche*. Soveria Mannelli: Rubbettino.
Finamore, Gennaro, 1893. *Vocabolario dell'uso abruzzese*, Città di Castello: Lapi.
Flórez, Luis, 1946. Reseña de American Spanish syntax. *Boletín del Instituto Caro y Cuervo* 2, 372–85.
Forestiero, Giuseppe, 1985. *Proposta per una grammatica calabrese*. Rome: Accademia degli Incolti.
Formentin, Vittorio, 1987. *Le lettere del 'Colibeto' (di F. Galeota)*. Naples: Liguori.
Freeze, Ray, 1992. Existentials and other locatives. *Language* 68, 553–95.
Gallelli, Nicola, 1987. *Nà vota succedia. Due atti unici in vernacolo calabrese*. Cosenza: Santelli.
Gemelli, Nino, 1990. *A porta 'e l'ortu*. Soveria Mannelli: Calabria Letteraria Editrice.
Gentile, Gino, 1992. *Le avventure di Pinocchio raccontate in dialetto calabrese*. Foggia: Bastogi.
Gentili, Angelo, 1897. *Fonetica del dialetto cosentino*. Milan: Rebeschini.
Giammarco, Ernesto, 1968–85. *Dizionario abruzzese e molisano*, 5 vols. Rome: Ateneo.
Gili y Gaya, Samuel, 1955. *Curso superior de sintaxis española*, 5th edn. Barcelona: Spes.
Giorgi, Alessandra, 1983–4. Toward a theory of long distance anaphors: a GB approach. *The Linguistic Review* 3, 307–61.
Giorgi, Alessandra and Pianesi, Fabio, 1997. *Tense and aspect. From semantics to morphosyntax*. Oxford: OUP.
Gioscio, Joseph, 1985. *Il dialetto di Calvello*. Stuttgart: Steiner.
Giusti, Giuliana, 1993. *La sintassi dei determinanti*. Padua: Unipress.
Gliozzi, E., no date. *Su' Calavrisi. Libro per gli esercizi di traduzione dal dialetto nelle scuole elementari della Calabria. Parte I – Per la III Classe. Proverbi – Indovinelli – Novelline*. Milan-Catania-Parma: Torino.
Goria, Ceclia, in progress. *The syntax of Piedmontese subject clitics*. Doctoral thesis, University of Manchester.
Granatiero, F., 1987. *Grammatica del dialetto di Mattinata*. Comune di Mattinata.
Green, John, 1988. Spanish. In Martin Harris and Nigel Vincent (eds), *The Romance languages*. London: Routledge, 79–130.
Grosu, Alexander and Horvath, Julia, 1984. The GB Theory and raising in Rumanian. *Linguistic Inquiry* 15, 348–53.
Guasti, Maria Teresa, 1993. *Causative and perception verbs. A comparative study*. Turin: Rosenberg and Sellier.
Guéron, Jacqueline and Hoekstra, Teun, 1994. The temporal interpretation of predication. In Anna Cardinaletti and Maria Teresa Guasti (eds), *Syntax and semantics 28: small clauses*. New York: Academic Press, 77–103.
Haare, Catherine, 1991. *Tener + past participle*. London: Routledge.
Hale, Ken and Keyser, Samuel Jay, 1992. The syntactic character of thematic structure. In I. M. Roca (ed.), *Thematic structure: its role and grammar*. Berlin: Foris, 107–44.
Hale, Ken and Keyser, Samuel Jay, 1993. On argument structure and the lexical expression of syntactic relations. In Ken Hale and Samuel Jay Keyser (eds), *The view from Building 20*. Cambridge, Mass.: MIT Press, 53–110.
Harbert, Wayne, 1995. Binding theory, control, and pro. In Gert Webelhuth (ed.), *Government and Binding Theory and the Minimalist Program*. Oxford: Blackwell.
Harris, Alice and Campbell, Lyle, 1995. *Historical syntax in cross-linguistic perspective*. Cambridge: Cambridge University Press.
Hastings, Robert, 1997. Abruzzo and Molise. In Martin Maiden and Mair Parry (eds), *The dialects of Italy*. London: Routledge, 321–9.
Hastings, Robert, 1999. Initial lengthening in abruzzese. Paper presented at the Incontro di dialettologia, University of Bristol 16–17 September.
Heine, Bernd, 1993. *Auxiliaries. Cognitive forces and grammaticalization*. Oxford: Oxford University Press.
Henríquez Ureña, Pedro, 1940. *El español en Santo Domingo*. Buenos Aires: Biblioteca de Dialectología Hispanoamericana.
Hernanz-Carbó, María Luisa, 1982. *El infinitivo en español*. Universitat Autònoma de Barcelona, Bellaterra.
Hoekstra, Teun, Hyams, Nina and Becker, Misha, 1999. Specifiers and finiteness in early grammars. In David Adger, Susan Pintzuk, Bernadette Plunkett and George Tsoulas (eds), *Specifiers. Minimalist approaches*. Oxford: OUP, 251–70.

Holmberg, Anders, and Platzack, Christer. 1995. *The role of inflection in Scandinavian syntax*. Oxford: Oxford University Press.

Hopper, Paul and Traugott, Elizabeth, 1993. *Grammaticalization*. Cambridge: Cambridge University Press.

Hornstein, Norbert, 1999. Movement and control. *Linguistic Inquiry* 30, 69–96.

Hualde, José Ignacio, 1992. *Catalan*. London: Routledge.

Huang, C.-T James, 1989. 'Pro-drop in Chinese: a generalized control theory. In Osvaldo Jaeggli and Kenneth Safir (eds), *The null subject parameter*. Dordrecht: Kluwer.

Iandolo, Carlo, 1994. *'A lengua 'e Pulecenella. Grammatica napoletana*. Castellammare di Stabia: Franco Di Mauro Editore.

Iannace, G., 1983. *Interferenza linguistica ai confini fra stato e regno. Il dialetto di San Leucio del Sannio*. Ravenna: Longo.

Imperatore, Luigi, no date. *Appunti sul dialetto napoletano*. Naples: Berisio.

Ingria, R. 1981. *Sentential complementation in modern Greek*. Doctoral thesis, MIT.

Ippolito, Michela, 1999. Pseudo relatives and existentials: towards a unified analysis. In Raffaella Folli and Roberta Middleton (eds), *Oxford University Working Papers in Linguistics, Philology & Phonetics* 4, 50–69.

Jackendoff, Ray, 1990. On Larson's treatment of the double object construction. *Linguistic Inquiry* 21, 427–56.

Jaeggli, Osvlado, 1981. *Topics in Romance syntax*. Dordrecht: Foris.

Jaeggli, Osvlado, 1986. Passive. *Linguistic Inquiry* 17, 587–622.

Jiménez Sabater, Max, 1975. *Más datos sobre el español en la República Dominicana*. Santo Domingo: Ediciones Intec.

Johnson, Kyle, 1991. Object positions. *Natural Language and Linguistic Theory* 9, 577–636.

Jones, Michael, 1988. Sardinian. In Martin Harris and Nigel Vincent (eds), *The Romance languages*. London: Routledge, 314–50.

Jones, Michael, 1992. Infinitives with specified subjects in Sardinian. In C. Laeufer and T. A. Morgan (eds), *Theoretical analyses in Romance linguistics*. Amsterdam: John Benjamins, 295–309.

Jones, Michael, 1993. *Sardinian syntax*. London: Routledge.

Jones, Michael, 1995. The prepositional accusative in Sardinian: its distribution and syntactic repercussions. In John Charles Smith and Martin Maiden (eds), *Linguistic theory and the Romance languages*. John Benjamins: Amsterdam, 37–75.

Jones, Michael, 1998. Inflectional ambiguities: a feature checking approach. Paper presented at *Au commencement était le verbe*, Maison Française, Oxford, 8 November.

Jones, Michael, 1999. The personal infinitive in Sardinian revisited. Paper presented at the Incontro di dialettologia, University of Bristol, 16–17 September.

Joseph, Brian, 1983. *The synchrony and diachrony of the Balkan infinitive*. Cambridge: Cambridge University Press.

Kany, Charles, 1951. *American Spanish syntax*. Chicago: University of Chicago Press.

Kayne, Richard, 1975. *French syntax: the transformational cycle*. Cambridge: Mass.: MIT Press.

Kayne, Richard 1984. *Connectedness and binary branching*. Dordrecht: Foris.

Kayne, Richard, 1989. Facets of Romance past participle agreement. In Paola Benincà (ed.), *Dialect variation and the theory of grammar*. Dordrecht: Foris, 85–103.

Kayne, Richard, 1991. Romance clitics, verb movement and PRO. *Linguistic Inquiry* 22, 647–86.

Kayne, Richard, 1993. Toward a modular theory of auxiliary selection. *Studia Linguistica* 47, 3–31.

Keniston, Hayward, 1937a. *The syntax of Castilian prose. The sixteenth century*. Chicago: University of Chicago Press.

Keniston, Hayward, 1937b. *Spanish syntax list. A statistical study of grammatical usage in contemporary Spanish prose on the basis of range and frequency*. New York: Henry Holt.

Koopman, Hilda and Sportiche, Dominque, 1991. The position of subjects. *Lingua* 85, 211–58.

Koptjevskaja-Tamm, Maria, 1993. *Nominalizations*. London: Routledge.

Körner, Karl-Hermann, 1983. Wie originall ist der flektierte Infinitiv des Portugiesischen? Eine Studie zum Subjekt in den romanischen Sprachen. In Jürgen Schmidt-Radenfeldt (ed.), *Portugiesische Sprachwissenschaft*. Tübingen: Narr, 77–103.

Koster, Jan, 1978. Why subject sentences don't exist. In Samuel Jay Keyser (ed.), *Recent transformational studies in European languages*. Mass.: MIT Press.

Koster, Jan, 1984. On binding and control. *Linguistic Inquiry* **15**, 417–59.

Kratzer, Angelika, 1994. On external arguments. *Occasional Paper 17*, University of Massachusetts, Amherst.

La Fauci, Nunzio, 1984. La formazione del siciliano nel Medioevo: uno sguardo oltre la storia della linguistica e la linguistica della storia. In Adriana Quattordio Moreschini (ed.), *Tre millenni di storia linguistica della Sicilia: Atti del Convegno della Società Italiana di Glottologia. Palermo 25–27 marzo 1983.* Pisa: Giardini, 105–38.

La Fauci, Nunzio and Loporcaro, Michele, 1989. Passifs, avancements de l'objet indirect et formes verbales périphrastiques dans le dialecte d'Altamura (Pouilles). *Rivista di Linguistica* **1**, 161–96.

Laenzlinger, Christopher, 1998. *Comparative studies in word order variation. Adverbs, pronouns, and clause structure in Romance and Germanic.* Amsterdam: John Benjamins.

Larson, Richard, 1988. On the double object construction. *Linguistic Inquiry* **19**, 335–91.

Larson, Richard, 1990. Double objects revisited: reply to Jackendoff. *Linguistic Inquiry* **21**, 589–632.

Lasnik, Howard, 1999. *Minimalist analysis.* Oxford: Blackwell.

Lass, Roger, 1990. How to do things with junk: exaptation in language evolution. *Journal of Linguistics* **26**, 79–102.

Launi, Giovanni, 1980. *U mbruogliu.* Cosenza: Silvio Chiappetta.

Ledgeway, Adam, 1995. *A diachronic grammar of the Neapolitan dialect. I: Phonetics and Phonology. II: Morphology. III: Syntax.* Ms., University of Manchester.

Ledgeway, Adam, 1996a. La ristrutturazione e i verbi modali-aspettuali in napoletano. In Robert Hastings (ed.), *Centro di dialettologia e linguistica italiana di Manchester, Quaderni di Ricerca* **1**, 62–82.

Ledgeway, Adam, 1996b. *The grammar of complementation in Neapolitan.* Doctoral thesis, University of Manchester.

Ledgeway, Adam, 1997 [1999]. Asyndetic complementation in Neapolitan dialect. *The Italianist* **17**, 231–73.

Ledgeway, Adam, 1998a. La ristrutturazione in napoletano. In Giovanni Ruffino (ed.), *Atti del XXI Congresso Internazionale di Linguistica e Filologia Romanza. Centro di studi filologici e linguistici siciliani, Università di Palermo 18–24 settembre 1995. Sezione 2 Morfologia e sintassi delle lingue romanze.* Tübingen: Max Niemeyer Verlag, 529–41.

Ledgeway, Adam, 1998b. Variation in the Romance infinitive: the case of the southern Calabrian inflected infinitive. *Transactions of the Philological Society* **96**, 1–61.

Ledgeway, Adam, 1998c. *Avé(re)* and *esse(re)* alternation in Neapolitan. In Olga Fullana and Francesc Roca (eds), *Studies on the syntax of central Romance languages.* University of Girona, 123–47.

Ledgeway, Adam, forthcoming. Dialect syntax and generative grammar. To appear in *UCL Occasional Papers.*

Ledgeway, Adam, in preparation. Adverb agreement in southern Italian dialects. Ms., University of Cambridge.

Lehmann, C., 1988. Towards a typology of clause linkage. In John Haiman and Sandra Thompson (eds), *Clause combining in grammar and discourse.* Amsterdam: John Benjamins, 181–225.

Leone, Alfonso, 1980. *La morfologia del verbo nelle parlate della Sicilia sud-orientale.* Palermo: Centro di Studi Filologici e Linguistici Siciliani.

Leone Alfonso, 1982. *L'italiano regionale in Sicilia.* Bologna: Il Mulino.

Leone, Alfonso, 1995. *Profilo di sintassi siciliana.* Palermo: Centro di Studi Filologici e Linguistici Siciliani.

Lepschy, Anna Laura and Lepschy, Giulio, 1988. *The Italian language today*, 2nd edn. London: Hutchinson.

Lipski, John, 1991. In search of the Spanish personal infinitive. In Dieter Wanner and Douglas Kibbee (eds), *New analyses in Romance linguistics.* Amsterdam: John Benjamins, 201–20.

Lipski, John, 1994. *Latin American Spanish.* London: Longman.

Lombard, Alf, 1974. *La langue roumaine: une présentation.* Paris: Klincksieck.

Lombardi, Alessandra, 1997. *The grammar of complementation in the dialects of Calabria.* Doctoral thesis, University of Manchester.

Lombardi, Alessandra, 1998a. Calabria greca e Calabria latina da Rohlfs ai giorni nostri: la sintassi dei verbi modali-aspettuali. In Paolo Ramat and Elisa Roma (eds), *Sintassi storica.*

Atti del XXX congresso della società di linguistica italiana, Pavia, 26–28 settembre 1996. Rome: Bulzoni, 613–26.

Lombardi, Alessandra, 1998b. Linguistic fragmentation in the Calabrian dialects: the distribution of the perfective auxiliaries in Latin Calabria and Geek Calabria. In Olga Fullana and Francesc Roca (eds), *Studies on the syntax of central Romance languages.* University of Girona, 149–69.

Longobardi, Giuseppe, 1994. Reference and proper names: a theory of N-movement in syntax and Logical Form. *Linguistic Inquiry* **25**, 609–65.

Loporcaro, Michele, 1986. L'infinito coniugato nell'Italia centro-meridionale: ipotesi genetica e ricostruzione storica. *Italia dialettale* **49**, 173–40.

Loporcaro, Michele, 1988. *Grammatica storica del dialetto di Altamura.* Pisa: Giardini.

Loporcaro, Michele, 1997a. Lengthening and *raddoppiamento fonosintattico*. In Martin Maiden and Mair Parry (eds), *The dialects of Italy.* London: Routledge, 41–51.

Loporcaro, Michele, 1997b. Puglia and Salento. In Martin Maiden and Mair Parry (eds), *The dialects of Italy.* London: Routledge, 338–48.

Loporcaro, Michele, 1998. *Sintassi comparata dell'accordo participiale romanzo.* Turin: Rosenberg and Sellier.

Lyons, Christopher, 1995. Movement in 'NP' and the DP hypothesis. *Working Papers in Language and Linguistics.* European Studies Research Institute, University of Salford.

Lyons, Christopher, 1999. *Definiteness.* Cambridge: Cambridge University Press.

Mahajan, Anoop, 1992. The specificity condition and the CED. *Linguistic Inquiry* **23**, 510–16.

Maiden, Martin, 1991. *Interactive morphonology: metaphony in Italy.* London: Routledge.

Maiden, Martin, 1995. *A linguistic history of Italian.* London: Longman.

Maiden, Martin, 1996. Ipotesi sulle origini del condizionale analitico come 'futuro del passato' in italiano. In Paola Benincà, Guglielmo Cinque, Tullio De Mauro and Nigel Vincent (eds), *Italiano e dialetto nel tempo: saggi di grammatica per Giulio C. Lepschy.* Rome: Bulzoni, 149–73.

Maiden, Martin, 1998. *Storia linguistica dell'italiano.* Bologna: Il Mulino.

Mandalari, Mario, 1881–83. *Canti del popolo reggino.* Bologna: Arnaldo Forni Editore.

Manzini, Rita, 1983. On control and control theory. *Linguistic Inquiry* **14**, 421–46.

Manzini, Rita, 1991. Frasi subordinate all'infinito. In Lorenzo Renzi and Giampaolo Salvi (eds), *Grande grammatica italiana di consultazione. Vol. II: i sintagmi verbale, aggettivale, avverbiale. La subordinazione.* Bologna: Il Mulino, 485–97.

Manzini, Rita, 1994. Locality, minimalism, and parasitic gaps. *Linguistic Inquiry* **25**, 481–508.

Manzini, Rita and Wexler, Kenneth, 1987. Parameters, binding theory and learnability. *Linguistic Inquiry* **18**, 413–44.

Marantz, Alec, 1993. Implications of asymmetries in double object constructions. In S. Mochombo (ed.), *Theoretical aspects of Bantu Grammar.* Chicago: CSLI.

Marinucci, Marcello, 1998. Aree linguistiche VIII. Abruzzo e Molise. In Günter Holtus, Michael Metzeltin and Christian Schitt (eds), *Lexikon der romanistischen Linguistik* **4**, 643–52.

Martin, Roger, 1992. On the distribution and Case features of PRO. Unpublished manuscript, University of Connecticut.

Martoglio, Nino, 1978a. *Nica.* Palermo: Il Vespro.

Martoglio, Nino, 1978b. *Scuru.* Palermo: Il Vespro.

Martoglio, Nino, 1979. *'U riffanti.* Palermo: Il Vespro.

Mastrangelo Latini, G., 1981. Note di morfologia dialettale. *Quaderni di filologia e lingue romanze* **3**, 241–49.

Mateus, Humberto, 1953. *El español en el Ecuador.* Madrid: Instituto Miguel de Cervantes.

McArthur, D. G. M., no date. *Il romanzo di Francia. Une version du Libro di Fioravante édité d'après le manuscrit unique conservé à la Bibliothèque nationale.* Doctoral thesis, Université de Paris.

Meliadò, Renato, 1994. *Le radici linguistiche e psico-antropologiche del dialetto reggino,* 2nd edn. Reggio Calabria: Jason Editrice.

Mennonna, Antonio, 1977. *Un dialetto della Lucania (studi su Muro Lucano). Grammatica e antologia.* Galatina: Congedo Editore.

Mereu, Lunella, 1986. Il controllo nelle frasi completive in italiano e l'approccio lessico-funzionale. In Annarita Puglielli (ed.), *Studi di grammatica dall'XI incontro informale di grammatica generativa.* Rome: LIS, 75–113.

Meyer-Lübke, Wilhelm, 1900. *Grammaire des langues romanes. Tome III: Syntaxe*. Paris: Slatkine.

Moore, John, 1994. Romance cliticization and relativized minimality. *Linguistic Inquiry* **25**, 335–44.

Morales, Amparo, 1988. Infinitivo con sujeto expreso en el español de Puerto Rico. In Robert Hammond and Melvyn Resnick (eds), *Studies in Caribbean Spanish Dialectology*, 85–96.

Moro, Andrea, 1993. *I predicati nominali e la struttura della frase*. Padua: Unipress.

Motapanyane, Virginia, 1994. An A-position for Romanian subjects. *Linguistic Inquiry* **25**, 729–34.

Oehrle, Richard, 1976. *The grammatical status of the English dative alternations*. Doctoral thesis, MIT.

Oliva, Francesco, 1970 (original 1728). *Grammatica della lingua napoletana*, edited by Enrico Malato. Rome: Bulzoni.

Ordóñez, Francisco, 1998. Post-verbal asymmetries in Spanish. *Natural Language and Linguistic Theory* **16**, 313–46.

Padrón, Alfredo, 1949. Giros sintacticos en Cuba. *Boletín del Institiuto Caro y Cuervo* **5**, 163–75.

Parascandola, V., 1976. *Vèfio. Folk-glossario del dialetto procidano*. Naples: Berisio.

Parenti, Giovanni, 1978. Un gliommero di P. J. De Jennaro <<Eo non agio figli né fittigli>>. *Studi di filologia italiana* **36**, 321–65.

Parkinson, Stephen, 1988. Portuguese. In Martin Harris and Nigel Vincent (eds), *The Romance languages*. London: Routledge, 131–69.

Parrilla, Angelina, 1990. *Il folclore a Longobucco*, Reggio Calabria: Gangemi Editore.

Parry, Mair, 1997. Piedmont. In Martin Maiden and Mair Parry (eds), *The dialects of Italy*. London: Routledge, 237–44.

Pascuzzi, Umberto, 1982. *'A vrigogna d'a gente*. Soveria Mannelli: Rubbettino.

Pasquali, Giorgio, 1942. Fu, furono. *Lingua Nostra*, **(3)**/5, 112.

Pellegrini, Giovan-Battista, 1975. Tra lingua e dialetto in Italia. *Saggi di linguistica italiana*. Turin: Boringhieri, 11–54.

Percopo, Erasmo, 1887. *I Bagni di Pozzuoli. Poemetto napolitano del secolo XIV*. Naples: Federico Furchheim Libraio.

Pérez-Vázquez, Yuya, 1997. L'infinito con soggetto lessicale in spagnolo europeo. L'infinito con preposizione (subordinata avverbiale). In Maddalena Angonigi, Lorenzo Cioni and Enrico Paradisi (eds), *Quaderni del laboratorio di linguistica* **11**, 127–38. Scuola Normale Superiore Pisa.

Pesetsky, David, 1995. *Zero syntax*. Cambridge. Mass.: MIT Press.

Picallo, Carme, 1984–5. Opaque domains. *The Linguistic Review* **4**, 279–88.

Piera, Carlos, 1987. La estructura de las cláusulas de infinitivo. In Violeta Demonte and Marina Fernández-Lagunilla (eds), *Sintaxis de las lenguas románicas*. Madrid: El Arquero, 148–66.

Pinker, Steven, 1989. *Learnability and cognition: the acquisition of argument structures*. Cambridge Mass.: MIT Press.

Plank, Frans, 1984. The modal story retold. *Studies in Language* **8**, 305–64.

Pitré, Giuseppe, 1875. *Fiabe, novelle e racconti popolari siciliani*, 4 vols. Catania: Clio.

Pollock, Jean-Yves, 1989. Verb movement, Universal Grammar, and the structure of IP. *Linguistic Inquiry* **20**, 365–424.

Posner, Rebecca, 1999. The present form in English and Romance – a diachronic view. In Raffaella Folli and Roberta Middleton (eds), *Oxford University Working Papers in Linguistics, Philology & Phonetics* **4**, 127–40.

Pountain, Christopher, 1995. Infinitives with overt subjects: a pragmatic approach. In T. F. Earle and Nigel Giffin (eds), *Portuguese, Brazilian, and African Studies. Studies presented to Clive Willis on his retirement*. Warminster: Aris and Phillips.

Pring, J. T., 1950. Notes for a phonetic analysis of the dialect of Naples. *Zeitschrift für Phonetik* **4**, 118–23.

Radford, Andrew, 1997. *Syntactic theory and the structure of English. A minimalist approach*. Cambridge: Cambridge University Press.

Radtke, E., 1988. Areallinguistik IX. Kampanien, Kalabrien. In Günter Holtus, Michael Metzeltin and Christian Schitt (eds), *Lexikon der romanistischen Linguistik* **4**, 652–68.

Ramat, Paolo, 1987. Introductory paper. In Martin Harris and Paolo Ramat (eds), *The historical development of auxiliaries*. Berlin: Mouton de Gruyter, 3–19.

Rapoport, Tova, 1995. Specificity, objects and nominal small clauses. In Anna Cardinaletti and Maria Teresa Guasti (eds), *Syntax and semantics 28: small clauses.* New York: Academic Press, 153–78.

Raposo, Eduardo, 1985–6. Some asymmetries in the binding theory in Romance. *The Linguistic Review* **5**, 75–110.

Raposo, Eduardo, 1987. Case Theory and Infl-to-Comp: the inflected infinitive in European Portuguese. *Linguistic Inquiry* **18**, 85–110.

Real Academia Española, 1973. *Esbozo de una nueva gramática de la lengua española.* Madrid: Espasa-Calpe.

Rigau, Gemma, 1995. Temporal infinitive constructions in Catalan and Spanish. *Probus* **7**, 279–301.

Rinaldi, Paola and Sobrero, Alberto (eds), 1974. *La città del sole.* Milan: Rizzoli.

Rivero, M-L., 1989. Long head movement and negation: Serbo-Croatian vs. Slovak and Czech,' *The Linguistic Review* **8**, 319–51.

Rizzi, Luigi, 1982. *Issues in Italian syntax.* Dordrecht: Foris.

Rizzi, Luigi, 1986. Null objects in Italian and the theory of *pro. Linguistic Inquiry* **17**, 501–57.

Rizzi, Luigi, 1988. Il sintagma preposizionale. In Lorenzo Renzi (ed.), *Grande grammatica italiana di consultazione. Volume I: la frase. I sintagmi nominale e preposizionale.* Bologna: Il Mulino.

Rizzi, Luigi, 1990a. Speculations on verb second. In Joan Mascaró and Marina Nespor (eds), *Grammar in progress. GLOW essays for Henk van Riemsdijk.* Dordrecht: Foris, 375–86.

Rizzi, Luigi, 1990b. *Relativized minimality.* Cambridge Mass.: MIT Press.

Rizzi, Luigi, 1998. The fine structure of the left periphery. In Paola Benincà and Giampaolo Salvi (eds), *Romance syntax. A reader.* Budapest: L. Eötvös University, 112–225.

Roberts, Ian, 1991. Excorporation and minimality. *Linguistic Inquiry* **22**, 209–18.

Roberts, Ian, 1994. Long head movement, Case, and agreement in Romance. In Norbert Hornstein and David Lightfoot (eds), *Verb movement.* Cambridge: Cambridge University Press, 207–42.

Rohlfs, Gerhard, 1956–61. *Vocabolario dei dialetti salentini* (3 vols). Galatina: Congedo Editore.

Rohlfs, Gerhard, 1966. *Grammatica storica della lingua italiana e dei suoi dialetti. I. Fonetica.* Turin: Einaudi.

Rohlfs, Gerhard, 1968. *Grammatica storica della lingua italiana e dei suoi dialetti. II. Morfologia.* Turin: Einaudi.

Rohlfs, Gerhard, 1969. *Grammatica storica della lingua italiana e dei suoi dialetti. III. Sintassi e formazione delle parole.* Turin: Einaudi.

Rohlfs, Gerhard, 1971. Autour de l'accusatif prépositionnel dans les langues romanes. *Revue de linguistique romane* **35**, 312–33.

Rohlfs, Gerhard, 1972. *Studi e ricerche su lingua e dialetti d'Italia.* Florence: Sansoni. (Reprinted 1997.)

Ronjat, Jules, 1937. *Grammaire historique des parlers provençaux modernes*, vol. 2. Montpellier SLR.

Rowlett, Paul, 1998. *Sentential negation in French.* Oxford: Oxford University Press.

Ruggieri, Donato and Batinti, Antonio, 1992. *Lingua e dialetto ad Anzi (Potenza). Note sulla situazione linguistica.* Potenza: Il Salice.

Safir, Ken, 1985. *Syntactic chains.* Cambridge: Cambridge University Press.

Salvi, Giampaolo, 1991. La frase semplice. In Lorenzo Renzi (ed.), *Grande grammatica italiana di consultazione. Volume 1: la frase. I sintagmi nominale e preposizionale.* Bologna: Il Mulino, 29–113.

Salvioni, Carlo, 1912 Note sintattiche II. *Zetischrift für romanische Philologie* **35**, 378–81.

Sandfeld, Kristian and Olsen, Hedvig, 1936. *Syntaxe roumaine. Volume I: emploi des mots à flexion.* Paris: Librairie Droz.

Satriani, Raffaele, 1953. *Racconti popolari calabresi.* Naples: Fratelli De Simone.

Savini, Giuseppe, 1881. *La grammatica ed il lessico del dialetto teramano.* Bologna: Forni Editore.

Savoia, Leonardo, 1997. The distribution of the dialects. In Martin Maiden and Mair Parry (eds), *The dialects of Italy.* London: Routledge, 225–34.

Scarpetta, Eduardo, 1992. *Scarpetta: tutto il teatro.* Rome: Grandi Tascabili Newton.

Scarpetta, Eduardo, 1994. *Qui rido io: commedie di Eduardo Scarpetta.* Naples: Torre Editrice.

Scerbo, Francesco, 1886. *Studio sul dialetto calabro con dizionario.* Bologna: Arnaldo Forni Editore.

Schmitt, Cristina, 1998. Lack of iteration: accusative clitic doubling, participial absolutes and *have* + agreeing participles. *Probus* **10**, 243–300.

Serianni, Luca, 1991. *Grammatica italiana. Italiano comune e lingua letteraria.* Turin: UTET.

Simpson, Andrew, 1999. *Wh*-movement, licensing, and the locality of feature checking. In David Adger, Susan Pintzuk, Bernadette Plunkett and George Tsoulas (eds), *Specifiers. Minimalist approaches.* Oxford: Oxford University Press, 231–47.

Skytte, Gunver and Salvi, Giampaolo, 1991. Frasi subordinate all'infinito. In Lorenzo Renzi and Giampaolo Salvi (eds), *Grande grammatica italiana di consultazione. Volume II: i sintagmi verbale, aggettivale, avverbiale. La subordinazione.* Bologna: Il Mulino, 483–5; 497–569.

Sobrero, Alberto, 1988. Italienisch: Regionale Varianten (italiano regionale). In Günter Holtus, Michael Metzeltin and Christian Schmitt. (eds). *Lexikon der romanischen Linguistik* **4**, 732–48.

Solà, Jaume, 1992. *Agreement and subjects.* Doctoral thesis, Universitat Autònoma de Barcelona.

Solà, Joan, 1973. *Estudis de sintaxi catalana* (2 vols). Barcelona: Edicions 62.

Sornicola, Rosanna, 1977. *La competenza multipla. Un'analisi micro-sociolinguistica.* Naples: Liguori.

Sornicola, Rosanna, 1996. Alcune strutture con pronome espletivo nei dialetti italiani meridionali. In Paola Benincà, Guglielmo Cinque, Tullio De Mauro and Nigel Vincent (eds), *Italiano e dialetto nel tempo: saggi di grammatica per Giulio C. Lepschy.* Rome: Bulzoni, 323–40.

Sornicola, Rosanna, 1997a. Campania. In Martin Maiden and Mair Parry (eds), *The dialects of Italy.* London: Routledge, 330–7.

Sornicola, Rosanna, 1997b. L'oggetto preposizionale in siciliano antico e in napoletano antico. Considerazioni su un problema di tipologia diacronica. *Italienische Studien* **18**, 66–80.

Speas, Maragaret, 1990. *Phrase structure in natural Language.* Dordrecht: Kluwer.

Sportiche, Dominque, 1982. Zibun. *Linguistic Inquiry* **17**, 369–74.

Steele, Susan, 1978. The category of AUX as a language universal. In Joseph Greenberg (ed.), *Universals of human language*, vol. 3. Standford: Standford University Press, 7–45.

Stehl, Thomas, 1988. Aree linguistiche XI. Puglia e Salento. In Günter Holtus, Michael Metzeltin and Christian Schitt (eds), *Lexikon der romanistischen Linguistik* **4**, 695–716.

Stowell, Tim, 1981. *Elements of phrase structure.* Doctoral thesis, MIT.

Stowell, Tim, 1982. The tense of infinitives. *Linguistic Inquiry* **13**, 561–70.

Suñer, Margarita, 1986. Lexical subjects of infinitives in Caribbean Spanish. In Osvaldo Jaeggli and Carmen Silva-Corvolan (eds), *Studies in Romance linguistics.* Dordrecht: Foris, 189–203.

Suñer, Maragarita, 1988. The role of agreement in clitic-doubled constructions. *Natural Language and Linguistic Theory* **6**, 391–434.

Szabolcsi, Anna, 1981. The possessive construction in Hungarian: a configurational category in a non-configurational language. *Acta Linguistica Academiae Scientiarum Hungaricae* **31**.

Szabolcsi, Anna, 1983. The possessor that ran away from home. *The Linguistic Review* **3**, 89–102.

Telmon, Tullio, 1993. Varietà regionali. In Alberto Sobrero (ed.), *Introduzione all'italiano contemporaneo. La variazione e gli usi.* Bari: Laterza, 93–149.

Thráinsson, Höskuldur, 1990. A semantic reflexive in Icelandic. In Joan Maling and Annie Zaenen (eds), *Modern Icelandic syntax. Syntax and semantics 24.* New York: Academic Press, 289–307.

Torrego, Esther, 1998a. *The dependencies of objects.* Cambridge. Mass.: MIT Press.

Torrego, Esther, 1998b. Nominative subjects and pro-drop INFL. *Syntax* **1**, 206–19.

Tropea, Giovanni, 1988. *Lessico del dialetto di Pantelleria*, vol. 2. Palermo: Centro di studi filologici e linguistici siciliani.

Trumper, John, 1996. Riflessioni pragmo-sintattiche su alcuni gruppi meridionali: l'italiano popolare. In Paola Benincà, Guglielmo Cinque, Tullio De Mauro and Nigel Vincent (eds), *Italiano e dialetto nel tempo: saggi di grammatica per Giulio C. Lepschy.* Rome: Bulzoni, 351–67.

Trumper, John, 1997. Calabria and southern Basilicata. In Martin Maiden and Mair Parry (eds), *The dialects of Italy.* London: Routledge, 355–64.

Trumper, John and Lombardi, Alessandra, 1996. Il ruolo della morfologia verbale nella determinazione di eteroglosse calabresi significative (ed eventuali ipotesi storiche). In Robert Hastings (ed.), *Centro di dialettologia e linguistica italiana di Manchester, Quaderni di Ricerca* 1, 83–101.

Trumper, John and Rizzi, Luigi, 1985. Il problema di *calmu* nei dialetti calabresi mediani. *Quaderni del Dipartimento di Linguistica Università della Calabria* 1, 63–76.

Tufi, Stefania, 1999. Auxiliary distribution in the Castellani Romani dialects. The case of Marino. Paper presented at the Conference of the Society for Italian Studies, University of Bristol 9–11 April.

Turri, C., 1973. *Grammatica del dialetto novarese.* Novara: La Famiglia Nuaresa.

Tuttle, Edward, 1986. The Spread of ESSE as universal auxiliary in central Italo-Romance. *Medioevo Romanzo* 11, 229–87.

Vaccaro, Gennaro, 1969. *Vocabolario romanesco Bellini e italiano-romanesco.* Rome: Romea Libri Alfabeto.

Varvaro, Alberto, 1988. Aree linguistiche XII. Sicilia. In Günter Holtus, Michael Metzeltin and Christian Schitt (eds), *Lexikon der romanistischen Linguistik* 4, 716–31.

Vespucci, Gerardo, 1994. *Terra nostra.* Piano Lago: Edizioni Nuova Comunità.

Vikner, Sten, 1995. *Verb movement and expletive subjects in the Germanic languages.* Oxford: Oxford University Press.

Villa, Eligio, 1992. *Grammatica e ortografia dei dialetti abruzzesi.* L'Aquila: Japandre.

Vincent, Nigel, 1982. The development of the auxiliaries HABERE and ESSE in Romance. In Nigel Vincent and Martin Harris (eds), *Studies in the Romance verb.* London: Croom Helm, 71–96.

Vincent, Nigel, 1987. The interaction of periphrasis and inflection: some Romance examples. In Martin Harris and Paolo Ramat (eds), *Historical development of auxiliaries.* Amsterdam: Mouton de Gruyter, 237–56.

Vincent, Nigel, 1988. Latin. In Martin Harris and Nigel Vincent (eds), *The Romance languages,* London: Routledge, 26–78.

Vincent, Nigel, 1990. The inflected infinitive in old Neapolitan. Paper presented at the University of Manchester.

Vincent, Nigel, 1993. Head versus dependent-marking: the case of the clause. In Greville Corbett, Norman Fraser and Scott McGlashan (eds), *Heads in grammatical theory.* Cambridge: Cambridge University Press, 140–63.

Vincent, Nigel, 1996. L'infinito flesso in un testo napoletano del Trecento. In Paola Benincà, Guglielmo Cinque, Tullio De Mauro and Nigel Vincent (eds), *Italiano e dialetto nel tempo: saggi di grammatica per Giulio C. Lepschy.* Rome: Bulzoni, 389–409.

Vincent, Nigel, 1997a. Complementation. In Martin Maiden and Mair Parry (eds), *The dialects of Italy.* London: Routledge, 171–8.

Vincent, Nigel, 1997b. Prepositions. In Martin Maiden and Mair Parry (eds), *The dialects of Italy.* London: Routledge, 208–13.

Vincent, Nigel, 1998. On the grammar of inflected non-finite forms (with special reference to old Neapolitan). In Iørn Korzen and Michael Herslund (eds), *Clause combining and text structure,* Copenhagen Studies in Language 22, 135–58.

Vincent, Nigel, forthcoming. Il gerundio in napoletano antico e in toscano antico. Ms., University of Manchester.

Vittoria, E. (ed.), 1990. *Le più belle canzoni napoletane.* Naples: Edizioni E.V.

Voci, Bruno, 1994. *Com'a ru focularu. Dizionario lessicale fraseologico calabro andreolese – italiano con elementi di grammatica descrittiva e centri d'interesse illustrati.* Soveria Mannelli: Calabria Letteraria Editrice.

Watanabe, Akira, 1996. *Case absorption and WH-agreement.* Dordrecht: Kluwer.

Wheeler, Max., 1988. Occitan. In Martin Harris and Nigel Vincent (eds), *The Romance languages.* London: Routledge, 246–78.

Wheeler, Max, Yates, Alan and Dols, Nicolau, 1999. *Catalan. A comprehensive grammar.* London: Routledge.

Williams, Edwin, 1980. Predication. *Linguistic Inquiry* 11, 203–38.

Willis, Clive, 1971. *An essential course in Modern Portuguese.* Hong Kong: Nelson.

Yoon, James Hye-suk and Bonet-Farran, Neus, 1991. The ambivalent nature of Spanish infinitives. In Dieter Wanner and Douglas Kibbee (eds), *New analyses in Romance linguistics.* Amsterdam: John Benjamins, 353–70.

Zagona, Karen, 1988. *Verb phrase syntax.* Dordrecht: Kluwer.

Zanuttini, Raffaella, 1997. *Negation and clausal structure. A comparative study of the Romance languages.* Oxford: Oxford University Press.

Ziccarelli, Vicenzo, 1988. *Cristina 'a spedesa.* Soveria Mannelli: Calabria Letteraria Editrice.

Zolea, Enzo, 1986. *Mo' veni Natali.* Soveria Mannelli: Calabria Letteraria Editrice.

Zubizarreta, María Luisa. 1985. The relation between morphophonology and morphosyntax: the case of Romance causatives. *Linguistic Inquiry* **16**, 247–89.

Zubizarreta, María Luisa, 1998. *Prosody, focus and word order.* Cambridge Mass.: MIT Press.

Zwart, C. Jan-Wouter, 1997. *Morphosyntax of verb movement. A minimalist approach to the syntax of Dutch.* Dordrecht: Kluwer.

INDEXES

GENERAL INDEX

INDEX OF LANGUAGES AND DIALECTS

INDEX OF AUTHORS